GREEK TRAGEDY
AND THE MODERN WORLD

Greek Tragedy and the Modern World

BY

LEO AYLEN

LONDON

METHUEN & CO LTD

11 NEW FETTER LANE EC4

FOR MY
FATHER AND MOTHER

First published in 1964
© 1964 by Leo Aylen
Printed in Great Britain by
Richard Clay and Company, Ltd., Bungay, Suffolk
Catalogue Number 02/2227/31

CONTENTS

PREFACE

AWARE that almost every issue is more complicated than it appeared to previous ages, our generation chooses the comparative safety of judgements made within a limited field of specialized knowledge in preference to large-scale syntheses of thought. But if we ban all attempts at such syntheses, then we must ban all discussion of tragedy. If it is a good thing that such attempts be made, then let the inevitable inadequacy of such attempts be forgiven. This essay is one person's synthesis of several very different disciplines. The material has been collected by working in theatres, discussing philosophy and talking to scientists, as well as by studying drama and poetry, both Greek and modern. It has been written in the hope that it may interest people engaged in any or all of these activities, those interested in the theatre, those interested in philosophy, and those interested in the Classics.

I have therefore tried to avoid technical terms and where I have been unable to do so refer to an appendix where their use, or my special use, is briefly explained. I have tried to avoid foreign languages as much as possible. In the case of critical and philosophical works in foreign languages I quote and refer to the standard English translation, unless there is no translation. I have used Kathleen Freeman's translation of the Pre-Socratic philosophers; her numbering of the fragments is the same as Diels' fifth edition. The remaining Greek references are to the latest edition of the Oxford Classical Text, unless otherwise specified. I quote in my own translation. I have tried to find equivalents of the Greek metre, since a prose translation inevitably distorts the sense. Iambic dialogue I have translated into blank verse, with occasional use of rhyme. Anapaests I have put into a stressed prosody with an equivalent number of beats to the original, using rhyme. I am sure that all choral lyrics must be translated isometrically. Far too much of the meaning depends on the rhythm. I have not done this, however, with fragments of a few lines only. The sign ω marks an isometric translation. With the Greek plays I refer to the title most commonly in use, whether it is Greek, Latin, or English. The *Supplices* is the play by Aeschylus, the *Suppliants* that by Euripides. I have tried to serve the convenience of the majority. With the modern plays I refer to the text of the original, except in the case of Ibsen and Strindberg. I have, however, only quoted French dialogue in the original. I have avoided chronological discussion, because to do this properly would take up too much space. I offer a provisional order of composition for the Greek plays, and put dates of first production in a note for the modern plays I mention. The sign * by a play's date means that it is the date of composition, not production. I have avoided synopses altogether, since they mislead more than they assist. References are given in footnotes, indicated by arabic numerals. Letters of the alphabet refer to longer notes, to be found at the back of the book, arranged by chapters.

Much of the material in this book was originally presented as a doctoral thesis in the University of Bristol. Of the many people who helped me in this undertaking I owe particular thanks to my supervisors, Professor H. D. F. Kitto of the Department of Classics and George Brandt of the Department of Drama of the University of Bristol. I am also grateful for conversations I have had on aspects of this thesis with Professor Glynne Wickham of the Department of Drama, Professor S. Körner of the Department of Philosophy, Dr C. R. Burch of the Department of Physics, Donald Watson of the Department of French, and for help on one particular point from Professor Powell of the Department of Physics, all these being members of Bristol University. I am also grateful for conversations with Professor E. R. Dodds, Christ Church, Oxford, and the Rev. Dr Austin Farrer, Keble College, Oxford, and with Bernard Williams, of the Department of Philosophy, University College, London.

INTRODUCTION

The one thing that is certain about a human being is that he will die. Confronted with this certainty we have two choices. We can try and forget it, hastily removing dying people from the sight of all but doctors and nurses, surrounding ourselves with things that will distract us from thinking about death, enjoying our life right up to the moment when we are surprised; or we can try to prepare ourselves gradually so that when we do die we shall not be quite so afraid. Now, however, distractions are useless. We cannot but be reminded of the possibility of our own death and the destruction of our society almost every time we pick up a newspaper. We cannot avoid facing our fear.

What is peculiar to our generation is the intellectual nature of our awareness of the destructive forces with which we are surrounded. We are more likely to think about wholesale obliteration of millions of human beings, less likely to see one actual dead body. We are more constantly forced to think about death than our grandfathers were; but we have almost nothing concrete to help us come to terms with the idea. One of the functions of tragedy is to help people to come to terms with the thought of death. We have a great and obvious need to learn how to live with this thought, but no means of doing so. Tragedy might be the means of filling this need. The Greek tragedies at any rate are conspicuous for their clear-headed acceptance of the fact of death. We may assume that the Athenians found tragedy to be an effective means of contemplating the forces of destruction that surrounded them and of learning to live with the thought. It is eminently worth while to try and see how they achieved this clear-headedness.

Because we are constantly reminded of the destructive forces with which we are surrounded, we are thoroughly aware of the limits to human power, thoroughly aware that if we perform certain actions, disastrous consequences will surely follow and there will no longer be anything we shall be able to do about it. Our ideas of what is right and wrong are bound to be affected. The fifth-century Athenians used tragedy to help them as they thought about right and wrong, and in all the Greek tragedies there is a constant awareness of the limits of human ability.

We are now forced to call into question the values of our tradition. Because of what people in the West have done for some centuries, we now have the power to do such good to the world as even our grandfathers could not have dreamt of; and we have the power to destroy the world completely. Because we feel that we are more likely to destroy it than to do the good, we are forced to wonder if the values by which our ancestors directed their lives are the right ones; we are forced to try and disentangle what is good and what is bad about our tradition. It is easy to see its distinguishing features; the Western tradition is the story first of one, united, Christian Church, and then of the practice of scientific method, which started under the aegis of the Church and then broke away. Clearly there is much that is wrong with our society now. Should we say that Christianity and scientific method are responsible for more human misery than all the quietist Eastern ways of life put together? Should we say that the troubles of our society are due to the split between the two unique parts of our tradition? If so, is this because the Church was wrong to try and keep the people in ignorance of the enlightenment scientists held in store for them, for fear that this enlightenment would reveal that the Church's dogma was nonsense? Is it because the scientists' vision became distorted through the specialization necessary to their craft? Is it because both Church and scientists forgot the whole community of which they were both members? Is it because the community was too lazy to think deeply about the aims of either Church or scientists? There are no obvious answers to these questions, but there is a clear need for us to ask them. There is a clear need to look at the history of our society, and try and see what it means, to look back and see what has gone wrong, so that we can reach a deeper understanding of what is going wrong now. Fifth-century Athenians used their tragic drama as a help in this sort of activity.

If we are to ask questions of this last sort we cannot treat our life now, or the history of our society, under the separate headings of art, thought, religion, and politics. Clearly the significant periods in European history involved changes in thought, political organization, and religious practice, at the same time. The artists followed the changes in thought. If we admit the need to question all the values of our tradition, then we are bound to be impatient with any outlook which treats artistic, moral, religious, and political matters as separate, not as different facets of the same activity. The idea that it was possible to treat these aspects of human life as separate had never occurred to the Greeks until after tragedy had ceased to be important.

We are forced, then, to be aware of the possibility of our own death, and the destruction of our society, to be aware of the limits of human power as well as its great potential, and to call in question all the values of our tradition in an inquiry which is neither a political, moral, religious, nor artistic activity, but something which combines what is usually meant by all of these things. We do look at life in a very different way from our grandfathers. This is principally due to the advances of the scientists. I have already spoken of the way in which we have been made to realize the danger that inevitably accompanies the benefits of scientific development; we are insecure. I shall discuss later the effect of quantum physics on our thought. I shall summarize here, and say that its effect has been to make us see that no intellectual system is certain. We do not know, but we see that we can learn, in every direction.

This kind of awareness is a recent development. Since the First World War people have begun to realize that the advances of science are only potentially, not inevitably, good. I hope to show that some significant changes in thought have occurred since the Second World War. Some far-sighted people may have had this awareness for a considerable time. But by now at any rate we cannot help having this awareness. We, who have been conditioned by what has gone on since the Second World War, have an outlook almost as far removed as it could be from those who died immediately before the First. To put it crudely, they were secure and certain; we are insecure and uncertain. But the kind of awareness which has been forced on us seems very similar in many ways to the kind of awareness which produced Greek tragedy. I believe we all feel a desperate need to ask questions about life in a particular way, and that the strength of Greek tragedy arises from a need which was somewhat similar to ours. Because of this I have tried to relate Greek tragedy to our society, believing that we are likely to appreciate much of Greek tragedy that our grandfathers could not appreciate.

I believe that our society has a need which only tragedy can fill. In addition, there have been a number of dramatists who have tried in one way or another to give us a tragic drama. As it happens they have mostly been inspired by the example of the Greek poets. I shall therefore try to reach some idea of what tragedy was to the Greeks, an idea based on the effect of all the plays extant, and then try and relate this to modern patterns of thought and theatrical practice, as well as to these modern plays. I have confined myself to tragedy in the theatre. What seems to separate our generation from those that preceded it is that we all, wise and foolish alike, have a particular tragic awareness forced on us. A hundred years ago this awareness was only found in exceptional, wise people. One might say that *War and Peace* had this tragic awareness; that is a matter of how one chooses to use the term "tragedy". But a novelist is not dependent on his audience as a dramatist must be. A "tragic" novel might be written in an age not conducive to tragedy; it would be less important to examine the general climate of thought in relation to such a novel; and it would be less reasonable to expect novels of such a nature to arise because the climate of thought was as it was. There cannot be tragic drama unless the audience to some extent shares the writer's preoccupations. I am asking whether our generation could see an age of tragic drama, because I think that our preoccupations are tragic ones. In this inquiry novels are irrelevant.

I shall ignore films for the most part, primarily because it is hard to get our perspective right if we compare a medium which is less than a hundred years old with one that is at least two and a half thousand. Clearly the cinema does not now fulfil a function for us comparable to that of tragedy for the Athenians. I doubt if it ever will, because the cinema at its best seems to give us a different sort of understanding from the theatre at its best. The cinema's appeal is primarily through pictures, the theatre's through words and the imagination. Some things are best done by one, others by the other, but it is too early to say very much more with any sureness. We need both media, and it would be rash to say that one was better than the other. But probably the need for tragedy which I have outlined will always require drama in which words are important, because the need is a need for enlightenment.

I shall only touch occasionally on comedy, when discussion of a particular play requires. Comedy has many more elements in it than tragedy, and has flourished more constantly. It is more complicated to decide what are its essential features. There is, however, one general distinction to be made. Sometimes a writer will take a theme which is highly serious and invite us to laugh at it. Often this will be juxtaposed with a serious treatment of the same theme. The grave-digger scene in *Hamlet* acts as counterpoise to the serious treatment of death elsewhere in the play. We can compare Chaucer's juxtaposition of the Miller's bawdy and the high romantic tone of the Knight. Both tell tales about sexual love, and the effect of the juxtaposition is increased by the references to astrology, seriously in the Knight's tale, ridiculously in the Miller's. Not all comedy is like this. *The Importance of Being Earnest* requires us to forget all serious issues if we are to enjoy it. I shall refer to the former kind as grotesque juxtaposition, and to the latter as sophisticated trivializing. The former is connected with tragedy; as far as we can see, it is the comedy of the Satyr plays which followed the tragic trilogy. It probably arises when everyone is aware of the seriousness of the issues involved. When First World War soldiers put a corpse at the entrance of their trench and shook its hand as they went past this was not mockery of the dead; it was merely an attempt to get a little light relief out of a situation clearly recognized as intolerable. Study of tragedy should be completed by study of its reverse and complement; but one thing must be tackled at a time.

I am trying, then, to see what it was that Greek tragedies had in common in order to see whether we could have a tragic drama similar to theirs. It seems likely that the impact of tragedy consists of various elements, and that the different groups of plays which are generally accepted as tragedies have these elements in different proportions. There is a similar feel about all plays called tragedies. But I am not going to examine these other periods of tragedy. Still less am I concerned to define Tragedy.

I should like to think that this book may serve as a corrective to some other books which have come out recently, in which the author seeks to define Tragedy, and see whether there can be tragedy today. I am thinking especially of *The Idea of a Theater*, by Francis Fergusson, and *The Death of Tragedy*, by George Steiner. Both of these books assume some essence of tragedy, which is never defined, and neither of the authors is very familiar with Greek tragedy. Steiner talks of a "progress from ruin to forgiveness which occurs at the end of the *Oresteia* and in the *Oedipus at Colonus*".[1] He cannot have read the plays. He also thinks that Greek actors "stood on lofty wooden shoes and spoke through great masks, thus living higher and louder than life".[2] It was Roman actors who wore the high-heeled buskins. Pickard-Cambridge has conclusively demonstrated that these high shoes were quite unknown to the theatre of the tragedians.[3] Fergusson adheres to the theory that tragedy began as the celebration of the death and rebirth of the year spirit. This theory was developed by Harrison, Cornford, and Murray,[4] on almost no evidence, and is now held by no serious Classical scholar. Drawing attention to these points is not a scholar's quibble; far from it. These three mistakes typify three misconceptions as to the nature of Greek tragedy. These misconceptions were spread by Classical scholars thirty or forty years ago, and have given people a particular, reasonably clear picture of what Greek tragedy is. It is totally wrong. To think that there is forgiveness at the end of the *Oedipus at*

---

[1] *The Death of Tragedy*, pp. 174–5.   [2] Ib., p. 246.

[3] A. W. Pickard-Cambridge, *The Dramatic Festivals at Athens*, pp. 228–34.

[4] Cf., eg., Gilbert Murray, *Aeschylus*, pp. 6–8.

Colonus is to misunderstand Sophocles; to fail to understand the end of the *Oresteia*, to say, as so many say, that Aeschylus turned away from tragedy at the end of this work, is to fail completely to understand Greek tragedy. Secondly, those who thought that the Greek actors stood on high shoes also thought that Greek tragedy was "heroic" and statuesque, something rather like French Classical tragedy. Let these people do the choreography for Aeschylus' *Supplices*, one of the earliest plays, or Euripides' *Bacchae*, one of the latest, and exhaust their imagination in inventing violent movements, and in the former play, moving enormous numbers of people. Then let them say there is a resemblance between Greek tragedy and Classical French drama. There is none whatsoever. Thirdly, the theory that Greek tragedy celebrated the year spirit has made critics think that the hero is important in Greek tragedy. With the possible exception of the *Oedipus Tyrannus*, no Greek tragedy has a hero in the modern sense. Certain features of Tragedy as it is often discussed are quite irrelevant to the Greek tragedies. If this is so, it is likely that we shall get different answers from those who ask whether Tragedy is possible today when we ask whether there can be drama like the Greek tragedies.

I hope this book will act as a corrective in another way. Fergusson and Steiner both assume an idea of Tragedy which they do not define, and most writers on this subject assume this, as do Chiari[1] and Henn.[2] They are all Idealist philosophers, and base their criticism on their philosophy. If Idealism has been shown to be a misguided philosophy, then criticism founded on it will be misleading. If no serious philosopher now is an Idealist, then we must assume that critics who still use Idealist terms are unaware of the implications of the recent developments in philosophy. This is by no means a trivial point. Our whole intellectual outlook will be different if we believe that there is some fixed Reality or Right, to be apprehended by intellectual intuition; our grandfathers did believe this; we do not. The collapse of Idealism typifies one of the fundamental changes that have come over our thought recently. I shall discuss this later.[3] Here I can state crudely that it seems obvious

[1] Joseph Chiari, *The Contemporary French Theatre*.
[2] T. R. Henn, *The Harvest of Tragedy*.   [3] Cf. Chapter Six.

that there is no such thing as Tragedy. There are only plays, some of which have always been called tragedies, some of which have usually been called tragedies; at certain times in history the atmosphere has been conducive to the production of such plays. If we want to find out about tragedy we must study the intellectual climate of the time when these plays were written, and perform the plays, rather than ask about the nature of Tragedy in isolation.

When I use the word "tragedy" I refer to the impact of the Greek tragedies, which is due to certain connected features which they all possess, and which I will try to isolate in discussion. I use "Tragedy" to refer to the idea of what tragedy should be, which has been discussed in literary circles since the Renaissance. In the same way I have used common words of criticism with a limited sense, and indicated the way I use them in the Appendix. I mean by this, words such as "religion", "humanism", "poetic", "Romantic". I have tried to treat all the generalizations I make like scientific hypotheses, statements which are at first meaningless except in so far as they direct our attention in a particular direction, and are then given increasing meaning, as we perform various tests to see whether they are reasonable or not.

I have undertaken this inquiry because we are all desperately questioning every value of our tradition. Because of this I cannot understand how it is possible to talk of politics without mentioning religion, or art without morals. All these things are related. The Greek tragic poets treated all these things as related. I shall therefore at no stage pay much attention to these artificial categories. My aim will be to try and bring all facets of my experience to bear on any one particular experience. Greek tragedy was a medium for illuminating this sort of aim. It can be further clarified now by considering aims which are opposed to it. There are those who say that religion appeals to the irrational in us. I am saying that religious beliefs should be tested by ordinary experience. There are those who say that in matters of moral action we can intuit what is right. I am not sure that I understand what moral action is; all conscious action is a result of decision between opposing courses, and in all decisions we use value judgements. There are philosophers who say that philosophy is independent of science. Ayer says of the relation between the two:[1]

> This is not to say that philosophers are not concerned with facts, but they are in the strange position that all the evidence which bears upon their problems is already available to them.

But when we practise philosophy, it can only be about the world we know, and our idea of the world is continually changing, precisely because of the new evidence that scientists are producing for us to bring to bear on the old problems. There are those who say that we should judge art by separate values from those of real life, presumably adhering to the Idealist belief in a separate science of aesthetics. Hobson says:[2]

> We have no right to resent in the theatre an author's philosophy merely because it is different from our own.

Of course we have a right to resent it, if we believe our own is right. If we are not to resent wrong-headedness in the theatre, then the theatre cannot be a place for serious issues. We are sometimes asked to abandon our values in the theatre. But "our values" is the exact equivalent of "the way in which we judge".

It used to be thought possible to reach objectivity. Now not even scientists talk in these terms. A scientist recognizes that facts are only his observations, and that he may be mistaken or biased; so he tries to understand himself in order to realize his biases and avoid mistakes. He recognizes that his hypotheses are adopted by a particular human being, brought up in a particular way at a particular time. If this is true of science, how much more necessary is it for a critic of tragedy, which touches on all the fundamental things of life, to realize that there is no objectivity. Surprisingly few critics have admitted the need for stating their own fundamental beliefs, not realizing that different answers may be given to questions about tragedy by people

---

[1] A. J. Ayer, *The Problem of Knowledge*, p. 1.
[2] Harold Hobson, *The French Theatre of Today*, p. 191.

9

of different beliefs. Criticism of Greek tragedy has been written from Christian, Marxist, or Liberal Humanist[1] viewpoints and by those who claim to write from no viewpoint at all. As this latter is impossible, they are presumably people who do not care very much which of the other three views is correct. As far as I can see, my own view is a Christian one, and as a result I shall no doubt say things with which people of other religions[2] will disagree. It could not be otherwise. We cannot understand more than a fraction of what the Athenians believed. We have to use our imaginations, and our imaginations are as they are, because we are as we are. We cannot do more than try and understand the past a little, and ourselves at the same time.

I am undertaking this inquiry primarily because I believe that tragedy will only be written in a society with a particular sort of outlook, and that this sort of outlook is a good one. I believe that we could make our society one in which tragedy could be written, and that the process of trying to write tragedy or prepare the ground for tragedy will help us a little in making our society better. Because I believe that this is the right way to perform criticism, I also believe that my method will reveal incidental merits in the plays I discuss which other methods have failed to reveal. So I hope at least to arouse enough interest in Greek tragedy to make people ask what it really is that makes so many people say that these works are masterpieces. There is only one way to answer that question: perform the plays. I am writing with a particular purpose in mind, since I believe that is the only way to approach tragedy. But I am also writing so that those who disapprove of this purpose, or who consider my philosophical outlook misguided, may yet find themselves drawn to return again to the masterpieces of Attic tragedy. As Goethe said:

One should not study contemporaries and competitors, but the great men of antiquity, whose works have, for centuries, received equal homage and consideration. Indeed, a man of really superior endowments will feel the necessity of this, and it is just this need for intercourse with great pre-

[1] Cf. Appendix.   [2] Cf. Appendix.

decessors, which is the sign of a higher talent. Let us study Molière, let us study Shakespeare, but above all things, the old Greeks, and always the Greeks.[1]

[1] *Gespräche mit Goethe in den letzten Jahren seines Lebens*, 1823–32. Wed. 21.3.1827, translated by John Oxenford. Quoted by Barrett H. Clark, *European Theories of the Drama*, p. 336.

PART I

GREEK TRAGEDY

CHAPTER ONE

THE BACKGROUND TO GREEK TRAGEDY

(i) THE RELIGIOUS BACKGROUND

Tragedy arises out of a need to come to terms with the fact of death, and the forces with which human life is surrounded. The tragic poet concerns himself with the same problems as the religious leader. Clearly, then, we shall need to try and understand the terms in which the Greeks expressed their religion. If we make this attempt we shall find that we can still learn from their insight into fundamental experiences, even though we do not accept the terms in which they described the experiences.

I would, however, hesitate to claim that I or anyone at the present time could imagine more than the tiniest fraction of what it meant to accept the religious framework of Aeschylus. Religious outlook is probably the most elusive part of anyone's mental activity, and in many ways Greek religion is very different indeed from our own. Among many possible examples I shall instance three. First, there is no word for "religion". If we could explain the most common use of this concept today, I suppose a Greek would translate with some phrase using the neuter plural of the definite article – "matters concerning the gods". By using the concept "religion" throughout this inquiry in such a way that everyone may be said to have a religion, I have tried to bridge the gap a little between the two notions. In addition, from Homer to the fifth century all mental and artistic activities were carried on within the religious framework. If we are comparing this with Christian culture we should think of the Middle Ages. In both periods religion was

15

more a colouring to the whole of life than something which concerned a part of life. But there was no equivalent to the dominance of the ordained ministry, nor was there any equivalent to the body of Christian dogma. Secondly, to use the word "God" means at least a transcendent being, and usually contains the notion of source of morality and Creator as well. The Greeks did not arrive at the idea of transcendence until after the age of tragedy, though I shall refer to certain glimmerings of this idea in the tragedians when I come to discuss their religious outlook. For the most part I shall avoid using the word "god" when translating "*theos*".[1] Thirdly, let us take as vivid an example as possible. The plays of Aristophanes were performed at a religious festival. In one of them Dionysus, the terrifying power of the *Bacchae*, is shown on stage, shitting with nerves. In the Annunciation play of the Miracle Cycles fun is made at the expense of St Joseph, and there are other saints who were sometimes shown as ridiculous in Medieval art. But there is nothing comparable to what we see in Greek drama.

To discuss Greek religion is a lifetime's study. Here I can only summarize crudely, in the hope that this may help some to perform the necessary feat of trying to imagine the religious outlook of the audience at the dramatic festivals; necessary, but ultimately impossible. Everyone, even perhaps serious Classical scholars, has to guard against being misled by the neo-classic representations of Greek gods, simply because he will so often see them. There is really nothing in common between Dionysus and Bacchus as depicted by Rubens.

A possible way to start is to imagine the primitive religious experience, roughly common to all cultures. Primitive man slips on a stone and stumbles, and so he says that there is a power in the stone which makes him stumble. He also looks at how the rain falls, and then the crops grow, and says that there is a power in the rain that makes the crops grow. Things out of his control are in the control of gods, and these things fall into two main categories, exceptional circumstances and observed regularities.

This is very largely the outlook of the Homeric poems. Exceptional circumstances are ascribed to various ill-defined

[1] Cf. Appendix.

powers. Teucer complains that a *daimōn*[1] has broken his bow-string,[2] though Homer tells us that in fact it was the work of Zeus. On the other hand, there are instances given of the action of powers to keep the world in order. When Achilles' horses start to speak the *erinyes*[3] cut them short.[4] Their task is to enforce *moirai*,[5] to see that everything keeps within its portion of life.

In addition, if we think of gods as the powers presiding over exceptional events and observed regularities it will be natural to assume that this is true of human events as well. This we find to be the case in Homer. There are constant references to the occasions when a particular hero becomes inspired in battle, because "some power put might in him". The important thing to notice is that it is not any the less to his credit because he is acting in the strength of a power other than his own. The impression we get is of various powers keeping the world roughly in order, by various means, including the actions of certain human beings. The easiest way of seeing this is to read Homer's appeal to the muse in the opening lines of the *Iliad*. Through the wrath of Achilles the plan of Zeus was fulfilled. The plan of Zeus is not announced beforehand, there is no suggestion that the action of Achilles is constrained, and yet in some way the action of Achilles, and its consequences, also free actions, is the plan of Zeus. Dodds[6] has coined the concept "over-determination" to describe this. We can express the concept in a sentence; the other-than-human powers that supervise the order of the world on occasions make use of humans in the performance of this supervision, and this for the humans, far from being a loss of freedom, is a mark of special attention. I shall not use "over-determination", because this suggests that the humans are less responsible. Instead I shall refer to this notion as "double determination". Men and *theoi* both are acting, it is the same action, and both are free. Basically it is not too hard for Christians to imagine; a Christian's aim is to act out the will of God for him; but if he does so he would not think of himself as constrained. It is much harder to imagine

---

[1] Cf. Appendix.   [2] *Il.*, xv, 461–4.   [3] Cf. Appendix.
[4] *Il.*, xix, 418.   [5] Cf. Appendix.
[6] E. R. Dodds, *The Greeks and the Irrational*, pp. 30 ff.

this from most other religious outlooks. But it is the most important aspect of the religious background to Greek tragedy.

To go further into this would be an endless task. The relation of this concept to questions of moral responsibility has been studied by Adkins,[1] to whom further reference should be made. Dodds[2] has dealt with the way in which actions are sometimes attributed to *atē*, which does involve a lack of control, a temporary madness or blindness, and which has something of the same relation to a given individual's responsibility as our reaction to drunkenness; the Greeks were prepared to say that an individual was less responsible for his acts under its influence, but if the consequences were serious were not prepared to excuse him. *Atē* also was attributed to external power. In other words, this primitive system did have ways of distinguishing between free and less free acts.

One further example may amplify the concept of double determination. Aegisthus and Clytemnestra are described as acting according to their *moira*, though there is no suggestion that they are not free in so doing.[3] A person's *moira* was his portion in life, and like the concept of "portion in life" seems to suggest a notion of the limits within which one is free, and also that of what we might call our "function in life". It was part of the scheme of things that Aegisthus and Clytemnestra should act as they did. Each person has a part to play in a total pattern. Disaster occurs when men try and step outside the limits of their *moira*; some power will intervene as the *erinys* did to stop horses talking. Adkins[4] says of this passage:

> Common-sense carelessness again preserves individual responsibility.

This is not carelessness; it is the central feature of their thought. Of course, to comply with your *moira* is to be responsible; it is, as it were, to be yourself. If you stray outside its limits anything may happen, and so perhaps you may not be so responsible; you may, for instance, be blinded by *atē*. The concept of a general overriding Destiny is far later than Homer, or the

[1] Arthur W. H. Adkins, *Merit and Responsibility*.
[2] E. R. Dodds, *The Greeks and the Irrational*, pp. 2 ff.
[3] *Od.*, iii, 269 ff.   [4] *Merit and Responsibility*, p. 23.

tragedians. It is significant that when this idea became current in Hellenistic times the word used was *Heimarmenē*, not *Moira*.[1]

Primitive man feels himself surrounded by a number of powers whom he can't really describe. This accounts for most of the religious experience of the characters in Homer. Most primitive peoples personify some of these powers, but the Greeks elaborated the personal aspects more skilfully than other races; they acquired a richer variety of stories. Because the stories helped to clarify the experiences, and because poets themselves welcomed the chance to make stories, more experiences became ascribed to personal powers. Greek *theoi* were always partly personal, partly impersonal, and the personal ones were like the top of the iceberg, evident but very much the minority. A good example of this mixture of personal and impersonal powers is found in the *Theogony* of Hesiod, where the daughters of Night are described: *Momos*, blame; *Oizus*, lamentation; and the Hesperides.[2] We shall find the same sort of thing in the fifth century.

We shall never be able to say exactly how the Greeks conceived the personal Olympian *theoi*, to whom they prayed and sacrificed. It was a less crudely anthropomorphic conception than has often been supposed. Athena plucks Achilles' hair[3] to stop his rage; but she is visible only to Achilles. She does not appear like a girl. These powers have certain rather ill-defined areas over which they exercise control. In the course of time the relation of these powers, one with another, came to seem more ordered. There is a considerable change between the *Iliad* and the *Odyssey* in this respect. Above all, Zeus, whose function has always been especially concerned with order, is considered as more and more powerful. All Greeks thought of the order of the world as having changed. First Ouranos had ruled, then Cronos, and then Zeus. Zeus had had to overcome disruptive elements before he was fully in power; this is represented by the battle of the Olympians with the Titans. In short, then, the Greeks believed that different parts of the world and different facets of experience were ordered by a vast number of powers other than human, some of whom were personal and

---

[1] *The Greeks and the Irrational*, cf. especially p. 7.
[2] *Theog.*, 211–16.   [3] *Il.*, i, 197–8.

could be affected by propitiatory action. Where they differed was over the extent to which they believed that all events were under the central control of one power. Perhaps the analogy of the Feudal monarchs may help. Officially they ruled the country. In fact, they often had very little power over some of their vassals. As time went on they saw to it that they did really control what happened in the country.

I see no reason to assume that the religious outlook of the fifth century was very different. Belief in the central order had increased, and there was a stronger feeling of personification. Both are natural developments. If Zeus really does rule, then it is hardly likely that he will let another power defy his rule, so more and more experience will be described as ultimately under his supervision, however indirectly. The latter's increase is also easily explainable. If you have an experience, and then hear some poet singing of a man whose experience seems similar, and the poet says that the man's experience was contact with Dionysus, you will naturally attribute your experience to Dionysus too, even though at the time you were not aware of any personality in particular. The stories therefore accumulated, and the accumulation was helped by the Greeks' enjoyment of stories.

In addition, however, there are two important developments in the religious atmosphere. Both are dealt with by Dodds.[1] First, there is a growing concentration on the individual. Before, it was enough that if a man did wrong his tribe should suffer; now men wanted to see that the wrong-doer himself should suffer. And they did not always see it. Secondly, there was a growing feeling of dread in face of the other-than-human powers. There is no very satisfactory explanation of this; it is, I suppose, somewhat parallel to the increasing emphasis on the macabre, and on death, in the later Middle Ages. Anyhow it was certainly the case. Both of these developments, while not changing the Greeks' idea of the powers that ordered their lives, certainly changed the way they felt about these powers; and both developments have an obvious connexion with the development of tragedy, where there is a far greater feeling of dread in face of the powers that order the world than in Homer,

[1] *The Greeks and the Irrational*, pp. 28–63.

and where the concern is with the individual wrong and the immediate reaction of the powers to it.

During the sixth century, in Ionia, another movement began which was to affect Greek religion profoundly; one after another the pre-Socratic philosophers attempted to find the basic substance of the universe. It was the beginnings of science, but at first the work seems not so much scientific as metaphysical or even mystical. What they had in common was an attempt to derive all processes from one process, all matter from one sort of matter. The answers they gave were different, but probably their effect on ordinary people, and for example on the tragic poets, would have derived more from the way they questioned than from their actual answers. This effect can, I think, be described in general terms. To try and account for all processes in terms of one process would lead to a general increase of interest in the search for purposiveness in the order of the world. Or perhaps we should say that this search for purposiveness would lead to the attempt to reduce all processes to one process. The interest in moral purposiveness which we shall discover in the tragedies is analogous to the scientist's questionings. In other words, scientists and poets are trying to do very much the same sort of thing. One preoccupation of the tragedians is the relation of the natural and moral order. Heracleitus also relates the tension in nature to the tension in the human soul. Later on the activities of the scientists and the poets diverged. It is easy to see why; the scientists became preoccupied with their special studies, and ceased to relate what they discovered there to their central idea of the universal order. When Socrates was accused[1], specialist study of "things under the earth" was related to the art of making the worse cause win. Science was not now conceived as part of the art of learning how to live.

The activities of the Ionian scientists have a somewhat similar purpose to those of the tragedians, and we can find parallels between Aeschylus and Sophocles and the work of Heracleitus or even Xenophanes.[a] There is no conclusive proof that the two older dramatists had read any of the pre-Socratic philosophers, but I should not expect to find quotations

[1] Plato, *Apol.*, 18B and 19B.

embedded in such carefully wrought plays as theirs. Especially after the Persian wars, when Ionians must have flocked to Athens as the head of the Delian league, I find it incredible that these ideas should not have immediately affected the intelligent Athenians. Euripides we know to have studied with Anaxagoras, but it is quite likely that Aeschylus knew his work too. At any rate there is a common outlook.

But the activity of the scientists left them with a different idea of the powers that ordered the universe, and their methods of thought made them opposed to the way in which the poets conceived these powers, and the stories they told about them, while at the same time their increase in special technical studies made them forget the original purpose of their first inquiries. The increasing influence of the scientists is one of the reasons for the change in the religious outlook of the Greeks that took place at the end of the fifth century.

Any account of fifth-century religion must mention Orphism and the Eleusinian mysteries. But there is so little reliable evidence that we can say almost nothing on this topic with confidence.[1] It seems likely that both Orphism and the Mysteries were individualistic practices, ritual designed to ensure the purification and the happy life after death of a man by himself, as opposed to that of the society as a whole. Probably therefore, these rites are not directly important for their effect on tragedy, which was so very much concerned with society as a whole. The growth of the mystery religions should be regarded as part of the increasing attention to the individual, parallel with the general focusing of religious and moral problems on the individual which also takes place in the development of tragedy. As that development went on, the action of the community at large became less and less relevant, and the peculiar tension between individual and community, which we find in the great tragedies, disappears.

The development of Orphism was also a development of doctrines about the fate of the soul after death. The beliefs about survival after death are extremely confused. But it seems likely that most Greeks did believe in some sort of after-life at

[1] Cf. Plato, *Crat.*, 400c; *Rep.*, 364e–365a; *Laws*, 782c; with which cf. Ar., *Frogs*, 1032.

all stages of their history. The matter has been examined in more detail by Adkins.[1] The most important evidence is the account of Polygnotus' painting in the hall of the Cnidians at Delphi, which shows an amalgam of all the beliefs about the after-life, juxtaposed without worry over the contradictions.[2] There is a Homeric Hades, there are sinners being punished, and there is some unhappy destiny for the uninitiated, as Pausanias interprets. Belief in some scheme of rewards and punishments after death is as old as the *Odyssey* and perhaps even the *Iliad*, but at no stage did any one view of the after-life oust its opposites. Even Virgil hardly presents a consistent picture in *Aeneid* VI. There are remarks expressing scepticism about survival after death in the tragedies, and there are also remarks expressing some sort of belief. It would seem probable that the tragedians did believe in some form of after-life, and almost certain that their audience did.

We must attempt to complete this picture of the religious background with some sort of sketch of the early Greek attitude to morals. This has been fully covered by Adkins.[3] There is no way of translating the concepts "good", "right", or "duty". The word "*agathos*", which is carelessly translated "good", is better rendered as "gentleman" or "appropriate to a gentleman". The noun with the same root, "*aretē*", should be translated "distinction" or "excellence", not "virtue". The sort of qualities that are commended depend on what sort of a man is needed for a particular society. Alcinous tells Odysseus that excellence means something very different in Phaeacia to what it means elsewhere, largely because the Phaeacians are peaceful, pleasure-loving people.[4] In Homeric times excellence was excellence in war; later, in the city states, it was the excellence of the just administrator. Socrates attempted to define a concept of virtue, but before him the nearest the Greeks got to this was to define the sort of things a gentleman would not do. This prevented one from spurning a suppliant, and included certain acts of unselfishness, though the motive of self-interest is never far absent; the man who turns away a suppliant may one day himself be a suppliant. Learning what you must not do

[1] *Merit and Responsibility*, pp. 140–8.   [2] Paus., X. 31. 1.
[3] *Merit and Responsibility*.   [4] *Od.*, viii, 236 ff.

was just a part of learning the skill of excellence in whatever station of life was yours; and this depended for its nature very largely on the society in which you were living. This is connected with the notion of *moira*. Excellence is the skill, which is partly a gift, of being able to develop to the full the potentialities of your *moira*, and wrong-doing is largely that of overstepping its limits. In the tragedies we shall come across examples of actions which appeal to our instinctive feelings of generosity and even self-sacrifice; and these actions were certainly meant to appeal to equivalent instincts in the original audiences. But it was an appeal for which no terms were ever found. People accepted that *theoi* punished action which overstepped the limits of the agent's *moira*. But then they felt a sense of goodness in actions like that of Macaria in the *Heraclidae*, which sense was developed by the compassion and sensibility of writers such as Euripides, and they asked that this sort of thing should be rewarded, in the same way that excess in wrong-doing was punished. In short, then, the development of the Greeks' moral concepts tended to make them see the sole function of *theoi* as punishers of wrong action, and finally to abandon a religious outlook of such terrible astringency. Hard thinking about virtue in terms of the religion I have tried to outline is almost bound to lead to what some call pessimism. Aeschylus grew up with the idea of democracy, something completely new in the history of the world. In this context his optimism becomes understandable. Sophocles was a fortunate man, but we find a stern view of life even in the *Ajax*, written before the Peloponnesian war. Herodotus seems from his writing to have been a very likeable, friendly, and happy man; but the tone of his history is desperately pessimistic. The jealousy of the powers is constantly stressed. Pindar thought that life gave two parts of bad to one of good, but that the good man turned the bad inside out.[1] Athenians whose brains had been sharpened by a generation of logical training, and whose outlook had been darkened by having grown up in a state of siege, denied the comforts of a tyrant's court, the interest of travel, or the consolation of a long successful life in the prized calling of a poet, abandoned belief in personal powers whose actions

[1] Pind., *Pyth.*, III, 82.

seemed only malevolent, and demanded that tragedies should entertain them with flights of fancy rather than show these intolerable powers at work in the actions of men.

That there was a change in religious outlook at the end of the fifth century is indubitable. The Olympian gods become irrelevant to thought about religious and moral experience. This change is often referred to as a growth of scepticism. There is some complete scepticism, but on the whole there is a great growth of superstition. In 432 it was declared to be against the law to teach astronomy or to disbelieve in *theoi*.[1] In 420 "Asclepius was brought to Athens",[2] whatever that exactly may mean, and from then on there was a great increase in a cult of magic healing. There is the custom, which started round about this time and increased during the fourth century, of inscribing potsherds with curses against enemies. There is the story of the Kakodaimonistai, a club which met on unlucky days to mock the gods and Athenian customs, all of whose members died young, except for one man who suffered an incurable disease. This story was told by an advocate,[3] and it was to his advantage to attack these people. But he must have assumed that the jury would believe his story. Finally, there is the reaction of the Athenians to the mutilation of the Hermae[4] and their instant recall of Alcibiades, whom they suspected of having had a hand in this sacrilege, even though this action endangered the success of the enormous Sicilian expedition. At the same time there is an increase among intellectuals of a feeling that god is separate from the world, and unlike humans. Xenophanes[5] had said:

There is one god, among gods and men the greatest, not at all like mortals in body or in mind.

Plato[b] seems to have developed this idea of god, a being far removed from the affairs of the world. But he realized that this idea was too hard for the ordinary man, and at the end of his life he was in favour of the worship of the Olympian deities,

[1] Decree of Diopeithes, Plutarch, *Pericles*, 32.
[2] Plutarch, Num. 3, Etym. Magn.
[3] Lysias, Frag, 73 apud Athen. 551e.
[4] Thuc., VI. 27–29, 53, 60.   [5] Frag. 23.

because this worship helped to ensure that men led good lives, even though he did not accept the stories as true himself. We can say that Plato's attitude became typical of the intellectual's attitude through the fourth century, because we find a similar idea of god in Stoicism, only one more fully expressed. The principal effect of this sort of religious outlook was to make philosophers search for some way of commending good actions without reference to *theoi*. "Morality" before had been a matter of complying with your *moira* so that *theoi* should not crash on you, and *theoi* were those powers that crashed on you if you transgressed the bounds of your *moira*. Definition was reference of one to the other. This was the moral scheme of the great tragedies, and all the available evidence suggests that later tragedies ceased to have the same moral interest.[e] This is understandable. Morality became a matter more for logical than imaginative discussion, for prose than poetry. Religion became a matter of abstracting oneself from the world, not of using human experience to imagine other-than-human powers.

This change in religious outlook is concurrent with the decline of tragedy as serious art form, and I have suggested that the two are basically connected. To imagine this change is therefore extremely important for our understanding of the relation of tragedy to religion. But the task is, strictly, impossible. Because of this I offer a model which has helped me to understand it. Let us compare these two attitudes with the two Christian Ways, Affirmative and Negative. These have, for instance, been defined by Charles Williams.[1] In the former Way the intention is to see everything that can be experienced as an image of the order that lies behind experience; in the latter to deny the relevance of ordinary experience to the understanding of what governs it. For those who practise the former Way, religion is much more a communal activity, for those who practise the latter an individual one. A change from the former to the latter on a large scale can be seen as part of what happened at the time of the Reformation, and in particular in the Protestant emphasis on the Communion as personal exchange of man with God, as opposed to the communal celebration as emphasized by the Catholic Mass. Neither Way can be practised

[1] Charles Williams, *The Figure of Beatrice, A Study in Dante*, pp. 8–11.

to the exclusion of the other, and the issues of the Reformation are much more complicated than that. But if we allow for this there are certain parallels. Medieval Affirmative Catholicism was an attitude of mind in which men saw themselves surrounded by immanent personal powers, both good and evil, the angels and devils, and aided by those men who had acquired more than human power by the virtue of their lives, the saints, in which spiritual progress was by means of a communal ritual, and whose dogma was illuminated by every form of imagery available. To the archaic Greeks and the tragic poets the Olympians are immanent personal powers, and religious activity is primarily a communal ritual. To Plato religion is a special private activity set apart from ordinary experience, and imagery is something pretty but irrelevant. The extreme Protestants, of course, ignored the prettiness and concentrated on the irrelevance of images. The most obvious point where the parallel breaks down is that Protestant Christians had the Bible as a common reference; I should not try to say that the Protestant movement was purely Negative. There was not the gulf between intellectuals and ordinary people that there was in the religion of Greeks of the fourth century and later. But the comparison is worth making, and has been made before. Coleridge[1] begins a lecture:

> It is truly singular that Plato, – whose philosophy and religion were but exotic at home, and a mere opposition to the finite in all things, genuine prophet and anticipator as he was of the Protestant Christian aera . . .

There is a feeling of Puritanism in Plato, and a sense of decorum. During his lifetime art became decorous, and merely decorative. It is interesting to compare the attitude in England during the eighteenth century, which was similarly Protestant and decorous. Nahum Tate, who rewrote *King Lear*, would have approved of Plato's condemnation of the poets for being depressing about the after-life, and for laughing excessively.[2] Can it be that these two things inevitably go together? At least

[1] S. T. Coleridge, *The Literary Remains of S. T. Coleridge*, ed. H. N. Coleridge (4 vols.), London, 1836, Vol. ii, p. 12.
[2] *Rep.*, III, 3862A–3889A.

they are found together in great poets, in Homer, the tragedians, in Chaucer, and Shakespeare. Of whom do we approve?

(ii) THE FORM OF GREEK TRAGEDY

Greek tragedy started with a riotous choral improvisation, out of which also grew the dithyramb. This is probably the most reasonable interpretation of the account in Aristotle.[1] The dithyramb was merely one way in which this performance was organized, and it was the earliest form to be governed by rules. In Athens during the fifth century it was a solemn religious choral work. We first hear of it in the first half of the seventh century, when Archilochus of Paros sings:[2]

> Dionysiac dithyrambs – I lead 'em fine
> When my wits have been thunderstruck with wine.

This must have been the undifferentiated choral improvisation out of which all the forms grew. On the whole these were connected with Dionysus, but there were choruses to Adrastus at one time in Sicyon,[3] and Alcman wrote a choric ode to Hagesichora which seems to have involved the same sort of performance.[4] Clearly once a chorus starts performing the element of improvisation will diminish, since choruses must work together. This seems to have been the case, and a highly elaborate form of choral celebration by means of song and dance was developed in the sixth century, largely in the Dorian states, traces of which remain in the custom of using Doric dialect in tragic choruses.[5] The lyric metres of tragedy are extremely complicated, which indicates that the performers must have had a very subtle sense of rhythm. What we know of Greek music suggests that their pitch was very subtle too; they certainly used quarter tones at least. And the generally highly allusive way in which the stories are told in Aeschylus or Pindar confirms that the audience was expected to listen very acutely. It is very likely that, like other primitive peoples, they had a

---

[1] Arist., *Poetics*, especially 1448a 29 ff., 1449a 9 ff., 1449a 38 ff.

[2] Quoted in A. W. Pickard-Cambridge, *Dithyramb, Tragedy and Comedy*, p. 5.

[3] Herodotus, V, 67.   [4] *Oxford Book of Greek Verse*, 114.

[5] *Poetics*, 1449a, 28–33.

very highly skilful mime. Study of Aristophanes particularly suggests this, and if the tragic choruses also used an elaborate mime technique, poetry which seems very obscure from reading the text would be less so in performance.

Soon after this already elaborate art form arrived in Attica, where performances took place in the country districts, Thespis began the custom of using a masked soloist speaking verse to help illustrate the story. At first the mask did not represent character; it may have had a ritual significance, or it may have been merely designed to increase the performer's remoteness.[d]

The Athenians were never very interested in character representation for its own sake. It was not until 420 that any sculpture except a few portrait busts showed character traits. We should not think so much of the actors as characters in their own right, but of the story, illustrated by the chorus and at first by one soloist, later by two or three. They would characterize, but in the same way that Homer must have changed his voice for different characters' speeches in his recitations. We should think of tragedy as much nearer epic, or our own ballads. As both of these break into dialogue when they need to, so the actors speak as need arises in the course of the choral telling of the story. Character is subordinated to the central pattern. The actor's task was to assist the choral meditation on the story, and make it easier for the audience to share this.

We need to understand this in order to understand why the Greeks never used more than three actors in tragedy; they preferred to emphasize basic pattern at the expense of the details of characterization. Sometimes the tragedians used the fact that two characters spoke with the same voice to make a definite point in the pattern of the play. The most significant examples are the *Ajax*, *Antigone*, and *Trachiniae* of Sophocles, and Euripides' *Hippolytus*. The audience would have taken note of this, having only three voices to attend to; it was not like modern doubling in a cast of forty.

If the function of the actors is to illuminate a central pattern, then it is understandable that they will often speak in narrative rather than dramatic form. For an actor to tell what has happened is only odd if the audience are trying to pretend he is not an actor, but the character he represents. In Greek drama actors often speak to the audience direct. Agamemnon on his entrance does not immediately address his wife.[1] Commentators worry about why he should talk to the chorus after ten years away from her. This is to get a wrong idea of tragedy's focus. He talks direct to the audience because there is much that must be said at this point and that is the quickest way of getting it over. There is the same direct address in Euripides' prologues, or, for example, at the opening of the *Clouds* of Aristophanes, when Strepsiades explains his predicament to the audience direct. There is no difficulty about this, once the audience is thought of as participators with the chorus and actors, rather than as mere spectators from outside.

Tragedy was fundamentally a chorus singing; we must not take remarks of the chorus as though they meant the same as what a prose paraphrase of the words would mean. It is easy to give examples of the difference of meaning music gives; the best one that I have myself found is in Comedy. Engaged on a production of Aristophanes' *Clouds*, I realized that the Unjust Cause during the stating of his case[2] would obviously be indulging in comic erotic business with members of the chorus. As this is so very erotic, it is disgusting if spoken. I accompanied it with grotesque music on a trombone, using an instrumental colour to provide the emotional colour that variations of pitch alone gave the Greeks. Immediately the effect was right; merely comic and grotesque. We should think, then, of the way in which the music and the formal elements of the dance distanced the action of the drama. The audience of Greek tragedy were invited to contemplate the totality, not to become involved with individual characters as they are in the normal modern theatre.

(iii) THE IDEA OF THE POET

The poet was regarded as a teacher, though in fact the word which we translate "teach" means also to put on plays. It is possible to translate every early use of this word, *didaskō*, as "show", if we allow ourselves to translate its use with the infinitive as "show how to", since English does not have the construction "show to". The primary idea of teaching is that

[1] *Ag.*, 810 ff.   [2] Ar., *Clouds*, 1068 ff.

it is by examples not admonition. Plays are one form of teaching, showing examples of how to live.

The poet was judged by his qualities as moral leader. Aristophanes gives us a very clear idea of the attitude of the Athenians to their tragic poets, and there is no doubt that such leadership was the first job of the tragedian.[1] The Homeric poems were used in education not so very differently from the way Christians use the Old Testament. The tragic poets were deemed to continue what Homer had begun.

We are also lucky in being able to see clearly how the Greeks regarded the nature of the poet's inspiration. Every time Homer calls on the Muse in the *Iliad* it is for special facts, numbers of ships, or names of the slain.[2] In the *Odyssey* Demodocus is said to be inspired because he knows the details of what actually happened at Troy, and in two other cases it is the knowledge of the stories, the ballads, which is the divine poetic gift.[3]

The primitive method of teaching is by example, and the tragic poets continued this method, showing examples of crucial decisions in the past, in order that their audience might understand what had gone wrong for themselves, and for themselves decide rightly in analogous situations. The effect of many of the tragedies can be expressed like an equation "if x, then y", where x is a wrong act and y is disaster. The poets are concerned with showing how natural it is that y should follow x.

The poet has two responsibilities, to his material and to his audience. He must get his facts right about the past, but he is at liberty to distort them in order to show the moral of the story more clearly. This idea of the poet fits with all the evidence; there is no doubt about it. It is salutary for those brought up with an aesthetic view of poetry to realize how uncompromisingly opposed the Greeks were to such a view.

(iv) THE MYTHS OF TRAGEDY

Since Plato, there have been two senses of the word "myth", and now it is normally taken as meaning an invented story, not

[1] Cf.., eg., Ar., *Frogs*, 1054.
[2] *Il.*, II, 484; XI, 218 ff.; XIV, 508 ff.
[3] *Od*, VIII, 487 ff.; XVII, 519; XXII, 347.

literally true, symbolizing some part of our psychological experience which cannot otherwise be described. This sense is unknown before Plato. The myths[1] of tragedy are the stories of ancient history, and were quite certainly believed in as literally true. This can be shown quite briefly. The only body of myth whose truth we have been able to test is that of the Trojan war, and what we have tested shows that the story basically is true. Secondly, we can read Thucydides, than whom there was no Greek more sceptical.[2] He believed the stories, and has a long argument about the size of the expedition to Troy, based on Homer.

On the other hand, the tragic poets took considerable liberties with the myths. They were probably allowed to do what they liked provided that the details they altered were not generally known.ᵉ Agamemnon kills a stag of Artemis in Sophocles' version of the story.[3] This has obviously been done to make Agamemnon less guilty, because Sophocles does not want his audience to be concerned with that. The introduction of Lycus into the *Heracles* should be considered with reference to the play.[4] In addition, they were quite careless about anachronism. To talk, however, of deliberate anachronism is surely a misunderstanding. Dodds[5] says that references to the *dēmos* in the *Agamemnon* are "more frequent than we expect in a Mycenaean monarchy". Grube[6] says:

> Medea's description of the lot of women is a clear anachronism; she is thinking and speaking as a fifth-century woman might.

It is more that the poets were trying to show the great events of the past in a way that their present audience could understand to the benefit of the present society. Aeschylus is concerned with the state of contemporary democracy, and the *Agamemnon* is partly designed to give an idea of society which will benefit contemporary Athens. Euripides is concerned with

---

[1] Cf. Appendix. [2] Thuc., I. 3, 9, 10.
[3] *El.*, 548 ff. [4] Cf. pp. 126–8.
[5] E. R. Dodds, Morals and Politics in the *Oresteia*, *Proceedings of the Cambridge Philological Society*, 1960, p. 19.
[6] G. M. A. Grube, *The Drama of Euripides*, p. 152.

the relation between the sexes in his own day. Homer wrote for the most part in terms of his own contemporary society; it is just that he had considerable material handed down in the bardic tradition from a different society. He made one sort of mixture of past and present, the tragedians another. This activity is immediately understandable if we remember the religious purpose, though hard to understand otherwise. We can compare the way in which the characters in the Miracle Cycles, who are not obviously Palestinians of a certain period, become Englishmen of the fourteenth century, though more of the latter is due to sheer ignorance. The fourteenth century was not interested in historicity, in the way that the Athenians were beginning to be during the course of the fifth.

We shall understand the Greek attitude to their myths best by examining the *Persae*, the one occasion in an extant play in which the poet created a new myth from near contemporary history. There was a strong sense among the Athenians at the time that it was not their own power alone which defeated the Persians. It was not in the order of things that Xerxes should rule Europe. So strongly could they sense this other power, that Aeschylus could take the same liberties in telling the story that he takes in telling more ancient stories. Stories of past history become myths suitable for tragedy when they arouse a general sense that the powers behind the world guided the event. The whole world order would have been different if the event had turned out differently. Naturally there will be few recent events that can be felt in this way. There will be many in ancient history.

(v) CONCLUSION

The evidence available about the development of Greek religious, scientific, and moral thought, the form of Greek tragedy and the attitude of the Greeks to the poet and the myths which it was his job to describe, all suggest that it will be wisest to assume that the religious and moral issues that the tragedies seem to discuss are indeed central to the writer's point. In other words, I shall on the whole assume that the tragic writers meant what they said. Many critics have thought that this is not the case, because they have thought that what the tragedians said was silly. I do not find it silly, and so I shall try and understand it, in accordance with the principles that seem to lie behind the impulse to write in this particular medium. I shall try and find the central action of the play, since, after all, Aristotle said that tragedy was the representation of an action, then discuss some of the issues that seem to be involved, then notice structural points of interest, and finally see how the characters fit into the total pattern. I hope in passing to draw attention to some incidental merits of these splendid works; if we wish to appreciate or understand them fully we must perform them; there is no other way.

CHAPTER TWO

AESCHYLUS

(i) LIFE

Aeschylus was born in 525 into a middle-class family, since he
fought as a hoplite at Marathon. For a long time he dominated
the tragic festivals, and after his death he was to remain so
popular that thirty years later, in 411, Aristophanes could write
the *Frogs*, knowing that Aeschylus' poetry would be familiar to
his audience; his plays were granted the unique honour of
revived performances at the City Dionysia; probably they were
also performed at the rural festivals, and possibly they were
circulated in manuscript. He must have been a friend of
Themistocles to put on the *Persae* in 472, the year of Themistocles' ostracism, and it is likely that he was in favour of those
who with Themistocles wished to ally with Argos rather than
Sparta during the 460s. It is also likely that he was sympathetic
to the radical party in home politics at this time, though he was
very careful with his political allusions, in the *Eumenides* for
example.[a] The reforms of 462 should be regarded as the final
establishment of the middle class in power, the class that won
Marathon, and Aeschylus was certainly regarded as the spokesman of this class, the back-bone of the state, later to acquire all
the connotations that phrase would have for us, but then standing for what was at the same time progressive and responsible.
His fame spread beyond Athens, and he died in Sicily at Hiero's
court two or three years after the performance of the *Oresteia*.

It is likely that he was familiar with the work of the Ionian
scientist philosophers, but it cannot be proved.[b] He must have
been in close contact with the intellectuals of Athens; and they
must have formed a small well-knit circle; most probably he

knew the work of the Ionians quite early in his life; certainly his thought has a similar pattern sometimes. His outlook is progressive, as befits someone living at a time of great changes. He was making innovations in his theatrical style when he was nearly seventy, and the work of his old age does not seem old in outlook. He wrote of the past and looked to the future.

The *Persae*, the earliest Greek play, complete in itself and not part of a trilogy, was performed in 472. The *Seven against Thebes*, final tragedy in a tetralogy on the Oedipus story, is 467. The *Supplices* is probably 463.[c] It is the first play of a tetralogy. The *Oresteia* was produced in 458, and probably the *Prometheus Vinctus* was the last work Aeschylus wrote. Our judgement on Aeschylus' form is inevitably incomplete; we have to base it on the tragic trilogy of one tetralogy, and one complete play. The rest are fragments.

(ii) DRAMATIC FORM

His main preoccupation was with order, and the way in which, once order is disturbed, disorder grows and spreads. As far as we can tell, he made the form of the tetralogy peculiarly his own, because his imagination preferred to move on a cosmic scale and it needed more than a single play to fit all the powers involved into their appropriate places in the pattern. He was interested in the way wrong-doing increases as wrong repays wrong, and so in the way in which wrong is handed from generation to generation. He frequently takes a story about a family curse.

His method is to take some central event, some central wrong action, which typifies all the tendencies and influences round it, and then group all the events with which he deals in relation to that central event. The background to the event is treated by allusive choruses. By this means he is able to make the central event more obviously central; it is what we shall see acted, as opposed to hearing about; but it also means that he is able to bring an enormous weight from the past to bear on the central event, because in his choruses he can cover so much so quickly. After the central action we see the consequences, the evil spreading until it destroys all around it, or, in the last great works, the disorder being checked, and a new order being made.

We hear sometimes of Aeschylus' "musical form". Obviously the actual music is more important in his plays than in either of the others, because the sung chorus parts are so much greater in proportion. Obviously too, the way in which stanza balances stanza in the choruses is always important in Aeschylus, in a way in which it is not in Euripides. Often we can understand the meaning of an obscure chorus passage when we see the equivalent passage in the balancing stanza, and realize that both had the same dance movement. When we try to think of a movement that could illustrate both passages equally well we discover that there is only one movement, and this will convey the meaning of the passage.

But the critics who talk of "musical form" usually mean more by this. There is something in the way in which Aeschylus organizes his ideas. They fall into patterns, like musical themes. Music became more specialized during the fifth century; probably Aeschylus did most of his own music, and so perhaps he had more of a musician's mentality.

Thirdly, we are told that Aeschylus is a profound thinker about religious and political issues. It is possible to extract serious thought from the texture of his plays. We can think of the *Oresteia* as showing the development of a democratic society.[1] We can read from it advice on how we should vote, though it is advice on what we should think before we cast our vote, rather than advice to vote for one political party. But if we think of the *Oresteia* as only that so much of it will appear irrelevant. It is all that, but it is much more. The advantages of this particular dramatic form, perhaps above all others, are that in it the dramatist is able to say more than one thing at a time. If we stop to think what an Aeschylus play is "about" we can find so many things which it is about.

We can say these three things, then, about Aeschylus' dramatic form; he is interested in the spread of disorder from an initial wrong act which he sets in the context of the relevant past, and whose consequences he then traces to their conclusion; he has a way of organizing his structure that seems

[1] George Thomson, *Aeschylus and Athens*, pp. 199–219 and 245–97.

like music, and he writes about serious issues in such a way that a particular event is about more than one issue at the same time.

I think these three statements can be related. The impulse behind his plays is to show a story which he sees as a type[1] of one or more than one aspect of history, so that his audience should get a clearer grasp of history as a whole. This relates all three, for the word "type" is important. The structure of the plays is a system of images,[2] and in the same way that the images used are both themselves, and represent many other things as well, so the events also are both particular events in themselves, and represent many other events as well. If this is so, we may more easily understand the structure of the plays by thinking of the actions as being subordinated to the pattern of images, though I do not mean merely the imagery. In Sophocles also we find everything fitted into a total pattern, but in Aeschylus this pattern can be seen as a physical thing. Let us take an example. The point of the first part of the *Oresteia* is to show how Orestes is driven to avenge his father's murder by killing Clytemnestra and Aegisthus, who by killing Agamemnon and Cassandra avenged the wrong Atreus did to Thyestes, the wrong Agamemnon did to Troy and Iphigeneia, the wrong Agamemnon did to Apollo by taking Cassandra, and the deceiving of Apollo by Cassandra. This is shown by the image of the net. Zeus threw a net over Troy,[3] Cassandra sees "the net of Hades"[4] just before her doom, we hear of how the net was thrown round Agamemnon,[5] and finally Orestes appears[6] holding the net, embodied in the physical cloth we can see, in Agamemnon's robe full of holes, and as he holds it up in front of him, goes mad before our eyes. All the doom has come upon Orestes.

This kind of structure is unique to Aeschylus; the pattern of Sophocles is not visible in this way. In the *Oresteia*, our only trilogy, all the imagery has this structural function, and as far as I can see this is so with all the other plays. But, as the example of the net shows, it is not merely a matter of verbal imagery. I

---

[1] Cf. Appendix.   [2] Cf. Appendix.
[3] *Ag.*, 355 ff.   [4] Ib., 1114–15.
[5] Ib., 1382.   [6] *Cho.*, 973 ff.

shall refer to the moment when a verbal image is shown physically on stage as "embodiment". It is one of Aeschylus' key
structural devices, and is obviously over-poweringly effective;
the audience have been prepared half-consciously by means of
the poetry, and then suddenly they are face to face with a real
thing.

I said that actions and events were types, images, as well.
Certain actions I shall call "poetic actions",[1] meaning by this
that they are especially rich in representative qualities. Agamemnon acts wrongly in sacrificing Iphigeneia; we only see the
sacrifice through the eyes of the chorus.[2] In order to show us
what he has done more clearly, we see an exactly similar free,
wrong, submission to admittedly considerable moral pressure,
in his walking on the purple carpet.[3] In a sense all actions in
Aeschylus are poetic actions in that they have this typifying
quality. I use the term for the ones he invents specially to sum
up a situation such as that in the *Agamemnon*, not for parts of
the story like Clytemnestra killing Agamemnon.

The pattern of events is something physical; doom is a net;
but at the same time it is the pattern of events. We are led to
understand the total pattern by having our attention drawn
to the image which summarizes it. There are moments in
the plays when we are made to imagine a particular picture,
which summarizes the total pattern. Later we shall see the
relevance of the picture, and conversely, the later events
will be felt as part of a pattern. I shall try and show how the
Persae in a sense is the embodiment of the dream of Atossa,
the *Oresteia* of Clytemnestra's beacon speech. This technique
gives us a kind of multi-dimensional understanding. It is a
highly theatrical technique, and Aeschylus is its greatest ex-
ponent.

There is likely to be more need for this multi-dimensional
poetry in relating the past to the main action. We may therefore
expect a far greater density of image in the opening play of the
trilogy. The *Eumenides* and *Seven against Thebes* are simple in
structure compared with the *Agamemnon* and *Supplices*. The
structure of the *Persae* is simpler, but the action is simpler.
There is no time for the sort of development that the trilogies

[1] Cf. Appendix.   [2] *Ag.*, 193 ff.   [3] Ib., 908 ff.

39

show. The *Prometheus* demands controversial argument, and will be discussed later.

(iii) RELIGIOUS THOUGHT

In the same way that it is only really possible to see what Aeschylus' poetry was like by considering the whole complex of story, poetic and physical images, and interaction of characters, as one, in the context of each play, so his religious thought cannot be extracted and put down in neat maxims. When a chorus sings to Zeus the words do not mean exactly what they would mean out of context, in cold prose. His religious ideas should be gathered from the effect of the total play, working as an image. Having said this, and added once more that to imagine the religious outlook of someone in an age very different from our own is, strictly speaking, impossible, I shall try and gather a few things together which seem to apply to his thought as a whole.

Opinions of Aeschylus' religion have changed considerably during this century. This is part of a general change which can be seen in our use of the word "primitive". At the beginning of this century to call religion or art primitive was to condemn it. Now it is to praise it. Most of my contemporaries agree that it is Archaic Greek sculpture that they really admire, that it is the Italian primitives, not the Renaissance painters; this is connected with our realization that in developing a sophisticated civilization we have lost one of the most important elements in our culture, which primitive culture possesses to some extent the world over. We can describe this only by talking of vague abstracts such as "awe" and "reverence", and by pointing to the fact that we are affected in much the same way by a Nigerian wood carving and a sixth-century *Kouros*. At the beginning of the century the general consensus of Classical critics felt Aeschylus to be a great religious thinker. In showing the nature of his greatness they made him out as having developed far more towards their own position than could be justified. For example, they tried to make out that Aeschylus had a "Zeus religion" in which Zeus could almost be described as benevolent. He was certainly "moral", by which they meant something like "conforming to the laws of decent, kindly behaviour". As a result a reaction set in, connected especially with Page[1] and Lloyd-Jones[2], to show that Aeschylus was not a "great religious thinker", but a primitive, whose sense of other than human powers was little different to Homer's or Hesiod's. This controversy now seems sterile. Aeschylus is certainly primitive, but his writing is one of the most coherent expressions of a primitive religious thought when it was beginning to be examined in the light of new modes of thinking.

The lack of sympathy with primitive thought comes out in most of the criticism of Aeschylus. D. W. Lucas says:

> It should cause neither surprise nor discontent that Aeschylus was untroubled by the contradictions latent in polytheism.[3]

It is also found for example in Thomson's attitude to Aeschylus' use of myth,[4] when he says that Aeschylus was trying to write about political issues in an age which had not yet developed the ways of expression for these issues. If Aeschylus' structure was merely an inadequate substitute for scientific thought, then I do not know why we bother to read him now.

Aeschylus' religion should be understood by means of his poetry. Everything is both itself and an image of something other than itself. The net is both net, and doom, the doom is the net. Themistocles is "some avenger or evil spirit".[5] More significant, because it has been misunderstood, is Clytemnestra's claim that it was not strictly she who struck her husband down, but the "ancient avenger, made manifest in his wife". This is in lyrics; it is quite clearly the climax of the stanza, and the line which balances it in the antistrophe,[6] performed with the same gesture, presents Iphigeneia.[7] Liddell and Scott translate the word I have translated, "made manifest" as "make oneself like someone", i.e. as middle, not passive. This occasion would be the only one at this period of a middle use; why should we sup-

---

[1] Denys Page, Introduction to the *Agamemnon*.
[2] H. Lloyd-Jones, "Zeus in Aeschylus," *J.H.S.*, LXXVI, 1956, pp. 55–67.
[3] *The Greek Tragic Poets*, p. 60.
[4] Eg. *Aeschylus and Athens*, pp. 317–20.   [5] *Pers.*, 354.
[6] Cf. Appendix.   [7] *Ag.*, 1500–1 and 1526.

pose that it is middle? The mistranslation reflects a misunderstanding of the centre of Aeschylus' thought. Clytemnestra is, not is like, the avenger, the recoil of the murder of Iphigeneia. This is double determination in the hands of someone whose imagination was extremely physical, and once we accept that in this passage Aeschylus actually means what he says, we shall find ourselves able more easily to imagine a system in which events are caused both by human intention and by will of *theoi*.

For a time it was fashionable to think that Aeschylus conceived *theoi* differently from Hesiod. But this was the attitude of a generation which thought the primitive conception was silly. The evidence of the plays suggests that Aeschylus did conceive *theoi* in much the same way as Hesiod. There are many other-than-human powers in the world; some of them are personal. The only difference is that by the time of Aeschylus more thought and imagination had been devoted to the nature of the personal powers and the way they worked. The amount of personality that they have clearly varies; it depends on the amount of contact with rational human affairs that they are conceived as having. Athena and Apollo have the most personal qualities; Ares has considerably less. The Olympian gods are immanent personal forces who cause events, but normally work through humans. They are not symbols,[1] as many critics have made out. Certainly Athena can be said in a sense to stand for the principle of trial by jury, Apollo for the process of purification, as Thomson says.[2] But they stand for much more besides that, and they have individuality. If they are forces as all agree, and they can be affected by prayer, as the plays show that they can, then they have personality in some sense. In addition, we are shown in the *Oresteia*, a progress like that implied in the myths of the *Titanomachia*, in which Zeus establishes his rule over the other powers. If the gods whom Aeschylus talks of and shows us are merely symbols of impersonal forces, which is what critics mean who talk of Aeschylus as having a symbolic religion, then we should see them gradually losing their identity as the force they represent is absorbed in the force that is Zeus. This by no means happens. Thirdly, is it likely that Aeschylus with his powerful sense of physical

[1] Cf. Appendix. [2] *Aeschylus and Athens*, p. 291.

imagining, who sees doom made manifest in a piece of cloth, would put Athena on stage in feminine form if he did not conceive her as in some sense personal and feminine?

The Ionian scientists were concerned to find some underlying order in the world, and the development of Aeschylus' thought also is very largely the development of his concept of this underlying order. All the Greeks had an evolutionary idea of the world; matter had come into being out of chaos, and had been ordered by a succession of powers. This fundamental attitude could manifest itself either as regret for a past Golden Age, as in Hesiod,[1] or as a belief in progress. Aeschylus was concerned with progress, but his was not a facile optimism. We may be more prepared for the end of the *Oresteia* as actually shown, not as gentlemen critics have tried to conceive it, by reading Heracleitus:[2]

> Fire, having come upon them, will judge and seize upon (condemn) all things.

This appears to be a vision of the same sort. The point of the end of the *Oresteia* is expressed perfectly in another passage:[3]

> They do not understand how that which differs with itself is in agreement: harmony consists of opposing tension, like that of the bow and the lyre.

There is a likeness in thought between the two writers.[d] Both present the goal of life as a balance, not a compromise. The end of the *Oresteia* does not say that we should be less rational to the extent we are passionate. We should be both, to the maximum extent. But we should use both elements, as a bow uses tension. Nor will everyone like the result of progress. Fire will judge, and once the Eumenides are working for the city, there will be absolutely no chance of the wrongdoer getting away with it.

For Aeschylus, as opposed to the scientists, this progress meant the way in which Zeus gathered all power under him. Lloyd-Jones[4] is concerned to show that Zeus did not "become moral", but Aeschylus could not have asked the question "Is Zeus moral, is the world order moral?" He had not the terms; and if we had been able to explain them to him, he would still

---

[1] *Works and Days*, 109–20. [2] Frag. 66. [3] Frag. 51. [4] *Zeus in Aeschylus.*

not have answered. Zeus is as he is, and the world is like that, would have been all that he could say. Clearly at the end of the *Oresteia* Zeus is permanently able to rely on the support of the Furies; before that, there was always the chance of a situation, like the dilemma of Orestes, when they supported the opposite course to him. Clearly also Zeus becomes Agoraios,[1] a power who can use the rational arts of persuasion, in a way which once he couldn't. Men have learnt from experience, Aeschylus saw. With his cast of thought he could only account for this by seeing this learning as first being done by some other-than-human power. Zeus was particularly concerned with order,[2] and he was the leader of the Olympians, whose worship was particularly involved with the city state. It was natural that he should think of the power of the Olympians increasing at the same time as the organization of the cities developed.

In addition, however, there are certain indications of something very akin to awareness of transcendent power, and this in Aeschylus is connected with Zeus.

> Zeus is the air, the earth, Zeus is the heavens,
> Zeus is the Whole, and all that is beyond it.[3]

> Zeus – who is that Being – if to him
> My addressing him as Zeus is well,
> With that name shall he be hailed.
> I have nothing to compare
> Though I measure everything
> Zeus apart – if in my mind I'm to make a projectile
> Out of this vague, pressing, weight.[4]ω

He is feeling after the notion of transcendence, feeling also that the total order of the world is related to the human moral instinct; he expresses this by making his chorus sing that they, eccentrically, do believe that it is sin, not just prosperity, that leads to disaster.[5] I find this as a strongly held instinctive conviction, colouring especially the *Oresteia*, and a conviction less strongly held in Sophocles, and doubted in Euripides. But even

[1] *Eum.*, 973.   [2] Cf. *P.V.*, 526 ff., especially 550–1.
[3] Frag. 70, from the *Heliades*.   [4] *Ag.*, 160 ff.
[5] Ib., 750 ff.

44

in Aeschylus it remains instinctive. As we have seen, the Greeks lacked terms for its expression.

There are a few indications to show that Aeschylus like his contemporaries believed in some form of after-life. The slave girls of the Choephori claim that there is consciousness;[1] this need not make us think any the less of death, which is an irrevocable fact.[2] Both Danaus,[3] and Pelasgus[4] are made to talk of punishment after death, and I am inclined to say that tragedy needs both these attitudes, a belief that there is some more abiding standard of judgement than the purely human, and also a recognition that whatever we believe, death is a horrible, irrevocable fact.

I have used the notion of "punishment". But we should try to avoid associating it with a Christian or post-Christian notion of sin. The world is of a certain nature, and if you do certain things the powers that organize the world recoil upon you, sometimes when you are alive, and sometimes after you have died. Morality for Aeschylus is understanding the nature of these powers, and so making the most of the limitations of your *moira*. We are shown two models of actions that are to be commended, those of Pelasgus and Orestes. Both are performed from fear.[5] We are shown the way in which Io flees from Zeus, and suffers, and told how when she capitulates she will be blessed. We must conform to the pattern or be crushed; but there is a positive side; we can learn to approve of the pattern. Aeschylus' idea of wrong action is best examined in the context of the plays, each of which gives a model of a wrong act, and shows how the agent is crushed. It is a very astringent morality, without much comfort, since there is no guarantee of happiness for those who do conform to the pattern; we are shown innocent people placed in intolerable positions. But innocent people are so placed. This is what life is like, and one of the first essentials of religious thought is to face this. Of course now we shall not accept the sketch of consolation that Aeschylus offers, that the power who now controls the world has in some sense himself learnt by bitter experience.[6] This idea is something that

---

[1] *Cho.*, 324–5. [2] *Ag.*, 1019–21. [3] *Supp.*, 230.
[4] Ib., 413–16. [5] Ib., 478–9 and *Cho.*, 276 ff.
[6] *Ag.*, 176–8.

Aeschylus is feeling after, and never finds. But the job of the tragic poet is more to clarify the way to start on this quest than to achieve its end, and the significance of Aeschylus as a religious thinker is that he has made use of a scheme of images to present a system in which the intolerable questions of religion can be posed.

(iv) PERSAE

The action of this play is the yoking of the Hellespont by Xerxes, an impiety committed by a man who thought to control the powers of nature for his own purpose, which had the result of loosing the powers against him; first they work through human agents, and then directly intervene in the course of nature, until the man who had ideas of greatness above his station is utterly humiliated. Xerxes clearly transgresses of his own free will,[1] and yet Darius and Atossa agree that some spirit must have helped him.[2] There are many forces in nature ready to assist an inclination to excess. Xerxes' action is a poetic one; his personal arrogant act in the face of the temptation of his own excessive power stands for the general arrogant action by the Persians of leaving their own continent to try and subdue another one.

The form of the play is shown very simply. It is all summarized in the dream of Atossa.[3] This is a completely static moment. All we have to do is to visualize what the poetry describes. Dreams anyhow were regarded as sent by *theoi*, and the account of a dream is always extremely significant, in tragedy, as in epic. Xerxes tries to control two girls, one Persian and one Dorian, who are fighting, and yokes them to his chariot. The Dorian resists, breaks the yoke, and throws Xerxes to the ground. Darius can only stand by and pity him. After Atossa woke she saw an eagle chased by a falcon. The falcon is Greece chasing Persia, and the fact that this image is not part of the dream, but what Atossa sees waking, corresponds to her departure from the play by the time that Xerxes arrives. It is unnatural to yoke girls in a chariot, and it is foolish to yoke two that are struggling. Disaster is likely, and disaster occurs. The function of Darius in the play is simply that, to stand by. The

[1] *Pers.*, 749.   [2] Ib., 724–5.   [3] Ib., 176 ff.

46

chorus sing of his achievements and restraint, but the point of this is to show that in spite of Darius' qualities disaster has struck Persia.[1]

The play opens with a resonant account of the greatness of the Persian armament seen from the slightly detached point of view of the old counsellors who form the chorus. But in the course of the dance we learn of the excessive ambitions of the Persians towards conquest,[2] and we hear the old men wonder if anyone can "escape the guiles of god".[3] We are prepared for hearing after the news of the disaster that Xerxes was badly advised.[4] As all Persia shares in the disaster, so it shared in the guilt.

In this action the Greeks are some of the divine instruments. First we learn that Xerxes has set himself a hard task of conquest, for Athens is far away, rich and powerful enough even to beat his army.[5] Later we learn of the avenger, the unnamed Themistocles.[6] The powers are against Xerxes, and we are prepared for the disaster, first the sea defeat, then the land defeat, then the troubles of the march and the discomforts of winter. Finally, there is the disaster at the Strymon caused by a *theos*.[7] Their arrogance in bridging the Hellespont is symmetrically repaid. They think that nature has provided them with a bridge by freezing the river, but the sun comes up, and their bridge is destroyed. As the Hellespont in this play stands for the natural right of each people to their own land, Greek to Greece, and Persian to Persia, so the breaking of the solid Strymon, the turning it back to a boundary again, signifies the return of the natural state, order established at a terrible cost.

The play is about the dangers inherent in power. If it was produced in the year of Themistocles' ostracism it was certainly intended to honour him. But the land battle is more important than the sea battle, and it is the "Dorian spear" that defeats Persia there.[8] It is a Dorian girl whom Xerxes tries to yoke, and Themistocles is not mentioned by name. The purpose of the expedition is to take Athens, but merely so that all Greece shall become subject.[9] I can see only one reading of this.

[1] *Pers.*, 852 ff. [2] Ib., 93 ff. [3] Ib., 107 ff.
[4] Ib., 753. [5] Ib., 232–44. [6] Ib., 354.
[7] Ib., 495 ff. [8] Ib., 817. [9] Ib., 231 and 234.

Aeschylus, aware of the aggressive policies being pursued at the time, writes this play as a warning. Look, he says, Persia fell through our instrumentality. But that was because we were under the protection of *theoi*; that was because we were defending the land to which we have a natural right. The Dorian girl has a right to Greece, the Persian to Persia.[1] This is stated very clearly. The play is about the right use of power. Darius had great power, and he used it moderately, keeping within Asia.[2] This distortion of historical truth, as Darius did in fact invade Scythia, shows Darius' function in contrast to Xerxes, whose wrong act we are told of quite clearly.[3] From a deluded sense of grandeur he felt that the great power which was his was not enough because he had inherited it and not won it; he yielded to evil counsellors, and invaded Greece. The implication is that power exercised within its limits is right and proper; if it steps outside it will be broken.

The play is obviously not written for the glory of Athens. None of the Greeks are mentioned by name, and the praise of Athens is in stichomythia,[4] the most matter-of-fact medium. It is hard for an actor to build tension when he is asking questions merely for information, and is in no way in conflict with the other actor. In addition, as I have said, the sea battle is made less important than the land battle, and the climax is the disaster in which Greeks have no hand.

It is, above all, a determined effort to show how the gods work through all events, even contemporary ones. Aeschylus distorts history very considerably. Xerxes left after Salamis, and the Strymon incident appears to be complete invention. There was a widespread feeling of divine deliverance at Athens, as we can see from Herodotus. The Athenians could accept Aeschylus' distortions as showing an intervention in which they believed, but in less articulate terms. Aeschylus could hardly argue for the fact that *theoi* were involved, by inventing an incident for them to control, but he could make physical a general belief that *theoi* were involved by means of this. Because it is contemporary history there is less awareness of any particular *theos*. Darius says that it is the work of Zeus, the

---

[1] *Pers.*, 186–7.   [2] Ib., 865.
[3] Ib., 751–9.   [4] Cf. Appendix.

punisher of the arrogant,[1] but in general it is nameless *theoi* who, however, in Aeschylus' mind, would not act independently of the will of Zeus.

There are two structurally important images. First there is the yoking, the bridge. Quite clearly the two are linked. Xerxes puts a "yoke on the neck of the Hellespont",[2] as he does on the neck of the girls.[3] The implication of slavery with the girls is clear, and ties with the reference to his enslaving the Hellespont.[4] These all clearly connect with the crossing of the Strymon.[5] Less important is the balancing of the list of names of Persians at the beginning with the list of the fallen given by the messenger,[6] and the final list over which the lament is sung when Xerxes comes. The lists serve to emphasize the large-scale aspect of the wrong and its result, the reference to Persia and so to everyone, rather than merely to Xerxes.

In this structure the characters' individuality has comparatively little function. Atossa gives the play the personal depth without which it will not make a real impact on our hearts. We see the disaster through her eyes, and because she is so sympathetic to Xerxes, the tension between our sympathy and our judgement is at its maximum. I find her remarks after the dream very moving. Xerxes is to go on ruling even if he has met disaster; he is not really answerable.[7] Our sympathy is deepened, and at the same time we are prepared for the appearance of the unkingly king.

For this is all the function Xerxes has. All that he has done, and most of what he has suffered, is more impressive for being seen through other eyes. All we need is to see his humiliation. Here there is a thinness in the writing. Almost certainly this means that the music and dance were more elaborate. This is reasonable; by the entrance of Xerxes there is nothing that needs to be said. On the other hand, we must not be allowed to miss the humiliation that follows arrogance. Music and dance was the obvious answer, and we can only regret that the one complete work we possess of Aeschylus turns out on examination also to be incomplete.

---

[1] *Pers.*, 827–8.   [2] Ib., 72.   [3] Ib., 191.
[4] Ib., 745.   [5] Ib., 495 ff.
[6] Ib., 303 ff.   [7] Ib., 213–14.

(v) THE SEVEN AGAINST THEBES

If it is right to consider Aeschylus' tragic form primarily as a developing pattern of images and events that typify, then we shall not learn much of this from looking at the third play in a trilogy. This play's action is the final working out of the consequences following Laius' wrong action in having a child against the will of heaven, which the first play, the *Laius*, will have shown, the second play showing what Oedipus did to make matters worse, leading up to the moment when he cursed his sons. Here the curse is fulfilled.

It is a tragedy without solution. In the usual version of the myth Eteocles breaks his word to Polyneices; they had agreed to rule alternate years; Eteocles will not give up after his year. But in this play we see Eteocles apparently a wise and good ruler, until he gives way to anger and goes to fight his brother, whom he should not fight.[1] At this stage in the story it is more that everyone is so far involved in wrong that no one can be said to be right, however wisely he may seem to act.

We have not enough evidence to say what issues were involved. The play concerns the relation of ruler and citizens. Thebes is saved, and so it would be interesting to know the relations between Laius and the city in the first play. There is the recurring image of the ship which is found eight times. In the second line of the play Eteocles refers to himself as helmsman, and the image finds its most effective use when the chorus describe the crisis of the city in terms of a storm,[2] and then the messenger says that it is in calm water again.[3] But soon we hear of the death of the man who held the tiller. That is how things are. This is the best play of all Greek tragedy for those who wish to talk of the Greek heroes as puppets of destiny. In a sense the captain of the ship is not free when the storm strikes him, and he is probably less free than the other sailors because he has to stick to the tiller. But even here we should notice, first, that it is a storm – there is no suggestion that people are permanently in the grip of evil events; and secondly, we are also shown Eteocles as it were slipping on the deck through bad temper. In some situations you are almost certain to crash,

[1] *Sept.*, 653 ff.   [2] Ib., 758–61.   [3] Ib., 795–6.

but Aeschylus shows the crash coming as a result of a particular action.

We should notice the emblem of Polyneices' shield.[1] He claims that he has *Dikē*[2] on his side. At this moment in the tragedy there appears to be a double *Dikē*, but this is not the final answer; for Polyneices is shown to be mistaken, and is destroyed; the city is saved. The logic of events means that the brothers will kill each other, each believing himself to be right; at least we can say that it is even more wrong to attack the city; and at least the city is saved.

In this play the only character to be noticed as such is Eteocles himself. Aeschylus' purpose is to show how even a wise man is over-powered in these circumstances, and so is careful to show Eteocles at first as strong and calm. It is not impiety that makes him tell the women of the chorus to leave the images of the gods,[3] but a desire to stop panic, and he reacts wisely to the news of each Argive champion standing at the respective gate. He can even pity Amphiaraus. Once again we hear of the ship.[4] If a good man embarks on a ship his goodness will be of no use if the ship is wrecked. It is what happens to Eteocles, a matter which has nothing to do with theories of men as puppets of destiny, but plain common sense. There are situations when whatever we do will be wrong, and there are situations in which we shall certainly be crushed.

(vi) SUPPLICES

The action of this trilogy is the wrong-headed flight of the Danaids from marriage with their cousins, and its disastrous consequences. Their action is quite clearly wrong-headed, but most accounts fail to mention this. At the end of this play the Danaids appear to be justified; the attempt at rape by the Egyptians is beaten off. But we know from the rest of the story that they finally did have to marry, and could only get rid of their cousins by murder.

Of the *Aiguptioi*, the second play of the tetralogy, we possess only three lines, which do not help with the interpretation. It must have shown the story of how the Egyptians got their

---

[1] *Sept.*, 646 ff.   [2] Cf. Appendix.
[3] *Sept.*, 185.   [4] Ib., 602 ff.

way, married their cousins, and were murdered on their wedding night. The third play, the *Danaides*, is more conjectural. We have two minute fragments. One is usually said to be part of an epithalamion, though it is in iambics, and the other is a speech by Aphrodite, usually said to be part of a trial scene in which she defends Hypermnestra, the one Danaid who did not murder her husband on the wedding night. We do not know if Aeschylus included the story of Hypermnestra. The most important evidence is the synopsis of the satyr play, the *Amymonē*.[1] Being in a waterless region, Danaus sends his daughters after water. One of them, Amymonē, aimed a dart at a deer, and hit a sleeping satyr, who woke up and tried to rape her. She was saved by Poseidon, who, however, had intercourse with her instead, and afterwards showed her the spring of Lerna. It has been suggested[2] that the trilogy ended with the Danaids marrying again, ignominiously, as in the version of the myth in Pindar.[3] But even if this is not so, the speech by Aphrodite is a clear indication that they are made to realize the claims of sex. We can be sure that Aeschylus, with his very strong sense of pattern, would hardly have chosen to write tetralogies in which the satyr play was on the same story as the tragedies unless he found that this practice served his purpose. We can also feel fairly sure that the comic possibilities of the satyr wanting the Danaid would have led to a climactic chase scene. So the story of the farce balances the three tragedies. We are more justified still in taking the fourth play as a clue to the total interpretation when we see the importance of the image of the hunt in the *Supplices*. It is a little difficult to see why the Danaid should start hunting deer when she is supposed to get water. If the point of the tragedies is to show timorous virginity as the prey of hunting animals, as can be shown to be the case, then there are obviously comic possibilities in seeing one of the virgins herself trying to hunt, with the same results as the tragedies showed.

The action is shown in miniature with reference to the story of Io. The Danaids' claim on Argos is that they are descended

[1] Cf. Apollodorus, *Bibliotheca*, ii, 13.
[2] Cf. H. D. F. Kitto, *Greek Tragedy*, pp. 19–20.
[3] Pindar, *Pyth.*, IX, 111 ff.

from Io,[1] their first song is their thoughts of Io,[2] and their strange appearance which so puzzles Pelasgus,[3] is obviously parallel to the strangeness of Io.[4] The centre of the play, and, I am sure, of the trilogy, is the chorus, in which, starting with a prayer to Zeus to help them, they consider how Zeus helped Io eventually, after her long wanderings.[5] It should be observed how very visual the geographical description of the third and fourth systems[6] is. The list of places is not merely for sonority as at the beginning of the *Persae*; we are meant to follow Io's travels in our mind's eye over the sheep country of Phrygia, past a city of the Mysians, through the hollows of Lydia and the mountains of Cilicia, so that, on the one hand, when the strange appearance of Io is mentioned we see the resemblance to the Danaids, and on the other, we have plenty of time to think of the point of the Io story. I should add that it is perfectly possible to make an audience visualize even during a sung chorus, if the music is not elaborate and there is little movement. A still chorus at this point, contrasting with the other active choruses, would emphasize the need for the audience to concentrate. When at the end of the chorus the Danaids pray again to Zeus to help them as he helped Io we remember that his way of helping Io at the end was to give her a child, with utter gentleness. They sing that all that happened to her was the work of Zeus; for everything is the work of Zeus. But earlier[7] they have attributed Io's sufferings to Hera; they are refusing to admit that Zeus is ultimately responsible. The unmistakable implication is that as Io fled from intercourse with Zeus, so the Danaids fled from their cousins; as Io was wrong, so were they. They themselves say that the marriage is "prevented by right".[8] Thomson[9] has some ingenious remarks about property; they are totally irrelevant. The Danaids are shown protesting against something which is natural. In fact, we should see in the second play that the marriage is not "prevented by right", because it is not prevented at all. This misunderstanding by the Danaids should be taken

---

[1] *Supp.*, 275.　　[2] Ib., 40 ff.　　[3] Ib., 234 ff.
[4] Ib., 565 ff.　　[5] Ib., 524–99.　　[6] Cf. Appendix.
[7] *Supp.*, 562–4.　　[8] Ib., 37.
[9] *Aeschylus and Athens*, pp. 302 ff.

with the speech in which Danaus advises them about not letting their fruit be picked.[1] He ends by saying they should value being *sōphrōn*,[2] more than life itself. But what they are to restrain themselves from is a perfectly natural marriage. Fruit is meant to be picked.

This is the significance of the chorus of handmaids at the end, who sing that Aphrodite also is to be worshipped, and that marriage on the whole is the lot of women.[3] The end of the play is a prayer by the Danaids that Zeus will give "the women mastery". This is mistranslated by Weir-Smyth as "victory"[4]. Women may win victories, but for women to have the mastery is clearly unnatural, and would have been more obviously so to fifth-century Athenians.

The play uses the way in which women submit to men as a type of the way men must submit to gods. All through the play we have allusions to the power of Zeus, who is clearly behind the action. But the incomprehensibility of Zeus is also emphasized. The Danaids do not understand the power on whom they call on every occasion. Io did not understand the power who pursued her and then soothed her. As the virgin fears to experience sex, and as the timid animals flee from the hunters, so man flees from Zeus, the predator god. But it is natural for animals to hunt, and for men to take their women, and for gods to crush their victims till they submit. The misconception of the Danaids is the misconception of men that they can have a god according to their own pattern, and the point of the play is that men must accept the pattern that exists; if they do, they may find it good.

This theme is worked out through the main image, the hunting of animal by animal. In the opening chorus[5] the Danaids think they may be mistaken for Metis, the nightingale wife of Tereus, now changed to a hawk and pursuing her. Aeschylus has changed the story. Normally the wife is Procne, and the nightingale is Philomela, Procne's sister. Often in fact Tereus is turned to a hoopoe, and so will not pursue to much effect. The usual story is that Tereus seduced Philomela, and then Procne

---

[1] *Supp.*, 980 ff., especially 996–1000.   [2] Cf. Appendix.
[3] *Supp.*, 1034 ff., especially 1050.
[4] H. Weir-Smyth, Loeb. transl., 1068–9.   [5] *Supp.*, 60 ff.

had her revenge by making Tereus eat a meal of their son, Itys.
There is wrong on both sides. Here all that is mentioned is the
killing of the child. We should expect the Danaids to give the
justification for the woman's act. In addition, Metis is made the
wife; there is no suggestion that the hawk is wrong. The audience would notice the linking of the Danaids' flight with the
horrible act of Procne in killing her son, and they would also
notice the change in the story which now gave no indication
that the husband was not entirely justified in pursuing, and
they would perhaps also think of the proverb, told by Hesiod,
of the hawk and the nightingale, in which the nightingale is
told it is foolish to complain of being in the grip of the
stronger.[1] The image recurs, though at one point it is a dove,
not a nightingale; still the Greeks had little ornithology; I
doubt if it is significant. The image is changed; it is also the
wolf chasing the heifer,[2] and the spider clutching its prey.[3] In a
sense it is the animals that eat fruit.[4] It is a highly diversified
representation of the idea of nature, and so the power who
orders nature. Because it is so diversified it is not possible to
know the way in which the image was gathered up at the end
of the trilogy. I shall hazard a guess. The opening line of the
speech of Aphrodite in the *Danaides* runs as follows:[5]

> The holy heaven desires to wound the land,
> Desire to be thus wedded takes the earth.

Is the final example of the image the way in which the rain
chases the earth? At any rate, as far as the religious implications
go, the final image is the child conceived by Io as a result of
the touch of Zeus.

There is one further structural point that illuminates the
play. Pelasgus persuades the chorus to leave their sanctuary
around the images of the gods, and come down on to level
ground. It is all right, he says. We shall protect you from your
cousins. He does, but only in the nick of time. This is a poetic
action of the same nature as that of Agamemnon walking on
the purple carpet. The chorus now trust in man, not Zeus.

We cannot be sure of the exact function of Pelasgus in the

[1] Hesiod, *Works and Days*, 202 ff.   [2] *Supp.*, 351.
[3] Ib., 887.   [4] Ib., 998–1000.   [5] Frag. 44.

total scheme, since we do not know if he appears in the other plays, or not. He is the type of the just king who respects the law of Zeus concerning suppliants, but who will take no action that will endanger his people without consulting them first. His relation to the Danaids is shown clearly by means of imagery. The Egyptians are made to be snakes, among other animals. When they grab hold of the Danaids the girls shout that the snake is catching them.[1] Pelasgus on his first appearance tells that the land which he has just called Pelasgian is called Apian after Apis, who purged it of a plague of serpents.[2] This story, by its apparent irrelevance, would stick in the audience's mind, and we are clearly to think of Pelasgus' act as parallel to Apis'; so as Apis is remembered in prayer, Pelasgus will be remembered also. It is likely that there was a battle in which Pelasgus was killed, because there is a tradition that Danaus took over the kingdom. Pelasgus anyhow acts rightly and suffers; he is to be commended, though this may seem a poor consolation; for though the law of nature is the law of natural selection and the survival of the fittest, men should rid the earth of serpents, even if the serpents' victims should learn to welcome their lot. It is a very stern picture of life that this play gives; but after all we know it to have a lot of truth. Even if we don't see wolves, we can all see spiders.

(vii) ORESTEIA

One of the greatest human delusions is that somewhere, at some time, some of our species will build a city of such an order that it will be seen that all evolution was intended to lead to the city. There have been visions of great cities; they have remained impalpable. The end of Aeschylus' life was the one moment in the whole of history when it was reasonable to believe the delusion that a physical city could be built under the aegis of an immortal power, made fertile and policed by other, grimmer powers, but where also, made more rational and more clear-headed by the awareness of all that was beyond their reason, actual men would meet together, and by process of peaceful discussion decide on what was just. The *Oresteia* is the moment

[1] *Supp.*, 895 ff.   [2] Ib., 249 ff.

when primitive man realized that man's end was to be a member of a community of freely associating individuals for an infinite purpose, and thought that he could actually touch this community's walls. The moment never occurred again, and in a few years Aeschylus' warning had been disregarded and his hope shown to be vain. Democracy did not come, and has not come yet. But those who have written of an intangible city have also written that the city will only be attained by those who have worked to the last limit of their powers to build a tangible one, and some of these deluded builders, as they stand by the ruined Parthenon, will see more clearly than Aeschylus himself what his vision really meant, and count him and Athens all the greater for their mistake.

The *Oresteia* must surely be our type of Greek tragedy, and here more than anywhere else in this book I am aware of the sketchy inadequacy of my judgements. The centre of the play is the killing of Agamemnon, king of kings, by his wife, Clytemnestra, and the consequent horrible duty of revenge laid on Orestes to kill his mother. This act is so horrible, and yet so necessary if justice is to be imposed on chaos, that gods themselves appear in court to plead a case which anonymous mortals judge, under the presidency of yet one more, ambivalent, power who finally reconciles the powers of air and darkness in a rational bargain to do the best they can for her city.

Agamemnon dies rightly, because he killed Iphigeneia. In an intolerable position he oversteps the bounds of his *moira*. "He put on the yoke of necessity."[1] If we visualize someone putting on a yoke, we see that this is quite clearly a conscious, intentional act, but we should notice that the gesture the chorus make as they sing this line is the same gesture as they make as they sing of how the chiefs disregarded the prayers of Iphigeneia. Agamemnon does to himself what the chiefs do to her, stifle an instinctive cry. We see the nature of the wrong act again, because he does exactly the same when Clytemnestra asks him to walk on the purple carpet she prepares for him on his arrival.[2] He knows he is wrong, that he is behaving as a tyrant, and arrogating divine privileges, but he yields. The chorus of old men have wondered all the time he was away

---

[1] *Ag.*, 218 ff.   [2] Ib., 908 ff.

about whether he will escape the consequences of his act, and are still worrying when he is inside, about to be murdered.[1]

But Agamemnon went to Troy as the instrument of Zeus' vengeance against the wrong of Paris.[2] It was Zeus who threw the net of doom over Troy.[3] It is Artemis who is angry with Agamemnon; she is angry at the two eagles feeding on a pregnant hare. Aeschylus does not have the story of Agamemnon killing a stag of Artemis and thus making her becalm the ships in anger. Artemis is angry at the destruction they are doing as instruments of Zeus, angry at the innocent victims who will be killed at Troy. Iphigeneia is in a sense a type of all the innocent victims of war. They all demand vengeance, but the war had to be waged. The world was out of joint.

Agamemnon brings Cassandra home as his mistress, dishonouring Apollo whose minister she is. Cassandra has suffered at Apollo's hands, but she has deceived him.[4] Clytemnestra, by killing her and her violator, is Apollo's agent, as she is in a sense also Artemis'.

Clytemnestra has joined with Aegisthus, who justifies his share in the killing as revenge for the brutal revenge Atreus took on his father Thyestes by cooking him a meal of his own children. But Thyestes had seduced the wife of Atreus. The family of the king of kings is rotten with feuds. It is not a matter of who is right, who wrong. All are wrong. In the same way, once war has begun, all become guilty. The world is out of joint, and can only be put right if the powers that supervise the world themselves agree more together. For whether they agree or not, they take care that he who kills shall be killed in his turn.[5]

The action of the first two plays, then, is innocent Orestes performing an act so horrible that he goes mad, but by that act avenging another horrible act, which in its turn was vengeance for a whole complex of wrongs. The way in which this action is shown is by the image of the net. First used of Troy, doomed by Zeus, it occurs in a passage of anapaests found oddly in the middle of the play. I suspect that there was some point of production, some action of the chorus with its robes perhaps, by

---

[1] *Ag.*, 783 ff., 1331 ff.   [2] Ib., 40 ff.
[3] Ib., 355 ff.   [4] Ib., 1208.   [5] Ib., 1018 ff.

which the mention of the net would be fixed in the audience's mind.[1] The obvious device would be for the chorus to march together on the audience, holding out robes like a cloud. Clytemnestra makes "careless" reference to it when she says that if all the war rumours were true her husband would be as full of wounds as a net of holes. We are suddenly reminded of the doom, and yet the whole phrase is so natural. Cassandra sees a net of Hades as she goes to her doom,[2] and then we hear how Clytemnestra cast the net about Agamemnon.[3] A producer who showed us Clytemnestra with it visible would have missed the whole point. We must imagine it more and more strongly until we see Orestes holding it, and going mad, while he exclaims that this, which was once the robe of the king of kings, is a net footpads might use. The point of the net is weakened if we see it embodied too soon. Aeschylus confuses robe and net, but they are obviously the same image. The net is also used to bring in Electra in a brilliant three lines which also illuminates Electra's character in a way that thirty pages of most natural-istic dialogue could not do.[4] "Children are like the corks that hold up the parent net." We feel such sympathy for Electra, and this increases the sense of horror as the doom focuses on Orestes.*

But this is not the action of the whole trilogy. The total action is assertion of new order. "Justice shines in smoky halls."[5] It is the turning of darkness into light. The key passage is the beacon speech of Clytemnestra.[6] We are asked to visualize with her the flame leaping from mountain top to mountain top, and we must remember that light before electricity was a flame; we picture a torch being carried at incredible speed; it is arriving in the theatre; but we do not see it, not for a long time. The function of the beacon speech is to make us long for light, and to realize at the moments in the play when they shout that light is come, that it has not come. Of course we do not see the light when the watchman sees it at the beginning.[7] Of course we do not see the light when the chorus shout "Now we can see the light" as Orestes appears standing over his mother's body.[8] A producer who followed Thomson's description of

---

[1] *Ag.*, 355 ff.   [2] Ib., 1115.   [3] Ib., 1382.
[4] *Cho.*, 505–7.   [5] *Ag.*, 773–4.   [6] Ib., 281 ff.
[7] Ib., 25.   [8] *Cho.*, 972.

Orestes standing surrounded by torches[1] would be a man who would hang his umbrella on the Apollo of Olympia; one can say no more. When light does come, it is not always to our fancy. The herald from Troy mentions the "sun who alone knows everything",[2] and soon after[3] describes the sunrise in an almost epic line, which holds up the action. Why? Because the sun showed a mass of wreckage, the ships of the men who had sacked the Trojan temples.[4] For some people fire and light are only doom; for Cassandra, who sees fire coming from the palace,[5] and who yet prays to the sun as she enters.[6] Each thinks that his personal hopes are the coming of the light, Aegisthus,[7] and Electra,[8] but they are all wrong. The light does not come until the Eumenides pray that Athens may prosper in the bright light of the sun,[9] after they have reached an agreement with Athena. The final hope is in the hands of powers other than human ones; then, and only then, does the light appear, embodied in the torches of the *propompoi*. Endlessly deluded, our eyes have been demanding the light to appear. It does, and we are satisfied.

Light and darkness are recurring alternatives, but the action of the play is an establishing of light, permanent, using the work of men to make the darkness bright. As in the earlier part of the work, light may mean disaster, so at the end we see the agents of doom, visible and manifest in the light. But they are now working for the good of the city, and this has come about because men have now advanced towards just institutions. For myself, I am sure how this should be expressed in production. When the Eumenides put on the scarlet robes, the sign of their acceptance by the city and of the city,[10] they should so act that their gesture recalls Orestes' gesture with that other robe, and thus both images are linked, and the one action, which seemed to be a growing doom, is seen to be part of the other, the light of justice starting to shine through smoky halls.

Clearly the play is about the growth of order, and equally clearly the growth is on all levels, that of men, and institutions,

---

[1] *Aeschylus and Athens*, p. 274.   [2] *Ag.*, 633.
[3] Ib., 658.   [4] Ib., 527, cf. 338–40.
[5] Ib., 1256.   [6] Ib., 1323.   [7] Ib., 1577.
[8] *Cho.*, 131.   [9] *Eum.*, 926.   [10] Ib., 1028.

and among the *theoi*. At the beginning we see Zeus requiring
war to avenge Troy, and Artemis opposing it, and also Apollo
seen as the tormentor of Cassandra. The world is in chaos, because the powers who should order it are at variance. Then the
king of kings is killed and chaos is threatened. Zeus and Apollo
now act together, and the latter is only Zeus' messenger when
he tells Orestes to kill the usurpers and regain his throne. But
matricide is the most horrible of all crimes, and all the primitive
powers, whose task it is to react instantly to such flagrant
violations of nature, band together against the criminal.
Athena, who is carefully not shown as involved in the Trojan
war, presides over Orestes' trial by a human, divinely ordained,
court, and then wins over the Eumenides to exercise their fear-
ful powers to preserve order within a total system. There have
been several critics who have totally misunderstood the end of
the trilogy. F. L. Lucas, for example, says:[1]

> Yet the Furies in the end are defeated; and there is some-
> thing very appropriate in their conversion by Athena into
> benign but shadowy goddesses of goodwill, "beautiful but
> ineffectual angels".

Here are the words of Athena, installing these "shadowy god-
desses of goodwill":[2]

> So for my city, readily
> I shall enact, establishing here
> These powers you'll not charm easily,
> Whose province will be to oversee
> All human affairs.
> He who meets them, when they are hard
> Will not know how his wounds appeared.
> All that his ancestors transgressed
> They add to his acts, and for all his boasts,
> Silent, unsmiling, they level him to the dust.

Confirmed in this power for ever by the sky goddess Athena,
they put on the scarlet robes, still wearing the masks at sight
of which women attending the first performance had mis-

[1] *Tragedy*, p. 63.   [2] *Eum.*, 927 ff.

carriages, and go out of the theatre to take up their domicile in Athens.

So the *Oresteia* is about the ideal society, based on a union of sky powers, the givers of order and inspirers of rational thought, and above all democratic practice, and the earth powers, the guardians of primitive instinctive morality. Quite clearly we are shown that neither side is enough without the other; and so we are also shown that individuals must develop both parts of themselves also, in order to be fit to live in this society.[g]

The main thing we learn about Aeschylus' sense of structure from this work is the different uses of the chorus. As in the *Supplices,* the Agamemnon chorus of old men are there to brood upon the past, to be aware of what has gone before which makes what happens now intelligible. The choruses are very complicated. In the *Choephori* Aeschylus is concerned to show us the tragic action at its highest point of tension. For this he needs to focus the dilemma upon one man. In order for us to feel the urgency of the command of Apollo when Pylades speaks his momentous three lines, we must be really inside the mind of Orestes.[1] The chorus of slave women is there to increase the pathos, to make us sympathize with Electra, and through her with Orestes. They only see one side, they pray for deliverance from the horrors of life under Clytemnestra and Aegisthus. In the third part we see the action from farther away in preparation for the solution. It is therefore less easy to compare its function with the chorus of the *Seven against Thebes*, whose task is partly to focus sympathy on Eteocles and partly to represent the city. Here the chorus' function is simple, one-sided, but very important. They contrast with all the other actors; they are a different class of being. It is significant that no actor sings in lyrics, not even Athena at the end. The power of the dancing, irrational Furies must not be weakened by letting us see anyone else dance and sing.

There are two other important connexions of imagery: the ministers of vengeance, even Aegisthus, are lions; he is only a weak one, admittedly.[2] And the Atreidae are eagles,[3] Orestes and Electra the eagle's young.[4] The eagle is the bird of Zeus,

[1] *Cho.*, 900–2.   [2] *Ag.*, 1224.   [3] Ib., 49.   [4] *Cho.*, 247.

and so the connexion is obvious. I think that this may include a clue as to the theme of the *Proteus*. Menelaus is the white-tailed eagle, the cowardly bird.[1] I would guess that the story of the *Proteus*, which must be Menelaus' experiences in Egypt, as told in the *Odyssey*,[2] is the story of a lazy idyll. While all this horror goes on, Menelaus basks in Egypt. If this is so, then the *Proteus* would not be so vital for the understanding of the *Oresteia* as the *Amymone* for the *Supplices* tetralogy.

Within this total scheme the function of the characters is enormously diversified, and the indications of characterization extremely rich. They must be looked for; Aeschylus has no time for a long demonstration of character; the actor may only have half a line of dialogue from which to build a significant aspect of his character, but this half line can be more pregnant sometimes than many pages. Agamemnon we must not see too closely, because we must not see the horror of the dilemma of decision until the action is focused on Orestes. We are not spared the horror of Iphigeneia's death; Agamemnon's worries and the preparations for the sacrifice are told with maximum visual force, and then the chorus, at the moment of sacrifice, as it were, cover their eyes;[3] but we do not see Agamemnon close at hand, and neither then nor later are we asked to sympathize with him personally, only as the lonely commander in a position where Odysseus was his sole friend.[4] Cassandra also, as character only, has function as someone caught up in events too big for her. Her scene is played diminuendo, once she has cast off her priestly insignia, until she enters the palace with an image of utter pessimism on her lips. A damp sponge wipes away her life, and she is nothing.[5]

Aegisthus' function is to emphasize how bad things are in Argos; this despicable weakling is now the ruler. He is also there to contrast with Clytemnestra. Her function in the story demands that she should be a woman of stature, and Aeschylus has created a magnificently well-rounded character. Notice her reaction to the news of her son's arrival.[6] "Bring me an axe," she says. Notice her reaction to the news of the victory at Troy;[7]

---

[1] Cf. Eduard Fraenkel, *Agamemnon*, vol. ii, pp. 67–70.
[2] *Od.*, iv, 435–569.   [3] *Ag.*, 191–249.   [4] Ib., 829 ff.
[5] Ib., 1329.   [6] *Cho.*, 889.   [7] *Ag.*, 330 ff.

at last the boys will get a good breakfast, and sleep in real beds. It is a great example of Aeschylus' range.

In contrast, Orestes' action is by virtue of his situation, not his disposition. He must do what he has to do because Apollo orders him, and because he is in debt, and because he hates the thought of Argos being ruled by two women, as well as because he honours his father.[1] He is appalled by his mission; when he does push his mother out he says, "Suffer what you should not suffer."[2] He has asked in the Commos[3] that he may kill her and then die.[4] His first act on stage is to pray. Because he believes the powers demand that he kill, he will do so. But he has no feeling of exultation. Our sympathy is roused for him by the characterization of the people round him, especially Electra and the nurse. The use of the latter is a brilliant and bold device. She has an ironic function in the structure, to increase the sense of triumph by her complete despair at the news of Orestes' death, news we know to be false. She helps to round out the character of Orestes. Through her we are aware of him as a child, wetting his nappies. In herself she allows us to get a nervous laugh or two, at her somewhat comical grief; she is one of Aeschylus' great creations, an example of his awareness of dirt as well as sunlight, an awareness that is the mark of the greatest writers of all.

Electra's character is most beautifully drawn. She is a little silly, lovable, and impulsive, drawn into a situation of horror. It is Aeschylus' genius that he can show us so well what her character is, although the only occasion we see her is such as to stamp out almost all the traces of her natural self. The business with the lock of hair and the footprints[5] connects very well with the image of the net;[6] she is impulsive and shy, eager at the thought, frightened at the the sight of her longed-for brother.[7]

We could speak at length on the other characters, and the incidental merits of this colossal work. For an example of a walk-on's greatest moment, could the three lines of Pylades be bettered? For an example of Aeschylus' great range, comparable to his use of the nurse, we should listen to the herald

---

[1] *Cho.*, 297 ff.   [2] Ib., 930.   [3] Cf. Appendix.   [4] *Cho.*, 438.
[5] Ib., 164 ff.   [6] Ib., 505-7.   [7] Ib., 212 ff.

from the Trojan expeditionary force,[1] as he tells what war is really like, that it is wet nights and lice in the hair. For all this human experience has a share in Aeschylus' great plan, in which we are shown his vision of the human paradox, in which somehow or other justice can come out of chaos. For the human paradox is only part of a wider paradox, in which we are reminded that the lords of air and civilization are Apollo, and Zeus, who bound his own father, and Dionysus, who snared Pentheus as one might a hare,[2] and that the powers of darkness and vengeance are those without whom no crops can flourish, no city prosper. We can know little of this strange order under which we live, except that it is a progress in which the lord of all, awful as he has always been, does not grow less awful as he gathers all powers into unity, but we are told that in this gathering our puny processes of human justice have a part. We see this as approaching light, light that reveals an ocean full of scattered wreckage, an effeminate adulterer standing over the body of a king who commanded the largest armament in the ancient world, a boy by the corpse of the mother he had to murder, and the final linking of sky and earth, male and female, reason and passion, young and old, as Zeus and *Moira*, in the persons of their representatives, come down off the raised stage, through the orchestra, and out into the city in a column of torches carried by the representatives of the new democracy. We ask no further questions, not because we have been answered, but because we have been blinded.

(viii) PROMETHEUS VINCTUS

The action of the play is the binding of Prometheus by the ministers of Zeus, in order to threaten him to hand over the secret which he knows; this is the way in which Zeus can be thrown from power. Prometheus had helped him to his power by allying with him against the Titans, but had then stolen fire and given it to men, thus angering Zeus.

We can only conjecture on the action of the whole trilogy. It is my own belief that the *Vinctus* is not the beginning, but the second play. It is now generally accepted that this was the

---

[1] *Ag.*, 555 ff,   [2] *Eum.*, 24–26,

last work that Aeschylus wrote, and we know that Sophocles and Euripides left incomplete work that was produced posthumously. This evidence is summarized by D. S. Robertson.[1] For myself, I can make no sense of the structure of the play if I compare it with the *Agamemnon* or *Supplices*, but it is very similar to that of the *Choephori*. There is no detectable pattern of imagery, but we should not be able to detect a pattern from the *Choephori*. There are no allusive choruses to include the action of the past. The chorus' function is to concentrate our sympathy on Prometheus, to pinpoint the tragedy, a function almost exactly the same as the chorus in the *Choephori*, and totally dissimilar to that of the *Agamemnon* or *Supplices*. If we say that, the *Purphoros*, conventionally thought to be the third play, is either the first or does not exist; in that case the reference to it would be a mistake for the *Purkaeus*, a satyr play which was put on with the *Persae*[2]. I am more inclined to the latter, because if we think of a structure somewhat similar to the *Oresteia*, then there would be many stories in the first play, the dethroning of Cronos, the battle with the Titans, and the theft of fire will be a comparatively minor event.

The action of the *Prometheus Luomenos* is easier to tell. We have some fragments. Thousands of years have elapsed, and the chorus of Titans, now freed by Zeus, come to visit Prometheus, now chained to a rock in the Caucasus. He is in great pain, and longs for release. His mother *Gē*, Earth, is in the cast. It is important to notice the passage in the *Vinctus*[3] where Aeschylus changes myth, and makes her the same as *Themis*, founder of prophecy. Perhaps she persuades Prometheus to give up the secret, which now seems of little use. Then Heracles comes, and Prometheus tells him of his future travels in a way that clearly parallels Io's, and a line of a prayer to Apollo survives, uttered as Heracles prepares to shoot the eagle that gnaws Prometheus' liver. Then I would suggest that the unusual linking of *Gē* and prophecy is turned to use. Earth herself prophesies the marriage of Heracles and Hebe, by which the strife between Zeus and Hera, which we have seen destroying Io, is reconciled, and prophesies the institution of the Prometheia,

---

[1] *Proceedings of the Cambridge Philological Society*, 1938.
[2] Scholiast on *P.V.*, 94.   [3] *P.V.*, 209–10.

the festival of Prometheus, which indicates the reconciliation of him and Zeus.

In that case the action will be the capitulation of Prometheus to Zeus. This is the obvious way to read the story, because that is the way that the story of Io ends, and Io is obviously parallel to Prometheus. The play will be then about much the same sort of issues as the *Supplices*; it will be the capitulation of nightingale to hawk, man to predator god. It is not a coincidence that both refer to Io. There is nothing unusual about the religious outlook of this play. Prometheus is in an intolerable position; but then so is Pelasgus, so is Orestes. Prometheus has gone wrong, he has overstepped his *moira* in giving the privileges of *theoi* to mortals. This is clearly stated, not only by Hermes[1] but by Hephaestus,[2] the chorus,[3] and even by Prometheus.[4] Yet this wrong is admirable, generous, and unselfish. We cannot fail to sympathize with Prometheus, and we see the responsibility of Zeus more clearly than in any other play. On the other hand, Prometheus is eventually honoured. The play is also about the uniting of the good that Prometheus represents and the good that Zeus represents into a co-ordinated whole.

This play offers little comfort, but there is the suggestion that things will never be as bad again, since Zeus eventually frees the Titans and will loose Prometheus once he is firmly in power. At the time of the play there is a strong sense of disorder. Zeus is called "captain"[5] and "chief",[6] never "king" of the gods. The Io story shows the disruptive influence of Hera, and Io's father receives conflicting oracles, a sure sign that the world order is out of joint. But we do not see the solution, and our instincts revolt against accepting what we are shown in this play.

One of the significant points in the play is the emphasis on relationship, especially marriage. Hephaestus alludes to his kinship with Prometheus[7] and Io's father, Inachus, is the brother of the Oceanids.[8] One chorus tells of Prometheus' marriage with Hesione, one of the Oceanids' own marriage. Probably we

[1] *P.V.*, 945. [2] Ib., 30. [3] Ib., 260.
[4] Ib., 266. [5] Ib., 96. [6] Ib., 169.
[7] Ib., 39. [8] Ib., 636.

shall never know the significance of this; certainly no one has yet explained it.

The function of all the characters is to focus sympathy on Prometheus. Hephaestus with his first words acknowledges the loftiness of Prometheus' aims, and then follows one of the greatest pieces of pathetic poetry ever written. Oceanus is there to emphasize the dignity of Prometheus, in contrast with the former's fussy and useless offers of help. Hermes is a contrast to the dignified Titan, a figure of unredeemed meanness. The chorus, innocent girls who have to get their father's permission before leaving,[1] but who left in such a hurry that they did not put on their sandals,[2] reflect the horror of the simple and pious at the brutal treatment of Prometheus. "All nature laments for you, they sing."[3] The climax comes when, for all their fears, they prefer to face the catastrophe with Prometheus, rather than leave him alone.[4]

Io is a parallel image of the cruelty of god; the wise man and the innocent girl are types of two people least deserving this sort of fate. It is near to the central Problem of Pain,[5] and here Aeschylus is moving in areas where he had no terms for his expression. I have called Prometheus "man". His status is ambivalent. If he were certain he was a *theos* he would hardly be so frequently drawing attention to the fact. And if he was, he would be a Titan, not on the side of Zeus. If this is so, then in the final acceptance of Prometheus by Zeus we are to think of the way in which human processes of justice are part of the progress shown in the *Oresteia*.

Our sympathies are all with Prometheus, but our reason sees that he is factually wrong, just as Io is ignorant of what really happened to her, judging from the confused narrative she tells.[6] He thinks that he knows the future, but he does not know that Zeus will escape his doom, because he under-estimates Zeus' ability to learn.[7] Zeus' power will at a point in time become coterminous with *moira*, and since that is the last line of the *Oresteia*, we must assume that the final vision of *Prometheia* and *Oresteia* are much the same. And if in the consummation of the *Oresteia* humans have a part, and if Prometheus in some

---

[1] *P.V.*, 130 ff.   [2] Ib., 135.   [3] Ib., 397 ff.   [4] Ib., 1063 ff.
[5] Cf. Appendix.   [6] *P.V.*, 640 ff.   [7] Ib., 511 ff.

sense stands for man, then we can see that part of the purpose of showing the cruelty of god to man in this play was to show that in the total scheme of things man could be divine.

(ix) CONCLUSION

The impression we get from the extant plays of Aeschylus is of someone passionately involved in the contemporary scene, and passionately concerned with the nature of the powers that order the world. His peculiar vision was to see the stories of the succession of overlord gods as being the same process as the development of city states, and living at the time he did, he was able to see this process as a continuous growth of order. He would not know how to answer if he was asked, is this a moral process? For to ask if the universe is moral, is to ask if it could be different. But it is a process related to human justice, for human justice has grown up as part of it. And it is a process to be welcomed. For it is life, not to be glossed over, not to be sentimentalized, but to participate in. This, perhaps, is the centre of his genius. He was so interested in gods and spiders, in fishing nets and constitutions, in Homer and private soldiers, that he could forget to be a poet to such an extent that his poetry is not mentioned on his epitaph. Let him be remembered for having fought at Marathon and Salamis. But let him also be remembered as the person above all who has made us always say that Marathon and Salamis were victories.

CHAPTER THREE

SOPHOCLES

(i) LIFE

Born of a good family in 495, and chosen at the age of fifteen
for the victory procession after Salamis, because of his great
physical beauty, Sophocles had a constantly fortunate career. A
friend of Pericles, and therefore probably of most of the notable
people in Athens, he was a general in the Samian war, and had
something of a public career apart from his poetry, in which he
was almost unbelievably successful. He competed at the Great
Dionysia first either in 470 or 468, and on an average every
other year from then on, never coming lower than second.
When the cult of Asclepius was introduced to Athens in 420
Sophocles was entrusted with the guardianship of the god.
After the Sicilian disaster he was chosen as one of the *probouloi*,
new officers designed to cope with the crisis; by then he was
eighty; the appointment was presumably made in order to add
the dignity of his name to the new office. From beautiful boy to
grand old man, he was a type of all that was most distinguished
in Athens of that time. While he was an aristocrat, we should
remember that his friend Pericles, the pioneer of the democracy, was one also. We should not expect necessarily to find
him praising the heroic, old-fashioned code. We cannot agree
with Whitman's thesis[1] that he was a religious rebel, and that
his audiences found him impossible to understand. They did
not; they voted him the prize constantly.

There are only two plays we can date confidently. The
Philoctetes was performed in 409, and the *Oedipus Coloneus* in 405,
posthumously. Presumably it was written just before Sophocles

[1] Cedric H. Whitman, *Sophocles. A Study of Heroic Humanism.*

70

died, 407–6. *Antigone* was written around 440 and *Ajax* is taken as the earliest play. If the *Electra* was written at the time of the break with Argos, since it is set in Mycenae; if it is earlier than Euripides' play, its date is about 417. The *Oedipus Tyrannus* is probably written soon after the plague, and therefore sometime in the 420s. The *Trachiniae* is the most doubtful, but I shall assume it to be a little earlier than the *Oedipus Tyrannus*, and take the order to be, *Ajax*, *Antigone*, *Trachiniae*, *Oedipus Tyrannus*, *Electra*, *Philoctetes*, *Oedipus Coloneus*.

(ii) DRAMATIC FORM

Sophocles, like Aeschylus, was concerned with the way in which *Dikē*,[1] the natural order, is disturbed and rights itself, but he did not think of this in evolutionary terms, or see it in the physical forms of his predecessor; it is easy to understand why Sophocles found separate plays more congenial than trilogies. Aeschylus could see doom handing itself from one person to another in the form of a net; Sophocles will talk just as much of doom, but his generation is considerably more sophisticated, and has lost the primitive age's power of seeing abstract process in concrete terms. Early in his career he abandoned the custom of presenting tetralogies; the evil in Aeschylus' tragedy is cumulative, but Sophocles, thinking of disturbance and its consequences as "if x, then y", is content to show one x and its consequent y. We can express the difference between them by saying that Sophocles writes from a closer viewpoint, a human bystander's, while Aeschylus, spanning more than one generation, takes more of a god's viewpoint.

We will discover that we are being shown things in his plays which will certainly make us think about political, moral, and religious issues. There is no difference in the intensity of his concern with such matters. But there is none of the obvious political interests of Euripides, or the enthusiasms of Aeschylus. This is not surprising; his career suggests that he was perhaps rather less involved in day-to-day struggles than the other two. But not very much less involved; every Athenian took an interest in politics, and we shall find much thought on

---

[1] Cf. Appendix.

71

how the individual ought to behave in the city, though little indication of support for any one political course.

Sophocles was not merely concerned in making "good plots". If his purpose is merely to keep our attention on a well-constructed story, then clearly he has not constructed his stories well enough. The ignorance of Jocasta about Oedipus' past, and the ignorance of Oedipus about the circumstances of the death of Laius would be both extremely implausible if we were thinking in terms of the detective story plot that some critics have tried to make the *Oedipus Tyrannus* into.[1] The important question as to who is really responsible in the *Coloneus* for Oedipus' exile, Eteocles or Polyneices, is left vague; important that is if we are looking at the play naturalistically. There are examples of a lack of accuracy about all the stories in Sophocles' plays, as, for example, in the *Philoctetes*, where Neoptolemus' knowledge about Philoctetes' wound seems to grow as time goes on.[2] Events in Sophocles are quite clearly subsumed to the pattern in the same way as in Aeschylus.

Secondly, if the object of Sophocles was to "create and display great personalities",[3] then his aim was presumably to get us interested in every aspect of their lives; in that case it is extraordinary that he should write in such a way that we are asked to forget characters as soon as the actor walks off the stage, as is the case with Deianeira and Antigone. The idea that a dramatist sits down to create characters in a vacuum is an odd one anyhow; they must surely be conceived in action. But presumably the notion behind this sort of judgement is that Sophocles wrote very instinctively and let his characters run away with him. This we shall find to be quite untrue. There are constant patternings of one sort and another through all the plays. He was an extremely conscious and careful artist.

We can see the way in which he subsumed his characters to a total scheme by considering the way in which he allotted parts to his actors. Taking the obvious, sensible allocation of parts, the actor playing Ajax will play Teucer, the actor playing

---

[1] *O.T.*, 697 ff.

[2] *Phil.*, 1–10, 191–200, 265, 1326; cf. H. D. F. Kitto, *Form and Meaning in Drama*, pp. 95–101.

[3] T. B. L. Webster, *An Introduction to Sophocles*, p. 83.

Antigone will play Teiresias, and the actor playing Deianeira
will play Heracles. Ajax betrays his heroic code, while Teucer
prepares for a hero's death, bastard though he is. The well-
meaning foolish action of Deianeira is in some way the same
as the excesses of Heracles, and it is the same power that confronts Creon in the instinctive act of an impulsive girl as that
which confronts him in the representative of Apollo.

Certainly Sophocles' aim is more than the mere naturalistic
representation of character for its own sake; we need only
consider the ritual basis of Greek tragedy to see that. But he
does provide a series of great character parts, parts which demand everything of an actor. There is nothing like Electra in
Aeschylus. I have said that he looked at events from a human
viewpoint, and we can see this best in his use of imagery as
opposed to Aeschylus'. His total pattern is abstract, not physical, and so there is no structural use of images. Instead he uses
them mainly to show character. Deianeira did not forget the
words of Nessus:[1]

> no, I kept them
> Like words engraved on bronze, hard to scrub out.

A conventional image suddenly becomes one of genius, revealing Deianeira's character beautifully; she is a homely woman;
who else would think of washing an inscription? We might
compare the sudden use of a very vivid verb right at the end of
a long speech without any imagery at all.[2] Electra has spoken
about her plight at length, and now announces that for the
future she will stay friendless at the gate, and "wither her life".[3]
This reveals Electra very clearly. It is also a very clear indication to an actor as to how to play that speech; the audience
should certainly be made to remember that image, and easily
can be.

Generally speaking then, Sophocles is a much less visual
writer than Aeschylus, and as a result makes far more use of
purely verbal poetry. He makes more use of balancing phrases;
his favourite figure of speech is anaphora; he is also able to
make use of confusion of imagery in a way that Aeschylus,
whose poetic aim was to make his audience visualize, was

[1] *Trach.*, 682–3.   [2] *El.*, 804 ff.   [3] Ib., 819.

unable to do. Agamemnon's threat to Teucer certainly has a confused image.[1]

You've got a dose of something coming to you.

A translation like that of Storr[2] conveys nothing at all of Sophocles' unique style:

A like corrective is in store for thee.

This example also shows something of his use of colloquial language, which we naturally find very difficult to gauge, but which is certainly part of his style. At a moment of extreme intensity in the *Coloneus* the summons for Oedipus is heard:

Hey you there, Oedipus! What's the delay?
You have been waiting for a long time now.[3]

It is a use of colloquial language without the slackening of the iambic line that we find in Euripides or Aristophanes. It is, perhaps, one more example of his ability to make everything into pattern, this combination of plain language and formal arrangement, and this is something which can be more easily extracted and analysed with reference to the verbal side of his poetry, but applies just as much to the whole synthesis of events and characters that make up his total dramatic form. Actions and dialogue take on significance in the appropriate context.

For all these developments, Sophocles is also a master of Aeschylean techniques when he needs them. The meaning of the great chorus on man in the *Antigone*,[4] very largely depends on the balance of a phrase in the strophe[5] with one in the antistrophe. And we could hardly find a more consummate example of the use of visual writing allied to the use of music and dance to express meaning than in the chorus which describes the winning of Deianeira.[6] The description of the power of love is balanced by that of the fight for Deianeira, and culminates in an epode[7] energetically showing the clash, and then suddenly changing in metre to describe Deianeira, quietly sitting apart

[1] *Aj.*, 1255. [2] F. Storr, Loeb edition.
[3] *O.C.*, 1627–8. [4] *Ant.*, 322 ff. [5] Cf. Appendix.
[6] *Trach.*, 497 ff. [7] Cf. Appendix.

74

on the hillside. She is the sort of person who is always fought over, and after this chorus we shall not forget that.

There are one or two critical misconceptions which ought to be noted, even if there is no justification for them. We can pass over the arrogance of remarks made by Waldock[1] that Sophocles ran out of material and had to make one plot out of two, or his description of the choruses of the *Antigone* as "tangential" and "arabesques".[2] According to his critical principles there is no reason why Sophocles should have written one thing rather than another, indeed why he should have written anything at all. His use of the term, "diptych form", coined by Webster to describe the first three plays is more instructive. He treats this phrase as if it gave an account of these plays, whose construction seems odd to people brought up on naturalism. But the phrase only states picturesquely that the plays concern two characters, not one. It provides no explanation why they are like that. We do better to consider whether they work on stage. We find that they do. We find also that in these parts the protagonist[3] played both the main parts, and that part of the point of the play lay in this doubling. At any rate nothing is gained by talking of diptychs.

A further misconception, equally foolish, is that which talks of the chorus as "ideal spectators". They shift from side to side in the *Antigone*, and on the whole support Creon, whom Sophocles clearly shows in the wrong, they agree with the admitted dishonourable stratagems of Odysseus in the *Philoctetes*. And if the message of the play is nothing but the pious platitude from the chorus with which most plays end, then why did Sophocles bother to write one and a half thousand lines lead in? The chorus represent the viewpoint of the ordinary citizens in a body, but on the other hand, we shall find that they are made to speak more than they themselves realize, because it is one of the functions of poetry to say more than one thing at once. I have found it helpful to distinguish what, as it were, they are thinking in character, and call it the "dramatic meaning", and what their words imply in the total context of the play, calling that the "poetic meaning".[4] This is to me the most significant

[1] A. J. A. Waldock, *Sophocles the Dramatist.*   [2] p. 121.
[3] Cf. Appendix.   [4] Cf. Appendix.

thing about Sophocles. His structure is a pattern, and all the parts of the pattern gain in significance once we realize the purpose of the whole.

(iii) RELIGIOUS THOUGHT

As with Aeschylus, Sophocles' religious thought and dramatic form are really one. He felt all things as part of a pattern, but was unable to express the pattern except as a pattern. In both Aeschylus and Sophocles we are constantly aware of *Dikē*, the natural order, being broken and reasserting itself, but in Aeschylus we are more aware of the exact way in which *theoi* take action in this. Sophocles, looking from a closer, human point of view, is less able to describe their actions all the time, with the result that we are more aware of the abstract process, which he asserts all the more strongly for being unwilling to describe it.

We can describe this sense of pattern as irony applied to all experience. Things turn out differently from what we expected, and sometimes it appears that they are turning out exactly as we expected. Clytemnestra prays to Apollo,[1] not quite daring to say that she wishes her son was dead, but clearly implying it, and the next thing that happens is the arrival of the Paidagogus to say that Orestes is dead. But we know that Orestes is alive, sent by Apollo, to whom Clytemnestra has been praying, to kill Clytemnestra. To talk of irony may not express the way in which this attitude of mind embraces all his thought. It is an awareness that we are ignorant of the total pattern, and that therefore our actions may have consequences opposite to those we intended. This is what happens to Oedipus' actions in the *Tyrannus*. This is what happens to Clytemnestra and Aegisthus in the *Electra*; they treat Electra in a particular way, trying to crush her, and by this very act they turn her into a power that crushes them.

In this total pattern *theoi* and mortals have a part. The example of Clytemnestra's prayer shows clearly that the action of Sophocles' plays also is doubly determined. There are natural causes for what happens, but it happens through the agency of Apollo. We should assume that Sophocles conceived

[1] *El.*, 634 ff.

76

of *theoi* such as Athena and Apollo in much the same way as Aeschylus, as personal immanent forces, though he may have been more reluctant to visualize their actual appearance. Even if Athena is intended to be seen by the audience at the beginning of the *Ajax*, she is not so seen by Odysseus.[1] It is reasonable that Sophocles' less visual imagination than Aeschylus was also less confident about the exact form of *theoi*.

But this is not to say that he conceived them as symbols. As in Aeschylus they respond to prayer, and therefore they can cause events and be affected. If they are symbols we may ask what they symbolize. Athena in the *Ajax* then will presumably symbolize Ajax' madness. But then what does she symbolize to Odysseus? Something completely different. The notion of symbol just does not make sense here. In the *Philoctetes* Heracles would have to symbolize Philoctetes' change of mind. But a change of mind is something that needs to be explained, and the appearance of Heracles means that no explanation is given.

For most of Sophocles' life the majority of people accepted the personal nature of some *theoi*. Sophocles was popular, and admired for his orthodoxy, as the episode of the care of Asclepius shows. The onus of proof is therefore on those who wish to say that Sophocles did not acknowledge personality in *theoi*, and most talk so far about symbolic gods has been too vague to do more than reflect an inability on the part of critics to imagine themselves into this sort of religious attitude.

We find indications of a belief in some form of after-life in the plays, and it is reasonable to assume Sophocles had the same sort of muddled thoughts on this as his contemporaries, or indeed as people of most ages. Oedipus[2] wonders how he could meet his father with eyes, and Electra wonders if the dead feel pleasure.[3] She has already declaimed that if the dead are to lie as nothing, and the murderers not pay, then all regard for men and fear of other powers will leave the earth.[4] Later, however, the chorus can describe Amphiaraus as reigning.[5] Perhaps in Sophocles as elsewhere the chief result of the beliefs is a feeling that acts done in life will always recoil, either in life or later.

[1] *Aj.*, 14 ff.   [2] *O.T.*, 1371.   [3] *El.*, 356.
[4] Ib., 245 ff.   [5] Ib., 837 ff.

This is the central notion of his moral thinking. Certain actions upset the order of nature, and then everyone is involved, innocent and guilty. Not all of these actions appear to us as obviously immoral; that of Ajax does; that of Oedipus does not. It is normally said that the "lesson" of these plays is that one should be *sōphrōn*, but this is to look in the wrong way. It is more that he is saying, If you are not *sōphrōn*, such and such things will happen to you; some people are naturally more *sōphrōn*, and others learn by bitter experience. There is a lack of moralizing; certain actions have disastrous consequences, and if you want to avoid the consequences you should avoid the actions. This is what is meant by saying that the powers of the world love those who are *sōphrōn*, and hate the wicked.[1] The difficulty of this is that being *sōphrōn* is not quite the same as conforming to notions of instinctive morality. We can translate only by a phrase, "clear-headed humility", and this will cover most of the examples of wrong action. Oedipus, for example, was neither clear-headed nor humble. But we are still bound to ask why some actions are punished so much more severely than others, and we are also bound to ask whether there is not something positive we can do. The answer we are shown by characters such as Odysseus in the *Ajax* or Creon in the *Tyrannus* is that we should learn to make the most of the limits in which we live. But there is more in the plays than he can express. There is a positive unselfishness about Antigone in the *Coloneus* which we must admire, though there are no terms in which to express this, and there is a general conviction that *Dikē* is related to human notions of justice, even though the relation cannot be expressed.

This is part of a general feeling about Sophocles' religion, which has made people call him a pessimist. It is general throughout his life, and is therefore not only brought on by the war, though it increases in the last two plays. The remarks of Philoctetes about those who have died at Troy tend to stand out of their context:[2]

> It would be so. Evil has never perished.
> The powers carefully look after that,

[1] *Aj.*, 132-3.   [2] *Phil.*, 446 ff.

And somehow wickedness and treachery
They love to turn away from death, but justice
And nobleness they always hurry down.
Where can I set these things, where praise, if by
Praising the gods I find the gods are evil.

One of the central morals of the plays is that the good life does not necessarily bring happiness, but that is not to say that it should not be pursued.

We cannot see the order of the world. All we see is humans who transgress it being crushed. We cannot see the gods. The nearest we ever come is a feeling of rhythm and order moving through mountains, plains, and light. Aeschylus was exceptional in his ability to see the gods and the order of the world. The apparent pessimism of Sophocles is part of his more human viewpoint. But from this human viewpoint, that can invoke mountains and plains almost more easily than gods[1] and feels time as something personal,[2] he creates as strong a sense of order behind the world.

(iv) AJAX

Enraged at the decision of the Greeks to award the arms of Achilles to Odysseus, Ajax decides to kill all the leaders. As he starts on this course, he is blinded with *atē* by Athena so that he kills a flock of sheep thinking them to be the captains. When he discovers this he commits suicide, and is finally buried at the entreaty of his enemy Odysseus. The action is supervised by Athena, who will relent her anger if Ajax remains inside his tent for one day;[3] but the message from Calchas the seer comes too late, and Ajax has already left. The point of Athena's action seems to be to make Ajax a laughing stock, and see if he can endure it for the shortest possible time. In naturalistic terms we would say that Ajax was not the sort of person that could. In the terms of Sophocles' religion we see that Ajax' act of suicide is of the same excessive nature as his original anger.

We are shown the dependence of all the characters on Ajax. Tecmessa was born free, and became a slave; but she contrasts her present lot as the mother of Ajax' child with the real

[1] Eg. *Aj.*, 859 ff.; *Phil.*, 936 ff.   [2] *O.C.*, 7.   [3] *Aj.*, 748 ff.

slavery that will be hers if Ajax kills himself.[1] The chorus, Ajax' sailors, also realize their complete dependence on him, and finally Teucer his bastard half-brother tells how he was protected by Ajax during the war,[2] and wonders what will happen to him now, without the hero's help.[3] Ajax ignores them all.

The play is about the way of life followed by Ajax, which we call heroic. The crux of this lies in his great speech, in which he claims to be a hero.[4] Critics have talked of this as a magnificent setting forth of the heroic code, and have failed to notice that it contains a most explicit betrayal of that code. He contemplates advancing on Troy and dying a hero's death before the walls, but rejects this because it would pleasure the Atreidae. This is a certain way he could have atoned for his disgrace, like the Spartan who stayed away from Thermopylae, and was held to have shamed himself until his violent attempts to attain a hero's death at Plataea.[5] Ajax instead decides to commit suicide.

In contrast we are shown Odysseus, with his different kind of behaviour. When Athena tells him to mock his rival he can only pity him. When they are disputing as to whether Ajax should be buried he says that it is not the mark of a just man to insult the dead.[6] He remembers that he himself will one day be in the same position.[7] This is the mark of the *sōphrōn*, to realize what you are, and to what you will come.

There are two facets of this: first, there is a political point. There are certain things which one should not do, whatever the provocation. To refuse Ajax' body burial will not do him any harm,[8] but it is an offence against natural law, and therefore is likely to recoil on the heads of those who act in this way. Secondly, the play contains a moral that *sōphrōn* conduct will not necessarily be recognized or rewarded. Odysseus offers to help Teucer with the burial rites,[9] but his offer is rejected. Just action must be its own reward; it is unlikely to get any other.

The centre of the play presents a crux of interpretation. Having convinced everyone that he is about to commit suicide,

---

[1] *Aj.*, 485 ff.   [2] Ib., 992 ff.   [3] Ib., 1006 ff.   [4] Ib., 430 ff.
[5] Herodotus, VII, 229–32 and IX, 71.   [6] *Aj.*, 1344,
[7] Ib., 1365,   [8] Ib., 1343.   [9] Ib., 1378–9,

Ajax reappears to make his great speech on mutability.[1] It is one of Sophocles' greatest pieces of iambic poetry, a speech that stands out of context. It seems wrong to give it to Ajax now. We should notice that the main point of it is to indicate that he should yield to the Atreidae, for all things yield in time. On the other hand, he ends with giving instructions to the chorus that make us realize that he is not going to return. Some critics have said that he takes in the chorus, but the ode which follows his departure is hardly one of relief, rather of nervous excitement. The point of the speech seems to be that Ajax would be right to submit to the Atreidae, and not kill himself; otherwise why should Sophocles spend such great poetry on a lie? We might say that the dramatic meaning is the attempt of Ajax to deceive the chorus, the poetic meaning is that in this deception he speaks the truth; his conscious decision is wrong, what he is pretending is right. There is a deliberate confusion of imagery which illustrates the point of the play:[2]

> the snowy
> Winters move out of fruitful summer's way.
> The endless wheeling of the night stands back
> To let the white-horsed day kindle its light.
> The blast of awful winds has put to sleep
> The troubled sea; and that all-powerful slumber
> Binds and then looses, grasps, but holds not always.

These verbs are strange ones, and above all we should notice that the *wind* does not put the sea to sleep. This definitely connects with Ajax' death; he uses the same word.[3] The point is that he is wrong, and yet the end is peaceful. It is paradox piled on paradox, and criticism stumbles before it. But in it is the centre of the play.

The natural distribution of the parts is: protagonist, Ajax and Teucer; deuteragonist,[4] Odysseus and Tecmessa; tritagonist, Athena; messenger, Menelaus and Agamemnon. Odysseus and Tecmessa are understanding, Ajax and Teucer intolerant. When Ajax is on stage Tecmessa is seen helpless, but later when instead of Ajax' splendid pride we see the taunting Teucer, Odysseus shows the strength that comes with

[1] *Aj.*, 646 ff.   [2] Ib., 670 ff.   [3] Ib., 832.   [4] Cf. Appendix.

understanding. The point of the play lies in the interaction or lack of it between Ajax and Odysseus, Ajax and Tecmessa, Teucer and Odysseus, and Teucer and Tecmessa.

Ajax is proud and splendid. In spite of the fact that he is wrong, we admire him; sympathy is not the same as judgement. But he is shown as having been noble, though we shall not see him thus. The chorus in the parodos[1] show what Ajax could be like,[2] and tell of his love for Tecmessa which we shall not see.[3] Ajax is not himself; Tecmessa describes his wailing, when he says that this is the mark of a mean man.[4] He loves his son,[5] and realizes the troubles the child will have if he is gone, but he kills himself on Hector's sword, which he has said that he will bury, since it is dangerous.[6] Except that he gets a quick death, none of the prayer he makes before dying is answered.[7] He hopes that Teucer will see that he is buried, but it is Tecmessa, the wife he does not mention, who finds him, and Odysseus, his enemy, who gets him buried.

Teucer will curse the Atreidae, tactlessly, since he is at the time in the presence of Odysseus, who has just befriended him, and to whom the Atreidae are friends.[8] But in the struggle to get the brother he admires buried, Teucer grows in stature, and prepares for a hero's death rather than give way.[9] This is another of the paradoxes of the play.

Odysseus knows that it is Athena who is behind the action, and his presence at the end will serve to remind us of the power that governs the pattern of events. But Tecmessa, though not so aware of what lies behind the action, is understanding in her own way. We should notice how Ajax cannot bear to be mocked,[10] and hear shortly afterwards Tecmessa telling how she will be mocked, if Ajax is gone. Of this he takes no notice. She is all the time ignored. When Teucer arrives, he talks only to the chorus, until he tells her to fetch the child. He delivers the speech of lamentation over the corpse, when it would be normal for the wife to do so.[11] Finally, when the burial begins, she is given no task.[12] Of course at this point she is played by a mute. But it is a superb use of the mute for poetic effect.

---

[1] Cf. Appendix. [2] *Aj.*, 134 ff. [3] Ib., 211–12. [4] Ib., 317–20.
[5] Ib., 545 ff. [6] Ib., 658 ff. [7] Ib., 823 ff. [8] Ib., 1389 ff.
[9] Ib., 1308. [10] Ib., 454. [11] Ib., 500 ff. [12] Ib., 1402 ff.

The dramatic function of the chorus is to show the stature of Ajax, by showing how everyone depends on him. Poetically they are there to emphasize the likelihood of his killing himself. They sing that if he killed the beasts he'll die,[1] though later the chorus leader, speaking, says that all will be well if Ajax is in his right mind.[2] After Tecmessa has attempted to dissuade Ajax from suicide their ode expresses the realization that whether they share in the hero's wrong act or not, ordinary people share in the resultant suffering. The most important ode follows the central speech of Ajax,[3] and carries on its ambivalent mood. It starts:

> I shuddered with desire, joyously I flew aloft.

It is an excited invocation to Pan. I have not seen this explained, and will indulge a guess. There was a belief current in Greece up to the present century that Pan slept at noon, and was terrible if woken. Ajax later[4] will call on the sun climbing the heavens, and the chorus refer to "white sunlight".[5] If this was a common belief in Sophocles' day, then the audience would shudder at the chorus attempting to wake Pan. It would be like trying to keep a werewolf in the house as the sun was setting. Anyhow we hear them say at the beginning of the antistrophe that Ares has freed Ajax' eyes from grief, and we know that Ares never does anything of the kind.

On the dramatic level, the chorus are mistakenly optimistic, and the poetic meaning implies disaster in the invocation to Pan or the reference to Ares. But there is a still deeper level in the poetic meaning. We can only explain this by saying that Ajax adds to the wrong he has done a greater wrong, the self-betrayal of his suicide. But by this greater wrong, order and peace are restored. The only way that I can apprehend this is to return to the image of Ajax' great speech which I have already quoted:

> The blast of awful winds has put to sleep
> The troubled sea;

The blast of winds makes a sea stormy. But we can visualize a wind passing over the waves and as it were smoothing them

---

[1] *Aj.*, 227 ff.   [2] Ib., 263–4.   [3] Ib., 693 ff.
[4] Ib., 845.   [5] Ib., 708–9.

down. It is an illogical image, but it is right. And in this lies
the point of the play, inexpressible in prose terms.

(v) ANTIGONE

Early on in this play [1] Creon says that only when a man is king
can one discover his real nature. This is the story of Creon, a
man who was too small to be king, because he did not see that
civic law must be part of natural law, must comply with the
basic human moral instincts, one of which is to bury corpses.
Thus he shows himself unfit to be king, and he who says that
private loyalty should give way to public not only brings confusion to the city but complete disaster on his own family.

Creon forbids burial to the body of the traitor Polyneices,
whose brave sister Antigone instinctively and immediately
reacts to this repulsive form of vengeance, and buries her
brother. Creon is first confronted with evidence that *theoi* are at
work, when the guard says that the beasts have not touched
the body.[2] This he disregards. Secondly, he is confronted with
Antigone and sees her natural reaction to this edict, that there
is some law higher than those of the city. Thirdly, he is confronted with Ismene, who had become so inspired by the rightness of Antigone's act that she is willing to share in Antigone's
death. At this stage we see how callous Creon has become. On
discovering that Ismene is innocent, he acquits her with the
casualness with which he would have condemned her.[3] Next he
is confronted with his son, who is driven to accusing his father
of being a tyrant for all his talk of private loyalty giving way to
the claims of the city:

> What one man owns cannot be called a city.[4]

The next stage is Creon's self-deception when he says that
Antigone shall be walled up, not stoned,[5] then the scene with
Teiresias which reduces him, the man who thought to rule, to
ask for advice from the chorus, to the shame of saying: [6]

> What must I do? Tell me, I shall obey you.

[1] *Ant.*, 175–7. [2] Ib., 257–8; cf 278–9. [3] Ib., 577–8.
[4] Ib., 737. [5] Ib., 883 ff. [6] Ib., 1099.

His ruin is completed with Haemon's suicide at the tomb and the suicide of Eurydice that follows.

The play is a conflict between a law and a fundamental moral instinct. Because of this fundamental instinctive quality, it is less obviously supervised by any one particular *theos*. All the time we are aware of other powers, but they are not defined. The effect is of a gradual bringing in of a great number. First we are not sure who is behind the preservation of the body from decay; then we learn that Creon has outraged *Erōs*,[1] and then finally we are to assume that Dionysus is involved.[2] But all the time there is the suspicion that Zeus is behind it, as Antigone claims.[3] The point of the burial is as follows: Antigone throws on a handful of dust, and some power takes a hand in her action, and keeps the dogs off as they would be kept off by genuine burial. The earth is removed, and the power, who in the sphere of physical law is neutral, accepts that Antigone's action has been countered. These powers are natural forces, and sometimes react in ways which displease themselves, as we shall see Poseidon does in the *Hippolytus*.[4] Or we may compare the way in which Xerxes is helped by some other power on the course of wrong which he has chosen.[5]

We should use the *Ajax* to help us understand the point of the play. We are asked to admire Odysseus for refusing to allow Ajax to lie unburied, because he realizes that one day he will be in the same position. It is not so much dishonouring the dead, who cannot be touched, but it is dishonouring *theoi*, as Haemon points out.[6] The fact that Antigone cannot adequately explain her position is irrelevant. She has responded instinctively to what the natural order of things demands; she happens to be right. The centre of it lies in her remark to Creon:[7]

> Of course I understood that I would die;
> Even if you kept silent.

The point of the play lies in its poetic climax, the great ode on man, which follows immediately after the first clear signs of *theoi* being involved in the action.[8] The dramatic point of this

---

[1] *Ant.*, 781 ff. [2] Ib., 1115. [3] Ib., 127, 604; cf. 450 ff.
[4] Cf. p. 123. [5] Cf. p. 46. [6] *Ant.*, 745.
[7] Ib., 460-1. [8] Ib., 332 ff.

chorus is that man can do anything if he keeps the laws. But casually Sophocles slips in that there is one hazard he cannot overcome, death. The poetic point is that man can do all these wonderful things provided that he remembers that he is mortal. Reverence for a corpse is part of this wider remembering of death, the common limit to everyone's *moira*. We are asked to admire Antigone for this instinctive reverence, not for any reasons she gives about burial.

The implication of this is that a ruler without reverence will be a bad ruler, and a city without it will be a bad city. It is one of the centres of Sophocles' thought, and it is therefore appropriate that it should be enshrined in one of Sophocles' and indeed Greek tragedy's greatest poetic triumphs.

The play also emphasizes the fact that those who do the will of *theoi* will not necessarily benefit. There is no comfort for Antigone, who is forgotten in the later part of the play, nor for Haemon, who realizes her claim is so strong that he goes so far as to threaten his own father. They are destroyed. There is nothing in Sophocles' thought to suggest that the bad cannot destroy the good.

We should regard Antigone as one of the instruments of heaven for bringing Creon's wrong action back on himself. We are helped in this if we consider the natural allocation of the roles, whereby the protagonist would take Antigone, Teiresias, and the two messengers, the deuteragonist Creon, the tritagonist guard, Haemon and Eurydice. Everything that the protagonist does then is to demonstrate the divine disapproval of Creon's act, while the tritagonist will be reacting in awareness of this disapproval. The most important effect of this is the entry of Teiresias, who is definitely in command of Creon, soon after the exit of Antigone.

A notable use of association of ideas by choral movement are the two pieces of anapaest[1] chant interspersed in the first ode.[2] The thanksgiving that the city offers for the defeat of the seven champions implies a warning against all who set themselves up against *theoi* as they did. This will, of course, be remembered with regard to Creon. There is a foretaste of it here. The first chant refers to the Seven; the second is an announce-

---

[1] Cf. Appendix.   [2] *Ant.*, 141 ff. and 155 ff.

ment of Creon's arrival. Although these are anapaests, I assume some balancing movement; the effect would be obtained equally if at these moments in the dance they stood still.

The function of the characters is very clearly subsumed to the central pattern, so that the timorousness of Ismene is used to emphasize the wrongness of Creon, when even Ismene comes out against him, and the nervousness of the guard, which makes a splendid opportunity for character acting, serves to emphasize the growing fear that Creon is becoming a tyrant. The coarseness of Creon, especially perhaps his remark to his son that with Antigone gone, there'll "still be other fields to plough", is part of the roughness of a man who is too weak for his job, not wise enough, and therefore rude. Antigone is the impulsive girl who cannot say what she is doing. The climax of this is the speech in which she tries to justify herself.[1] It is a strange reason for her act, to say that she could get another husband, or bear a child to another man, but with parents dead could never find another brother. Whitman says this is an actor's interpolation;[2] he can never have spoken to an actor. No one would conceivably damage his part by interpolating this badly reasoned speech, which would be bound to lose sympathy. The point of it must be to show that she cannot express her reason, and this can easily be done on stage; it is pathetic and groping, not convinced at all. It could then be very moving.[a]

The centre of the play is an action which is right whatever reasons are given for it. Therefore it is likely that the function of the chorus, the old men of Thebes, will be to suggest the rightness of the action in spite of themselves. The dramatic meaning of the first ode is thanks for victory over the Argive boasters, the poetic meaning is warning against all boasters. After Antigone is condemned they sing of the contagiousness of evil.[3] They think of Antigone, caught in it, but we think of Creon. They sing of the "tricks of impulsive desire"[4] and think of Antigone's impulse. But "desire" refers more naturally to Haemon's love, which will be an instrument of Creon's ruin. When Antigone is finally led away they sing of three people

[1] *Ant.*, 891 ff.   [2] *Sophocles*, p. 92.
[3] *Ant.*, 582 ff.   [4] Ib., 617.

who were imprisoned.[1] That is the dramatic connexion. The poetic meaning is a reference to three men who did not escape; the ode appears to refer to Antigone, actually it refers to Creon. Acrisius imprisoned the innocent Danae because an oracle warned that through her he would be killed, but in spite of what he did, the oracle came true. Lycurgus suffered for chasing a nymph of Dionysus, for interfering with a person under the protection of *theoi*. Phineus, who imprisoned Cleopatra, suffered as a result; his second wife, Eidothea, stabbed his sons, as Haemon will stab himself, and put out their eyes, so that they were blind, like Teiresias, who appears immediately as the chorus finishes singing. An audience trained in the extreme allusiveness of early choral lyrics would be able to follow this. It is necessary to follow it, because the next ode is an invocation to Dionysus to come to Thebes.[2] Creon's action is compared with an offence against Dionysus, and the action that follows the invocation to Dionysus is the messenger telling of the death of Haemon. This use of song to make the ordinary people's reaction say more than they know is more important in the Antigone than in the rest of Sophocles. When we understand this central function of the chorus there will be no more remarks that the ode to man is inessential. It contains the message of the play, but the message is poetry, and cannot be extracted.

(vi) TRACHINIAE

The real course of the action of this play is not immediately obvious. The story is the consequences of a wrong action of Heracles, but in the beginning we are asked to look from the point of view of Deianeira and a chorus of her attendants. Their hope is that Zeus will protect his son Heracles, but in the course of the story we learn that what has come about has done so because Zeus is angry at the arrogance and violence of Heracles. Our hopes are dashed at the same time as we discover good reason why they should be dashed. Heracles, angry at being insulted by Iphitus, hurled him from a cliff.[3] This premeditated deed of violence, as opposed to an immediate reaction of anger, made Zeus punish Heracles, for all that he was

[1] *Ant.*, 944 ff.   [2] Ib., 1115 ff.   [3] *Trach.*, 269 ff.

his son. Heracles had to serve Omphale for a year. Enraged at this indignity, Heracles determined to sack the city of Eurytus, though he was also moved in this by his love for the daughter of Eurytus, Iole. If Zeus had punished his excessive vengeance on Iphitus, how much more likely is it that he will punish this worse excess of destroying a city because of one person.

The course of the play is the gradual revealing of Heracles' callousness to those who love and admire him. First we see the neglected and forgotten Deianeira, then we learn what he did to Iphitus, then of his love for Iole, the cause of the procession of slaves we have seen cross the stage. Then we learn how he killed Lichas, as violently as he did Iphitus, and finally we see him calmly telling his son to marry his mistress, as if this was the most natural thing in the world.

At first we will have thought of Heracles the hero, because we see him through the eyes of Deianeira and the chorus. This feeling will be strengthened when we see the triumphal procession of captives,[1] but it will finally be shattered when we see Heracles himself, for he collapses completely under his suffering, in strong contrast to the quiet resignation with which Deianeira bears what comes to her. He cries for instance:[2]

> pity me
> Who am so pitiable, who like a girl
> Blubber in misery,

This is what the great hero has become.

In natural terms the play is about the recoil of wanton violence on its originator's head. If you are violent you will cause people to react; they may not mean to do you harm, but that in the long run may not matter. A man who is strong physically is more likely to be brought down by other than direct physical means.

In the terms in which Sophocles shows the action the play is about Zeus, who clearly supervises the events in a more direct way than, for example, in the *Antigone*. Zeus is constantly mentioned, but his effect on the action can be summed up by noticing that Deianeira attributes Heracles' return to Zeus,[3] and then immediately afterwards Lichas brings on the captives,

---

[1] *Trach.*, 225 ff.   [2] Ib., 1070 ff.   [3] Ib., 200.

the result of Zeus' action, so he says. The result of this victory is to make Deianeira try the charm to get back Heracles' waning love for her, and Heracles puts on the robe when he is sacrificing at Zeus' altar. Heracles has done things for which nothing can atone, and even the fact that he is Zeus' son cannot prevent him suffering for them.

Heracles is so violent that something would have happened to him even without Deianeira; she is incidental to the underlying action. But his sympathy for Deianeira makes Sophocles come very near to making a different sort of play, something much nearer to what we would call the Problem of Pain. Our sympathies are entirely with her; she does not blame Iole or Heracles;[1] her reaction is entirely that of the *sōphrōn* who does not fight the gods. She is the sort of person who is fought over, as we learn in the chorus following this discovery;[2] and this has happened more than once. Nessus tried to rape her.[3] In a sense the trouble has sprung from that, and that is not her fault. We are bound to ask what justice is there in a world that lets her suffer. She does not know, and Hyllus curses her when he does not know,[4] and that is why she suffers. This is why Hyllus must chant the last emphatic word, that it is all the work of Zeus. This play is the acutest expression of Sophocles' realization that good intentions do not bring good fortune. It is not the Problem of Pain, because the suffering is all attributable to Heracles' violence; but it is not far from this central challenge to any religion which includes moral injunction, and it is as bleak a play as any of Euripides'.

The natural distribution of the roles is: protagonist, Deianeira and Heracles; deuteragonist, Hyllus and Lichas; tritagonist, nurse, messenger, and old man. Deianeira and Heracles are the same actor. Feminine foolishness and masculine arrogance come to the same thing. Brutal man is loved, and loved for his brutality, by good-hearted woman. That is the way things are. But Deianeira faces adversity with silent courage, Heracles with womanly tears. This again is a paradox that speaks to us, though we cannot paraphrase what it says.

Heracles is loved by Deianeira and adored by Hyllus,[5] but

[1] *Trach.*, 490 ff.   [2] Ib., 497 ff.   [3] Ib., 555 ff.
[4] Ib., 734 ff.   [5] Ib., 811.

we only see his good qualities through the eyes of others. Lichas' death is designed to remind us of Iphitus'; we should think that Heracles tends to be like this, that it was a perpetual danger he would act like that. Lichas and Hyllus have parallel functions; they are Heracles' victims. The impact of the play, whether we see it detachedly as the natural consequences of Heracles' action or as an affront to the belief that gods look after the good, centres on the character of Deianeira. If she was not interesting and admirable there would be no play. She emerges as immensely understanding and sympathetic, a woman trying to grow old gracefully, and the beautiful imagery of some of her lines[1] show that Sophocles enjoyed creating her.

Her hope, which is based on lack of knowledge, is the centre of the play. This is what we find in the chorus. There are references to the power of love; these are taken up in a song of wonder at this power. There are references to oracles, and the chorus develop this aspect of the way all things are ordered.[2] The words mean something different to us who know or suspect the whole course of events, and to them, who only know a little. Sometimes this is obvious, as when they sing, after Lichas has arrived with the captives, that "maddened Ares" has ended Deianeira's sorrow. The audience would know that Ares never did anything of the kind. Generally the tone of the chorus is to insist that there are powers all round, and that the powers will see that all goes according to plan. Yes, the chorus are right, but the plan is not as they hoped. Their attitude and its limitations is expressed well by the way they end their first ode.[3] "Who has seen Zeus unmindful of his children," they sing. They are right; Zeus is mindful. But they are wrong in thinking that to be mindful necessarily means to be kindly.

(vii) OEDIPUS TYRANNUS

Oedipus tried to evade the fulfilment of the oracles, and by his action, brought about their fulfilment. This play has had so much praise and so little performance that it is likely that a generation of critics brought up on the naturalistic theatre may

[1] *Trach.*, eg., 693 ff.; cf. p. 72.   [2] Ib., 821 ff.   [3] Ib., 139–40.

misunderstand it. In our judgement, as opposed to our sympathy, Oedipus is clearly wrong-headed. He is doubtful about his parentage, and goes to inquire of Delphi. On arrival there he is told nothing of what he asked, and so is still doubtful about his parents, but he is told instead that he will kill his father and sleep with his mother. Immediately he runs away, panicking, and comes straight to the cross-roads where he kills Laius. This is all told in one speech, by Oedipus himself.[1]

Once this has happened there is little that can be done, but in these dangerous circumstances he does not behave with circumspection. Ignoring Teiresias' warning, he presses him to speak, when the latter is prepared to remain silent, and when Teiresias does speak, Oedipus attacks him violently. He becomes convinced on no evidence that Creon is plotting, and will not listen as Creon attempts to defend himself. He threatens him not even with exile, which would be severe enough, but with death.[2] It is understandable that he should feel the urge to press on with his inquiries when he becomes aware of the implications; it is understandable that he should wish to know; but it is not the mark of a *sōphrōn*.

As the course of the *Trachiniae* shows us the admired hero, Heracles, brought low, so also we see Oedipus brought low. It is the development of someone who thought that he could get round the oracles, who thought that he was in control of events, into someone who is not considered even capable of looking after his own children.[3]

The action is supervised by Zeus and Apollo working together. These are the two powers above all concerned with order, and Oedipus and Jocasta think that they can defy the principles of order, typified in the oracles at which they mock. After Oedipus has told how he came from Corinth, Jocasta says that she cares nothing for oracles now, since the oracles said that Laius would die by the hand of her son.[4] The chorus then sing a prayer that they may be holy, and not violent, since violence is the mark of a tyrant. They end by wondering how there can be any order if oracles do not come true, and end by calling on Zeus to show his power. The answer is that Jocasta comes out, and more or less prays to Apollo to make his own

[1] *O.T.*, 774 ff. [2] Ib., 623. [3] Ib., 1522. [4] Ib., 857–8.

7

oracles false;[1] and the reply to that is the arrival of the messenger from Corinth who appears at first to show that yet another oracle is false, that of Oedipus and his father, but who ends by showing that all the oracles are true. Zeus has shown his power, and Apollo has answered the prayer.

It is a play about intellectual cocksureness. Oedipus falls because he thinks he knows. His wrong-headedness could be shown quite easily as sin in Judaistic or Christian terms; it is not nearly so blameworthy in Liberal Humanist or Marxist terms, in fact in these terms he is an innocent man in an intolerable position. The difficulty of the play is that our sympathies are roused for him, because he is splendid at the beginning and because he suffers so horribly. But we are never asked to identify ourselves with him, and the chorus viewpoint is less close to his than it is to Deianeira's in the *Trachiniae*. This play, though close to the Problem of Pain, is less near than its predecessor.

It is also about the right way to govern. This is expressed in the contrast between Oedipus and Creon. The former behaves as a tyrant, the latter explains how he'd much rather not be one.[2] The former is careless about oracles, the latter is scrupulous. When he is challenged by Oedipus as a traitor his reply is to suggest that they inquire at Delphi.[3] When Oedipus, impulsive as ever, demands to be thrown out of the country, blind and polluted, Creon replies that he will see what Delphi says,[4] and when Oedipus repeats his demand, replies that to do that sort of thing is to usurp the privileges of a *theos*.[5] The implication is that if the government of Oedipus is tyranny, and part of what makes him a tyrant is disrespect for oracles, then part of good government is respect for oracles. It is the same theme as the *Antigone*, the need for reverence.

Oedipus is shown in his weakness as blind. One of the chief functions of Teiresias is to appear at the beginning as the one who really knows, who is really strong. His physical blindness is contrasted with Oedipus' moral blindness, and with Oedipus' knowledge, after he has blinded himself. Jocasta is another type of the sceptic, more convinced than Oedipus of the lack of order in the world. Creon is not shown as a very colourful

[1] *O.T.*, 911 ff. [2] Ib., 583 ff. [3] Ib., 603 ff.
[4] Ib., 1436–9. [5] Ib., 1518.

character; it is part of Sophocles' practice of not overweighting his advocacy of the people and the actions he approves. Creon is, above all, a careful, humble man. Twice he says: Where I don't understand I'm silent.[1] The point of the play is well brought out by the two messengers. They come expecting one thing to result from their actions, and the opposite happens. They show in miniature the fall of Oedipus.

The chorus of old men of the city present the city's point of view. The play is as much about Thebes as about Oedipus, in spite of what some critics say. It starts with plague, with innocent men and women suffering and dying because of the folly of their rulers. We may wonder if this is what Sophocles was thinking about the leaders of the war party at Athens. They plan, but the people suffer. The chorus pray to all the powers that there are to help them. Running through all that they sing is the plea that Zeus and his attendant powers will settle the matter, and make all things well. As the action develops there is a gap between dramatic and poetic meaning; according to the former, they are hoping that all will be well with Oedipus and with the city; according to the latter, as we understand it, they are foreseeing the disaster that will come to the man who flouts the oracles, who is not holy but violent. The details of these choruses repay endless study, but one detail in the first ode seems to sum up the play most movingly. The action of this story is the disaster and misery caused by man's arrogance and folly. And yet in all this arrogance and folly there is something wonderful. Sophocles describes the disasters and disease. People are dying; it's like – a flock of birds, there are so many of them. But Sophocles has too much triumph in his heart to describe it like that. In a piercingly visual passage he asks us to focus our eyes not on the flock, but on one bird:[2]

> One on anoth-
> er you can observe, like a high-flying bird
> Mightily riding the invincible fire
> To the shore of the western god.

Somehow or other, in ways not to be explained, victory may be won in the squalor of death.

[1] *O.T.*, 569 and 1520.   [2] Ib., 174 ff.

(viii) ELECTRA

Clytemnestra and Aegisthus killed Agamemnon, and by their action make it come about that Orestes and Electra will take vengeance and kill them in their turn. In the *Oresteia* we see the ways in which people act, confronted with the net. In this play we are asked to ignore all that Aeschylus wrote about, and look at the process of turning a girl into an avenger. In Aeschylus we see wrong breeding wrong, as more people get involved. In Sophocles we are asked to concentrate. The evil act of Aegisthus and Clytemnestra recoils upon itself, because it makes the chief sufferers into particular sorts of people. It is the process of making Electra into a *theos*, a remorseless super-human creature, and that is why all our attention is focused on Electra, because it is in her that the process can be most easily shown, since she is in daily contact with Clytemnestra and Aegisthus. The action of the play might be said to be the hope of the two criminals that Orestes should die. This culminates in Aegisthus standing over the corpse of Orestes.[1] Only it is not Orestes, it is Clytemnestra. Their action has exactly the opposite result to their intention.

All that happens is supervised by Apollo, though we should notice that Orestes had decided to avenge his father first,[2] and only asked Apollo how it should be done. Men and gods work together. In a sense it is Sophocles' most ironic play. Right at the beginning we can see that the action of Clytemnestra and Aegisthus has had the effect they did not want, and ranged both gods and men against them. Their remaining actions have opposite results to those intended, and so act as miniatures of the total action. This is the importance of the sequence[3] in which Clytemnestra prays to Apollo, more or less asking that Orestes should be killed, and then immediately the Paidagogus arrives to say that he is killed. From there the action builds naturally to the moment when Aegisthus sees who the corpse really is.

A third way of viewing this is through the character of Electra. At first we learn that her passionate lamentation is a periodic thing. She is someone of strong temperament, anyhow.

[1] *El.*, 1466.   [2] Ib., 32–35.   [3] Ib., 634 ff.

But events are driving her, as we see in her argument with her mother,[1] and she is pushed over the edge by the news of Orestes' death. Now she will actually try to avenge her father alone, even without the help of Chrysothemis. This is what they have made of her. The climax of his development is when we see her at the moment of her mother's death. Hit her again, she shouts to her brother.[2] That is all; she is avenger, pure and simple, a terrible fury.

I am no doubt naïve; but I believe that it is wrong to kill one's mother. I am sure Sophocles thought so too. Critics who have thought that Sophocles approved of matricide have done so because of taking too close a view. Sophocles is very detached from his main character, as he is from Oedipus, as he is from Antigone. It is easier to understand his sympathetic detachment from the latter than his moral detachment from Electra, but they are all part of his method. His point is that the two criminals will get their deserts, and his method is to isolate this aspect of the story from all the other aspects. This is why he has a different story of Iphigeneia, so that Agamemnon should be clearly innocent,[3] so that we should be less disposed to question the need for Orestes to act. This is why the climax is Aegisthus standing over Clytemnestra's body; and not the other way round; if there was a moment when we saw her weep for her lover we might start to feel sorry for her, and question the need for her death. The way we are meant to see the matricide is the way Sophocles shows us. The girl we have seen turning into a fiend stands shouting, "Hit her again." In terms Sophocles is anxious to avoid we could say that Electra's punishment and triumph are the same. She has now become that sort of person. In the terms he does use this is the way things are; people can become like this.

There is another theme which will appear in the remaining plays, a preoccupation with the power of suffering. There are three people who are terrible in Sophocles: Electra, Philoctetes, and Oedipus in the *Coloneus*. They become terrible because of what they go through. As this naturally takes time, this preoccupation with the power of suffering goes with a preoccupation with the power of time.

---

[1] *El.*, 516 ff. [2] Ib., 1415. [3] Ib., 565 ff.

I said that this is the most ironic play we have. It is full of balancing actions. We should notice especially the way in which Electra and Clytemnestra pray at the same altar, to Apollo, and the way in which their prayers are received. We understand much of Sophocles' intention when we see that Clytemnestra and Orestes are played by the same actor. It emphasizes the detached way in which we are to look at the action, and gives an added twist to the climax over the corpse.

Only people of a certain stature can become *theoi*, and so it is necessary to show the full range of Electra's character. This, too, is the reason for the introduction of Chrysothemis, to show that events such as these will not turn everyone into what Electra becomes. Chrysothemis increases the stature of her sister by contrast. Electra is the greatest part for an actor in Greek drama. She runs through every human emotion from a simple joy that has to point out the obvious to her neighbours, when she realizes her brother is alive,[1] to the bottomless grief of the urn speech,[2] all of which is necessary to show what she could have been, what love was in her. It is this widely ranging being who is turned into the grim automaton of the end. Because this is the way in which Sophocles wants us to look at the logic of events we do not see Orestes too closely. He is to be seen through Electra's eyes, the heroic minister of *Dikē*, and we are to concentrate on the way in which Electra urges on his ministrations. In the same way, Clytemnestra and Aegisthus are mainly of interest as the wrong-doers. Clytemnestra is shown clearly to be wrong, in the sequence at the altar, but she is subordinate to Aegisthus in the murder, so that we are prepared for the killing of Aegisthus to be the climax of the play, a necessary step in view of Sophocles' treatment of the story.

The function of the chorus also is simple. They are frankly partisans of Electra, her girl friends. They sing that justice must be done. Their first ode is to *Dikē*, a feeling that the *erinys* will come.[3] Their next ode also refers to the coming judgement, though here they think of it as coming from Zeus.[4] Finally, before the killing, they call on Ares, the *erinyes*, and Hermes to

[1] *El.*, 1227-9. [2] Ib., 1126 ff.
[3] Ib., 473 ff. and 489-91. [4] Ib., 1058 ff.

aid the attempt.[1] There is less sung chorus than in any other
play of Sophocles; Electra and Orestes both sing. There is less
need to distinguish poetic and dramatic meaning, since we are
meant to see this partisan eagerness for a bloody vengeance,
and the complete confidence that this is according to the will of
all the powers, as part of a remorseless total natural order, in
which certain actions will spark off reactions as surely as con-
necting two electric wires. The pun that Sophocles was two and
a half millennia too early to make is one more clue to the centre
of this forbidding play.

(ix) PHILOCTETES

The Greek army under the leadership of the Atreidae and
Odysseus threw Philoctetes on to an island, because he was
physically repulsive through a snake bite. At the end of the
Trojan war they discovered that his presence was necessary in
order that Troy should be conquered. Their action recoils on
their own heads. Their treatment of him proves their undoing.
They have made him into the sort of person who is bound to
affect any normal man who goes to try and persuade him to
come to Troy. They have turned him into a *theos*.

Sophocles, however, is careful to show that this numinous
quality in suffering does not come about without outside
powers as well. *Theoi* are necessary for the making of man into
theos. Philoctetes is suffering because of what he did on Chrysē.
We are never told exactly what this was, but we gather that it
was some impiety which was punished with this gangrenous
infection. The vagueness is necessary here, because this is something about which we cannot but be vague.

We are asked to regard this action through the eyes of
Neoptolemus. It is the nearest a Greek tragedian ever comes to
asking us to identify ourselves with a character. Our understanding of what is happening advances as his does. We cannot
see ahead as much as in the other tragedies. The development
of the action is the process of Neoptolemus coming to the
decision that he must not try and take Philoctetes against his
will to Troy. What Neoptolemus is asked to do by Odysseus[2]
is to behave in an unholy way for one day; it is put very subtly

---

[1] *El.*, 1384 ff.   [2] *Phil.*, 79 ff.

of course. What Heracles, appearing *ex machina* at the end, commends is holiness.[1] This formulation of the virtue in question is important. One would have thought that the motive for siding with Philoctetes was irrational pity. Sophocles uses the word connected with the worship of the gods. It is the decision of Neoptolemus to side with what he does not understand as opposed to what he does. But as in the *Antigone*, this instinctive reaction is shown as conforming to the will of heaven.

These three strands are united at the climax of the play, when Philoctetes threatens Odysseus with the bow and Neoptolemus stands with him. Philoctetes is shown in power, as a result of what has been done to him. He has been made so obstinate by his wrongs that nothing will make him change his mind; except of course a god. Heracles apparently has very little function in the play, except to change Philoctetes' mind for him. But this is of extreme importance. The action of the Greek captains has turned Philoctetes into *theos*, and this is shown by making him so resolute, so much of a *theos*, that he needs the appearance of another *theos* to change his mind for him. Secondly, Heracles appears to show that the action, which has so far seemed to have had only natural causes, has been under supervision in the same way as the action of all the other plays. If Sophocles had wanted to write a purely naturalistic play he could so easily have made Philoctetes change his mind by whim. Thirdly, the appearance gives a temporary relief in the theatre. We have been shown a wrong action, that of the Greek captains, having intolerable results. But we have been involved in them in a way we are not in other tragedies. Our sympathy is drawn more into the action; we want Philoctetes to be cured, and Neoptolemus not to be endangered when Odysseus returns with the Greek army. And so in the theatre we welcome the relief. When we get outside we realize that these actions do have these intolerable results, that we have to decide as Neoptolemus decided, even without the hope of a miracle to extricate us from the consequences. The exceptional ending may make us reflect even more on the point of the play, a point which applies generally, on occasions where there will be no miracles.

[1] *Phil.*, 1441.

99

The play is about political morality, the claims of the better-ment of the group against the instinctive response of sympathy for the individual. We should notice the way in which Neopto-lemus blames Odysseus less for the imagined theft of Achilles' arms than the leaders in general,[1] and Philoctetes also includes the Atreidae in his curses.[2] The wrong done him is done by the whole group. Since all ethical thought in Sophocles' day was in terms of the group, this is a new idea.[3] But even now the point is worth making. Sophocles is also careful to make the further point that we must do good in this way, but not expect the consequences to be pleasant. It will not be to Neoptolemus' advantage to act rightly in this way; it needs a miracle.

Secondly, the play is about the power acquired by suffering. The bow of Philoctetes is called a *theos*,[4] and this is what Odys-seus fears; but it is more the suffering itself which convinces Neoptolemus. In a sense the bow is part of the complex pheno-menon that is Philoctetes. He is somewhat numinous, by being repulsive. It is not a Problem of Pain play, because we are given to understand that in some sense he deserves the suffering, though the vagueness of the story of Chrysē prevents us asking quite how. In other words, everything possible is done to stop us thinking of this in the theatre.

The action is advanced by making Neoptolemus become more and more reluctant to take the bow, as he becomes more successful in his stratagem. It is sound psychology, that often we do not discover that something is wrong for us until we have achieved it. In this development the scene with the sea captain is important. We know that all he says about the Greeks coming in pursuit of Philoctetes is false, but the scene shows Philoctetes now completely ready to flee with Neoptolemus, and Neoptolemus now unwilling to make use of his advantage.

Odysseus in this play has little to recommend him. He is the type of the unscrupulous politician, though he does know that he is doing wrong.[5] Philoctetes is deliberately made pathetic; he cannot even make good wooden cups.[6] At the end Neopto-lemus tries to persuade him in spite of everything to go to

---

[1] *Phil.*, 385 ff.   [2] Ib., 314 and 406.
[3] Cf. Adkins, *Merit and Responsibility*, pp. 172–89, esp. 183 and 189.
[4] *Phil.*, 657.   [5] Ib., 79 ff.   [6] Ib., 35–36.

Troy. He resists, obstinately. It is not a heroic resistance; it is the dignity of the tramp, clinging to the last thing he can call his own. He even clings to his sickness, as a sign of independence; cure would be "terrible".[1] The greatness of this play is the demonstration that this last central dignity is the most god-like part of human nature, and that an abject creature can be a god.

Neoptolemus carries the main character interest. He it is who develops. He is an ordinary chap, son of a very noble father. This latter is constantly stressed. He is not very ambitious for himself; Philoctetes is surprised that the matter of the arms does not anger him more. His ordinariness is designed to help us to see that his problem is ours. This also is the function of the chorus. They share their leader's doubts, and urge him to pity Philoctetes more. They do not bear the divine meaning of the play, because in this the divine meaning is kept to the end. Their function is to focus our attention on the wretchedness of Philoctetes, and so to make us face the agonizing political and moral decision that is Neoptolemus', a decision which we still find ourselves facing today.

(x) OEDIPUS COLONEUS

Aeschylus' greatest work is an attempt to show us a cosmic pattern in which the actions of gods and men and states complement each other. The end of Sophocles' work is a meditation into the mystery of what it is to be alive. Aeschylus brings a whole city on stage. Sophocles ends with a solitary girl, dragging her feet away from a spot to which she feels rooted. Granted that Sophocles wrote the ode on man in the *Antigone* and Aeschylus showed Orestes' plight at the end of the *Choephori*; nevertheless, this does typify the difference between them. We think of Aeschylus as the man of wide vision, Sophocles the man of deep understanding.

There is a meditative quality about the writing of the *Coloneus* which makes people use the term "dramatic poem" which I do not find very helpful. More helpful is to see that the action of the play is the almost passive development of Oedipus.

[1] *Phil.*, 1380.

It is the making of man into *theos* that we have seen before, but the making is done by time, and the accumulation of suffering. In this play Oedipus is shown as an innocent victim, so that we shall not ask about his early acts. Now we are simply to see a process in which suffering is a necessary ingredient. We see Oedipus, shown apparently more and more helpless until the moment when Creon is about to capture him. From then on we see the power growing. Creon is discomfited, Polyneices is cursed, and finally Oedipus is called by the thunder to go to his death, which is wonderful, and which will leave his body in the ground, a force even more powerful. When he still does not quite realize what is happening to him Oedipus asks Ismene:[1]

> When I no longer am, am I then man?
> Yes, for the powers now raise you whom they felled.

So Ismene replies. This is the action of the play, the realization that when Oedipus seems nothing then he is strong.

There is, however, a sense of power about him from the beginning. When he reaches the grove of the Eumenides he knows that he has come to the end of his travels.[2] He is in touch with other powers. He impresses the chorus as "terrible".[3] He instantly impresses Theseus, and sees through Creon's pretences. The development of the play is only the culmination of his development which has taken many years, much wandering, and much pain.

There seems to be a gathering into one of all the themes that preoccupied Sophocles. As in the last two plays, we are asked to think of the power of time and the numinous power attendant on great suffering. Oedipus makes a speech to Theseus which has a likeness to Ajax' great speech on time. Oedipus speaks of the decay caused by time to all except *theoi*, and then goes on to speak of the power that will continue to flow from his body in the ground, implying that it will be a *theos*. The image of the single bird in the plague chorus from the *Tyrannus* develops in the *Coloneus* into a more general sense that somehow there is some victory over decay.

It is necessary to underline what is obvious to those who

[1] *O.C.*, 393–4.   [2] Ib., 146.   [3] Ib., 141.

actually read the play, as opposed to just writing about it, that there is no hint of peace; there is none of the resignation of old age, no feeling of forgiveness. When Oedipus curses Polyneices it is the most violent curse in all Greek tragedy.

It shows a type of the *sōphrōn*, the most powerful representative of this type that we see in Sophocles. Theseus, a man who has himself suffered, understands Oedipus, and does not fear his power. Nor does he fear the Eumenides. While others will not enter the sacred precinct, Theseus has no fear. I cannot imagine that any poet could write about the Eumenides at Athens without conjuring up memories of the *Oresteia*, and ever since then it must have been recognized that an essential part of *sōphrosynē* was coming to terms with them, by coming to terms with the dark irrational parts of one's nature. This coming to terms that is *sōphrosynē* can either be acquired naturally by gift and understanding, as is the case with Odysseus in the *Ajax*, or by suffering, as in the case of Oedipus.

The implication is that Theseus has suffered, but he is shown more as the type of the natural understander, who in himself acquires a stature almost equal to Oedipus. He at any rate alone can watch the death.

One would expect this play to embody Sophocles' view of society, because of the connexion of thought with the *Oresteia*. Theseus is the type of the king. He is constantly referred to as *anax*, the Homeric word for king, the word with the primitive ritual associations. There is constant reference to Athens. But it is to the old reverent Athens, who receives suppliants and is governed by ritual. The ritual element is very strong in this play. Aeschylus writes of a society which he thinks could grow, a democracy which yet reveres all the old irrational sanctions. Sophocles writes of an ideal society. The democracy had been overthrown once, and Athens was nearly defeated. But he still writes of a balance between ritual and commonsense. Theseus comes from a sacrifice to save the girls when Creon orders them to be carried off.[1] There is no point in mentioning the sacrifice, except to show that Theseus knows when ritual claims must give way to practical morality. It is an image of the balanced life. We are reminded of how this should apply

[1] *O.C.*, 887 ff.

to Athens when Creon says that the Areopagus would never accept a wanderer like Oedipus. We think of the time when it did accept Orestes. Sophocles' ideal society is based on ritual, but it is ritual used intelligently.

It is, above all, a play about death. Oedipus in the *Tyrannus* seems very much Sophocles' type of arrogant, impulsive man who brings about his own downfall. Here once again, he becomes a type of man, weak, suffering man, whose death is yet wonderful, a mystery. It is the death itself, not any thought of life afterwards. There is little suggestion here of personal survival.

Once again the chorus have central importance, carrying the play's meaning in a way they do not do in the *Philoctetes*. Their function is to react to Oedipus, and to feel his impact on Athens, and this gives opportunity for multi-dimensional poetry. When Theseus has said that he will accept Oedipus into Athens they sing the great ode about Colonus.[1] It is in a sense a meditation on the glory of Athens, but it never mentions either the city or the people. It does mention the countryside, and each stanza mentions a god or gods taking part in ritual celebrations. It mentions the horses,[2] and we shall remember this in the later account of the battle.[3] The ode appears to talk of peace, but there are overtones of war. Above all, it mentions the olive[4] as the symbol of Attica. We must remember that this was written at a time when the corn was being destroyed every year by the Peloponnesians. They were at this time trying to destroy the olive trees too, but they can't have quite succeeded. The olive is an image of the indestructible earth. The play is so written that we are able to see the battle[5] through the eyes of their imagination, eyes of old soldiers who long to fight, and have the excitement of it in their frustration at not being able to fight. At the same time this is a way of showing us the battle while making it a foregone conclusion. Antigone returns and makes no mention of it.[6] But the ambivalence of the play is summed up in the terrifying ode on old age.[7] The chorus link themselves with Oedipus, and sing what folly it is

[1] *O.C.*, 668 ff.	[2] Ib., 714-15.	[3] Ib., 1044 ff.
[4] Ib., 700-1.	[5] Ib., 1044 ff.	
[6] Ib., 1096 ff.	[7] Ib., 1211 ff.	

to live long. There is nothing in life but suffering. It is an expression of such utter pessimism that it is bound to set up a reaction in the audience. Granted the Athenians were defeated; but if they accepted that they would commit suicide *en masse*. The ode comes too when Oedipus' power is beginning to be shown, and immediately after it we shall see him crushing Polyneices to despair. The epode with which the song ends is brilliantly ambivalent. Oedipus is like a wave-lashed cape, battered by troubles. But the implication of a cape is of something that resists troubles. There is more than a hint of power in this song, though it is a very grim picture. In all this Sophocles is moving on the edge of language. This play, and especially the choral parts, express his own kind of mysticism, one of the most austere religious outlooks that there have ever been. This is summed up in the last set ode of all, to death, death whom they hardly dare address, not so much Hades, as a mysterious nameless being, to whom is addressed the last line of Sophocles' last set ode: [1]

On thee I call, the giver of endless sleep.

In this pattern, this development of a mystery, Oedipus is the centre, the pivot, the focus. His innocence is necessary so that we should merely think of the working out of some divine plan, should worship and not question. Creon is shown as a small-minded villain by contrast. The function of Polyneices is to show Oedipus' power. Sophocles changed the myth so that he should be the most guilty, and most deserve the curse, though there is a vagueness about the whole arrangement of the government of Thebes, intended to stop us asking questions irrelevant to the point at issue. Polyneices is so crushed that he arouses our sympathy, and he creates the opportunity for a great scene of pathos with Antigone. She is the character who seems to turn the meaning of the play upside down. With Theseus she is to be wholly admired; he is admired in his office, as the just king of a just people; she is admired in her person. All her life she helps Oedipus, and gets little thanks for it. At the end of the play Theseus offers her a home in peaceful

[1] *O.C.*, 1578.

Athens. But she will not accept; she will return to Thebes. We know what will happen to her there. She has no consolation. She cannot see the father she has followed die; she may not even see the body, or where he died. It is an image of utter despair. But we are told the words of Oedipus to his daughters as he said good-bye.[1] Because in a sense these contradict all that I have said of this play it is necessary to quote them. May the necessity forgive the presumption of a translator:

> My children,
> This is the day on which you'll have no father.
> For all that's mine is gone, and now no longer
> Need you bother with looking after me.
> I know, it was hard, wasn't it, but one
> Syllable balances those years of boredom:
> Love – you'll never – not from anyone –
> Have more than from this man who now leaves you
> To spend the rest of your life far from him.

(xi) CONCLUSION

Every extant Aeschylus play demands a sumptuous décor and brilliant colours in the costumes. Aeschylus was well known for his love of scenic display. None of the extant Sophocles plays demand colourful costume. Aeschylus is the poet of the startling image, Sophocles of pattern, in the sounds of his words, the structure of his thought, the arrangement of his action. Aeschylus makes what we had thought was impalpable visible and tangible. Sophocles sees through the visible to some intangible pattern beyond. Aeschylus shows us an image of what man might be. Sophocles looks right through man, through all his follies and wickedness, and maintains, contrary to all the apparent evidence, that man is a worthy part of a wonderful pattern which is beyond our understanding. The energy of his middle age expressed in the ode on man in the *Antigone* derives its strength from the same total lack of illusion that made him write the ode on old age in the *Coloneus*. Because it is total, his disillusion is positive. Fully aware of the uselessness of human

[1] *O.C.*, 1611 ff.

effort, possessed of no comfort, and offering none, he nevertheless ends his work in a chant of complete affirmation:[1]

> Cease now, and do not move
> Yourself to further tears.
> For here lies total proof.

[1] *O.C.*, 1777–9.

CHAPTER FOUR

EURIPIDES

(i) LIFE

According to tradition, he was born in 480, the year of Salamis
at Phlya in the fertile centre of Attica. He was first granted a
chorus in 465, but was not successful like Sophocles in the competitions, only winning the first prize five times, once posthumously with the *Bacchae*. His mother is represented as a
greengrocer by Aristophanes. We do not know the basis for
this joke, though it is certainly not literally true. But he does
not seem to have moved in the same upper-class circles as
Sophocles. We do not hear that he was a friend of Pericles, for
example. He was a pupil of Anaxagoras, and so was introduced
to the new intellectualist way of thinking at an early age. He
was also a friend of Timotheus, whom we know to have been
the composer most chiefly responsible for elaborating the
music used in the theatre. If some of Euripides' choruses seem
thin in poetic texture compared with those of his predecessors,
this is largely because music was beginning to gain an ascen-
dancy over words. The anonymous life describes him as "showing no ambition in things of the theatre". Of course he is a
master of theatrical technique; he has a far wider range than
Sophocles. I assume that this comment refers to what we notice
ourselves, that sometimes it seems that he was in such a hurry
to get his ideas down that he did not bother to polish the
presentation. After his death and indeed for six hundred years
afterwards he eclipsed the other tragedians in popularity.
Partly this is due to his sense of the theatre. Aristotle thinks
that the *Iphigeneia in Tauris* is his best play, and it is certainly not
his most serious. The *Hecuba, Orestes,* and *Phoenissae* were all

popular through Hellenistic and Roman times; all they have in common is theatricality. But the *Suppliants*, to judge from the references to it in fourth-century authors, was also popular; it is above all a play of ideas. But Euripides' ideas are more easily extractable and quotable than those of the other dramatists. It is the very fact that he has assimilated them less deeply that makes him an easier writer to understand.

I enjoy the story that Euripides used to sit alone in a cave on Salamis to write his plays. There is a romantic[1] feeling about the country in his poetry, which is different from the simple acceptance of natural rhythm in Sophocles, and is more like a townsman's outlook. Much more of Euripides' life must have been spent in the town, and Athens during the war, in a state of siege, must have been more like a modern town where it is not easy to get out of the sight of houses. Euripides is far more quick-witted than his predecessors; he changes his viewpoint rapidly, and that is why he was unpopular. Associated with the progressive thinkers, he attacks narrow-minded rationalism, and was prosecuted by Cleon for impiety, probably for political reasons; we can assume that for all the radical views of his writing he did not approve of the extreme democrats. Misunderstood and embittered, he left Athens finally, and wrote the *Bacchae*, his last play, in Macedonia, just before his death in 406.

Several of the plays are lighter in tone, and have indeed been called tragi-comedies. I shall only deal with these cursorily. The comedy is trivializing, not grotesque juxtaposition, and it is clear that while these throw light on Euripides' theatrical technique, they do not illuminate his idea of tragedy. The earliest is the *Alcestis*, in 438. This was a substitute for the satyr play. Some of the later ones do not appear to be necessarily the fourth play. The distinctions of tragedy and satyr play became blurred at the end of the fifth century. The details of the chronology of all the plays is conjectural, depending much on internal evidence. I am convinced by Zuntz[2] that the *Heraclidae* was almost certainly produced in 430, right at the beginning of the war, and the *Suppliants* near the end of the first war, and find this helpful

---

[1] Cf. Appendix.

[2] G. Zuntz, *The Political Plays of Euripides*, pp. 81–94.

in the interpretation of these plays. The *Troades* was produced in 415, the year of the Sicilian expedition, the year after the massacre of Melos. It is important that this violently anti-war play was shown just when Athens was beginning to become eager for war again. Otherwise the dates do not matter. The plays about war are all written during the war, and I shall deal with them all together. I shall first take his three early, more psychological plays, *Medea*, *Hippolytus*, *Heracles*, then the four war plays, *Heraclidae*, *Suppliants*, *Hecuba*, *Troades*, and then the last play, the *Bacchae*, ending with some remarks on the other plays.

(ii) DRAMATIC FORM

I am attracted to the idea of Euripides as townsman, Sophocles as countryman, because it seems to express succinctly the main difference between them as poets. Euripides is closer to the objects of his vision. The issues of his plays are often immediate issues; he is less able to stand back from the events he is describing. Everything in Sophocles is subsumed to the pattern. Euripides takes less trouble over the final shaping of the pattern, because he cannot stand back far enough to see it. Some people, ignoring the inconsistencies and awkwardnesses of Sophocles' plots, have tried to make out that he was only concerned with telling a story. The inconsistencies and awkwardnesses – if we take this line with Euripides – are so obvious that no one can say this of him. Obvious examples are the entry of Aegeus in the *Medea*, totally unmotivated, and the whole structure of the *Suppliants*. Events do not grow out of each other, as they do in most other dramaturgies.

We can express this another way. Euripides writes more naturalistically. There is less opportunity for the characters, and especially the chorus, to carry a poetic meaning in overtones, because there is less multi-dimensional poetry and less ritual atmosphere. On the one occasion when Sophocles did not allow the poetry of his chorus to rise above the plane of the rest of the action he brought a god on at the end of the play, just to state that there was more than one plane of action. This we shall find in Euripides constantly. In Sophocles the pattern of events can usually show us what the play is about. In Euri-

pides we often have to be told. This confirms us in thinking
that Euripides did believe in some pattern behind events, but
he was unable to see it as Aeschylus did, or feel its rhythm as
Sophocles did. We have a sense of jerky rhythm in Euripides,
the rhythm of the town, not the country. On the other hand, he
is more flexible; he can get more into his plays, because he is
less concerned with the way everything fits together.

I have used this metaphor of distance because it can sum up
all the differences in style between Sophocles and Euripides.
The latter has a brilliant sense of detail. For sheer description
he is unsurpassed. The messenger speeches are a great feature
of all his plays. As with Aeschylus, we are asked suddenly to
see with our imagination instead of with our eyes, and this is a
very effective theatrical device. But while Aeschylus puts the
point of the play over in visible form, Euripides uses this
device for showing the climax of the action, feeling perhaps
that this made it more vivid for the audience, because it meant
that they were using their faculties to the maximum extent. A
virgin is brought to life, and her futile death foreshadowed, in
three lines, as the messenger in the *Medea* tells of Creon's
daughter who:[1]

> Placing the gold crown in her curls, and shaping
> Her hair before the brilliant mirror, smiles
> At that reflected body with no breath.

But examples of this sort of memorable detail can be found in
all the messenger speeches.

The audience is expected to respond very much more quickly
to changes of mood than in the other dramatists. I would not
worry, for example, about stopping the audience laughing at
Iolaus' antics with the arms in the *Heraclidae*.[2] And yet soon we
are to take him seriously. People, after all, are ridiculous and
magnificent in quick succession in real life. It is only when an
artist wishes to emphasize one aspect of life so as to make his
audience think more about it that the natural kaleidoscopic
pattern is simplified. This goes with the desire of Euripides to
shock his audience into awareness. The jerky rhythm and lack
of transitions is part of this desire. We notice it in details of

[1] *Med.*, 1160–62.   [2] *Heracl.*, 720 ff.

the poetry. Andromache describes what a wife she was to Hector:[1]

> I often gave my breasts to your bastards.

Sometimes Euripides may seem tasteless; but it is because he is so passionately concerned with making his audience feel. Talthybius is trying not to hurt Hecuba too much, as he describes the death of her brave daughter Polyxena, but this is how things are:[2]

> Chosen and picked Achaeans were in attendance
> To hold your struggling kitten down.

Another consequence of his closer view might be expressed like this. Sophocles may have thought about a particular action and eventually arrived at a story which would help him to understand how that action could take place. He would think, How can men get into these situations? Euripides would go a stage further. He would say that for a person to perform a certain action he must be of a certain character. Then if the action is abnormal the character must be abnormal. Only certain people could do the things that Electra and Orestes do, and Euripides shows us in both his plays on this subject, and especially in the *Orestes*, the sort of characters he thinks could do these actions. The point of the *Oresteia* is that this situation would make anyone, whatever the character, act as they do. The play has a universal point because it suggests that our reaction would be the same as that of the characters involved. If the characters are shown as abnormal, then we will say that we would not do anything of the sort. This is the beginning of a decadence in tragedy, because the play no longer affronts our vital beliefs or involves us in the action. It means that the chorus, whose function is to involve the audience in this way, by presenting the ordinary point of view of society, and implying the wider pattern, become less and less necessary; the ordinary man's viewpoint becomes detached from that of the main actors, and there is less feeling after the wider pattern. But this is only true of a few of Euripides' plays.

Events, images, and words take on extra significance from

[1] *And.*, 224–5.   [2] *Hec.*, 525–6.

their context in Sophocles. It is important for the interpretation of a choral ode to know what has happened just before the chorus sing. With Euripides this is less true. There is less careful integration of each part into the total pattern, and therefore less relation between each event and the total action. Accordingly, we often find that the chorus is singing something only generally relevant, not relevant to the exact moment when they sing it. Sometimes this gives a chance for Euripides to open out and generalize the action, as in the *Hecuba*, when the chorus sing the great ode about the fall of Troy.[1] Sometimes the result is mere decoration, as in the *Helen*.[2]

In general, the texture of Euripides is thinner than that of the other two. This may have been partly because his dialogue was delivered faster, for certainly the average length of his plays is longer. Sometimes this apparent thinness has point on the stage. We hear on occasions of a character being sighted, and then there is a discussion for several lines about him before he appears. On stage this can be used to build up suspense, though obviously it is boring to read.

In addition, there is an increase in decoration for its own sake, another natural outcome of his less concentrated sense of pattern. The increase of decorative adjectives in the choral parts is probably largely due to the more elaborate settings, in which the words would be less noticed. The most conspicuous example is the *Iphigeneia in Aulis*, which is the most operatic of Greek tragedies.[3] But this sort of language occurs in the dialogue also. I can see no purpose in this line from the *Alcestis* except a love of decoration for its own sake:[4]

He drinks unmixed the juice of the dark mother.

Heracles is on the booze; that's all. Nor can I see anything more than a kind of journalistic elaboration in the description of a passage of time, while the princess is dying, in the messenger's speech in *Medea*:[5]

Meanwhile a good goer – shifting himself –
Would have achieved a circuit of the track,

[1] *Hec.*, 905 ff.   [2] *Hel.*, 1451 ff.   [3] E.g. *I.A.*, 1036 ff.
[4] *Alc.*, 757.   [5] *Med.*, 1181-2.

I cannot resist ending the list of places where Euripides seems to have failed in poetic control, by noticing the first words that the chorus in the *Helen* sing.[1] In several very decorative lines they sing that they heard the cry when they were doing the washing. Perhaps Euripides intended this as parody. We need to be sure when we laugh at him that he is not laughing at himself.

Of course, Euripides is a very great poet, and a master of the techniques of choral writing when he wants to be. The *Bacchae* choruses are full of elaborate patternings which recall Sophocles and even Aeschylus. But I find the greatest satisfaction in moments of significant detail which seems to sum up in a phrase the whole point of an episode or a whole play. Medea is described by the nurse as "goring her children with her eyes",[2] and this prepares us for what is to come. And could there be a better indication of the peace and terror of the Dionysiac life than the description of the Bacchants after the battle having the blood licked off their cheeks . . . by snakes?[3]

(iii) RELIGIOUS THOUGHT

The metaphor of closer viewpoint will also help to explain the difference between the religious outlook of Euripides and Sophocles. In all the tragedies we see innocent people involved in suffering which is the result of some wrong action. But sometimes in Euripides our attention is so focused on the innocent sufferers that the power through whom the suffering comes is made to appear malicious. Malice is cruelty for which we cannot see the reason, and, being so close to the action, we cannot always see the reason. Some critics seem to have thought that Euripides makes his powers more cruel than those of Aeschylus or Sophocles, but no writer could go much further than Aeschylus' account of Prometheus or Sophocles' of Deianeira.

Euripides was concerned to make points about religious matters and took good care to see that his audience got the points that he was trying to make. No one can fail to see that his gods are intolerable; some people seem to have failed to see this with the other dramatists. I suspect that the real implications of nearly all religions worth respect are frightening, and

---

[1] *Hel.*, 179 ff.   [2] *Med.*, 92; cf. 187–8.   [3] *Bac.*, 767–8.

that it is the people who probe the implications of a particular religion much more than its opponents who are pilloried. We have an example of how Euripides suffered as a result of the shock tactics he used. The line from the *Hippolytus*[1] was quoted against Euripides,[2] as showing that he did not care for oaths:

My tongue has sworn, my mind remained unsworn.

But the development of the play shows that Hippolytus died rather than break the oath. Euripides was definitely misrepresented.

The evidence of the plays is that Euripides conceived of the world, and the powers that ordered the world, in much the same way as Aeschylus and Sophocles. His serious plays could be rewritten as naturalistic stories; the action is doubly determined. He seems to have accepted the existence of a great number of *theoi*, some of them personal, in the same way as his predecessors. For otherwise why could these beings so constantly appear? It is clear that the Olympians are both causative forces and personal, since in Euripides as well as the other two they can be influenced by prayer. On the other hand, it is likely that if one starts thinking of a personal being who appears to have very wide powers indeed, caught up in the vastness of the power, the sense of personality will be lost. How many Christians would dare to say that they had a clear apprehension of the personality of the Holy Spirit? There is an increased sense of the vastness of the powers. We see the traces of it in Phaedra's nurse, who thinks that Cypris may perhaps be more than a *theos*.[3]

It is often said that the gods in Euripides are symbols of psychological forces. The evidence of the plays is all against this. Teiresias definitely contrasts Dionysus with internal psychological forces.[4] We should notice the beginning of the *Hippolytus*. Aphrodite says that she does not mind Hippolytus honouring Artemis. If Aphrodite and Artemis are opposite psychological forces, as is sometimes said, then to honour both gods would be to compromise between the two forces. But

[1] *Hipp.*, 612.　　[2] Cf. Ar., *Thesm.*, 275-6 and cf. *Frogs*, 1471.
[3] *Hipp.*, 359-60.　　[4] *Bac.*, 314-15.

then if you "honoured one god" you would automatically be honouring the other less. So Aphrodite should be angry that Hippolytus honours Artemis, for that act of honouring is automatically dishonouring her. But if they are not psychological forces, but external powers, it is obviously possible to honour both.[1]

What is unique to Euripides is the beginnings of a new idea of the ultimate power, a new reaching after transcendence. In the *Troades* at a moment when she is confronted with ultimate questions, Hecuba says:[2]

> Holder of earth, whose seat is on the earth,
> Whoever you are, incomprehensible
> Zeus, whether law of nature or the mind in men,
> Accept my prayer.

We should compare fragments 935 and 1007, which are quoted by Lucian and Cicero respectively as representing Euripides' belief:[3]

> Look at these boundless spaces up above
> Enfolding earth within their fluid grasp;
> All this consider Zeus, claim this for god.

> Our mind in each of us, that is our god.[4]

Lucas deals with this more fully.[5] It is probably right to take these quotations as reflecting Euripides' actual belief, since he is made to believe in Air by Aristophanes.[6] There is a different feel about these two passages from the superficially similar ones in Aeschylus. Euripides starts with the air, and claims it as god, and Aeschylus starts with Zeus as generally understood and says that this being is all-pervasive as air. They can be taken as an argument for those who wish to say that he did not accept the personal, external reality of the forces called Olympian gods. But this is not necessarily so any more than a Christian mystic practising the Negative Way need be assumed to disbelieve in angels. But it is unlikely that the old modes of apprehension would survive very long, once beliefs such as these became

---

[1] *Hipp.*, 20.　　　　　　　　　　[2] *Tro.*, 884 ff.
[3] Frag. 941.　　　　　　　　　　　[4] Ib., 1018.
[5] D. W. Lucas, *The Greek Tragic Poets*, pp. 235–8.　　　[6] *Frogs*, 892.

current. It is possible that Euripides might have said that he did not consider the Olympian gods as personal, external forces, though I do not see why we should say this. If, however, he did not so conceive them, it is reasonable that he could still make plays in which they must be so treated; for he had been brought up for most of his life to accept them as such. Modes of religious apprehension involve much more than conscious thought. To put it in terms inappropriate to it, I can conceive of Euripides writing the *Bacchae* having "lost his faith" in Dionysus. I cannot conceive of anyone writing the *Bacchae* who had always been brought up to think of Dionysus as a symbol of a psychological force.

People who have wished to say that Euripides did not "believe in the Olympian gods", have either said that he thought of the gods as symbols, that he satirized them, or that he didn't care one way or the other, but used the divine machinery for theatrical effect. The symbolist view is held by Dodds,[1] and I think by Grube.[2] I would sum up my argument against it by saying that we have to believe in the actual, not the symbolic, existence of these powers, during the plays; Euripides could without much difficulty have rewritten the plays without introducing the powers in person. Since we have so little evidence, it seems more reasonable to take what we have at face value; we do not know enough to be subtle safely.

Neither of the other views need to be taken seriously. To say that he satirized the Olympians may mean that he made fun of them, which is certainly true. But it is also true of Sophocles, in the *Ichneutae*, of Aristophanes, and of Homer, especially in the story of Ares and Aphrodite.[3] No doubt Aeschylus did so also, in his satyr plays. This was the way the Greeks thought. If it is meant that he made them out to be spiteful this is also true. But it is attributable to the closeness with which he looked at suffering. If it is held, as it sometimes is, that to say the gods cause suffering is to satirize them, then all significant religious writing is satiric. The truth of the matter is that for some time in the wealthier Western countries there has been a belief that God is kindly. Within the Christian Church people bowdlerized

---

[1] E.g. *Introduction to the Bacchae*, p. xlv.
[2] *The Drama of Euripides*, pp. 60–62.   [3] *Od.*, viii, 266 ff.

the Bible, and outside it they believed in general human progress towards sanity and goodness. Critics who held either of these religions resented the destructive gods of Euripides, and because they approved of Euripides they said that he could not have meant what he said. It is the view of Verrall, who spent fantastic ingenuity in explaining that Euripides meant the opposite of what he said, and made nonsense of most of the plays, especially the *Troades*. It is the view of Greenwood,[1] whose comment on the *Hippolytus* is illuminating. The only moral of the *Hippolytus* he says[2] is "that the traditional story, with its callous, jealous, revengeful deities, is intellectually incredible and morally repulsive". The linking of the last two is important. He means that it is morally repulsive that a god should destroy an innocent man. It may be unpleasant, but it is hardly intellectually incredible. Anyone who believes in any form of personal theism will have to face it every day, as he picks up his newspaper. To take this attitude to Euripides' religious outlook one has to be an upper-class Edwardian, and there are not very many of these left now, though perhaps there is a higher proportion among Classicists than among the total population.

To those critics who said that Euripides did not care about the religious apparatus of his drama, one cannot reply that the *Bacchae* is a profound image of religious experience, because they presumably cannot understand it. But they all say that he was only concerned to write a "good play", and we can point out places in all the plays where he quite clearly was not simply concerned to write a good play, where he spoilt the symmetry of his plot in order to make his point.[3]

In conclusion, then, I assume that Euripides meant what he said. He views the world as ordered in more or less the same way as his predecessors. He, like them, gives indications of belief in some after-life,[4] but like them finds it no consolation for the suffering of the innocent. His ideas are confused because he is trying to put into language what will not go into language.

[1] L. H. G. Greenwood, *Aspects of Euripidean Tragedy*.
[2] Ib., p. 48.
[3] Cf. D. W. Lucas, *The Greek Tragic Poets*, p. 233 and cf. *Aspects of Euripidean Tragedy*, p. 30.
[4] E.g. *Hec.*, 422.

He had a different idea of the ultimate order from Sophocles, and he wrote in anger, not with Sophocles' austere and detached acceptance. He shows more violently the futility of unselfish action, but commends it more eagerly. Instead of Antigone in the *Coloneus*, we have the willing sacrifices of Macaria or Polyxena. It is the same contradiction between reason and instinct, only expressed with more passion and bitterness. This is not surprising. The Olympian religion, once the interest in the relation of wrong action to suffering had shifted from the family to the individual, was to our minds almost inconceivably comfortless. The surprising thing is not that Euripides raged, but that he could write at all of peace in the dionysiac life, as Sophocles could write of the dance of the gods at Colonus.

(iv) MEDEA

Jason, a mean-minded calculator who thinks that mean-minded calculation is rational action, decided to marry the daughter of Creon, king of Corinth. This action so angers Medea, his wife, that she reveals herself as a creature more than human in her revenge, more horrible, and more powerful. She becomes a *theos*, by virtue of what is done to her, and in this context we would translate *theos* as "fiend".

She is shown throughout the play as having a strange and horrifying power. The nurse describes how she "persuaded" the daughters of Pelias to kill their father[1] and fears that she will kill the new bride.[2] Medea herself wishes that Jason and all their children may die[3] and hopes to see Creon and his daughter "scraped to bits" in their halls.[4] But we do not yet know if this is more than the desperate screams of a wronged woman. However, the development of the story is the development of her power; over Creon, whom, having charmed into allowing her to stay for one day in the state, she mocks;[5] over Jason; over Aegeus; and when she has won for herself a refuge, so that she is out of the reach of the weak men ranged against her, she reveals herself in power. D. W. Lucas[6] comments that there is a feeling in *Hippolytus*, *Heracles*, and *Bacchae* of divine power guiding the action, but that the feeling in the *Medea* is not very

[1] *Med.*, 9. [2] *Ib.*, 39–43. [3] *Ib.*, 113–15.
[4] *Ib.*, 164. [5] *Ib.*, 371. [6] *The Greek Tragic Poets*, p. 222.

different. This is because Medea is herself the *theos*. Half-way through the play[1] she reveals herself in a manner very similar to that of Aphrodite or Dionysus. She cows the chorus almost immediately; before they were on her side, because she was wronged. Now she is announcing murder. An actress must make this speech a moment for causing panic. We should notice how the speech ends with three sibilants in the last three feet.[2] She ends in a hiss, and the chorus retreat in fright. The chorus may cry to the Sun to prevent her whom they now call *Erinys* from committing murder,[3] but it is her ancestor the Sun who sends the fiery chariot in which she escapes at the end. Jason can cry, "How can you look on the Sun!"[4] Medea can, with easy assurance. The point at which Jason arrives on the scene of action might be described as "just too late". Grube thinks Jason's cry is a slip by Euripides. It contains the whole point of the play. As he arrives he says that she will need to burrow or fly to escape him. In a moment we shall see her fly. Everyone is powerless before Medea; even "chance" plays into her hands.

The Devil looks after his own. There are people like this, before whom ordinary men are helpless, and Euripides puts this point across in his vigorous and blatant manner. It is a play about the conflict of rational and irrational, and we shall find elsewhere that Euripides often conceives of this as a conflict between man and woman. He probably used the image of the quarrels between Hera and Zeus for this also. We have seen that Hera does stand for disruptive elements in the world order from Aeschylus' treatment of the Io story,[5] and we can see it in the *Iliad*.[6] She is, of course, with Zeus, the patron of marriage, but apart from that function and her care of childbirth she occurs as a disruptive influence. Here we notice that Medea will bury her children at Hera's shrine.[7]

It is said that this play provides an example of Euripides' attack on rationality.[8] But it is clear from the rest of his writing that he did believe in trying a rational approach to life. Surely it is better to say that he is here over-stating the case for the other side. It is a fact that usually people who act instinctively

---

[1] *Med.*, 764 ff. [2] Ib., 810. [3] Ib., 1251–4.
[4] Ib., 1327. [5] Cf. p. 72. [6] E.g. (Ib.), xiv.
[7] *Med.*, 1379. [8] Cf. especially 1078–80.

are stronger than those who act rationally, but that does not mean we should not try to act rationally.

Even "chance" plays into Medea's hands. This is the point of the dramatically awkward arrival of Aegeus, so convenient for Medea. The chorus end their song with a curse against those who do not honour friends,[1] and on this Aegeus enters, saying, "Hail, for thus it is right to greet friends."[2] Aegeus will fulfil the honourable duty of friendship, and the result will be safety for a murderess. It is like the ode following this scene,[3] when the chorus contemplate the wisdom and peace of Athens, which is about to receive Medea.

The dominance of Medea will be emphasized if all the people she dominates, by charm or terror, are taken by the same actor. This will leave the tritagonist a small part, only the nurse and messenger, but it is an early play, and if Jason, Creon, the tutor, and Aegeus are all played by the same man this will underline the main action, which is the manifestation of Medea's horrible power.

No actor in Greek drama will be completely lost in his part. He must stand outside it to varying extents. We can most easily see this, in the portrayal of irrational women. The psychology of Medea's opening speech[4] is splendid, but it is the psychology of a narrative. No woman would ever say, "It's an insult to our sexuality that makes us run amok",[5] because this is so deep inside a woman that she cannot express it. If it is to be shown in dialogue there has to be this unnatural presentation. This device, often referred to as Euripides' rhetoric, is necessary to show parts of Medea that otherwise could not be shown. In the scenes with Creon and Aegeus she acts according to the logic of a desire not fully conscious, more like an ordinary person, and the scenes are beautiful naturalistic portrayals.

We see an example of how Euripides, having shown characters as evil, will then write a great scene to establish sympathy for them, in the moment when Medea says good-bye to her children. We see what love she had, what her passion could have done for good.[6] She talks to the children, then sends them off, then talks as if they were there.[7] They do not return for this,

[1] *Med.*, 659 ff.   [2] Ib., 663–4.   [3] Ib., 824 ff.   [4] Ib., 214 ff.
[5] Ib., 265–6.   [6] Ib., 1019 ff.   [7] Ib., 1069 ff.

which would be intolerably fussy, and much less moving. This is a great moment for the actor, and gives added depth to the play.

Aegeus, humdrum and fussy, and Creon, outmanoeuvred at every point, are foils for Medea. Jason is an image of how Euripides the rationalist argues against himself. People who claim to be rational are so often mere schemers. He is now at any rate rather less than a man.[1] He can even say that a woman who was *sōphrōn* wouldn't mind about having no sex-life.[2]

The function of the chorus of Corinthian women is to universalize the action. At first they represent the normal woman's reaction to a wronged woman. When they do not understand they agree to the idea of vengeance.[3] After the scene with Creon[4] they sing first that the natural order is overturned and that honour will come to women, and then, making the balancing movements, they sing that the old songs will cease, since Phoebus has not made women poets. In the second system they turn to Medea and sing how she sailed here in passion, and in the balancing stanza refer to the overthrow of justice and the keeping of oaths, thus linking all women in Medea's own personal passion for vengeance. Later they will turn against the murder,[5] and be disregarded; one more example of the way Medea's exceptional power overrides all round it. Their reaction to the actual killing is to escape into generalization.[6] Ino was the only other woman to kill her children, but only after having been driven mad by Hera; and Ino killed herself. Medea will fly away in triumph. There are awkwardnesses about the function of the chorus in this psychological play, summed up in the scanty motivation of their arrival, but they have a function to show how near the reaction of Medea is to that of a normal woman, and how, fortunately, the normal woman does not live up to her first reaction.

(v) HIPPOLYTUS

Phaedra, madly in love with Hippolytus, is repulsed with disgust by him, and in revenge writes a letter to her husband

---

[1] *Med.*, 555 ff., especially 569–70. [2] Ib., 1369.
[3] Ib., 267. [4] Ib., 410 ff.
[5] Ib., 811 ff. [6] Ib., 1282 ff.

Theseus, saying that Hippolytus has assaulted her, as a result of which Theseus brings about the death of his son. On the naturalistic level it is that a woman desiring to be raped pretends that she has been, and a man drives his son away to be killed in an accident. On Euripides' level of double determination it is that Aphrodite is angry with Hippolytus for honouring only Artemis and not her, and sees to it that Phaedra should fall in love with Hippolytus. Aphrodite in her prologue says that she will tell Theseus, though in fact it is the nurse who brings about the telling of what Phaedra had kept secret. The nurse should be thought of as a tool of Aphrodite. There is something sinister about her. It will be seen that this play almost suggests that the human beings involved are helpless in the clutches of powers stronger than themselves. We almost feel that Aphrodite has set everything in motion herself [1] rather than that *theoi* and mortals are working in parallel. Phaedra need not have reacted in the way she did, and Theseus is wrong to have cursed Hippolytus at once; [2] but their actions are all very excusable when we see the powers ranged against them.

It shows us more detailed images of how the gods work. Zeus allows the two opposing *theoi*, Aphrodite and Artemis, each to retaliate on each other's devotees, if these are too one-sided in their attentions. This is the way things go; attention to one of the principles of nature will bring disaster; it is necessary to be aware of them all. *Theoi*, too, are neutral powers; on occasions we can make use of them, but then whether we use them for good or evil is up to us. Theseus has been granted three prayers by Poseidon. He prays that Hippolytus may be destroyed; Poseidon grants his prayer, even though it is a terrible one, and one that Theseus will regret. *Theoi* take us at our word, and one action may undo the good of a lifetime. The point of the play is the combination of the sense of reverence which Hippolytus feels for Artemis, which is certainly commended in the strange peace of the ending, as it was in the poetry of the beginning, and the fact that it seems to be the prayers with evil intent that are answered, and the powers cannot always help their devotees. [3] The pitiless, inhuman, nature of these powers is beautifully brought out when Artemis must

---

[1] *Hipp.*, 24 ff.   [2] Ib., 1296.   [3] Ib., 1328 ff.

go at the end, since she cannot stay to see a man die,[1] any more than she can weep.[2]

In the face of these powers true *sōphrosynē* is much more than mere innocence. There is an important image of this when Hippolytus offers Artemis a wreath of flowers picked from an uncropped meadow, where none but the chaste can go.[3] An uncropped meadow is useless, and this would be more quickly realized by Greeks than by Englishmen after the Romantic Movement. Hippolytus does not understand enough, and so he may protest his innocence, but it is of no avail. That is the point of the messenger speech.[4] Hippolytus called on Zeus to let him be killed if he was guilty of the rape; Zeus did let him be killed, and he was not guilty. The world is not as easy as we make it out to be. When Hippolytus lays a wreath on the statue of Artemis his servant urges him to honour Aphrodite likewise, and when Hippolytus refuses, lays a wreath on her statue himself, praying that she will forgive, for *theoi* must be wiser than mortals. This they may be, but they do not show their wisdom by forgiveness.

This aspect of the play is well put over by the sight of Theseus' reaction to the news;[5] he tears the wreath off his head. We see the two statues of Aphrodite and Artemis, both wreathed. No one will tear the wreaths from them.

The point of the action will be helped by consideration of the natural distribution of the parts. The protagonist will play Hippolytus and the messenger who announces his death. The deuteragonist will play Aphrodite and her two tools, Theseus and the nurse, leaving the tritagonist with the servant, Phaedra, and Artemis. In particular, we should be made to feel the presence of Aphrodite in the nurse; she is bawd and temptress.

Hippolytus is someone who thinks that the balance which is *sōphrosynē* is to be achieved by repressing one side of his nature. Some critics dwell on the fact that he is a bastard. It is reasonable that a bastard should develop an antipathy for sex, and also reasonable that he should take elaborate pains to preserve not only his chastity but his reputation for chastity. But Euripides does not give the bastardy great prominence. More people are

---

[1] *Hipp.*, 1437. [2] Ib., 1396. [3] Ib., 73 ff.
[4] Ib., 1173 ff, especially 1191. [5] Ib., 806 ff.

like Hippolytus than are bastards. In his mistrust of women he is somewhat like Jason,[1] that is to say he is definitely represented as excessive in his mistrust. This explains the unnaturalness of the dialogue between him and Theseus. This rhetoric is the only way they can communicate.

Phaedra is brilliantly characterized, though as with Medea some of her character has to be shown in an unnaturally explicit way. We see that she is more concerned for a good name than for chastity,[2] because that is how she ends her long speech in her defence. In this she has protested too much. May she die rather than be bad, she has said.[3] She herself is unnatural, not properly *sōphrōn*, and if we understand this we will be prepared for her action, which is even worse than yielding to her desires would have been. This wrongness of Phaedra is brought out by means of the nurse, the most subtly evil character in Greek drama. She has said, Let us not have friendship that reaches the marrow,[4] and cunningly gets Phaedra to tell, by making the telling appear the noble gesture of granting a boon, a boon Phaedra really wants to grant.[5] Then after pointing out that Phaedra's case is not unique[6] and accepting Phaedra's overdramatic antithesis of death or yielding,[7] she says that to give way is pleasant and cites other people who have done so. Finally, she accuses Phaedra of pride, and calls for instant action.[8] She says she has a charm for love, but we know that there is nothing, for she cannot say whether it is ointment or medicine.[9] When she has betrayed the matter to Hippolytus she defends herself by saying that if matters had gone well no one would have blamed her, and leaves the stage hinting at the "one way left". Euripides has given us the paradigm of the temptress.

Against these we see Theseus, a healthy sceptic, who does not believe in the fulfilment of his curse, and so exiles his son as well. But the powers involved in this play are there whether we believe in them or not. Because the play is concerned with showing the enormous strength of these powers, the function

---

[1] *Hipp.*, 616 ff. [2] Ib., 373 ff., especially 426–30.
[3] Ib., 419. [4] Ib., 255.
[5] Ib., 333–5. [6] Ib., 437.
[7] Ib., 442. [8] Ib., 491. [9] Ib., 517.

of the chorus of attendant women is to wonder, and later to pity. The odes, especially the one directly on *Erōs*, are of general relevance, rather than relevance to the particular point of the play reached at that moment. Their function, however, is important; it is to make us realize, with tears if necessary, the continual presence of the terrible powers in the lives of uncomprehending men and women.

(vi) HERACLES

The development of this play is the story of a great man brought low. The suffering arises out of the direct intervention of *theoi*, notably Hera. It is the first clear instance of tragic victims rather than tragic agents. The sufferings of the first part are brought about by Heracles' noble action in offering to atone for his father's presumably accidental killing of Electryon,[1] and those of the second by direct intervention from the agents of Hera. We can say that the central action is that Amphitryon killed and had to leave Argos, thus making Heracles offer to serve Eurystheus in atonement, and thus letting Lycus seize the children. But we are never told why Lycus acts as he does. It is better to say that both first and second parts are caused by Hera, not acting through any mortal action, but on her own, from hatred of Heracles.

Euripides has changed the myth to emphasize this. Normally the labours are a result of Heracles' wrong action. Here Heracles is shown as acting from extreme unselfishness. In addition, he is made less violent than normal, and there is obviously enormous justification for his rage with Lycus, which is shown as springing out of his love for his children. Thirdly, Euripides invented Lycus to emphasize the point even further.

Both Sophocles and Euripides have been concerned to show that goodness does not always bring happiness, but sometimes the reverse, if a good man is caught up in the consequences of some evil act. Here Euripides goes further, and shows the good man suffering, but not as a consequence of any human wrong. It is the nearest Greek tragedy gets to the Problem of Pain. This point is shown most clearly at the moment when the deified abstraction of Madness protests at the task of madden-

[1] *Her.*, 17.

ing Heracles.[1] It is something akin to the numerous allusions in European literature to sky and rocks feeling pity, but it is even more extreme. Sky and rocks do not cause events. The order of events protests at itself, and goes on as before. So little have pity and sympathy got to do with the running of the world.

This is a very pessimistic conclusion. It is in a way a meditation on the hopelessness of just and rational activity as ever being able to achieve much. The exact emphasis of the whole play will depend on how we take the end. Grube[2] calls the end "the triumph and the glory of true friendship", while Byrde[3] puts the matter more pessimistically when he says that "the answer" is friendship. Theseus advised Heracles against killing himself; he should live, thus accepting the lot Hera has laid on him, for *theoi* themselves have had to bear suffering. The world is pitilessly ordered, in a way we cannot understand. We should pay attention to the remarks of Theseus because they go with an expressed disbelief in the extravagances of divine misdeeds.[4] It is the same attitude as that of Teiresias in the *Bacchae*.[5] The stories about the powers are made less crude, but the powers are in no way diminished. In this cruel world Theseus acts admirably, and looks after Heracles. This at least we can approve, and we are left with two irreconcilable facts, that the world is savage, and yet that it is good to be just and civilized.

The point of the first part of the play is ironic. It leads up to the moment when Lycus goes into the house where Heracles is waiting for him; the chorus sing that justice is being done and the plan of the gods is being revealed, for they care for justice.[6] Everything has been designed to appeal to our sense of pity, and we have heard Amphitryon saying that he is better than Zeus, who is either fool or knave.[7] Later Amphitryon can say to Lycus, when he is playing with him,[8] that Heracles could only return if a god raised him from the dead. As Heracles has returned, we are to see the hand of the gods in this. But the

---

[1] *Her.*, 843 ff. [2] *The Drama of Euripides*, p. 260.
[3] O. R. A. Byrde, *Introduction to the Heracles*, p. xv.
[4] *Her.*, 1313 ff. [5] Cf. pp. 141–2.
[6] *Her.*, 757 ff., 772 ff. and 814.
[7] Ib., 342 and 347. [8] Ib., 719.

return is only for the further evil. He might as well have let Lycus kill his children, as kill them himself.

The function of Theseus is to show us sanity, a man like Heracles, more just than the gods, when after having seen the havoc Heracles has caused we are inclined to forget his goodness. Theseus is not afraid to touch Heracles; others would fear pollution. Lycus, for whose villainy Euripides finds no mitigation, serves to increase the pathos of Amphitryon and Megara's plight. This, too, is the principal function of the chorus of old men. They are helpless, and though they have come to help, they can only sing like a white bird.[1] They cannot serve to universalize the action of the main character, because he is victim rather than agent. They do, however, sing the ode on the labours of Heracles.[2] This is very important; we never see Heracles in power, and his power has to be shown through this song instead. It is not one of Euripides' greatest lyrics, but I suspect that it did not need to be. It was presumably a great display of mime. This would have balanced the play where modern critics feel that it is lacking, and made us realize that it is the story of a great man. Reading this ode in the text, we tend to get the balance wrong. I find the theory of Blaiklock convincing, that Heracles is an epileptic.[3] It is often the case that men of genius are epileptics, and this disease seems a very good image of the way a great man is at the mercy of powers outside him, who can suddenly bring him down. Epilepsy attacks without any warning. It may easily have provided a starting-point for this play whose course is enough to make a god groan, if gods could feel pain.[4] But we think of Artemis who could not weep. The greatest man is a wild creature, frothing at the mouth, when they strike.

(vii) HERACLIDAE

It would be possible to describe this play as having a central action like those of Sophocles' plays, and its course as being the development of the consequences of that action. Eurystheus being afraid of the sons of Heracles drives them from

[1] *Her.*, 110. [2] Ib., 348 ff.
[3] E. M. Blaiklock, *The Male Characters of Euripides*, pp. 122 ff.
[4] *Heracl.*, 1115.

Argos. Under the care of Iolaus, the comrade of Heracles, they come and ask help from Demophon, king of Athens, son of Theseus. He agrees to receive the suppliants, and when Eurystheus demands them to be given back, refuses, even though this means war. In the ensuing battle Eurystheus is defeated, captured, and handed over to Heracles' mother, Alcmena, who has him put to death. Violence breeds violence.

That is not, however, a very satisfactory account of the play. We never see into Eurystheus; we are given no reasons for his action which might partly excuse him and he is by no means central in the development of the story. The function of the chorus of old men of Marathon is to focus our attention on the decision of the Athenians, as represented by their king, Demophon. His action in going to war is what we are invited to consider as the main issue of the play, but not all the development of the story could be said to spring from it, Alcmena's action at the end, for example. Our interest is concentrated on the people of Athens going to war, and the way in which the action is clearly supervised by Athena, here very much the patron saint of Athens, confirms that this is the best way of looking at the play.

It is concerned with the question as to whether a democracy, a society based on law, that is to say the substitution of peaceful, rational discussion for violence as a method of settling disputes, may use the violence of war for settling disputes outside its frontiers. The play gives the answer that sometimes it is right, but that war is always horrible. But it is important to see the sort of society that Euripides presents to us as justifying its defence by fighting.

We are not shown the Athens of 430, but an ideal Athens which never existed, governed by a king, and founded on ritual, but yet with all the new advantages of democracy. Like the *Suppliants* and Sophocles' *Oedipus Coloneus*, it shows us the combination of the old virtues and the new. After the victory, the chorus sing, "You have a way that is just, Athens, to honour the powers."[1] Justice, the virtue of democracy, is linked to honouring *theoi*, the old virtue. This linking is found all the way through. Iolaus at the beginning cries for help, linking

---

[1] *Heracl.*, 901–3.

the dishonour that would be shown to the gods, if he and the suppliants were torn from the altar, to the disgrace of the city.[1] The chorus on their entrance equally link justice with the ritual honouring of suppliants.[2] Demophon receives the suppliants out of respect for Zeus, because of his relationship with Iolaus, and because of the "disgrace of not doing so".[3] These are all aristocratic motives, not the sort of motives of advantage discussed in Thucydides. But he links this with the word associated above all with democracy, "free",[4] and the word had much fewer associations apart from the political in Greek. When the herald lays hands on the suppliants[5] Demophon threatens violence. But the chorus restrain him from violating a man whose person is protected by the old ritual sanctions, under any provocation whatsoever. Iolaus, speaking in thanks,[6] praises the aristocratic virtues. Athens at this time did not generally value "noble birth".[7] The chorus sing in defiance of Eurystheus, who "comes to drag suppliants off by violence, not yielding to kings, or saying *anything else just*".[8] This last phrase is extremely odd unless it is a deliberate attempt to draw attention to this linking of the democratic virtue of justice and the old ritual virtue, now unnecessary at Athens, of yielding to kings.

The importance of the ritual society to Euripides is contained in the image of sacrifice. The play is full of sacrifices.[9] Four times Athens is mentioned as sacrificing before the battle, and Demophon links sacrificing with gathering the troops; they are both equally important. We are prepared to hear that oracles demand the sacrifice of a maiden.[10] Demophon, a modern humane man, will not kill any of his citizens, and Iolaus offers himself to be handed over to the Argives. But we know that Eurystheus fears the children, not him. The offer is in vain. Then Macaria, the best of Heracles' daughters, offers herself, willingly, as the sacrifice. As willing victim she will bring no pollution on Demophon. She plays down her sacrifice, knowing she would find it hard to get a husband; she is a

<hr />

[1] *Heracl.*, 72. [2] Ib., 104. [3] Ib., 238–46.
[4] Ib., 244. [5] Ib., 269. [6] Ib., 297.
[7] Ib., 298. [8] Ib., 365–70.
[9] Ib., 340, 399–402, 673, 821–2. [10] Ib., 406 ff.

rational, democratic heroine. We know nothing of Macaria except for the sacrifice. She is a type of all the innocent lives willingly offered in wartime. It is important that Iolaus has offered himself first, and that Hyllus will offer himself to fight in single combat, so as to avoid the mass slaughter.[1] The point of the play is that war is only justified if it is taken in the spirit of sacrifice, on behalf of a society in which the spirit of sacrifice is clearly understood through the ritual framework of life, and it ends with a clear warning. The chorus end their song of triumph by praying not to have a "grasping soul",[2] and immediately Alcmena, by ordering Eurystheus, her prisoner of war, to be put to death, reveals herself as having precisely that. The tone of the play is more optimistic than any other of Euripides' works, and this is reasonable if the *Heraclidae* belongs to the first year of the war, and also if Athens was not responsible for starting the war, as now seems likely.[a] For example, it contains the most confident reference to immortality in Euripides.[3] It is the optimism of someone who thought that under the stress of war a better idea of society might emerge. But it is very heavily qualified.

Iolaus is the most important character in his own right. He is a good old man, and indeed holds up an extreme idea of justice as living for one's neighbour.[4] He is pious, and refuses to leave the altar,[5] until he actually prepares himself for the battle. His old soldier's pride that Eurystheus is really pursuing him, not the children, is both amusing and rather touching. All the time he is a bit ridiculous, and this has its climax when he struggles into the dedicated arms, and is helped off to battle. His capture of Eurystheus in the battle is definitely represented as a miracle, the result of a prayer to Zeus and Hebe, but after all he is an old soldier. He might take some time to get used to his armour again, but then he might be successful; the miracle need not be made an impossibility.

Demophon is important in his office, not his person, in the same way that Macaria must typify, not be too individual. Alcmena also represents wrong action. We do not see into her enough, and her violence with Eurystheus is only intellectually

---

[1] *Heracl.*, 802 ff.   [2] Ib., 926–7.   [3] Ib., 320 ff.
[4] Ib., 2.   [5] Ib., 344.

understandable, not dramatically gripping. I feel that here we do need a greater roundness of characterization than the schematic structure of the play allows Euripides. Eurystheus is utterly contemptible, so contemptible that he arouses pity. He is shown very skilfully.

The function of the chorus is to represent Athens. But the old men of Marathon will convey to Euripides' audience a very strong image of the "good old Athens". They serve to universalize the decision of Demophon, and constantly insist on their ritual life. They pray to Pallas to protect them, for they perform her sacrifices and dances,[1] and when they have won the victory they sing to the city to dance, since it honours the gods.[2] But they allow Alcmena to have her will with Eurystheus, which is surprising. The last words are "the kings will be free of pollution". Surely this leaves the implication that the people will not be. Perhaps most of the audience would not notice that, sung as the chorus went out. But at any rate it was in Euripides' mind. All the optimism about an ideal society in this play is conditional, and soon Euripides was to see the impossibility of fulfilling the conditions.

(viii) THE SUPPLIANTS

Adrastus preparing to invade Thebes with the seven champions would not wait until the oracles were favourable, but attacked and was defeated. In this play it is suggested that he had some justice on his side for attacking, but definitely disobeyed the will of heaven in going when he did. After the battle the Thebans refused burial to the fallen champions, and the play is the request of the Argives' mothers, led by Adrastus, who escaped death, and helped by Aithra, mother of Theseus, to persuade Athens to go to war to recover the bodies. The central wrong action and its consequences is less the form of the play than ever. It is a pathetic[3] tragedy more than any we have come across so far. Our attention is focused on the plight of the chorus of mothers, wanting the bodies of their sons. In front of them a series of debates take place, but they are debates with dramatic significance, since on their result depends the satisfaction of the women. The climax is a pathetic climax.

[1] *Heracl.*, 770 ff.   [2] Ib., 892 ff.   [3] Cf. Appendix.

First, after the Athenian victory the chorus sing that sorrow is mixed with joy, and gradually the sorrow overmasters the joy, until they wish that they had never married.[1] After the funeral speech Theseus dissuades the mothers from looking at their sons' bodies. The whole point of their request was that they should be able to see their sons again. Now it would be too horrible, and they submit. All we can do is say with Adrastus, Why do men fight?[2]

Apart from the tone, which is thoroughly pessimistic, this play is very similar to the *Heraclidae*. It is about the question whether a democracy can go to war, and it is about the ritual society. The answer given is the same as in the *Heraclidae*, that it is sometimes right to go to war, but the implied warning of the earlier play is now clearly explicit, and the effect is of an anti-war play.

It starts with Aithra praying to Demeter for a blessing on Theseus her son, and the city of Athens, while the mothers lie on the altar steps. Of all Euripides' prologue, this is the one most obviously put there for a purpose, not because he could not convey the information otherwise. The opening is to give the strong religious emphasis that is needed. Thebes is dishonouring divine law.[3] The Theban herald can point out that *theoi* were against the Seven;[4] that makes no difference; now they are dead. It is the point of the *Ajax* and *Antigone*.

This is why Athena appears at the end, when Adrastus has agreed to remember Athens for the favour. Greenwood thinks that the enterprise of "chivalrous" Athens is "degraded" by Athena, in that she makes Athens exact an oath from Argos.[5] Theseus makes a request; Athena appears, and gives this the sanctity of ritual. There is nothing degrading about this, unless all ritual observance is degrading. This is the way the old kings conducted their affairs. Here for the last time Euripides tries to show how it could be applied to democracy.

Athena also prophesies another war, which the sons of the Argives will fight. One implication of this is that wars will continue, but at least let Athens and Argos remain friends. The other implication is more conjectural, because it depends on the

---

[1] *Sup.*, 778 ff.   [2] *Ib.*, 950–1.   [3] *Ib.*, 19.
[4] *Ib.*, 494 ff.   [5] *Aspects of Euripidean Tragedy*, p. 106.

state of mind of the audience. The play was produced after nearly ten years of war, during which there had been the plague. Athens was war-weary. Surely the prophecy of Athena would reflect the mood of the audience; wars go on, they are pointless, but fools start them, and innocent people have to fight. It is a protest against the whole custom. This war-weariness may explain the funeral speech by Adrastus.[1] Critics are agreed that it is weak and rather dull. But suppose that it was meant to be a parody? A good example in our own day of the way interpretation depends on the state of the audience is to be found in some of the left-wing plays, produced at the Royal Court Theatre, which mention the Royal Family or the Union Jack, and immediately get a laugh, because that is the mood of the audience. In the same way a war-weary audience would recognize this speech as intentionally hollow. The ending must be ironic.[2] "So educate your sons," says Adrastus to the chorus. The chorus' sons are now mangled corpses. If we take this as the tone the Evadne–Iphis scene is merely an extension of this mood, a grim parody. Euripides is very careful not to end on Evadne's hysteria but on Iphis' prosy comments, which in the context, where we are sick of heroics, are very moving. Nor is Evadne less sympathetic for not being an operatic heroine, only a victim of war neurosis; she is made genuine, by being made pathetic and a bit ridiculous. There is a great clearness of honesty about the writing all through. Democracy is accurately criticized by the Theban herald,[3] because democracies rush into war. This the Athenians would know well now after the activities of Cleon. But in spite of all this, without democracy, law is flouted, replies Theseus, and this is still the impact of the play. Degrading as war is, we may have to fight.

We are clearly meant to approve Theseus' action. He is shown at first as the type of the rationalist liberal. He appears to take a very detached view of Adrastus' trust in oracles.[4] He believes in progress, in the predominance of good over evil. But he starts his account of this to Adrastus[5] by praising "whatever power it was who ordered progress", and later[6] he instances soothsaying as an example of man's ability to know

---

[1] *Sup.*, 857 ff.   [2] Ib., 917.   [3] Ib., 476 ff.
[4] Ib., 221.   [5] Ib., 201–2.   [6] Ib., 212.

things invisible – hardly typical of a normal rational liberal. Later still, he says that we should be content with what the powers have given us and not think ourselves greater than they are.[1] But this is what he says Adrastus has done. He is inconsistent, and Aithra tells him he is wrong to despise divine matters, though right in everything else.[2] Finally, however, he decides to fight, so that "the powers will have nothing to complain of".[3] But the final decision must be taken by the citizens. He decides to defend the suppliants for the old ritual reasons, but the process of decision is taken by the democracy. Having decided, Theseus is vehemently firm. Streams would flow upwards if the decision was reversed, he tells the Theban herald.[4] He recognizes himself as complying with natural law, and orders the army to make ready in the knowledge that nothing avails without the goodwill of the powers.[5] Wise and humane his conduct in fighting a limited war shows him to be; kindly his attitude to the mothers; but he is also, in spite of himself, the head of the ritually governed society, king Theseus.

Aithra is more obviously pious, and serves as a link between the chorus and Theseus. The remaining characters, in their different ways, are there to emphasize the pathos or the brutality of war. This is the simple function of the chorus, the cry to heaven of the innocent victims of the degrading process, typified by the sordid hysteria of Evadne. The difference of ten years' war is the difference between the willing sacrifice of Macaria and the enforced victimization of these women. But in the later plays there will not even be altars where they may cling and weep.

(ix) HECUBA

We have seen the result of war: a grotesque group of hysterical women. This next play shows how an innocent victim can become brutalized. Hecuba, driven crazy by the discovery that on top of all her other troubles her son Polydorus has been murdered for money by his host Polymestor, blinds Polymestor in a wild lynching scene with her women. There is a strong feeling of powers other than human being involved, but they are not

---

[1] *Sup.*, 216–18.   [2] Ib., 301–3.   [3] Ib., 346–53.
[4] Ib., 520–1.   [5] Ib., 592 ff.

brought so much to the fore. The play opens with a speech by the ghost of Polydorus, who conveys the need for revenge in terms vaguer than the more usual mentions of *Dikē* by the Olympians. It ends with the prophecies of Polymestor, blind, and so possessing that strange power that great suffering conveys. Hecuba will be turned into a dog, and Agamemnon, who has permitted her brutality, will be murdered on his return home. Hecuba is almost a beast already, but the reminder of the death of the leader of the Greeks is necessary to emphasize that everyone is going to suffer for the Trojan war.

Some critics have spoken of the play as "breaking in half". This is merely because at first we are asked to sympathize with the plight of Hecuba, and having sympathized, we then see her behaving in a way for which there is no justification. But if we watch from less close than the normal state of drugged identification with the characters that modern naturalistic staging encourages, then we shall find no difficulty. The point of the play is that everyone, sympathetic or not, is brutalized. We see this happening in the case of Hecuba.

Like the *Suppliants* and *Troades*, this is pathetic tragedy. They could be said to be less tragic, because they do not affront our fundamental beliefs. They simply say that war is horrible, though in many ages, both our own and the beginning of the second half of the Peloponnesian war, this simple message still needs stressing.

The sacrifice of Polyxena is superficially like that of Macaria, but the point of it here is its pointlessness, for all its nobility. The only reason that Odysseus gives is that of honouring Achilles, but Achilles could be honoured by the sacrifice of a sheep.

Because of this pathetic atmosphere, the structure is again loose, and the chorus of Trojan women, about to go with Hecuba into slavery, sing odes more relevant to the general point of the play than to the particular moment in the action.

Hecuba is a victim of circumstance. Her dream, of which she chants as she comes out of her tent, tells us what is coming; but her inability to understand it shows her relation to the events in which she is a part. She is the least rational of Euripides' main characters, as we can particularly notice in her speech requesting help from Agamemnon after she has dis-covered the murder.[1] Her attempts to make Odysseus sacrifice her instead of her daughter, and then her request to be killed with her daughter are very moving. From her violent curses[2] to the end she should be acted with frequent abrupt changes of mood. She is, in effect, mad. Polyxena, in contrast, shows ex-treme restraint. She even asks the villain Odysseus to bear with the anger of parents.[3] Her "lament" is in stichomythia. Be-neath this brave façade she is breaking down, and she has to ask Odysseus to cover her head.[4]

Odysseus is the unscrupulous demagogue. He speaks half a line in which he regrets the need for the sacrifice, and otherwise shows no sign of grief.[5] Agamemnon is the war-weary com-mander. He does not want to know, either about his future or the atrocities which are going on. Talthybius, who is not, after all, the man who takes decisions, can afford to be more pitying.[6] There is nothing to be said for Polymestor's action, which offends every moral instinct, and was done for money. But when we have seen him crawl out on all fours from the tent with blood pouring down his face, and hear how the women set upon him with their brooches and tore out his eyes, we are bound to feel sorry for him too. That scene is one of the greatest representations of the ugliness of war ever written.

The function of the chorus is to insist that Hecuba is only one of many women. Inevitably they will reduce the tension a little, since the disasters affecting Hecuba are played at such a high level of tension. After Hecuba has collapsed and Odysseus has led Polyxena off, they sing meditatively, wondering to what place they will be taken as slaves. The language is decorative, and therefore I suspect that the music may have been elaborate, designed to relieve the unbearable focus on Hecuba. After Hecuba has won a pledge of non-interference from Agamem-non they sing the great ode on the fall of Troy. This again is not relevant except in general, but it serves to make us think of the universal plight of the victims. Having asked us to pity all the chorus as we pity Hecuba, Euripides then firmly aligns the chorus with Hecuba's disgusting revenge. With them as with

---

[1] *Hec.*, 787.   [2] Ib., 716 ff.   [3] Ib., 402-3.
[4] Ib., 432.   [5] Ib., 395.   [6] Ib., 488 ff.

her, we are not allowed to go away from the theatre having had a good cry, and feeling better. We are not to feel better; we are to be horrified.

(x) TROADES

The Greeks have dishonoured Athena by burning her temples as they sack Troy, and by such acts of sacrilege as that of Ajax raping Cassandra. Anyhow, Poseidon is angry with them for all that they have done. He and Athena decide to join forces and send a storm on them as soon as they sail. The course of the play shows a general panorama of what they have done and are doing. Its construction is lyrical rather than dramatic, a series of scenes of gradually intensifying pathos on the central theme of the degradation of war. Aeschylus might have taken any one of these actions and shown it as typical of them all. Euripides tries to keep the focus as general as possible throughout.

The theme is as it were the reverse of the *Heraclidae*. There war was considered justified if it was conducted in defence of a special society, and in a spirit of sacrifice. Here the wrong done by the Greeks is the exact opposite of the way the society of the *Heraclidae* should conduct itself, and instead of sacrifice we have the sight of the war victims. But as we were asked to admire Macaria, and as her death was shown as having more honour than all the other actions, so here there is a recognition that the true heroes are the Trojans who have died for their country. Such nobility as there can be in war rests in the sacrifices made. The soldier's glory lies in dying not killing, and without this dying there would be no honour.[1] This is a most revolutionary idea at the time, and it must have hit home at Athens when the play was first produced, at a time when the Athenians, recovering from their hate of the war, were preparing to send their largest force ever embarked against Syracuse.

When a state is defeated it believes that its gods have deserted it. There is some doubt expressed by the characters as to the existence of the gods, or their nature. It was therefore necessary to show two Olympians on stage to redress the balance. We should notice that Poseidon has to leave the beaten city.[2] His power has no longer anywhere in which it can take hold.

[1] *Tro.*, 1240 ff.   [2] Ib., 25–27.

We are clearly not meant to think of this as a cowardly act, as it would be if a human being acted thus. Poseidon is a power who needs conditions, in which to be effective; *theoi* should not be conceived as in every way like humans. The unequivocal warning of his last words[1] shows, however, that where there are the conditions, then *theoi* are just as effective as ever. It is against this that we should take the beginnings of doubt shown by Hecuba[2] and even Cassandra.[3]

The chorus of Trojan women is central anyhow, but they were probably made even more important by elaborate choreography. I can see no dramatic point in having two semi-choruses, but it would obviously lend itself to more elaborate patterns. The total focus of the play is maintained by such devices as the refusal of Talthybius to tell where everyone is going, once he has told the fates of Hecuba, Polyxena, and Andromache.[4] If he had enumerated them all it would have been boring and anti-climactic; if he had only mentioned the main characters we should have lost touch with all the minor victims, about whom Euripides is really concerned. The principal function of the chorus is to emphasize the apparent uselessness of worship. Three odes carry as the main point the contrast between the ritual performed and the sorry fate of the performers of the ritual.[5] They were sacrificing to Artemis when the Greeks broke in.[6] But nevertheless they will not blame Zeus.[7]

Cassandra, rushing on stage like a maenad and "celebrating" her forthcoming marriage, demonstrates the blasphemy of the Greeks but also serves as reminder of the doom waiting for them at home. For she prophesies how she will be the cause of Agamemnon's death as well as her own.[8] Let the women rejoice at that. She also talks of the advantages the Trojans enjoy in dying for their country in a place where their women may lay them out for burial. It is one more reminder that all the advantage is not with the blasphemous victors.

Euripides uses Andromache with extreme skill. She first appears with the news of Polyxena's murder, but this is played down, and the tension is lowered so that the action can be once

[1] *Tro.*, 95–97. [2] Ib., 884 ff. [3] Ib., 356.
[4] Ib., 246 ff. [5] Ib., 511 ff., 799 ff., 1060 ff.
[6] Ib., 551 ff. [7] Ib., 845–6. [8] Ib., 359–60.

again universalized. She is worried at the problem that will trouble all the young captives. She fears that through sleeping with her master Neoptolemus she will come to love him. This is a superb psychological study, though here, as in the *Medea* or *Hippolytus*, feminine psychology is revealed in a too explicit way if we think naturalistically. Hecuba tells her not to worry, but to concentrate on bringing up Astyanax. Then we learn that Astyanax is to be killed too; this is what Hector's heroism has led to, Andromache cries.[1] Finally, she is led away to sail with Neoptolemus early, and Hecuba has to perform the burial rites. With this careful move Euripides avoids having two centres for the pathos, and at the same time increases our sorrow.

The scene in which Helen persuades Menelaus not to kill her immediately, and so not to kill her at all, for we know that she is not going to get killed by him, is splendidly written. Its point is to show that it was *this* that all the lives were lost to recover, this worthless scatterbrained creature, fit mate for her weak husband. All is designed to show the futility of war, and the development of the action is seen in the gradual disintegration of the noble queen Hecuba, until the terrible moment when weeping over Astyanax, she resolves to throw her ornaments over his corpse since fortune "is leaping around like a madman". This is fit preparation for the final catastrophe when the chorus sing of their approaching slavery, as they watch their city go up in flames, and this development has moved even the Greek Talthybius to pity, to offer to share in the funeral of innocent Astyanax. Foes join in unnecessary office; perhaps there is some hope for them, there is none for those who have brought them to it. But in spite of all this, there is something intangible called glory, not as the patriots know it. I do not find the end of the *Troades* so much in the flames of Troy, the final grimace by the people who thought themselves to be the most civilized in the world at the powers that would soon destroy them, so much as in one moment when Hecuba runs her finger round the rim of Hector's shield, and feels where it has been stained with sweat.[2] It is in these actions that weak human beings defy corruption.

[1] *Tro.*, 742.   [2] Ib., 1194 ff.

(xi) BACCHAE

In his last play, written in exile away from the city of Athens for the primitive society of Macedonia, Euripides returns to a far more closely patterned structure. The action grows out of an initial action, and the chorus have a function more like that of most of Sophocles' choruses. Their odes have relevance to the exact moment at which they are sung, rather than to the play as a whole. Thebes has refused to accept Dionysus, and he manifests himself to the city. The women who mocked his mother Semele's claim to have slept with Zeus have been turned into bacchants and wander the mountains living the ecstatic life. Dionysus now turns his attention to the king, Pentheus, who despises him. The story of the play is the gradual crushing of Pentheus. Teiresias realizes that this power is that of a *theos*, and prepares to worship, while Cadmus joins him largely out of family pride, since if Dionysus is *theos*, then Semele is really the bride of Zeus. For the rest of the characters their punishment depends on their repression of the power. None, except the chorus of devotees, are truly *sōphrōn*, because none have come to terms with this part of nature.

Scant attention need be paid to those who cling to the outdated notion that this play is satirizing Dionysus, any more than any other of the plays satirize their respective powers. We worship from terror, not because we think that gods conform to our ideas of human decency. Dionysus is a power we ignore at our peril, whether we are civilized or not. He is a principle of nature, the beast who is both hunter and hunted, the sap in the trees as well as the juice in the vine. He is the power who is worshipped by the rite of eating raw flesh on days which were unlucky.[1] The attitude of Teiresias is important. Told by Pentheus that he only approves the new god in order to get more money from divination, he replies that Dionysus is indeed a power. He confuses age-old bread and wine with their respective powers, Demeter, and now Dionysus.[2] Winnington-Ingram[3] believes that this is sleight of hand on Teiresias' part.

---

[1] Cf. E. R. Dodds, *Bacchae*, Int., pp. xvi–xx.
[2] *Bac.*, 272 ff.
[3] R. P. Winnington-Ingram, *Euripides and Dionysus*, pp. 49–53.

If it is, it is very poor sleight of hand, because no one who did not accept Dionysus would accept the wine which had always existed as proof of Dionysus' power. It is illuminating as showing the way in which the intelligent man who accepted the personal qualities of these powers saw them as both personal and natural forces. It is also illuminating to see how Teiresias modifies the story of Dionysus' birth. It is said that he makes it less violent, but this is nonsense. There is not a whit less violence in Teiresias' story, but it is less crude.[1]

The power of Dionysus is shown all the way through the play, though Pentheus and even the chorus do not see it at first in the gentle, even effeminate Lydian. We see it, for example, at the moment when Pentheus orders him to be bound, and Dionysus simply says, No. No bonds are laid on him.[2] Then at the moment of his manifestation, when the chorus see the palace walls totter, Dionysus describes how Pentheus chased a bull, while he, Dionysus, stood by and mocked; and he describes this in trochaic tetrameters,[3] the metre of the dance.[b]

The play is about understanding, *sōphrosynē*. The implications of what the chorus sing are as savage as what the bacchants do, but the chorus are in control. They know what happens to them. The first messenger also accepts the power of Dionysus.[4] He can speak only in terms of the things he knows, of wine and the joys it brings, but although he cannot express the power, he has seen it in action, in the battle he has just described, when unarmed women put armed men to flight. The chorus, as soon as Pentheus has revealed his intention of resisting Dionysus, sing a prayer to Holiness,[5] in which occurs the line, "wiseness is not wisdom".[6] They end the ode by praising the point of view of the ordinary man. The point of the *Bacchae* is that people who try to be clever stifle parts of themselves governed by a power that brings destruction if repressed, but that some, small, people can live with it in beautiful, dangerous harmony.

At the end of the fifth century the cult of Sebazius was introduced to Athens. This was an orgiastic religion, something like the original worship of Dionysus, which had now become in-

[1] *Bac.*, 286 ff.   [2] Ib., 503 ff.   [3] Cf. Appendix.
[4] *Bac.*, 769 ff.   [5] Ib., 370 ff.   [6] Ib., 395.

stitutionalized. The *Bacchae* is about a society which has gone wrong, through repression. Having seen the preoccupation of Euripides with the ritual life, and his final despair at the possibility of combining it with rational democracy, and knowing of his retirement to Macedonia before he wrote the play, we must take Pentheus and the repressed women of Thebes as standing for Athens, and think of the joy expressed in some of the odes as the joy Euripides found in a return to the primitive simplicities. It is significant that the man who starts the pursuit of the bacchants is a townsman.[1] The countryfolk are content to watch. They are aware of the splendour and the terror of nature; it is not to fill out the line that Euripides describes the cattle as "horned".[2] It is the same vision as that of the balance of peace and terror that is the dionysiac life, which I have mentioned as summed up in the image of the snakes licking the women's cheeks.[3]

The point of the play is carefully worked out in a system of pattern throughout, and especially in the choral odes. Highly significant is the first song in which the chorus balance descriptions of the peaceful joyous ritual with the violence of the story of the birth of Dionysus.[4] More significant still is the ode sung after Pentheus has left for the hills with Dionysus.[5] In the first strophe they sing of themselves dancing like a hunted fawn in the hills, in the antistrophe of the gathering *Dikē*. The hunted fawn is *Dikē*. We need to remember that to wear a fawn skin it is necessary to kill a fawn. This is one of the focal points in the development of the animal image which dominates the play. The hunt is constantly referred to. Key places are the reference to the captured Dionysus as "the prey",[6] and Agave's claim to have killed the lion.[7] With dangerous animals it is always difficult to know whether one is hunter or hunted. This is the significance of the image.

There is considerable use of word patterning. The places where Euripides uses the words for "wise" or "violence" are important. The wands of the chorus are described as "violent", for example,[8] and it is said to be "wise" to beat one's enemies.[9]

[1] *Bac.*, 717.   [2] Ib., 691.   [3] Ib., 767–8; cf. p. 114.
[4] Ib., 73 ff.   [5] Ib., 862 ff.   [6] Ib., 434.
[7] Ib., 1168 ff.   [8] Ib., 113.   [9] Ib., 877 ff.

There is a horrifying use of embodiment, when Dionysus promises Pentheus that he will have a "glory pinned to the sky",[1]
and later we see through the eyes of the messenger the struggling man, trapped in the top of the pine tree.[2] There is a poetic
action. Pentheus cuts off a lock of Dionysus' hair. I do not
know why, but on stage this has a most ominous effect.[3] We
are reminded of it later when Dionysus, charming Pentheus in
one of the most magical scenes in all drama, straightens a lock
of Pentheus' woman's hair.[4] It is a fit preparation for Pentheus'
journey to the hills, there to be killed by the terrible, gentle,
god.

Pentheus is clearly shown as acting wrongly of his own decision. Dionysus offers quite definitely to bring back the women
from the hills, without violence.[5] Pentheus out of his warped
mind may suspect the stranger; but we have no reason to suspect Dionysus. As soon as Pentheus refuses the offer, the
stranger shows his power and starts to charm Pentheus, who
will now no longer be free. His function is to represent the
repressed rationalist, the man who will not accept what he cannot see, and refuses to see what he cannot accept. It is one of
Euripides' best character portraits. I find especially illuminating
the moment when Cadmus tries to put a wreath on his head,
and Pentheus cannot bear to be touched.[6] Cadmus, fussing over
his family's honour, and Teiresias, the ecclesiastic who thinks
he owns his god, not the other way round, are characters we
can smile at. But it is these slightly ridiculous people who are
often right. We are reminded of Iolaus. Agave's appearance is
necessary to show the bacchants on stage, for up to now we
have only heard of them. Her madness is a fitting climax to the
accounts of all that they have done, and contrasts with the
chorus who remain the centre of the action. We may say that
this is a pessimistic play. It seems to show the powers of nature
mostly as destructive of civilized man, and it was written in the
conviction that they could not but destroy the society that was
supposed to be the best that there had ever been. But the final
vision of the *Bacchae*, if a terrible one, is also a clear one. It is
the vision of the messengers who can describe horror with

[1] *Bac.*, 972.   [2] Ib., 1063 ff.   [3] Ib., 493.
[4] Ib., 928–9.   [5] Ib., 804.   [6] Ib., 341–3.

lucidity, the vision of the countryman who can treat death as an everyday thing, and at the same time worship its mystery.

(xii) THE OTHER PLAYS

Of the remaining plays five could be described as comedies, and six as something less than tragic. The qualities we admire in them are theatrical ones; they could not be described as being about issues, and they do not ask us to re-examine fundamental moral presuppositions. The chorus is less important; it takes up less time, and when it does sing its function is decorative; it does not carry the main significance of the action. The action is not doubly determined, and *theoi* are used as theatrical conveniences, or for decoration. We might classify them as three ways of avoiding serious issues. One is that of escapist comedy. The point of the tragedies is to look at the way things are, not to allow any wishful thinking. With these comedies the natural human desire for wishful thinking is indulged. They are deliberately escapist. A second way is to exploit horror for its own sake. In the theatre the audience are stimulated and excited; afterwards they realize that the horror has nothing to do with their lives. Thirdly, sheer theatricality can be exploited; exciting spectacle, large casts, processions, battle preparations, and elaborate solo singing are all enjoyable in themselves, apart from their use in underlining the poetic point of a play.

In the first group we may put the *Alcestis, Ion, Helen,* and *Iphigeneia in Tauris.* The *Cyclops,* a more normal satyr play than the unusual *Alcestis,* is in a class of its own. All conventions are treated as excuse for laughter, and all we need say of this rollicking piece is that Euripides knew how to enjoy himself. The remaining four are based on what amounts to invented plots; so radically has Euripides changed the story. The happy endings are the endings we wish would happen in some harrowing tragedy. The *Ion* makes fun of Apollo, but it is not a very serious satire; Euripides is more interested in Ion.

In the second category I should include the *Andromache, Electra,* and *Orestes.* The first is described by the Alexandrian commentators as a "second-rate drama". It is similar to the *Heracles,* but there is a sense of pettiness, and it suffers from the violent hatred of Sparta that shows through the writing. The point of the Orestes story is to show a situation in which the only solution seems to be that of killing one's own mother. Once there is the slightest doubt about the necessity of the killing, the story becomes merely horrible, and therefore of no universal interest. The interest in the *Electra* lies in the sort of people Electra, Orestes, and Clytemnestra might have been, and as such it contains some fine character writing. The *Orestes* is a melodramatic study of neurotic characters, full of exciting theatrical moments, but a much less serious play than the *Electra*.

The *Rhesus* is usually thought not to be by Euripides, and is probably a fourth-century work. But the *Phoenissae* has something of the same epic quality about it; it is a series of scenes strung together without an underlying theme, and stemming from no central action. The *Oedipus Tyrannus* and Aeschylus' Theban tetralogy had shown Athens the Oedipus myth twice on stage; after Aeschylus and Sophocles, the appearance of Jocasta alive at the beginning of the play, when in the myth she would be dead, would warn the audience to take the play in a different spirit from that in which they would take the tragedies I have discussed. The *Iphigeneia in Aulis* is clearly not tragic as the plays discussed as tragedies are. Its central action must be the decision of Agamemnon to sacrifice Iphigeneia. This is lightly passed over, so that we should not think too much about it. Menelaus "persuades his brother to face the music".[1] That is all we hear of what Aeschylus takes a trilogy to resolve. The *Iphigeneia* is full of suspense, and the ending is exactly that of wishful thinking. Above all, the part of Iphigeneia clearly is a great singing part. Opera is not easily combined with serious thought.

(xiii) CONCLUSION

In the last section I have not tried to denigrate those plays of Euripides which can be distinguished from his tragedies which follow the method of Aeschylus and Sophocles. Far from it; I have tried very briefly to indicate the width of his range. Consideration of a play like the *Helen* will show him a master of theatrical craft. It is clear proof that if he wanted to, Euripides

[1] *I.A.* 97–98.

could write well-made plays. Study of plays such as the *Suppliants* shows that he was not always concerned merely to write well-made plays; it is a conclusive argument against all those who talk as if the arguments or the religious images are put there purely for theatrical reasons. It is therefore best to take the obvious view of his development. He was a superb theatrical craftsman, but a man with a particular vision of society which he tried to impose by means of his plays. So enthusiastic was he to convey the vision that he allowed the form of the plays to suffer. He strove for a society in which the rational and sophisticated strains in man which had produced the Athenian democracy were balanced with the primitive explosive passions by means of ritual and law. His Athenian contemporaries were less and less able to understand his vision, and he distorted his plays more and more in order to present it, while at the same time developing his technique and entertaining them with plays that involved no thought. Meanwhile the course of the war convinced him that his vision was a hopeless dream. We say that drama is a social art, and that great drama depends on a great society. But we should also remember Euripides. Gradually becoming more and more embittered with his failure in the society he loved, gradually more and more convinced of its inability to appreciate anything but exquisite triviality, he left Athens for ever, and lonely among the unthinking tribesmen of Macedonia produced—his masterpiece.

CHAPTER FIVE

THE COMMON GROUND
OF TRAGEDY

When we consider all the extant Greek tragedies we find that they have various features in common. If we took these common features as the starting-point in a general discussion of tragedy we should stress certain aspects of tragedy which definitions based on Shakespearean or French tragedy ignore, and ignore aspects which such definitions stress. It may be that we shall find the Greek kind of tragedy to be more suitable than any other kind to the problems of our own time. It is at least useful to amplify ideas of tragedy derived from European drama since the Renaissance with reference to the original idea.

We could say of every extant Greek tragedy that it was a lively meditation, conducted in public, into some issue of permanent significance, using song and dance and verse dialogue to represent an event in ancient history which embodied the particular issue, so that the audience's understanding of the issue should be deepened. This is the common ground of tragedy.

It is necessary to remind ourselves that the Greeks regarded the poet as a teacher, someone who was specially gifted with insight into the past, and therefore specially good at understanding all societies and society in general. So it was natural to expect him to unravel the complexities of contemporary society. We can obtain a clear idea of the ordinary Athenian's attitude to the tragic poets from Aristophanes. The ideas of the tragedians were discussed and evaluated in practical terms, in terms of their effect on society. Their plays were judged in accordance with the way in which they showed people how to live.

We should remind ourselves, in connexion with this, that the stories of tragedy were stories from the ancient history of the whole Greek race. The events they described were believed to have actually happened, but they were listened to by an audience seeking enlightenment on contemporary issues, who therefore allowed the poets considerable liberties with the details of the story, in order that the point of the story should be put over with maximum force.

There are three fundamental points to notice about all the tragedies I have discussed in detail. First, in every tragedy the action is initiated by both men and *theoi*. Every tragedy represents action that is doubly determined. This must have been done by deliberate choice, because it is so easy to see how the plays of Sophocles and Euripides could be rewritten as purely naturalistic stories; and to rewrite Aeschylus in a similar way is only harder on account of his larger scale, which would involve a naturalistic paraphrase in the use of abstractions like curses. The world view of the Greek tragic poets is one where men's actions are complemented by the actions of other beings, and men's actions are given significance by fulfilling the purposes of other beings.

Secondly, in every tragedy the chorus is central. The action is universalized with reference to the reactions of a group of ordinary people to whom is given poetry which means different things on different levels, which, for example, means something different to the comparatively ignorant people who say it, and to the audience, who are aware of the wider pattern. The chorus speak beyond their own understanding, and thereby enlighten ours.

Thirdly, the poetry, especially that of the choruses, has multiple reference. It is possible to see these plays as offering thought-provoking images of religious, moral, and socio-political issues. But the images have application at one and the same time to all these categories. The great period of tragedy was a period when there was no philosophy in prose. The tragedians' attitude of mind was determined by a desire to bring all facets of experience to bear on the issues about which they were concerned, with the result that it is impossible to say if an issue is religious, political, or moral. It was all these things together, for at the time they wrote the idea of separating these categories had never occurred to anyone.

I have excluded from this account some plays by Euripides. Apart from the two submitted as satyr plays, these are all late, produced after the outbreak of the war. One of the fundamental points about fifth-century drama is the clear distinction between tragedy and satyr play. The poet submitted three serious works, and then a farce. At the end of the century the distinction becomes blurred. We do not know if the *Helen* was submitted as the fourth play; there is no reason to suppose that the *Iphigeneia in Tauris* was not submitted as a tragedy, and its tone is similar to that of the *Helen*, or indeed of the *Alcestis*. With some of Euripides' plays, the distinction between tragedy and farce becomes blurred. There is an element of fantasy about the *Helen*; it has the effect of an invented plot; and round this time Agathon submitted his *Antheus*, the earliest play with an entirely invented plot. All the available evidence suggests that fourth-century tragedy was decadent, and probably most of the plays were romantic and escapist in tone, following the example of these Euripidian tragi-comedies. The question has been more fully discussed elsewhere.[1] Here we need only remark that it is not necessary to account for these plays in the same terms as fifth-century tragedy, and that in these plays all the important features of tragedy are missing. The action is not doubly determined; the chorus are decorative, and no longer central to the action; and the plays involve no issues. These plays, which are clearly not tragedies, which are more typical of the following age which did not produce tragic drama like the fifth century, should confirm that all the features of Greek tragedy as defined are interconnected.

We are certainly aware of differences in religious outlook between the three poets. But the fundamental activity in which they engage throughout their tragedies is remarkably similar. They have a determination to feel after some ultimate, inexpressible order behind human experience and the powers of nature, personal and impersonal; they have a hope that some-

[1] H. D. F. Kitto, *Form and Meaning in Drama*, pp. 231–45.

how this order and the process of human justice can be related. The experiences of tragedy affront our belief in the order, or our hope in its relation to human justice.

They differ in the way they conceive this ultimate order. They wrote at a time when the notion of transcendent power was just beginning to be formulated in Europe. It is natural that they might have had different images of this as yet inexpressible notion. Aeschylus was the most articulate. He saw one of the immanent powers, personal Zeus, gradually bringing all other powers under his control, until finally his power was hardly of the same order. Sophocles certainly thought of Zeus as the lord of all the powers, but we never find in his work anything like the attitude to Zeus in the *Agamemnon* or *Supplices*. In the *Trachiniae* Zeus supervises the action closely, but there are good reasons for this; Heracles is Zeus' son. In Sophocles we are more made to feel all powers, human and divine, moving within a rhythm which includes them all, *Dikē*. Since this is an impersonal force, in our sense of the word Sophocles is the nearest of the three poets to an atheist. Euripides, the youngest, nearest in outlook to the Ionian scientists, was further advanced, reaching after an idea of transcendence, to which the images of the Olympians would soon seem increasingly irrelevant. In modern terms this difference is less important in their tragedies than we might expect, because tragedy is concerned with the preliminaries to religious experience, rather than the ultimate religious experience itself. In terms of the fifth century we can see that moral problems were all formulated with reference to images of immanent, not transcendent power. The important images for the tragic poets, therefore, were the shared images of the immanent Olympians, not the vague, hardly formulated belief in something beyond them all, which would not yet have penetrated the consciousness of the ordinary people, and for expression of which there were no myths or images.

They differ also in the confidence with which they believe that the ultimate order is related to human morality, that *Dikē* includes justice. Adkins has shown that terms for this relation were never really found.[1] But though they could never express

[1] *Merit and Responsibility*, Chs. *IX* and *X*.

their belief that the ultimate order was moral, they certainly felt that it was, or at least that it ought to be. Aeschylus believed in the relationship most confidently. *Dikē* for him was a progress towards greater order, and in this progress the institution of the city, and therefore the processes of human justice by which the city is governed, were an essential part. Sophocles and Euripides were less confident, and became less confident towards the end of their lives as they saw their society disintegrating. Sometimes we are made to feel that it is utterly profitless to act rightly, but in the theatre we are so moved by Antigone in the *Coloneus*, or Polyxena in the *Troades*, that we cannot help feeling that it is still worth acting like this, even though it is profitless. All three poets harrow us by showing men who have acted rightly being crushed; all three exalt us with examples of right action. The proportions are different; that is all. On the whole we are more harrowed by Euripides, more exalted by Aeschylus. Euripides has the least confident hope that justice is a part of *Dikē*. That is why Euripides is called the most tragic of the poets. This is not very important for our understanding of tragedy. The important thing is that all three have some sort of hope, and that all three both exalt and harrow us.

All three poets engage on a similar religious activity by means of their tragedies. In their political outlook also they are very alike. This may best be seen by considering the plays in which we are confronted with a society we are clearly meant to admire. As it happens, we are only shown this three times, once by each poet, by Aeschylus in the *Eumenides*, Sophocles in the *Coloneus*, and Euripides in the *Heraclidae*. We might possibly add the Argos governed by Pelasgus in the *Supplices*. In the accounts of these societies we are forcefully made to notice that they are democracies governed by the rule of law, and yet permeated with the old ritual observances. Sophocles and Euripides place their ideal society under a ritually appointed king. They were portraying a society they knew to be only a dream; Aeschylus was presenting one that he thought might conceivably become real. The significance of the king can only be to embody an idea of consecrated government, and this idea is even more clearly shown in the *Eumenides*.

We can either say that the tragic poets depicted the old ritually governed society in terms that their democratic audience could understand, or else we can say that they presented an ideal society combining the virtues of old and new. This idea of society is very illuminating for the understanding of the tragic poets. It typifies their ability to combine ritual and reason, primitive passion and intellectual analysis, in a synthesis, not a compromise.

It is necessary to add that Greek tragedy is not "patriotic". Shakespeare too is not as patriotic as some have said. The speech which everyone quotes as an example of his patriotic writing is Gaunt's.[1] The sentence, whose beginning everyone remembers, ends with what is often forgotten. Our "precious stone set in a silver sea":

> Is now leased out (I die pronouncing it)
> Like to a tenement or pelting farm.

Certainly there is no flag-waving in Greek tragedy. The greatest piece of lyric poetry about Athens is the Colonus ode.[2] It is set in the middle of a play that represents the greatness of an Attica of the past; it sings of the glories of the countryside, not of the town, not of the people; it was written two years before Athens suffered the most crushing defeat in her entire history. The *Persae*, written at a time when, in spite of acute civil strife, a more optimistic spirit might be likely at Athens, most carefully avoids any opportunity of waxing lyrical about Athens. Her advantages in the war with Persia are stated in matter-of-fact tone, and conveyed in stichomythia, the least lyrical medium possible.[3] The *Oresteia* praises what Athens might be, but the image Aeschylus takes is the Areopagus, which had just then lost its effective powers as a governing body. What would our reaction be if the House of Lords lost all its governing powers, and remained solely as a supreme court, and then a playwright who approved of this reform wrote a play in which the House of Lords was shown being instituted in the reign of a Saxon monarch, by an angel, solely as a court? We should hardly assume that he was praising contemporary England.

We can summarize the outlook of the tragic poets as a world

[1] *Richard II*, Act II, i.   [2] *O.C.*, 668 ff.   [3] *Pers.*, 232 ff.

view in which humans and powers other than human, personal and impersonal, moved together in a rhythm which evaded description; as a resolution to test this ultimate order in the light of experience which seemed to contradict it; and as a belief in the possibility of combining what is best in the primitive, passionate, ritual life with what is best in the rational and democratic life.

Some of the things which are normally discussed with reference to tragedy are not relevant to the Greek tragedies. I shall not bother with defining too closely the points that I mention, since, on the one hand, they are not precise matters, and, on the other, it should be easy to see what I mean.

First, the Greek poets are not concerned primarily with "making a good plot". They allow inconsistencies, and fail to fill in gaps in the story. How could Aeschylus miss the obvious trick of building suspense over Salamis in the *Persae*? How crude it is that Aegeus should arrive when he does in the *Medea*. Few would dispute that Aeschylus and Euripides had other intentions beside that of making exciting stories, but some say that plot was the main concern of Sophocles. But from this point of view there are crudities about the plot of the *Oedipus Tyrannus*. Oedipus is made to know nothing about Laius' death. The story tails off at the end after the obvious climax. In addition to other inconsistencies, Sophocles needs to bring on a god at the end of the *Philoctetes* to tie the story up. What is the plot of the *Coloneus*? The *Ajax*, *Antigone*, and *Trachiniae* all "break in half". The first two miss the obvious climactic endings. Critics have had great trouble in trying to explain away these crudities and inconsistencies, and at the same time claiming that these writers are among the world's greatest. The claim becomes much easier once we see that the criticism is in the wrong terms. We should remember that the word, *muthos*, which Aristotle considers the most important part of tragedy, does not mean "plot" as it is usually translated. It means "story". To say that the most important element in the tragedy is the story which the writer chooses out of ancient history is not the same as saying that the most important thing is "plot", in our sense of the word.

Secondly, these are not plays of "character". Characterization is subordinated to the general pattern. When the pattern demands complex characterization all three poets can rise to the occasion. They are not like Shakespeare; but has French Classical tragedy any characters as lively as Clytemnestra in the *Oresteia*, or Sophocles' Electra? Characterization is shown often by means of highly pregnant lines of poetry. It is easy to miss and if the actor misses it and fails to build his character round it the audience will not have this aspect shown to them again, as in a naturalistic play where the writer has less to express, and so more time to spend on showing character. A typical example of this significant characterization is the use of the net image by Electra in the *Oresteia*, or Pentheus' hatred of being touched. The actor must use these lines to make himself a character which he can exhibit by movement and gesture whenever he appears. He is given the indication, but very briefly. When, however, the action does not require complexity of characterization there is none. It would be distracting if we saw too much of the personality of Theseus in the *Coloneus*. His function in the play is to present an office, not a person. We hear comments sometimes to the effect that Aeschylus should have shown us Agamemnon and Clytemnestra alone together. That is to demand a "play of character", and not Greek tragedy.

Thirdly, all talk of the "tragic hero" is irrelevant. Probably the fourth-century writers saw that a greater concentration was obtained if the tragic action and its consequences were all shown with reference to one man, once the religious purpose which gave unity to fifth-century tragedy had evaporated. If you do not attend to the chorus it is possible to talk of Oedipus as the "hero" of the *Tyrannus*, and Aristotle based his detailed criticism of fifth-century tragedy solely on the *Tyrannus*. But there is no other play in the entire extant corpus which has a "hero". The development of Sophocles' Electra is quite different from what is supposed to happen to a tragic hero. Who would be the "hero" of the *Philoctetes*, Neoptolemus or Philoctetes? Oedipus is certainly not the "hero" of the *Coloneus*. Hippolytus is a victim; and clearly there is no sense in asking who is the "hero" of the *Medea*, or the *Troades*, the Sophocles plays that "break in half", the *Persae*, or any trilogy. The viewpoint is communal; the development of the action is traced in a pattern to which all parts contribute, and in most plays it is more clearly shown in what the chorus sing than in anything else. As a result, we are never asked to identify ourselves with the principal character, except at a particular moment of decision, as with Orestes in the *Choephori*, when we have been prepared by a gradual closening of focus, or when the chorus reflect the decision of the main character as they do for Neoptolemus in the *Philoctetes*. Our sympathy for the sufferings seen on stage is always that of spectators; we are able to detach our sympathy from our moral judgement. I use modern terms, to correct a modern misapprehension. It was part of the outlook of the fifth-century Greeks to be able to see the reason for suffering at the same time as pitying it.

Those who have thought that Greek tragedy depicts a story with a hero have also conceived it as "heroic". I use the term roughly: Wagner's operas are heroic; French Classical tragedy is heroic. The audience is required to accept conventions of behaviour as natural which it would normally consider ridiculous. Suicide is a notable example. In Greek tragedy we are never asked to admire the suicides. We can be impressed by the heroic stature of Ajax, but are never asked to forget that he is a selfish monster. We can feel wrenched by Phaedra's plight, and yet say that her death is the worst crime she could commit. We can be swept away as much as we like by heroic sentiments, but at any moment we can apply common-sense detachment as well; that is the way the play is written; it is not the way of *Le Cid*, or *Tristan*. This notion of the "heroic" might be said to stem from Plato. It is at any rate a Stoic notion, and therefore affected Roman thought, not Greek. It is certainly not current in the age of tragedy which was a democratic, anti-heroic period. Because the plays do not survive, we tend to forget the farce which followed each poet's group of three tragedies, and gave the audience an opportunity to mock what they had taken seriously earlier in the day. We can also see an anti-heroic outlook in the tragedies themselves. The end of the Trojan war is the triumph of the beacon flame, but it is also the fact that soldiers will be able to get rid of the lice in their hair. Orestes, child of the eagle, minister of Apollo, once wet his nappies. It would spoil our picture of Le Cid if we thought of him wetting his nappies.

Because the focus of the plays is communal, the question of the happy ending is irrelevant. When Aristotle talks in these terms he seems completely out of touch with fifth-century tragedy. He condemns the ending where a good man is killed, calling it "repulsive".[1] Is this not exactly the end of the *Antigone*? People who say that tragedy must end unhappily have to say that the *Oresteia* ceases to be tragic at the end. I find it very unhelpful to say that the crowning glory of Greek tragedy is not quite a tragedy. The happiness or unhappiness of the ending is not something that affects us at all, in contact with the plays. For an Athenian audience does the *Persae* end unhappily? The *Ajax* and the *Coloneus* end in resolution. But the question, "Is this happy, or unhappy?" is not a question any normal person would ask at this point. You might as well ask whether a Bach fugue was ending happily or unhappily.

The purpose of the tragic poets was didactic; they were concerned to show the way in which a person should live, and the limits of human power; they were especially concerned with life in the society they knew, and used their drama to present images of what that society could be. Their method was historical and ritualistic, a use of poetry to understand the way in which the world's order had worked in the past, as the best, or only, way of understanding how it works now. Their means was drama put on at a festival for the entire population. It was an all-purpose drama, including song and dance and verse, ritual and slapstick. The centre of the drama was an image of the community, a dancing, singing chorus. It was often highly spectacular, especially in the hands of Aeschylus; we think of the *Supplices*, the end of the *Prometheus Vinctus*, the end of the *Eumenides*. It was a means for everyone to discuss and ponder the important issues of life and death, and at the same time a union of all social activities. I have given this chapter an ambiguous title on purpose. I refer to what the tragedians have in common, but I also intend to refer to the fact that it is common. Tragedy is vulgar; it is blatantly theatrical; it is for the ordinary people; it is about vulgar things like death.

[1] *Poetics*, 1452b, 34–36.

157

Discussions of Tragedy hardly mention any of these features as important. The picture they give is almost totally different. There is, however, one other body of dramatic writing about which remarkably similar things could be said, the Medieval corpus, and in particular the Miracle Cycles. The purpose of the Medieval poets was didactic; they used historical material; their drama was founded in ritual, and used as a means for understanding the way in which the world's order works. It was put on at a festival, and it, too, involved song and verse and spectacle, ritual and slapstick. It was popular and communal in outlook, and a means for pondering on the mystery of life and death. There was no chorus, partly because northern Europeans are less good dancers than southern ones, partly because the drama developed differently. The mimetic element, comparatively late in Greek drama, came in right at the beginning of the Medieval tradition, with the *Quem quaeritis*. The communal focus of the chorus is provided by the far wider variety of scene and character in the Cycles. The remarkably similar purpose of the two different dramas can be well seen by comparing their two respective climaxes. Is the mixture of triumph and grim warning with which the *Oresteia* ends not an image in terms of Aeschylus' religion remarkably similar to the mixture of triumph and grim warning in the Christian image of The Last Judgement with which the Cycles end?

We shall not understand much about Greek tragedy unless we realize how much its nature depended on its purpose. We are helped in this when we see how very similar was the impact of the Miracle Cycles, granted the difference between Archaic Greek religion and that of Christianity. If this is so, then the question whether there can be modern tragedy is the question whether our religion or religions can be dramatized in the way that Greek or Medieval religion was dramatized.

I think it possible to relate criticism of Greek tragedy to that of the other bodies of tragic writing by considering one more fundamental aspect of tragedy, not yet mentioned in this summary. Tragedy represents wrong actions and their consequences. The task of the tragic poet is to show us how to live our lives; but it is very difficult to say clearly of many actions, even in the past, that they were clearly right. It is easier to say of many more that they were clearly wrong. Tragedy principally teaches us by showing us examples of individuals or societies going wrong, and how they went wrong. Roughly speaking, there are three ways in which tragic poets have looked at this process of wrong action and its consequences.

The Greek poets described an action which disrupted the order of things, where a person overstepped the limits of his human *moira*. As a result catastrophe follows, and innocent human beings suffer. This cannot be avoided; but natural order will reassert itself. The Greek poets never show a real example of the Problem of Pain, because their religion was not one in which it could be formulated. The nearest approach to it is in the *Heracles*, where the wrong action is initiated by Hera. But Euripides does not necessarily suggest that the total order of things is wholly malicious, only that the total order is sometimes broken by disruptive forces. Our sympathies are roused by the predicament of the innocent sufferers, but the poets do no more than show us the reasons why they suffer, comfortless as these often are.

A Christian poet may likewise show a wrong action and its consequences, a process in which innocent people suffer, and continue to suffer, until the process destroys itself or is checked. Belief in a force of utter evil, usually personal, will make his view of the process somewhat different; the evil will seem to grow, not merely spread. But the immediate effect will not be very different from that of the Greek tragedies. As Christians we can ask in cosmic terms, Why does God allow Cordelia to suffer so? But in a sense the answer is straightforward; she suffers as a result of her father's idiotic decision. This is the way of Shakespeare. He did not need to ask the cosmic question, because this had been the purpose of the Miracle Cycles which were still fresh in the minds of his audience, though censorship put an end to their performance in 1576,[a] when they were at the height of their effectiveness. As a result his tragedies are more personal and individual, less a search for meaning in history; that search had already been performed, with complete success, for his age. He did perform one such exploration, in the sequence of histories from *Richard II* to *Richard III*, which is more like an Aeschylean tetralogy than anything else in

Elizabethan drama is, though of course not designed to be performed at a sitting. A wrong action is shown, and its consequences, a process of wrong and misery that grows for several generations, crushing and corrupting innocent people, until it finally destroys itself. It is not customary to call Shakespeare's histories tragedy; this is because his "tragedies" are the work of his full maturity, and it is usually thought that "tragedy" is the highest art. We can account for Elizabethan tragedy in the terms of this discussion by regarding it as a closening of the focus of the Medieval drama. As we have seen with regard to Euripides, a closer focus naturally involves more "harrowing", less "exalting".[1] This is not the whole account of the development of Medieval drama into Elizabethan drama, because during the Tudor period a number of other influences were assimilated, some consciously. But what is tragic in the Greek sense of the word is what continued from the Medieval tradition. Elizabethan tragedy would not be such a significant phenomenon if it were not for the unique genius of Shakespeare. The material and formal possibilities happened to suit his genius in the same way probably as the lays of the Ionian bards happened to suit the genius of the man who gave shape to the *Iliad*. Without Homer or Shakespeare we should have a very different, and less interesting, Ionian epic, or Elizabethan drama. But Aeschylus did not always win the Dionysiac competitions. Elizabethan tragedy should be regarded as a special development from the more cosmic drama of the fourteenth century, but there is a different emphasis in the treatment of evil and wrong, which has led to the one being called tragedy, the other not.

We can most easily see this when we understand that Shakespeare concentrates on one aspect only of the Christian doctrine of evil, that in which it is most like other doctrines. Roughly speaking, it would seem that a Christian has a double duty. He has to accept that the universe is in human terms unjust, that people suffer not only because of their own wrong actions; he has to say each week, I believe in one God, maker of heaven and earth, and of all things visible and invisible, such as the process of cell reduplication which produces all living organisms,

[1] Cf. pp. 114 and 193.

including cancer cells, the force that holds the nucleus together, which can be used to make hydrogen bombs. And so he has to spend his life exactly as the holder of any other religious belief, trying to fight this injustice, in which fight writing tragedies as an attempt to understand the injustice is one part; other parts might be searching for cancer cures, or campaigning for peace. On the other hand, he has also to realize that his activities cannot but fail; suffering can neither be explained to human beings nor totally abolished; or Christ would have explained and abolished it, instead of suffering Himself. He has to realize that his own vocation is finally to welcome the suffering that comes to him, when he can no longer prevent it, to welcome physical disability, moral disintegration, and death. This is my crude attempt to paraphrase Christ's words: "Take up thy cross" and "He that loseth his life shall find it". Only through this process of welcoming physical and moral disintegration can one become fit to live eternally. Coupled with this belief is the realization that in history, in events which we can see from a detached point of view, the greatest good can only come out of the greatest evil. If we see a woman having learnt to look after a paralytic husband who can no longer respond to her love, and whose habits are filthy, and see her acting with the radiant love of a saint, we must still try and stop the conditions for the practice of this greatest love, because the conditions are horrible. But looking at it detachedly, we must also say that this radiant love could only have come about as a result of these disgusting conditions. Without the worldly ambitions of priests, the cowardice of a ruler, and the hysteria of ordinary people, Christ would not have been crucified. Christian history in cosmic terms would show evolutionary progress, and every now and then particular people turning the great evil with which they were confronted into a greater good, by this activity of welcoming their own disintegration, which has been called "sacrifice". This positive side to the Christian attitude to evil is what is shown in the Miracle Cycles, whose stories are those of people whose main action can be seen as a type of Christ's main action. Whether we call this "tragedy" or not is a matter of choice. On the whole, people have not called this "tragedy", in the same way that they have shrunk from calling "tragedy" Aeschylus' equivalent attempt in terms of his own religion to present a cosmic, positive vision of the function of wrong.

It is only possible for a Christian to see this evolutionary progress as a victory of good over evil in terms of the entire history of the universe from its creation to its future dissolution and the second coming of Christ. On any smaller scale history does not show the victory of good over evil. Even the Crucifixion did not result in everything being all right from then on. The final victory lies in the future. With the divisions in the Church came an inevitable increase in unorthodox doctrine, because there was no longer a clear idea of the central tradition with which to compare new formulations. One of these unorthodoxies was a tendency to think that history on a smaller scale could show the victory of good over evil. This sentimentality, clearly incompatible with Christian dogma and the teaching of Christ, produced a tradition of bad, so-called Christian art, whose badness was very largely due to its unChristian sentimentality. In this tradition are a number of so-called Christian tragedies, telling the story of a saint's martyrdom. Most of them are bad, because they distort the Christian idea of evil, and show victory of good in terms less than cosmic. The few good plays of this nature, one of which I shall discuss, *Murder in the Cathedral*, show carefully that the victory is conditional, only in terms of the saint concerned, and is achieved at maximum cost. The majority of these plays are bad tragedies, because they represent the religion on which they are based incorrectly, in that aspect which is most fundamental, the attitude to evil and suffering, and which is especially the concern of tragedy.

In short, then, the difference between Greek tragedy and the Miracle Cycles is the formal difference between a chorus, and a vast cast in many settings, and the intellectual difference between two ways of looking at the story of wrong and suffering that makes up history. The intellectual difference between Shakespeare and the poets of the Cycles is that he, on the whole, concentrates first on simply showing the wrong action and its disastrous consequences, though there is some sense of a new state emerging at the end of *Hamlet*, and a greater sense of this in *Macbeth*; secondly, he shows this process of evil on a smaller scale, with a closer, more intimate focus; the earlier poets were concerned to present the total cosmic picture, and so could end on conditional triumph. "Can there be Christian tragedy?" is often asked. I shall return to this question later, with reference to modern attempts to write Christian tragedy. Here it is sufficient to say that if the attitude to evil and suffering of the Greek poets is considered necessary by definition to tragedy, then of course there can be no Christian tragedy, and what is Christian in the tragedies of Shakespeare is untragic. If it is asked whether a Christian poet can present stories of past events representing the process of wrong action and its consequences, in accordance with his own notion of evil, but otherwise like the Greek tragedies, then the answer is clearly yes. Moreover, this has been done, by the fourteenth-century writers, though their work happens not to be called tragedy.

I shall conclude this general discussion by offering a few "definitions" of tragedy, attempts to summarize in a sentence certain aspects of what I find in tragedy, or what I think a tragic poet tries to do. I shall first offer a translation or paraphrase of Aristotle's definition.[1] Tragedy is the representation of an action, artificially isolated so that its limits are clearly defined, involving serious issues, and presented by means of heightened language, rhythmic organization, and song, before an audience with a view to affecting them in a way in which they could not otherwise be affected. Aristotle, writing long before the age of naturalism, stresses the artificial[2] nature of tragedy. I shall not investigate the notion of *catharsis*. The tragic poet aims to affect his audience in a particular way which has something to do with the fact that they are all present in a group together. But to say more seems doomed to failure. Different people react in different ways to the same experience; I react in different ways to similar experiences on different occasions. The effect of the actual physical audience on actors and each other is extremely important; it is especially interesting to discover its nature now, when television means that drama need not involve a physical audience. But I do not see how this investigation can be performed.

[1] *Poetics*, 1449b, 24–28.　　　　[2] Cf. Appendix.

The tragic writer looks at a mess, a group of people killed for no apparent reason, and tries to find some reason. There were apparently occasions during the last war when British ships left torpedoed Germans to drown when they could have picked them up. The reason for this apparently unnecessary cruelty lay in an Admiralty order of the First World War, forbidding the practice of taking up enemy survivors, because the Germans had started shelling the ships which stopped. One wrong breeds another; horrible, but understandable.

We are asked to wonder at the process of nature. Why does a song-thrush smash snails? A waterfall gives hydro-electric power, holds us spellbound with its constantly changing beauty, and can kill a man in a few seconds. In tragedy we are asked to watch men being swept down waterfalls, not only the man, the waterfall too. In Greek tragedy, which has no heroes, we are asked more to watch the waterfall, in Shakespeare, more to watch the man.

For a Christian it is part of the practice of the Affirmative Way, in which all experience is to be seen as experience of God. All experience is an image of something beyond experience.

> All images are, in their degree, to be carried on; mind is never to put off matter; all experience is to be gathered in.[1]

Clearly it is easy to gather in all pleasant experience. It is easy to praise the God who made all things bright and beautiful. It is considerably harder to praise the God who made mosquitoes and polio viruses. Practice of the hard part of the Affirmative Way will be similar to the activity of tragedy.

The viewpoint of tragedy is the viewpoint of death. Not quite every tragedy contains a death. The *Philoctetes* does not, and the *Prometheia* can hardly have done, since the characters are mostly immortal. But in general the action has reference to death, the issues are issues for which people face death, and the attitude we are asked to take to life as shown on stage is the attitude we would take to the whole of life, if we were going to die. Certain things become much less important, others much more. We become aware of a desperate need for life to shape itself into a pattern, and as the pattern forms we discover with

[1] Charles Williams, *The Descent of the Dove*, p. 59.

horror that we have to make a choice, to accept the pattern as real, or deny it as illusion. We have to declare or deny our relationship with the avalanche as it crushes us, the lion as he tears us, our own invention as it explodes on us. It is because this seems to be the fundamental part of the activity we call tragedy, and this is what we are being forced to do so constantly now, that I have dared to undertake this inquiry.

PART II

THE POSSIBILITY OF
MODERN TRAGEDY

CHAPTER SIX

TRAGEDY AND PHILOSOPHY

(i) THE END OF CERTAINTY

I believe that our generation may possibly see the growth of a drama somewhat like Greek tragedy. And I believe this primarily not because there have been a number of writers influenced by Greek tragedy, but because there has been a change in our whole way of thinking. To put this into words while it is still happening is impossible; to try and summarize it in a chapter of a book about plays will be considered by many impertinent. But I shall still commit this impossible impertinence. Great drama does not arise from conditions in the theatre, but from conditions in society. I shall summarize my own reactions to the recent developments in thought, if only to emphasize the limits to dramatic criticism such as I undertake in Part III.

Greek tragedy was written before there was such a thing as "philosophy". Dramatic poetry was the only medium known to the fifth-century Greeks for practising that activity which has usually been called philosophy, coming to terms with the meaning of life. Since then there have been many philosophers who have thought about the meaning of life, and some who have formulated these thoughts in a system. What philosophers have done recently is to cast discredit on all systems. It is not an exaggeration to say that as Euripides saw the beginning of "philosophy", so we have seen its end. We are in a position to see why the old Greeks used poetry. It is not that it is prettier or more pleasant than prose philosophy; it is more rational.

In Western Europe our ways of thought are conditioned by what scientists are doing and saying. The philosophy of the last three centuries is often considered as consisting of two streams,

169

the Rationalist and the Empiricist. The difference between them is well analysed by Walsh.[1] Both developed as it became apparent that science was a system of laws, connected causally. The Rationalists concerned themselves with asserting the independence of human reason from these laws, and the Empiricists with trying to develop a philosophy which should be independent of a particular human mind in the way that science was thought to be independent. The Rationalists therefore tried to reduce all statements about the world into statements about consciousness, the Empiricists to reduce all statements, including those about consciousness, to statements of direct sense experience, independent of the mind of the observer. Both were attempts to found a philosophical system which should have the certainty of science. In the Rationalist group is Descartes, trying to prove his own existence with the same certainty as that of a mathematical theorem, and all those who thought of consciousness as the ultimate reality, down to the Idealists. On the other hand are the Empiricists, especially Hume, and their successors, Russell, the Vienna Circle, and the Logical Positivists. The greatness of Kant is his attempt to embrace both streams. The inspiration of both sides was belief in the certainty of mathematics and the objectivity of science. The two views of consciousness are seen at their most extreme in the difference between Descartes' "Cogito, ergo sum", and Hume's definition of the self as a series of impressions.

But now we can see that both these inspirations were misguided. After the work of Peano, Whitehead, and Russell, we can see that the certainty of mathematics is only the certainty of tautology.[2] Euclid's geometry, for example, is based on an arbitrary choice of a fundamental proposition, that parallel lines do not meet. Other geometries, based on different assumptions, are needed for less usual kinds of space.

By "scientific objectivity" I refer to the assumption that the world was made up of particles which existed independently of the observer. This concept is irrelevant to contemporary physics. It does not make sense to ask whether electrons exist.

[1] W. H. Walsh, *Reason and Experience*.
[2] Cf. Bertrand Russell, *An Introduction to Mathematical Philosophy*, especially pp. 5–6.

The term "same electron" has no meaning, since we cannot observe the position and weight of an electron at the same time. Observing it means bombarding it with a photon, and this automatically changes its course. For the last three centuries philosophy derived from people's reactions to the laws of Newtonian physics. Our way of thought is bound to derive from the Indeterminacy principle.

It is in this light that we should see the developments in philosophy during the last forty years. The story has been told by Urmson[1] and Warnock.[2] I do not wish to disagree with their arguments. No serious philosopher in England today calls himself either an Idealist or a Logical Positivist. The collapse of both these systems is clear and irreversible. I have no space to go into the arguments, but I wish to stress the conclusions, since much of what I shall say in Part III depends on them. It is important, for example, to realize that much literary criticism is still based on Idealism. If Idealism has been discredited, then criticism based on it is less useful.

The achievement of the Logical Positivists was to insist that language has meaning in so far as it refers to actual or possible experience. The Idealists wrote of a supra-sensible Reality, and said that the task of philosophy was to lead men to understand the nature of the Absolute by a process of intellectual intuition. Most of them used an Intuitionist system of ethics; one intuited the Right.[3] But if we can intuit the Right, why do men disagree over what is right? The Absolute is by definition beyond experience. How, then, can we say anything profitable about it? With this kind of question Idealism was not so much disproved as passed over.

The centre of Logical Positivism was the attempt to reduce all knowledge to statements which were certain, either with the certainty of mathematics and tautology or as being statements of immediate sense experience, which could not therefore be falsified. This accounts for their concern with the problem of perception. It was fundamental to their philosophy that they should be able to reduce statements about the world to

[1] J. O. Urmson, *Philosophical Analysis.*
[2] G. J. Warnock, *English Philosophy since* 1900.
[3] Cf. H. A. Prichard, *Moral Obligation.*

statements of immediate sense experience which could not be falsified.

But now it is accepted that no statement of sense experience is certain in the sense they required.[1] Furthermore, their account of perception, with the sense-datum theory and its development into Phenomenalism, was misguided. It assumed that we were passive recipients of perceptual sensations, instead of actively discriminating in the very act of perception. And the objects of perceptual experience, introduced for the purpose of making certain statements, proved impossible to define. Were sense-data public or private? How many did one see at a time? These questions could not be answered, and so this kind of reduction has been abandoned.

Philosophers are now concerned with the analysis of concepts, and insist that it is not their task to lead people to understand the meaning of life. What we now call philosophy can be practised by people of all outlooks; but to be an Idealist meant having a particular outlook on life, and to be a Logical Positivist meant having an opposing one. The end of certain systems means the end of philosophy as an influence on life.

We can, however, live without this concept of certainty. We can formulate hypotheses to explain our experience. We cannot say of any hypothesis that it is finally certain, but I can say that some hypotheses clarify more than others, and why they do so. We can give reasons for our actions. No set of reasons are conclusive, but I can say that for me some reasons are better than others, and why they are better.

For the past three centuries philosophy was practised in order that life might be founded on an intellectual system that was certain. This activity can be understood by contemplating, on the one hand the Rationalists' act of intellectual intuition, and on the other the Empiricists' reduction of knowledge into statements of immediate sense experience. I shall now suggest a few intellectual actions that might be thought typical of our ways of thought.

We do not ask whether light is made of waves or particles. We accept that some experiments suggest that light behaves as if it was a stream of particles, and others as if it was a series of

[1] Cf. A. J. Ayer, *The Problem of Knowledge*, pp. 36–83.

waves. We use two, apparently opposing images in so far as they help us to understand. We do not try to reconcile them.

We do not think of intellectual activity as possible except with reference to experience, nor do we think of sense experience as something separate from rational activity. The two are inextricably linked. We hear, for example, some eight-part counterpoint by Byrd. We are just aware that it is in eight parts. We can follow the bass and the treble. We cannot really hear the second alto. If we had the score we could follow the second alto; we could really hear it; if someone then took the score away and the choir sang again we would be much more successful at humming, that is at really hearing, the second alto part; it would not be a matter of remembering the look of the music; it would be that we had heard its function in the harmony; we understood it, and so we heard more. If we know more we perceive more. And, further, knowledge is often more a matter of understanding than of acquiring facts.

Our perception of gestalt objects is another important image of our intellectual activity. What happens when we look at something like Wittgenstein's duck-rabbit, a line drawing which can be seen either as a duck or as a rabbit.[1] At one moment we see a duck, at another a rabbit; but the picture does not change. At first we cannot control which we see; but we can learn to do this. If we had never seen a bird we would never see the duck aspect. We do not just perceive, we perceive something as an *x*. This "perceiving as" is partly the result of learning; it is at first something that comes; later it can be controlled to some extent. If we think of a painter seeing a tree stump *as* a witch we realize that this "perceiving as", this "seeing of aspects", is akin to artistic inspiration, something which is partly a matter of will and partly something that just happens.

There is little point in trying to explain the world in terms of entities that we can experience and understand. Scientists freely posit entities if thereby our understanding of some process is enlarged. In the 1930s quantum electro-dynamics developed, giving a good account of many features of light and its relation to electricity, by describing the force between electrified bodies as the absorption and remission of quanta of the field of light.

[1] Ludwig Wittgenstein, *Philosophical Investigations*, part II, p. 194.

When scientists came to study the nuclei they discovered that they were influenced by even stronger forces. In Japan Ukawa suggested that here, too, quanta were being exchanged; he went on to suggest that unlike the quanta of light these had a rest-mass, and were in fact 200 $\times$ the weight of an electron. Further experiments confirmed that the positing of this entity, later known as the meson, were justified. But the entity was posited, and even described, by analogy with other experience, because it seemed to increase awareness.[a]

These are the activities by which our understanding of ourselves and the world increases. So these are types of rational activity. In contrast therefore with philosophers of past generations we shall not try and separate knowledge, perception, and choice; we shall admit that they are all part of one activity. We shall not so much ask, Is this real? but, Which fits better with the whole pattern of my experience? We shall not necessarily decide whether the world is x or y. We may prefer to treat it sometimes as x, sometimes as y.

Philosophical systems are useless as guides to life. Scientific method has achieved results. Our best hope of acting rationally is to follow scientific method as closely as possible in all branches of life. Fundamentally this seems to be the activity of formulating and testing hypotheses in the belief that things can be explained. A scientific hypothesis when first adopted may make its point in an almost poetic way, and is often reached by a similar process to that of an artist's inspiration. For example, we may say that the history of life on this planet is governed by the law of Natural Selection. The scientist then goes on to show what he means by drawing attention to the experiments he has made, and perhaps indicating a line for future experiments. By this he gives content to a statement which would otherwise be vague and meaningless. As the hypothesis is seen to account for more facts, so it acquires more meaning. If it conflicts with experience it is discarded as useless.

Two aspects of this are important. First, we cannot distinguish absolutely the concepts of meaning and truth. A generalization is shown to be true by experience; but it is also given added meaning by experience. I do not myself really know what it means to say that the earth goes round the sun. If I practised astronomy, and performed experiments to show that this belief was true, I should also have a much clearer idea of what it really meant.

Secondly, this activity involves evaluation at every stage. We have to ask, Does this explanation or that one give me a clearer understanding? Which theory is more useful, more likely to lead somewhere? These questions can only be asked with reference to some end, some purpose. In the past it has been said, first, that the business of science was with truth, philosophy with meaning; secondly, that the notions of evaluation, end, and purpose are part of the separate discipline of moral philosophy. If we are to apply scientific method to the whole of our lives the traditional categories of philosophy will have to merge in one unified activity.

The aim of rational activity is to develop self-awareness. I cannot know the world independently of myself, or myself independently of the world; but by learning about the world I learn more about myself, and vice-versa. I learn to fit my experiences into a pattern, explain them in more general terms, and then test the explanation with reference to future experiences.

We do not, of course, provide all the explanations ourselves. At first we accept the explanations we are given. To acquire self-awareness is to pass judgement on inherited explanations. It is to act and accept explanations for reasons and not from causes.[1] If a man is told by his mother that he is descended from John of Gaunt we would say that the cause of his belief is his mother's repetition. This would have no value as evidence when we decided whether to accept this or not. If he produced wills and so on we would say he had reasons for believing it, and these reasons would be equally helpful to us in assessing the claim, even though we might decide differently from him. All our beliefs are at first accepted from causes. To become self-aware is to discover that we hold a particular belief from causes, to inquire whether there are reasons for accepting it, to evaluate the reasons, and then to decide whether to accept, reject, or modify the belief. Once we understand why we hold a belief, and can evaluate and then accept or reject it, we are freer in

[1] Cf. J. O. Urmson, "Motives and Causes", *P.A.S.*, Supp. xxvi, 1952.

respect of the belief, because our acceptance or rejection is a matter of conscious choice. This is the sense of "freedom" in which Sartre says that the aim of man is to be free. It is the point of a recent book by Stuart Hampshire, *Thought and Action*, the first major attempt to combine the outlooks of British empiricism and Existentialism. He says that his purpose is to trace the connexion of knowledge and freedom.[1] He admits, however, that this activity is inevitably speculative, in contrast to Sartre, to whom I shall return. It is not only speculative in the sense that there is no certainty. It is much more imaginative than logical. I must use my own experience to understand the statements of others, and my experience can never be more than analogous to theirs. I must see in what way my experience is typical, and in what way unique. Since I can remember times when I was mistaken, there is no special reason for relying on my own experience. Sometimes we shall accept the explanation of others or one read in a book rather than rely on our own. We pay attention to the experience of experts in fields where we are ignorant. We do not evaluate a statement independently of the speaker.

I have now offered some models of rational activity, and suggested that its aim should be, on the one hand, to approximate as closely as possible to scientific method, and on the other, to develop self-awareness. The models suggest that the most useful intellectual skill is that of inventing or discriminating between images and analogies for our experience. The aims suggest that the activity should be imaginative, speculative, eclectic, provisional, and, above all, not specialized. Prose philosophy with its certain systems is not a sensible medium for this activity. Rational poetry such as Greek tragedy is.

This sort of attitude is much the same as that of Existentialism in so far as Existentialism is also a reaction against Idealism and is an attitude which starts with one's own consciousness of the world, and then works outwards. The Existentialists are also right in saying that we cannot discover much about the nature of decision unless we examine our own, important, decisions. It is not much use talking about decision in the trivial terms of Professor Ryle's *The Concept of Mind*, for

[1] *Thought and Action*, p. 133.

example. In my own experience it is just the case that important decisions are different from trivial ones. In all this Existentialism is valuable.

For this discussion I shall base my account on Sartre. The disadvantage of the system is that its basic proposition "Existence precedes Essence" can be taken to mean two things. Either it is, as Sartre says, merely an attack on the eighteenth-century notion of man as static, on an Idea of Man subsisting in a Platonic heaven; we first exist, and then discover what we are. This is a position with which very few would wish to quarrel. Or it is an atheist statement of faith: man is not a created being. I shall return to this aspect of Existentialism later.

Sartre's thought is based on a proposition we all accept, and he has drawn our attention to priorities in our thinking. But his philosophy, in so far as it is a system, is thoroughly muddled. It is based on the Cartesian Cogito. The Cogito was evolved in response to a notion of mathematics which we now see to be misguided. In addition, the Cogito is not adequate as a foundation for a philosophy.[1] There is no sense in which I *prove* the existence of myself by thinking. To say anything of anything implies something to say it about. Ayer goes into this in detail; I accept his arguments. Descartes went on to deduce the existence of God, and through that to deduce the existence of others. Sartre claims to reach a Cogito for others in ways analogous to the original Cogito. But he will not use the notion of God, and without this, the deduction is impossible.

It is perfectly reasonable to say that we are first aware of ourselves, and then of other people. But this is not by a process of logical deduction. And if it is not, then Sartre's system has no more validity than the uncertainties of common sense. It is easy to explain psychologically why Sartre wrote as he did. If you start with the Cartesian doubt and the Cogito, you are forced into a solipsist position, unless you follow Descartes' introduction of God. Sartre does not want this; for he is committed in morals and politics, and he believes in democracy. But if atheist Existentialism was a certain system, it would have to be solipsist. Sartre has another inconsistency. If we accept the

[1] Cf. A. J. Ayer, *The Problem of Knowledge*, pp. 45–54.

experience of others, why should we not accept the experience of the past? But to Sartre the point of view of history, like the point of view of science, is the point of view of Bad Faith. Sartre has said some important and useful things. But he has tried to make his thought look as though it formed a certain system like the Cartesian one. In this he is clearly misguided.[1]

I have tried in this section to summarize what seems to me a reasonable reaction to the main trends of thought of our time. This is the position from which I shall criticize the writers that I discuss in Part III. I am making two claims. I do not pretend to have substantiated them completely, because complete substantiation would take a lifetime. But I believe they will be substantiated soon beyond all argument. The development of quantum physics has meant an end of certain philosophical systems. Before this the most important rational activity was the understanding of logical connexions; now it is the making of relevant images. Secondly, if there are no certain systems, there is only me, and my experience, and the experience of others in so far as I can understand it by analogy with my own. Profitable discussion therefore will be in terms of analogies and images. And the medium for this is rational poetry.

(ii) THE PROBLEMS OF TRAGEDY

I shall consider the nature of this "poetry" in the next chapter. Here I wish to outline the results of the changes in thought I have been talking about as they affect those questions which have been considered the province of the tragic writer: the nature of human freedom, the nature of moral action and the nature of the order of the universe. I wish also to claim that when we examine these problems in the light of recent changes in thought, we shall find that here also traditional philosophy is a less useful medium than what I have called rational poetry.

We now think differently of the nature of the self and the freedom of the will. Hume defined the self as a series of impressions; we cannot define the self at all. We have to start with our consciousness and work outwards. We aim to act for reasons and not from causes. This is the sense at which we are aiming at freedom. To ask whether man is free is a funny ques-

[1] Cf. Iris Murdoch, *Sartre, Romantic Rationalist.*

tion. We cannot say of anyone that he is absolutely free. We can only say that one man is freer than another with reference to an end. Is the peasant freer than the industrial worker? If the aim is to be independent of money, the peasant is freer. If the aim is choice of leisure occupation, the industrial worker is freer. I can say that I can become freer by coming to understand why I act in a particular way, and acting more for reasons and less from causes. And I can tell with a degree of correctness that some people are more self-aware than others. But no one is anything like fully self-aware. If someone asks, "I see all that, but is man really free?" he can only be implying that this process is all illusion. I can only reply that the process achieves results.

The problem of freedom is a vast one, and needs discussion. But it does not need discussion in terms of the nineteenth century, the controversy on Determinism. To understand this point is vital for our understanding of Ibsen for example. Our notion of scientific law has changed. Because "law" normally implies constraint, it was feared then that if man could be shown as moving in total accord with scientific law he would be seen to be constrained. It was thought that if a man's actions could be completely predicted, then they could not be free. But now we see, first, that scientific laws merely describe, they do not constrain, and, secondly, we conceive them as statistical generalizations, not universal laws. Furthermore, predictability does not necessarily imply constraint. If I see Fred on a crowded bus, and predict that he will give up his seat to a woman with varicose veins, we would still call his action free. We would never say that an action done consciously for charitable motives was not free, however predictable it was. This example also shows that the notion of freedom is inextricably linked with the notion of right action, just as the example of the peasant and the industrial worker showed it to be linked with the notion of an end.

We hear it said that modern science may show that man is not free. But this is a generalized reaction to several very different discoveries. First, we realize that often a man is not fully in control of his actions, and sometimes this is not his fault. There are times when the law is more lenient, because a defendant was not fully in control. But that is more an acknowledgement that those for whom it is very hard to act socially should not be punished as severely as those for whom it is easy. It carries no implications that because A has been punished less, B, a man of similar background and handicaps, could not have overcome his difficulties and avoided the crime.

Then there are the findings of psychology, social psychology, and genetics. We are often moved to action by forces we do not understand, sub-conscious impulses and desires. But we can learn about these forces, and finally control them. Psychology has shown us that we are less free than we thought, but it has also shown us how to become freer. Social psychology has shown how much of our action is explainable in terms of our environment, and genetics how much in terms of inherited physical characteristics. But we can also see how it is possible to overcome the deficiencies of environment or inherited physique. A boy may be born of weak parents, so that he has weak shoulder muscles, and pants a lot. But if from the age of ten he pulls up to a bar twenty times every morning, and runs a number of miles every afternoon, when he is twenty he will be far better than most of his contemporaries at precisely those things at which once he was defective. A boy who has grown up in an area where everyone steals, and somehow has acquired the ability to avoid stealing, will be unlikely ever to steal in later, more prosperous life. Someone who has grown up in a comfortable middle-class home, in sudden need may succumb to a temptation he had never before experienced. These discoveries have influenced the way we praise and blame; but they are separate from the problem of freedom as it used to be conceived.

Modern fears about the nature of human freedom are given most concrete form by the discoveries in neuro-physiology of the brain. For some classes of mental events it is now possible to show corresponding physical events, patterns of electrical charges; it is reasonable to suppose that eventually it will be possible to show this for all events. We are forced to realize that body and mind are one. But in a sense this has always been clear; the discovery that someone's mental outlook can be changed by the operation of leucotomy is not different in kind from our knowledge that we think better when sober. If we do become able to explain all consciousness in terms of electro-magnetic waves, then we shall have to re-examine our notions of personality, in which is included the question of human free-dom. At the present stage of the development of this science we simply cannot tell what we shall have to think.

It is not even easy to say what it is that we fear. Clearly people feared an explanation of consciousness in physical terms, when "physical terms" meant the terms of mechanistic physics and causal connexion. But our notion of physical terms is com-pletely different now. Perhaps it is more that we fear for our chances of surviving death; if this looks less likely now it is bound to affect our notions of human freedom. We may decide that this is a much more vital question for tragedy to pose than the question, Is man free?

This possibility underlines the difference between us and the nineteenth century. Perhaps we shall be able to analyse con-sciousness in terms of electro-magnetic waves. We can analyse the universe in the same sort of terms. The distinction between the physical and the moral has broken down. To understand moral action we must understand psychological motivation. Psychology requires knowledge of physiology, and physiology is ultimately a matter of patterns of electro-magnetic waves. The problem of freedom disintegrates into a number of other vast, interconnected problems about the entire moral–physical universe, now seen as one.

If this is so, then what used to be called moral philosophy is merely an artificially isolated part of the individual's total pro-gress towards self-awareness. All consciousness, even percep-tion, involves choice and therefore value judgements; and what we thought were specially moral parts of us, the will, the con-science, and so on, will probably be analysable soon in terms of electro-magnetic waves. That part of my growth towards self-awareness which used to be called moral philosophy is now seen mainly to be either a psychological inquiry, seeing how I took decisions in the past, examining them more clearly than I could at the time, and seeing where I went wrong, and partly a religious activity, trying to discover more clearly what is my ultimate aim.

If I want to become self-aware I can only do so fully in a

society that is also developing in this direction. If we as a society want this awareness, each of us must develop it for himself as well. If this is the agreed aim of the society, then the more aware have a responsibility towards the less aware. There will therefore be no absolute distinction between morals and politics, or between the moral philosopher and the moral leader. We shall return to the notion of morality as a skill, partly a gift, partly the result of training. We shall be chary of judging that one person is better than another; but confident that for us, individually, to become better involves learning to understand more clearly. One of the best ways of understanding our own mistakes is to consider the mistakes of others; one of the best ways of understanding our ultimate aim is to contrast it with the aims of others. Indeed, it is impossible to be clear about our aim, except by contrast with that of others. We say, "I don't know what I want to be, but at least I don't want to be like him." So perhaps the best way of learning to take decisions which will be right for us in our society is to enter into the decisions of other people which can be used as analogies of our own moral and political problems. And no one has ever found a better medium for this than the Greeks in their tragedy.

Unless, like the Idealists, we claim to be able to intuit the Right, we can give no sense to the notion of "right action" except in relation to some end. Nor is it possible to discuss freedom without bringing in this notion. All I wish to imply by this notion is that I act with varying degrees of purposiveness, and am trying to become more purposive, and more articulate about the purpose. But it is the case that the majority have a very similar purpose in their lives. We have the idea of an end for ourselves in our society, and this relates to our idea of how the universe is ordered. This is what I mean in this inquiry by the word "religion".[1] To help people understand their religion is very much the task of the tragic writer.

We hear it said that tragedy depends on a common religion, and there is no common religion in the West at the moment. This is only partly true. Our adherence to democracy is non-sensical unless we believe in the virtues of free choice. If we believe this, then we must surely all believe that it is a good

[1] Cf. Appendix.

thing to develop towards self-awareness, both personally and as a society. We also believe in the efficacy of scientific method. We believe that the workings of the universe can in principle be explained. This is the common basis of all religions in the West today.

Everyone perhaps would agree that his aim was self-awareness, and that he lived in a rational universe. And over a very wide field of action we all agree about the general principles for deciding what is right and wrong. But people differ radically in the final analysis of what they mean by "self-awareness" or the "rational universe". Here, I think, there are three main religions in the West at the moment, with many small variations. To present these religions, and to help people decide between them, is surely an eminently suitable task for tragedy.

Confronted with a world in which some people are rich, intelligent, or talented, and others are poor, stupid, or undistinguished, where some people suffer and others seem happy, and there is no clear relation between any of these things, we can adopt one of three aims. Abandoning the attempt to make sense of this situation, we shall choose to enjoy ourselves as much as possible, developing towards awareness and helping those who come into contact with us, in so far as it helps us to enjoy ourselves more deeply. We can call this trying to achieve happiness or freedom; the name will vary, but the end will be much the same. This is the aim of atheist Existentialism. Alternatively, we may choose to work for one of two more clearly defined goals, both expressed in terms of an ideal society. The first involves working for a special sort of society which will eventually be established for the benefit of our descendants, even though we shall see none of these benefits, being dead. This, also atheist, is the Marxist attitude. Alternatively, there is the Christian aim, to train ourselves so that we can be members of a society which goes on for ever in a different temporal dimension. If we were rational in this choice our aim would depend on which of the three accounts of the world we think most reasonable.

I have left out those people who would be surprised to think that religion involves an idea of an end for society. There are theists, both Christian and non-Christian, who have a Negative religion, whose idea of God is unaffected by discoveries in biology, or the way they feel they ought to vote. I leave them out not because I think theirs is an inferior way, but because their religion is a private, not a communal matter. They need little from society except freedom from distraction and cannot be expected to give so much to society because its aims seem irrelevant to theirs. Tragedy will be of no special use to them. The tragedian can confine his attention to the three main groups.

Our society contains rational men who adopt each of these three outlooks on life; if we are to be rational we must adopt one of these positions ourselves. The questions we have to ask can be phrased quite simply, though the asking is the hardest thing we can do and the answering may take a lifetime. We all believe in an ultimate order in the universe. To be an atheist is to say that this is an impersonal force. To be a theist is to say that as the activity of a particular group of electro-magnetic waves can be called my consciousness, so the activity of the entire complex of electro-magnetic waves which make up the universe is the activity of something analogous to consciousness on an infinite scale. The first question we must ask is whether there is something of this nature.

If we answer no, we have to choose between living for ourselves and working for some social end. The real question here is whether we shall choose to suffer when we could avoid it, and when we shall gain nothing ourselves by doing so. The answer will vary with the person concerned, and the degree of suffering. It is very much a matter for decision according to the particular situation.

If we answer yes to the first question we shall then ask whether we survive death. In the West the answer to this almost invariably depends on the person's attitude to the question whether Christ rose from the dead. There are three questions involved in choosing or rejecting Christianity; did Christ return to life? Shall I, personally, live in some other dimension when my body decays? Is this related to the Christian life on earth, the activity of the Mass, Communion, or Lord's Supper, however it is described? Normally, however, those who answer yes to the first of these three questions will do so to the other two.

Full self-awareness involves awareness of our ultimate aim. And that involves asking and attempting to answer these questions. They ramify; our ideas of God are affected by what we discover about astronomy, and also by what we understand of the experience of the mystics. The other questions involve discussing discoveries in physiology and psychology, the nature of history and historical evidence, people we know and societies we hear about. We do not know what will provide the influencing factors when we start. Trying to clarify our ideas on these matters touches our whole personality; it is a frightening activity. We are more likely to be helped in this by the personal decision we are shown by a tragic poet than the abstract arguments of a philosopher.

I have tried in this section to outline what seems a reasonable attitude for us to take to the traditional problems of tragedy. It is from this basis that I shall criticize the presentation of these problems by the writers I am discussing in Part III. I also hope that this section has shown that we cannot separate these problems. If the traditional divisions of philosophy are admitted to have been a mistake we shall be confirmed in our view that what is required is a mental attitude of imaginative synthesis, not of logical analysis. That is the mental attitude of a tragic poet, not a philosopher.

CHAPTER SEVEN

POETRY AND THE THEATRE

(i) RATIONAL POETRY

Philosophy has come to an end, and philosophers no longer claim that their craft can illuminate experience in the way that people need. Scientists, when they talk in ordinary words about the nature of the world, can only use analogy. Moralists, when they claim to intuit the Right, are confronted with different and conflicting claims. The wheel has come full circle, and we now see that primitive cultures which thought analogy was the best way of understanding the world were right. To master the method of analogy is the craft of poetry. If we do not create the conditions for the practice of such a craft, then we will not begin to understand the world. In the meanwhile it is worth seeing how a poet might react to this situation.

The difference between the idea of poetry in fifth-century Athens and now can be expressed in two words. They wrote about fact, not fiction. They told stories which had actually happened; they believed in the world view they presented; they were concerned with making their society a better place, and enlarging the moral–religious outlook of their audience. They were judged by their quality as moral leaders. The strength of their plays derives from this factual quality and social purpose. Until poets are judged by their quality as moral leaders, we shall not have tragedy in the full Greek sense. That is a matter for critics and ordinary people. But we equally need poets prepared to shoulder this social responsibility. That is what is important. The form of the poetry will be dictated by the way they go about their newly rediscovered purpose. I do not know whether this will lead to a poetic drama like that of the Greeks;

writers are rediscovering their social responsibility, and some
have turned to the theatre, attracted by the social nature of the
art; but it may be that the poets as teachers will function better
in another medium – novel, film, or a different sort of poetry;
or their efforts will be spread over different media. Here, however, encouraged by the fact that most of the writers I shall discuss in Part III have something of the purpose of the Greek
poets, I shall assume that the medium in which the poet as
teacher will function best is a theatre similar to the Greek
theatre, and discuss three aspects of the form of Greek tragedy
with reference to modern conditions. In this discussion I hope
also to show the advantages of this medium, as opposed to the
other possible ones.

(ii) ARTICULATE DRAMA

We develop towards awareness by learning to act for reasons
and not from causes, by coming to understand that we have
always done certain things, or accepted certain beliefs, as a result of our upbringing, and then questioning whether this is
reasonable or not, in order that we may decide to accept, reject,
or modify our behaviour. We grow in awareness by understanding our processes of decision. Drama is clearly a medium
for showing decision. But when we take decisions, especially
important ones, it is very difficult to put into words what we
are doing. It is difficult to see what is going on when someone
else is taking a decision. In order to illuminate the process of
decision the dramatist will need to make it more articulate than
it is in real life.

If the dramatist then is to enlarge his audience's understanding he will have to represent decision in an artificial way. This
has never been doubted except for a short period in the recent
past, the age of naturalism. Naturalism is being abandoned in
the theatre; it is useful to see why it should be.

The notion of tragedy as the representation of an action is
inherently and avowedly artificial.[1] "Action" is anyhow an
artificial concept,[2] one which has meaning only in terms of the
observer describing. What is part of a particular action, and

---

[1] Cf. pp. 164–5.
[2] Cf., e.g., G. E. M. Anscombe, *Intention*, pp. 7–15.

what is not, is a matter of convenience in the context of the conversation. If I hit someone in the stomach, a normal observer would consider the drawing back of my upper arm, and the pivoting of my shoulder, as all part of the one action. But a boxing instructor or a teacher of anatomy might want to say that there were several actions. Once we talk in larger terms still, in terms of historical events, for example, the concept of "action" becomes even more obviously artificial. What is essentially part of Hitler's action of invading Poland? It will depend on our point of view. A biographer of Hitler would list quite different things from a historian of Poland.

Naturalism in the theatre was connected with naturalism in philosophy. It was part of the idea that "showing things as they really are" was the truest mode of representation. If we now tried to show things "as they really are" we would not know how to begin. I suppose the nearest we could get would be to show everything and everyone as patterns of light. The naturalistic theatre is now seen to be a convention, suitable for some purposes, but no more true to life, and much less manoeuvrable. It was introduced because it was thought to be true.

If I tried to describe naturalistically how I had spent a day, with a factual report of what I had done and said, it would convey very little. My state of mind would be omitted; it would seem that every moment was equally important, but we all know that some moments have more in them than complete days; to describe what happened takes longer. Once we think in terms of our own experience, not in terms of "objectivity", we realize that this is plain fact, and testable. Naturalistic reporting is further from what really happened than a more poetic account.

The whole aim of "photographic realism" was misguided. Even a photograph makes its effect because a craftsman decides what to show, and in what light. It is easy to understand this once we understand the recent discoveries in the psychology of perception to some of which I alluded in the previous chapter.[1] The aim of naturalism was connected with an idea of science, and of perception, now clearly shown to be wrong.

[1] Cf. p. 173.

A writer may grant all this, and yet decide to use a naturalistic convention; to disguise the artificiality of his method by keeping as close as possible to the inarticulateness of ordinary life. It is best to judge the value of this in terms of actual plays.[1] But there is a general argument against this sort of drama in the twentieth-century theatre. The cinema is an infinitely more flexible medium for this kind of task. If we want to see inarticulate people taking decisions, and thereby acquire illumination, it must be by means of facial expression and so on. The camera can show minute detail, and the director can use the camera to point out exactly what he intends us to notice. Those who want to write naturalistically will be better advised to use the cinema.

We cannot yet distinguish to any great purpose the difference between the two media. One basic difference, however, will illuminate further what I mean by "articulate drama". That part of an actor's craft concerned with projection is necessary in the theatre, but in films it is more a matter of the camera coming to the actor than of the actor reaching out to the audience. Projection involves a certain distortion, makes conflicts and emotions "larger than life". It is very easy for stage actors to distort a conflict so that the audience gets a point. It is also easy for an actor so to charge words by his delivery that they are remembered; this is not unnatural in the artificial atmosphere of the theatre. Nor do we mind focusing our attention on one man making a long speech in the theatre, because our eyes are free to wander over the stage. The camera cannot wander round like our eyes; it draws our full attention wherever it goes. But it is intolerable if it remains focused on the speaker for very long. In the theatre it is easy to listen to words, and easy to build up tension by means of dialogue, neither of which is easy in the cinema. It therefore follows that a story involving issues which need words to express them will be better represented in the theatre.

Greek tragedy was a medium for illuminating contemporary issues. We may get an analogous tragedy, if everyone acknowledges the need for a similar medium. We shall clearly not get a tragic drama in the theatre because of a desire to see "deeds of

[1] Cf. pp. 248–51, 297–304.

daring do". This is already met by films. We sometimes hear it said that tragedy has to do with heroism, and that the present time is not a heroic age. This latter fact is patently untrue. It is our generation that has climbed the big Himalayan peaks; we hear constantly of new records of endurance, new explorations, new opportunities for bravery. We are shown innumerable deeds of heroism on the screen. This is a valuable thing; but it is quite different from tragedy. The object of the director is to make the audience imagine that they are actually present where the characters are. To make them think of issues would fight against making them imagine themselves present; the characters are not thinking of issues, but of the danger. The audience of Greek tragedy are there to understand what is happening, not to be involved in the danger themselves. The film audience is intended to feel the danger. Danger is not a time for words, and if a writer wishes to represent a scene of extreme danger he must beware of intruding on the scene like a B.B.C. commentator at an accident. In the theatre, where more words are needed to establish the scene, this is likely to occur; we find it, for example, in *Morts sans Sépulture*.[1] In the cinema all that is necessary can be conveyed, sometimes with no words at all. I instance at random Jacques Becker's *Le Trou*. Roland and Geo are tunnelling when the rubble falls in on Geo. Roland is seen, furiously working, hurling rubble around, until at last we see Geo's arm. The camera tracks in, and we see their hands clasp. Then it cuts. Nothing more is needed. If tragedy is merely to affect us with Pity and Fear, or to show us heroism, then we are better provided than ever the Greeks were; it would not matter if the theatres all closed down tomorrow.

The aim of naturalism is to make the audience feel that they are actually present at the scene depicted, that they *are* the character in danger. The cinema fulfils both these aims better than the theatre; someone who wants to write naturalistically will be better advised to work in the cinema. Naturalism, and especially that of the cinema, can make more of an emotional impact, but it does so at the expense of clarity. The dramatist who wishes to enlighten his audience as the Greek tragedians did must develop means of distancing his action, so that his

[1] Cf. pp. 299–300.

190

audience may remain spectators, able to judge as well as feel. Broadly speaking, there are two ways of doing this. He may present his story in a setting well removed from the normal experience of his audience, in a far country, an unusual society, or in another period; or he may use stylized speech, verse, song, and dance, possibly masks. These two methods I shall now examine.

(iii) MYTHS

If a story is set in a distant time or place the audience will not know too much detail, and will therefore be free to concentrate on the point of what the writer is trying to say. For this, distance in time and space are roughly equivalent, as Racine remarks in his preface to *Bajazet*. This is partly the reason why Aeschylus set the *Persae* away from Greece.

But we have seen that there was more reason than this for the Greek tragedians to use the stories they did; it is impossible to conceive Greek tragedy without its myths, stories of seminal events in ancient history which typified contemporary issues, presented, if necessary with distortion, in such a way as to illuminate the issue.

If a writer wanted to do for a modern audience what the Greek poets did for their audience he would take a story out of European history which showed some important action, clearly wrong, and analogous to an aspect of modern society which is wrong also. There is no reason why this should not be done, and provided that he makes it clear what he is doing, there is no reason why his audience should not understand the point.

There are many advantages in this mode of writing. First, there are events in history which we can now see in perspective, as we cannot see contemporary events. At least some things have happened which are clearly wrong. From our own point of view we can see more clearly what were the important issues. If we understand how things went wrong then we may be slightly more capable of understanding how things are going wrong now.

I used the word "seminal". One of the most obvious ways in

which a past event can be seen to typify a present situation is if its consequences are still with us. For a story to be myth for us as it was for the Greeks, it must be part of our history, though I am not sure how we should paraphrase "our"; sometimes it seems as if it is European history, sometimes English. I shall suggest that the French Revolution is not the same myth for Englishmen as it is for the French or Germans.[1] But this is something we cannot answer yet. Nor does this affect the discussion, except by making it hard to point out in the abstract the body of our myths.

Secondly, however we define "our", we can see that almost any period of our history is morally more articulate and morally more direct than the present time. By the first I mean that other periods were better equipped with objective standards of moral judgement; life was "more black and white". By the second I mean that the more complicated society becomes, the more people there are, like lawyers and policemen, professionally concerned with taking decisions that in a more primitive society the individual took for himself. A good example of objective reference can be found in a story of the late Middle Ages.[2] A man was condemned to execution, and in addition, though penitent, was refused absolution, so that he should be damned. The evil action of the man who refused him absolution could no doubt be paralleled in our own time, but it would be much harder to find an example. By "moral directness" I refer to the difference between a society where you kill the man who killed your father and one where you call the police.

The Greek poets interpreted history from a definite point of view which their audience shared. Without some shared point of view there can be no myth in the Greek sense; for one can only say that an action is wrong, with reference to some idea of what is right. It is usually said that now there is no common point of view. This is not the case. We are agreed on the virtues of scientific method, and on the fact of individual responsibility. The question is whether this belief can be applied precisely enough in individual cases, and whether it excites people as the religions of the past did. But it does provide a viewpoint

[1] Cf. pp. 232–3.
[2] Cf. J. Huizinga, *The Waning of the Middle Ages*, pp. 15–16.

from which we can say that certain events in the past were wrong. This challenge is an immensely important one, but it has not yet been understood. It is therefore too early to make a firm judgement. There are two very significant plays which show an event in history that we can see to be wrong from this common point of view, and to embody contemporary issues. They are *Galileo* by Brecht and *The Crucible* by Miller. I discuss neither of them in detail, because we are not yet in a position to put Brecht's work, or this aspect of Miller's, in perspective.[1] But that is not because I think they are unimportant. It may very well be that as writers turn to myth this is the line on which they will work. But it has not happened yet.

There is no point in the activity of looking at the past, unless one believes in history having meaning, in it being possible to interpret events as part of a pattern. Here again there is a common point of view; we all realize that history is evolutionary, that human history is part of a cosmic process of evolution. But it may be that myth in the Greek sense requires a more precise view of meaning in history, a more detailed religion. If this is so, then there may be tragedy based on the myths of a particular religion, on history seen from a more specific point of view. Clearly the writer will derive his impulse to write from his religion, and clearly a more specific religion should produce greater clarity of judgement over the issues involved than the necessarily vague belief in scientific method and individual responsibility. He will have to choose whether to write only for those who share his religion or to write for his opponents as well. Possibly this latter can be achieved. Anouilh does not quite understand what he is doing with the myth of St Joan, but in a sense *L'Alouette* is a play of Christian myth. The chorus figure of Warwick gives expression on stage to those who choose not to believe that Jeanne was called by God.[2] This question also cannot be answered yet.

A rational man in the West now holds one of three outlooks. I have called them atheist Existentialist, atheist Marxist, and Christian. Not all who hold a particular attitude would describe themselves by these names, and the distinctions should be elaborated to fit the true state of affairs. But they will do as a

[1] Cf. pp. 256–7.   [2] Cf. pp. 289–90.

rough classification. Superficially one would have thought that atheist existentialists can have nothing to say about the meaning of history, and it is surprising that Sartre should have written plays of myth. Marxists trace a meaning in history, but their account is in impersonal terms. Their outlook makes them inclined to talk as though abstract nouns were entities, and even to represent these abstractions, such as Class Warfare, as causing events. It is also hard at the moment to say what for a Marxist is "our" history, in the sense of the word I have used earlier. This again is a question we cannot answer yet.

The situation is different for a Christian dramatist. There is a Christian way of looking at history: evolutionary progress leading up to the events of Christ's life on earth, and continuing by means of the action of the Holy Spirit through those people called to be part of the eternal society; this progress is detectable in a small degree through the distortions of human greed and stupidity; it requires that people should turn the evil with which they are confronted into good. Clearly this is a much more specific view of history than any other, and one much more difficult to express except by myths. Part of Christianity cannot be understood without myths, so a Christian audience is likely to be much more responsive to a drama of myth.

There is a body of historical material which would serve a Christian writer in almost exactly the same way as the Greek myths served the Greek tragedians. We have very much the same attitude to the history of the Middle Ages as the fifth-century Athenians had to the period of their myths. We look back from a sophisticated, rational, urban, and democratic culture to a primitive, irrational, rural culture governed by kings. We look back from a time when everyone goes to law, on a time of moral articulateness and directness, when gods walked the earth. We interpret life analytically, and look back on a time when it was interpreted through ritual. The situation at Athens in the fifth century was very similar in all these points. There is a further resemblance. The history of the Middle Ages is European history, not English. The stories of Greek myth were not specially Athenian. Euripides, writing the *Heracles*, takes as his type of the great man, the principal

Dorian hero, when the Athenians were at war with the Dorian states. Letters has made this comparison already:[1]

> The Hellenes were conscious of a strong bond distinguishing them from the outer world and giving them a unity roughly analogous to the deeper spiritual communion of disunited mediaeval Christendom.

I doubt if it will be possible in the same way to use history after the Church broke up, since I doubt if it will be possible to see what was the Christian interpretation of a period in history when there was no one Christian Church to interpret it. I am also assuming that most Christians will soon admit what anyone interested outside the Church has long realized, that no one faction of Christianity has all the truth. But the enormously increased efforts towards reunion show that this is likely, and should indeed stir people to try and rethink their ideas of history, and so create a desire for presentation of Christian myths. Here again we can only speculate, because there have not been enough attempts at Christian drama of myth for us to reach any firm conclusions.

Myth as I have used the term, and as it was regarded by the Greek poets, is a story of ancient history typifying the way history works. We can argue about its presentation. Did the writer really put over the point? Was it the right point? We can discuss his view of the issues; we can even discuss his entire world view. There is another sense of the word now current. Stories are called "myths", which are fictitious. Argument about them is impossible, since they did not happen. This sense of "myth" is as old as Plato, whose dialogues often contain a story which expresses a point he could not express in rational discussion. The only argument about such stories is aesthetic. We can ask, Do they touch us? Are they beautiful? But there is no way of showing someone why they should affect him, if he says he is unaffected. They are metaphors, the others are analogies. Some religions think metaphor and analogy are the same; when the distinction is blurred, and the factual nature of analogy is not understood, writers will indulge their fancy. This is what happened in the fourth century, and at some time

[1] F. J. H. Letters, *The Life and Work of Sophocles*, p. 3.

variously specified in the last three centuries. It is connected with the belief that there can be a separate aesthetics. This idea of "myth" is hostile to tragedy as the Greeks understood it, though it is the idea of several writers who have tried to revive Greek tragedy, notably Cocteau.

(iv) VERSE

Recently there have been one or two experiments in the use of masks. The importance of song, dance, and mime is being recognized. But in England these developments have taken place after the plays I shall discuss. I shall therefore confine myself to verse. We live in an age which does not enjoy "style", which is impatient of flowery language. Now is not a time for so-called poetic prose or ornate verse. So many people think only of Shakespeare, and equate verse with flowery language. I have argued elsewhere that Shakespearean drama was the product of special circumstances.[1] I shall suggest here that his work is not necessarily a sound model for a writer today.

I define verse as language arranged in units other than those of the sense. If the reader is not to make some infinitesimal pause at the end of the line, then the piece might as well be prose. There is, however, writing on the borderland between the two. If a piece of verse is written with uneven lines, and the break in the sense comes constantly at the end of the line, then what was conceived as verse may come to sound like rhythmically tautened prose. Conversely, if prose sentences tend to repeat themselves rhythmically, then they may be heard as verse. There is also a kind of writing which is organized in sentences, but ones which are conceived in a very isolated way, without connexions of sense that prose demands. The effect will be to encourage an incantatory delivery, similar to that of verse. In Eliot's later plays the effect, though not the prosody, is a line of uneven length, and most lines end with a break in sense. In Lucky's speech from *Waiting for Godot*[2] the effect of the short rhythmically repetitive sentences is very much that of verse. Disjointed sentences with incantatory effect can be found in the English psalter, or the dialogue of Claudel. These are

[1] Cf. pp. 159–60.
[2] Samuel Beckett, *Waiting for Godot*, I, pp. 42–44.

exceptions. Generally we can distinguish two different modes of organization.

We can also distinguish by the way the two media should be spoken. Verse requires attention to the rhythm, but also that it should not obtrude. The speaker will best effect this by using much more variety of pitch in his voice than he would when speaking prose. He can thus make clear that he is speaking verse, without using the nauseous "poetry speaking voice". Good verse speaking will be the discovery of a tune hidden in the words which will most clearly express the meaning. My own experience in productions suggests that this "tune" varies with the voice speaking; it is not the same for any voice, but each person can discover it, and learn it. It needs to be learnt, because we lost the art of speaking verse when it became customary to read it off the page. But it is an art that can be recovered, and we are now returning to the primarily oral idea of poetry as a result of the gramophone.

To describe the effect of verse as opposed to that of prose brings us to the edge of language. It is something that is partly speech and partly song. It is more universal than ordinary speech. It is the same sort of effect as that which I mentioned with reference to the *Clouds* of Aristophanes. Disgusting erotic dialogue, when music was added, became merely grotesque buffoonery. The use of verse makes the events described be felt as part of a wider whole. This is best understood by examining examples where rhythm and sense, by appearing to contradict, unite to form something whose meaning is beyond prose paraphrase. Donne ends "Go and catch a falling star":

> Yet she
> Will be
> False, ere I come, to two or three.

The words are savage; the rhythm is a light-hearted dance. Which is the meaning? Both together, in a unity only separable in thought. Nor is it the case that the words are any the less bitter for being set to a dance. It is that the bitterness is included in something bigger.

We need verse in the theatre as elsewhere to express this sense of all people and things moving in a rhythm which includes them, and which is in itself good. The arts which express this sense are verse, music, and dance, verse being the most articulate, less ecstatic than singing, less abandoned than dancing. Those who disapprove of verse in the theatre are presumably those who never feel this sense of rhythm, as tone-deaf people cannot understand why one should sing. The dispute has something to do with religious outlook. Passions are roused by arguments for and against verse drama, which suggests that more is at stake than a method of speaking. A sense of people and things included in a rhythm goes naturally with a belief in an order behind the world; in primitive societies poet, priest, and magician are connected; there are obvious connexions between poetry and ritual; in England recently the movement for verse drama has been largely the work of those who were at the same time trying to introduce a Christian drama. But part of the objection to verse has been simply that several bad verse dramas have been written by literary men with no knowledge of the theatre. What was not noticed was that they were not only bad theatre but bad verse also.

The need for verse is a need for rhythm, connected with the need for song. I have argued in the previous chapter that we need poetry in the sense of thinking synthetically by means of analogy, not analytically by means of logic. The poet's task is to satisfy our need for rhythm while at the same time presenting thought-provoking images. Words in themselves are unimportant. What is important in Homer or Aeschylus, Chaucer or the ballads, is sound and content. This is what is fundamental to poetry. To return to this primitive attitude was the aim of the Imagist movement at the time of the First World War, of whom the most important writer is Pound, though Eliot was associated with him. We have not yet fully assimilated Pound's reforms because we have only just realized their justification. He revolted against a poetry which demanded a set response to particular words. It was based on Idealism. If you believe that Beauty and Reality have existence in a world of Ideas, then you can write "Beauty", and expect your reader to perform an act of intellectual intuition, and experience Beauty. The writer has no need to refer to any particular experience. Pound attacked this sort of poetry for depending on stock responses, as being a worn-out convention. Now, since the collapse of Idealism, and especially since the later work of Wittgenstein, we can see that it was a totally misguided way of looking at experience. The best justification for Imagism is the *Philosophical Investigations*. New ways of thought reveal yet again the rightness of primitive poetry.

We need poetry which is concrete, a process of thinking in image and analogy, conveying through its rhythmic organization more than could be conveyed by prose, not poetry which relies on high-sounding abstract nouns, beloved of Idealists, which a modern audience realizes to be only abstractions, referring to nothing. In addition, if we are rediscovering what is essential to poetry it is unlikely that poets will be wise to use much decoration or rhetoric.

I shall offer a few examples to show what I mean by this new, or old, poetry. This poem by Pound has also an example of what I mean by "rhetoric". He is writing of the corrupt Western civilization and the idiocy of the First World War:[1]

> There died a myriad,
> And of the best, among them,
> For an old bitch gone in the teeth,
> For a botched civilisation,
>
> Charm, smiling at the good mouth,
> Quick eyes gone under earth's lid,
>
> For two gross of broken statues,
> For a few thousand battered books.

The last two lines express in concrete terms, as no other image could do, the whole idea of Western degradation, down to the auction implications of "two gross". The "old bitch" expresses, magnificently, Pound's personal anger. Another image would have done. Someone who does not approve of Pound, or that style of writing, can get up and say, "There he goes again," and take no notice. But with the last lines we have to ask, "Well, if not for that, what did they fight for?" The effect of the poetry has nothing to do with the poet.

The great moments in the ballads are of this nature; we

[1] "Hugh Selwyn Mauberley", v.

listen, and we see a scene, and we shall be able to think about that scene for the rest of our lives.[1]

> Mony a one for him maks mane,
> But nane sall ken whar he is gane;
> O'er his white banes, when they are bare,
> The wind sall blaw for evermair.

There is no need for an age which delights in fine language in order that poetry of this nature may be written; indeed, a delight in fine language may distract the poet from writing with this purity.

Shakespeare was able to indulge his delight for fine language, because his characters naturally spoke like that. Elizabethan England must have spoken much more like the Irish. Shakespeare's writing is often decorative:[2]

> There's nothing in this world can make me joy:
> Life is as tedious as a twice told tale,
> Vexing the dull ear of a drowsy man;
> And bitter shame has spoil'd the world's sweet taste,
> That it yields nought but shame and bitterness.

There are other things as tedious. Shakespeare's simile is magnificent, but not absolutely essential. He is, of course, full of essential poetry as well. Nothing could convey the point of *Antony and Cleopatra* so well as the moment when she, whom we have seen as a faded tart, gets up and says:[3]

> Give me my robe, put on my crown; I have
> Immortal longings in me:

And lest I seem to oversimplify Shakespeare, I instance one example of many in which he uses the convention of flamboyant language to enrich his characterization. Lorenzo and Jessica sit embracing, and Lorenzo says:[4]

> ... Such harmony is in immortal souls;
> But while this muddy vesture of decay
> Doth grossly close it in, we cannot hear it.

[1] "The Twa Corbies", *Oxford Book of Ballads*, no. 67, v, p. 293.
[2] *King John*, III, iv. (Lewis speaks).
[3] V, ii.　　　　　　　[4] *The Merchant of Venice*, V, i.

As he says this he is touching his beloved; it is a chance for an actor to show humour, and therefore an added dimension of tenderness. The "muddy vesture" is a decorative phrase, here used with clear structural function, and so no longer merely decorative.

This richness may not be possible for a modern writer. But all uses of poetry in Greek drama are possible; whether Aeschylus' image, his embodiment of the point of the play, first in verbal, then in physical form; or the Sophoclean sense of pattern and the use of imagery to suggest character; or the sheer sensuous accuracy and awareness of detail that we notice in Euripides. The intellectual needs of our time, the significant developments in modern non-theatrical poetry, and the methods of the Greek tragedians all combine to suggest a particular sort of verse as suitable for the modern theatre.

Verse is needed in drama; certain things cannot be conveyed without it. It is also a far faster medium for telling a story. I shall return to this later. If verse is defined as being half-way between speech and song, and the advantage of verse is speed, then it would seem likely that the best verse form will be a strict one. Eliot decided that verse should be unobtrusive, and most critics have followed his dicta. But the theatre for which he wrote *The Cocktail Party* is dead. There is no need for a dramatist now to pay attention to the worthless conventions of upper-class drawing-room comedy. *The Cocktail Party* has moved me as few other plays have done. Its second act has an austere beauty unlike anything in English, though perhaps there are resemblances in French Classical Tragedy. But the conditions which made Eliot develop this form are no longer with us.

The modern theatre is turning against naturalism; fluid staging and many scenes are now more usual. With this kind of form there is no reason why the writer should not change from verse to prose in one play, or even in one scene. Eliot and Fry both thought that if a play was in verse, then it should be verse throughout, because they wrote for a theatre where the audience kept the same point of view all the time. A more fluid staging necessarily involves a continual changing of viewpoint. There is also no reason why there should not be several sorts of verse, giving different effects of distance. On the whole, the stricter the verse and the nearer to song, the greater the distance. This would be similar to the different effects of the dialogue and the lyrics of Greek tragedy. Once this variety of verse form and the mixture of verse dialogue with ordinary speech is allowed, then the main reason for unobtrusive verse is gone.

Free verse is the most complicated verse form, rhythmically the most subtle. I doubt if it is very suitable for the stage, since an actor needs to make so many different kinds of pause anyhow, that the end stop is almost bound to get lost. It will only be suitable for a narrator, or for a static speech, where the actor is addressing the audience direct, and can concentrate simply on projecting the poetry. A good example of this is the speech of the third priest in *Murder in the Cathedral*, which begins:[1]

> For good or ill, let the wheel turn.

The function of the priests is more poetic than dramatic; their ritual impersonality discourages too full a characterization, and this speech is delivered at a moment when we pause and take stock of what has happened in the drama. We think also of some of Brecht's verse, that of the narrator in *The Caucasian Chalk Circle*, for example. But this is not a typical situation in the theatre. Most of the time actors talk to each other, and free verse is probably not suitable for that.

A strict verse form tells a story faster. To convey in prose what happens in the course of one ballad stanza, with all the right emphasis, would probably take three times as many words. Imagine this in a prose version:[2]

> O laith, laith were our gude Scots lords
> To wet their cork-heel'd shoon;
> But lang or a' the play was play'd
> They wat their hats aboon.

Spender's translation of *Dantons Tod* is well written, in taut dramatic prose. There are no unnecessary words. It may be worth comparing one speech in it with a transcription I made into blank verse. For reasons of space I do not reproduce the

[1] *Murder in the Cathedral*, Part I, p. 18.
[2] "Sir Patrick Spens", *Oxford Book of Ballads*, 75, xviii, p. 331.

Spender version. It contains 609 words. Marion speaks to
Danton:[1]

> Leave me alone now.
>   I was well brought up.
> My mother was a lady. She'd purse her lips
> Repeating, Modesty's a virtue dear.
> If she had guests and the conversation turned
> To "certain matters", I'd be sent upstairs,
> And if I asked the meaning I'd be told
> I ought to be ashamed of myself. And every
> Book I was given had forbidden pages.
> Except the Bible. All of that was holy.
> But all of it I couldn't understand.
> My only adviser my own mystery.
> Spring came, an infinite blooming, but for me
> No blooming. In this stifling atmosphere
> A second person grew within my body,
> Then melted into me again. Round then
> A gay young man came calling, he'd say such
> Silly things to me, I'd be always laughing
> Although I didn't often understand.
> Mother said, Do come often. We both liked him.
> What's the difference, we thought, in lying together
> Between two sheets, from sitting on two chairs.
> Why not the greater pleasure with the lesser?
> Constantly, but in secret. I was sea
> For ever swallowing. Deep. Deep. All men
> Who've ever lived and died sank in his body.
> That's to be woman. In the end he noticed.
> His arms crushed round my neck one morning. Stifled
> By such kisses I did feel terror.
> Laughing he let me go. I nearly did
> A silly thing, he said. Keep your dress,
> Use it, it soon wears out. It's all you have.
> Fun lies in dreams. And then he went away.
> That evening, still unknowing, at my window
> I sat, feeling my grasp on all around me

[1] Stephen Spender and Goronwy Rees, *Danton's Death*, I, v, pp. 43–45.

Sinking into the sunset; waves of crowd
And children rippling down the street, the women
Watching at windows. Down there, in a basket,
Him, damp hair, pale forehead in the moonlight.
He'd drowned himself, and I broke in weeping.
Days do not change for me, no six days work
Then Sunday prayers, no sentimental birthdays,
And no New Year.
I am one thing unbroken. Longing and desire,
A flame, a stream. My mother died of grief.
Fools' fingers point at me. But wise men know
You can worship saints, wine, sex, flowers or toys,
But to worship deeply means to have deep joys.

This contains 378 words, and is therefore about two-thirds of the length of the prose version.

Blank verse at its best has been an ornate form. In their different ways both Shakespeare and Milton are highly elaborate. The line lends itself to decorative repetition:

This royal throne of kings, this sceptred isle.

The subtlety of its rhythm, and its closeness to ordinary speech necessitates some ornamentation to distinguish it from ordinary speech. It is interesting to read Gilbert Murray on translating Euripides. He argues that Greek tragedy needs a simply direct diction, combined with a formal style. "In blank verse the language has to be tortured a little, or it will read like prose".[1] This led him to use couplets. We can ignore his practice; he wrote very ornately himself, adding many adjectives not in the Greek. But his theory is sound. There are moments in the Greek tragedy where the effect of the verse cannot be conveyed without using rhyme. The repetitive formality and simple language of the opening of the *Coloneus*, for example, demands rhyme:

Oedipus:
Child of an old blind man, Antigone,
To what place have we come, to what city?
Who now will take in wandering Oedipus,
Or who has any gift to give to us?

[1] *Euripides and His Age*, p. 132.

Asking a little, getting even less,
I shall be happy if it will suffice.
The suffering, the time who's lived with me,
Have been my teachers . . . and nobility.

On the other hand, it would be clearly impossible to translate an entire tragedy into such a static metre as couplets; and heroic couplets have more aristocratic associations than blank verse; they would be unsuitable in a modern play.

A comparatively plain blank verse has been used to some effect in plays mostly or entirely in verse. But there is a general feeling that this is not very satisfactory; it is usually expressed as an admission that Shakespeare exhausted the possibilities of dramatic blank verse, and Milton turned it into a non-dramatic medium. It is not usually sound practice to introduce blank verse into the middle of a prose play, since this has been done so often, unintentionally, by a writer waxing rhetorical. I suppose Tennessee Williams ends *The Glass Menagerie* with a page of blank verse unintentionally, and not by design. Otherwise he would have written it as verse. We should notice this passage; it brings out most of the things in favour of blank verse and against it, as a medium in the modern theatre. It is very near ordinary speech. I have heard it said by critics that modern English people no longer speak in a rhythm like blank verse; but I have also heard many people of all classes produce lines of blank verse in ordinary speech today. A writer can slip into it without noticing, and his audience will hear no difference. But if they hear no difference at all, then the advantages of verse are lost. Finally, this example shows the habitual association of blank verse and the purple passage. The arguments for verse have nothing to do with the desire for purple passages, and so this association is a dangerous one. Let each for himself judge the passage; I reproduce the latter half of the speech, in lines, but otherwise exactly as written. The first half could also be written as verse, though it is freer.[1]

> Tom:
> I would have stopped, but I was pursued by something.
> It always came upon me unawares,

[1] Tennessee Williams, *The Glass Menagerie*, sc. vii, pp. 62–63.

Taking me altogether by surprise.
Perhaps it was a familiar bit of music.
Perhaps it was only a piece of transparent glass –
Perhaps I'm walking along a street at night,
In some strange city, before I have found companions.
I pass the lighted window of a shop
Where perfume is sold.
The window is filled with pieces of coloured glass,
Tiny transparent bottles in delicate colours,
Like bits of a shattered rainbow.
When all at once my sister touches my shoulder.
I turn around and look into her eyes . . .
Oh, Laura, Laura, I tried to leave you behind me,
But I am more faithful than I intended to be!
I reach for a cigarette, I cross the street,
I run into the movies or a bar,
I buy a drink, I speak to the nearest stranger –
Anything that can blow your candles out!
– For nowadays the world is lit by lightning!
Blow out your candles, Laura – and so good-bye . . .

The effect of the iambic pentameter is to summon up all the associations of five centuries of perhaps the richest literature in the world; to do this unconsciously is always disastrous. But because the line is so rich in associations, and the user must be so much aware of the tradition, it is bound to be somewhat self-conscious. Perhaps it can only be effective now at moments, when it is right to be self-conscious, and aware of the tradition. Many prose plays end with a blank verse line, which produces an impressive cadence:

> I've lost
> The only playboy of the Western World.

This is surely the way to speak the last line of Synge's play. The film version, not the stage one, of *The Prisoner* by Bridget Boland ends:

> Try not to judge the priesthood by the priest.

But it is right to end these plays with a conscious summing up.

If blank verse can only be used in this sort of situation, its use will be very limited.

The quickest way of showing a modern English audience that you are speaking verse is by rhyme. The conditions of our society make our sense of rhythm, and our aural awareness very crude. A better verse form for drama may be one which uses rhyme more frequently than would be possible with iambic pentameters, and one which is rhythmically less subtle than blank verse with its mixed prosody, partly stress and partly syllables. I wish to draw attention to the advantages of the line scanned purely by stress, usually with four stresses and a caesura, as in most ballads, and similar to the Old English alliterative line, which ceased to be used after Langland. The advantages of the iambic pentameter are flexibility of rhythm, the subtle stress variations possible. The advantages of the ballad line lie in the variety of the number of syllables. In "The Outlandish Knight", for example,[1] we find eight syllables:

> Pull off, pull off your silken gown,

and twelve:

> For six pretty maidens thou has drowned here before,

and this range is often found.

Secondly, this line is even nearer to song than the iambic pentameter. At moments of great lyric intensity it would be more suitable than a line of ten syllables. Apart from Chinese, English is the most monosyllabic language there is. We think of the inevitable translation of one of the supreme lines in the *Commedia*:[2]

> e la sua volontate è nostra pace:

This can only be: "His will is our peace" – three stresses, five and a half syllables.

Thirdly, the line can approximate very closely to the iambic pentameter. There might be an occasion when the writer wished to summon up the associations of all our literary history since Chaucer, and use blank verse. He could slip into it very easily.

[1] *Penguin Book of English Folk Song*, pp. 80–81.   [2] *Paradiso*, iii, 85.

This verse has been used once to superb effect in theatrical dialogue, by Eliot in *Murder in the Cathedral*. Eliot says that the verse had "no positive novelty",[1] and that his aim was to avoid Shakespeare and even more the nineteenth-century imitators, and to achieve a "neutral idiom". In the theatre it is a novelty, and, as so often happens when an artist talks of his work, Eliot has not realized that this dialogue verse is one of his greatest formal achievements. It has great range and flexibility; far from being something of a stop-gap, suitable for this play only, its potentialities have hardly begun to be realized. And surely, once already it has flowered, in the most memorable moment since the death of Webster, where poetry and drama join, in a "condition of complete simplicity Costing not less than everything" over Becket on his knees after his temptations as he says:[2]

> Now is my way clear, now is the meaning plain:
> Temptation shall not come in this kind again.
> The last temptation is the greatest treason:
> To do the right deed for the wrong reason.

I am suggesting, then, that while a writer may arise to demonstrate that, in spite of the literary associations that blank verse has acquired since the time of Milton, it may still be used to provide memorable dramatic dialogue, a more profitable discipline may be for English writers to return to the English poetic tradition that stretches from *Beowulf* to *Piers Plowman*, the tradition of the ballads, down to their debased modern successors. That dramatic verse should arise from popular verse is no new thing. The metre of tragic dialogue that was to ring with the god-like anger of Prometheus' call to winds and infinitely laughing sea[3] was doggerel, the metre used for the archaic Greek equivalent of election songs.[4] Eliot ends his thoughts on verse in the theatre by providing an image of what he would like to think poetic drama could be.[5] May I do the same, and think of a possible moment in a modern play, when

[1] T. S. Eliot, *Poetry and Drama*, p. 24.
[2] *Murder in the Cathedral*, Part I, p. 44.   [3] *P.V.*, 88 ff.
[4] Cf. Arist., *Poetics*, 1448b, 30–2 and 1449a, 19–24.
[5] T. S. Eliot, *Poetry and Drama*, pp. 34–35.

some ordinary person will be allowed to say, under pressure of all the complex issues of our time, among the inflated emptiness of politicians and the propaganda of tycoons, something that will sing with the simplicity of Hecuba, feeling the stains of her dead son's sweat, and present our England with an image of itself, simpler, but no less passionate than the words of dying Gaunt. I have argued that we will have no tragedy unless writers and audiences are prepared for intense, clear-headed thinking, free from all illusions. But we will still not have tragedy unless writers and audience also remember the words of Tagore:[1]

> that training is most intricate which leads to the utter simplicity of a tune.

[1] Rabindranath Tagore, *Gitanjali*, 12.

PART III

MODERN TRAGIC WRITING

CHAPTER EIGHT

INTRODUCTORY

Can there be modern tragedy? I have tried to show that it is possible that there can be, that our outlook has changed or is changing from one hostile to tragedy to one that is more favourable. Clearly there is no large body of tragic writing in any way comparable to that of the Greeks, but there is good reason to treat the plays I shall discuss as models for future developments.

We think and feel very differently from our grandparents. First, we are insecure, aware of death as a community. The great periods of drama in Europe were insecure also. Periclean Athens had fourteen years of peace only, from the Peace of Kallias in 446 to the outbreak of the Peloponnesian War in 432. The great flowering of Medieval drama came during the Hundred Years War and the Black Death. Elizabethan England only just escaped invasion by Spain, and was often in danger of the civil war that came later. These three periods were also ages of social change. People were uncertainly questioning how society ought to develop, not accepting that it should stay as it was.

Secondly, we are in a position to see the way in which scientific method has been increasingly misunderstood over the last three centuries, until quantum physics blatantly upset this misconception. We can see that certainty and objectivity are impossible; there is only me and my experience. The only way in which we can universalize experience is through analogy. We are in a position to realize that poetry is not only more desirable than philosophy; it is more rational.

Thirdly, we have begun to understand how much our

culture has lost by becoming sophisticated. A new sympathy for primitive culture is spreading, and the most important cultural phenomenon of this century is clearly primitivist, the spread of jazz. All important artists have been very much aware of their dependence on the primitive exponents of their art. We think of composers returning to their countries' folk song, or to plainchant, or to the ages of counterpoint, Stravinsky, Bartók, Vaughan Williams, and Britten. We think of Henry Moore. We think of Pound and Provence, Lorca or Brecht and their countries' ballad tradition. Now, we are also in a position to see why primitive art is so often better than sophisticated art. The primitive artist was under fewer misapprehensions about life.

Because of this situation we are in a better position to understand Greek tragedy. Our generation should be able to see how reasonably is tragedy as it is. We can better appreciate the conditions which created the need for it, and its essential, connected features: that it was a presentation of a historical story with moral–religious point; that the poet was a teacher, gifted with insight into the past, into the way society works, and judged for his qualities as moral leader; that the poet's purpose was to impose a vision of human beings and society that should balance rational and passionate elements; that the setting was a festival attended by the citizen body, not people interested in the theatre; that this audience attended to a performance of verse, song, dance, and spectacle, for three plays with an attitude of worship, and a fourth with an attitude of buffoonery. The Greek poets wrote fact, not fiction, within a religious system of double determination; they thought as hard as any philosopher, but they had a synthesizing, analogical outlook, not a specializing, analytic one; for them drama was to do with society, not aesthetics.

We shall have no tragedy like the Greeks unless writers work with as strong a sense of purpose as theirs. Most of the writers I shall discuss do have a social purpose which has guided their writing. But there are still critics who deliver aesthetic judgements, although for thirty years it has been found impossible to define aesthetic terms. I came across a discussion of Sartre, which illustrates this attitude perfectly.[1] The writer had been

[1] Robert Kanters, *L'Express*, 22 June 1961.

saying that Sartre's philosophy was peculiarly appropriate to being expressed in dramatic terms:

> Se demander s'il a réussi, c'est se demander d'une part si son théâtre est l'expression fidèle de sa philosophie, d'autre part si ce théâtre existe avec force en lui-même, en tant que théâtre. La réponse à la première question est un travail de philosophe, qui confrontera les pièces avec les romans, les essais, les écrits théoriques: à première vue, je crois que sur ce plan, la réussite de M. Sartre est certaine et c'est peut-être même dans son théâtre que son intuition philosophique va le plus loin. Mais cela ne préjuge pas la réponse à la seconde question: si les drames philosophiques de Renan, par exemple, expriment sa pensée, cela ne leur confère pas *ipso facto* une valeur scénique. Le critique théâtral, qui ne peut pas s'empêcher d'être impressioniste dans une large mesure, est obligé de nuancer.

There is no indication that it ever occurred to Kanters to pass judgement on the philosophy itself, the view of life from which Sartre wrote in the first place. And I have only bothered to quote this piece, because this attitude is a common one, not only among journalists. If we pass over the specialist ignorance of a critic who thinks he is capable of delivering judgement on work that embodies a particular philosophy without bothering to try and evaluate the philosophy, and pass over the gross insult to any writer's effort of ignoring what he made the effort for, we cannot pass over the fact that the Greek audience did not care whether a writer expressed his philosophy well; they cared whether it was beneficial to the community. And we cannot pass over the strength and excitement of Greek drama.

The idea of a separate aesthetics is part of the basically irrationalist revolt of the Romantic movement; it goes with an idea of the artist as responsible only to himself and the claims of his Art. Cocteau said [1] that the true poets were angels, "Disinterested, selfish, tender, pitying, cruel, shrinking from contacts, pure in the midst of debauchery, taking a violent delight in, and at the same time despising, earthly pleasures, naïvely

[1] Jean Cocteau, *A Call to Order*, translated by Rollo H. H. Myers, p. 143.

amoral . . ." The true poets have had their naïvely amoral way, and have been responsible to no one. Society has had its revenge, and now they are read by no one. We are in a position to see the disastrous consequences of the irrationalist Romantic revolt, and are beginning to realize that aesthetic terms have no meaning in isolation. Gradually, fewer and fewer people will pay attention to critics who judge in aesthetic terms, as they have paid less and less attention to artists who claim only to be responsible to their Art.

There are three further obstacles to tragedy in our intellectual climate. There is still a mistaken idea of what scientific method is, there is still much Idealist thinking among literary critics, and there are large-scale misunderstandings of Greek drama. I have tried to see how scientific method as we understand it now can be applied to thought in general, and so to art. What I mean by the mistaken idea of science is the belief that we are still living in the Newtonian age. We get this expressed for example in Steiner's book.[1]

> The myths which have prevailed since Descartes and Newton are myths of reason, no truer perhaps than those which preceded them, but less responsive to the claims of art. Yet when it is torn loose from the moorings of myth, art tends towards anarchy.

But we must relate our thought and our myths, not to Newtonian, but to quantum physics. Steiner is out of date when he thinks that since tragedies became harder and harder to write during the Newtonian period, they therefore cannot be written now. The same feeling pervades Fergusson's book. He has a section entitled "The Diminished Scene of Modern Rationalism".[2] "Modern" rationalism is no longer modern; it is not diminished; it has come to an end.

Secondly, it is clear that many of the writers I am going to discuss are Idealists. Philosophy is bound to have an effect on one's writing, and the effect of Idealism can be seen in the work of Eliot and Giraudoux. If Idealism is a misguided philosophy, then it will have a bad effect on art that relies on an intellectual

---

[1] *The Death of Tragedy*, p. 321.

[2] Francis Fergusson, *The Idea of a Theater*, pp. 64–67.

content. The principal effect of Idealism is to inculcate an idea of static reality, independent of time, and one which does not develop. If there are Essences, then there are Essences of people. There are moments when the Essence of a Giraudoux character is revealed, and this seems unnatural. People develop gradually; in Giraudoux they either are or are not. Secondly, if one believes that one can intuit the Right directly, there is much less need to study history and other people's decisions in order to clarify one's own. If one can intuit the Right, one can decide rightly however ignorant one is. Thirdly, there is the mistaken idea of artistic creation expressed so well in Eliot's "The Hollow Men":[1]

> Between the idea
> And the reality
> Between the motion
> And the act
> Falls the Shadow

It is the belief that the artist becomes aware of something independent of ordinary life, which he then puts down imperfectly, due to struggling with his medium. Eliot has himself contradicted this and admitted that often the course of a poem will be changed by the discovery of a particular rhyme. But he has not seen that this opposes the Idealist conception. The artist uses his medium to help him clarify his original vague impulse. The process is dynamic and two-way, like the scientist giving meaning to his original vague hypothesis.

Thirdly, there are some important, and widely held, misconceptions about Greek tragedy. This is less significant in England than in France, because it is only in France that there is a significant body of writing based on a conception of what Greek tragedy was. Because Classical themes were used as the basis of drama throughout French history from the seventeenth century onwards, there is still an air of neo-classicism about some of the writing of this nature. The background to this can be well understood by means of Nostrand's book.[2] He says that the purpose of his inquiry is to discover what is *l'esprit de*

[1] "The Hollow Men", v.
[2] H. L. Nostrand, *Le Théâtre Antique et à l'antique en France de 1840 à 1900.*

l'antiquité in the works in question.[1] He finds it necessary, however, to say that we must realize that the spirits of Greek and of
Roman thought are different. We must not consider them both
as *l'antiquité*.[2] The implication is that some people might. If
they are treated as the same, then almost none of the spirit of
either will survive. The most important aspect of this is in the
two religions. At a particular point in history, during the Punic
wars, the Romans more or less consciously introduced a state
religion, based on gods who were given anthropomorphic
qualities by using the fact that most of their functions were
similar to those of Greek gods, and therefore that the myths
about the Greek gods could be borrowed. At this time the
Greeks had ceased to treat the worship of the Olympians as
outlets for their religious energy. Dionysus was once a god.
Bacchus was hardly more than a convention, ever. The Romans
had an animistic, not an anthropomorphic, religion, and borrowed myths when their culture was too sophisticated to use
them in worship. To confuse Greek and Roman religion is
totally to misunderstand Greek religion. To misunderstand
Greek religion is to misunderstand Greek tragedy. Nostrand
divides up the period he is studying into four sub-periods. But
his careful classification of the different approaches in the nineteenth century supports the opposite conclusion to that which
he had intended, that there was really a fundamental similarity
in all this work. We can refer to his conclusion. All the writers
tried:[3]

> chercher dans l'antiquité la patrie idéale des plus hautes
> aspirations de l'âme;

But this was done because they despaired of the future of the
human race and sought beautiful remote themes. There was no
awareness of the way in which the Greek poets were thought
of as spokesmen on pressing contemporary problems; there
was no awareness of the political implications of the Greek
tragedies. In other words, all this writing was trivial, and the
effects of this misunderstanding continued into the twentieth
century. The gods in *La Guerre de Troie* remind us of Rubens,

---

[1] *Le Théâtre Antique*, p. 1.   [2] Ib., p. 5.   [3] Ib., p. 187.

neo-classical fountains, and Offenbach; this will inevitably make the impact of the play very different from that of the *Troades*.

In addition to this, there are two, linked misconceptions of the nature of Greek tragedy, which have permeated French thought since the time of Corneille. No modern writer has fully understood the function of the chorus, and only Ghéon has come anywhere near understanding it. And because the function of the chorus has been underrated there has arisen the belief that Greek tragedy shows heroes at the mercy of Destiny, puppets moved by an impersonal force. The Greek poets were concerned to show how an event had happened which everyone in the audience knew had happened. They were not concerned with whether it could have been otherwise. That was how it was. Ever since the seventeenth century the French concentrated on the hero, not the chorus, did not realize the importance of the fact that the tragedies dealt with ancient history, and invented some reason for the events having to have happened as they did. This they called Destiny, for which there is not really a translation into Archaic Greek.[1] I instance an example of this sort of thinking:[2]

En particulier, les Grecs considéraient volontiers, dans les événements representés, la marque du destin. Ce destin, les Dieux y présidaient, les générations se le transmettaient, le chœur le commentait.

De Romilly goes on to say that Racine transmuted the notion of an external Destiny into an internal, psychological one.

In fact, this misconception has had less of an effect on the drama than on criticism in twentieth-century France. This is because all the writers concerned have a peculiar idea of the theatre, a strong awareness of the theatre as theatre, artificial by nature. They encourage us to remember that it is a play we are watching, and that the people are actors. The necessity that constrains the characters is simply that they are in a play. De

---

[1] Cf. pp. 18–19.
[2] J. de Romilly, "Légendes Grecques et Théâtre Moderne", *Mercure de France*, 1 May 1954, p. 72.

Romilly thinks that this is to miss the point of the Greek plays:[1]

> Profitant d'une necessité que l'on pourrait appeler lit-
> téraire, ils ont en quelque sorte triché avec la destinée, usé,
> abusé du caractère traditionnel des thèmes.

But this is much nearer the Greek necessity, which consisted solely in the fact that the story had happened. The instinctive practice of the craftsman is nearer to the truth than the theories of the critics.

Writers will write whatever the conditions. In the intellectual climate of the time it is still a little like living in a lumber room where everything is broken; but once you give up pretending broken things are whole, new arrangements reveal themselves. They have even managed to write for the bourgeois theatre, an institution kept going by executives on expense accounts, entertaining guests who bore them, at a show they do not properly watch, in seats which do not give enough room for the legs; while the interested audience watch from the gallery, while there is no common purpose uniting writer, technicians, and actors with those in the auditorium, except that the former are there to make money, while the latter pay to be entertained and taken out of themselves, it is unlikely that anything resembling the effect of Greek tragedy can be created. But the dedication of actors and technicians sometimes triumphs over these totally unpropitious conditions.

The worst result of the present situation is the separation of the writer from the other craftsmen concerned with putting on the play. He has been thought of as an outsider, whose job was done as soon as he had submitted his script. This attitude is changing, but is not wholly changed; it is difficult to see how a real sense of unity can be achieved without a common overriding social purpose to which all the craftsmen, including the writer, must submit. Certainly in the works I shall discuss there are things due to diffidence on the part of the writer over his content, dilutions of his social purpose due to his enforced acceptance of the theatre as a place of entertainment, where one must not be too serious. One example of this is the comedy of

[1] *Mercure de France*, p. 72.

sophisticated trivializing which softens the impact of much of what Eliot says in *The Cocktail Party* or Giraudoux in *La Guerre de Troie n'aura pas lieu*. And the development of Eliot's later verse is due to this lack of co-operation between poet and actor; the latter has been unable for so long to check what the point of writing verse is that he has given up learning how to speak it. I was interested to see a performance of *Brand*, by Ibsen, translated by Michael Meyer, at the Theatre Royal, Bristol.[1] The programme commended the translation for escaping from the Ibsen rhyming verse; there was no thought that perhaps there was reason for that verse. The production was in most respects quite good, but the play was a travesty, because what Ibsen had written in highly stylized rhyming verse was spoken in prose that veered into blank verse on occasions. Action which Ibsen had conceived at a distance was brought too close, and sometimes became embarrassing. A producer who could so produce *Brand* could never show more than a parody of Greek tragedy.

There are, then, a number of obstacles to the creation of modern tragedy; some of them are weaker than they were before the war, and are weaker for young people than for old. Some of these obstacles are being destroyed by writers who write with some overriding social purpose. It needs a sense of purpose, for example, to discover the deficiencies of the naturalistic convention. Once a writer has been able to infuse director and actors with his purpose, it will probably be seen that the play gives greater pleasure than one designed purely to give pleasure. Serious theatre is better entertainment. Even if we omit Shakespeare, a tragic tetralogy or a Miracle Cycle offers more action, spectacle, movement, colour, music, and sheer fun than the typical "comedy" of the small-scale sexual incapacities of three aspiring gentlefolk. And so it is worth studying modern tragic writing, even if we have as yet no theatre comparable to that of the Greeks.

I have been arguing that we are in a privileged position, able to see the misconceptions on which the thought and art of previous generations rested. I wish therefore to start this discussion by showing briefly the difficulties which the nineteenth-century tragic writer had to face. This can be quickly

[1] May–June 1962.

summarized. We have now a different attitude to the Principle of Causality, and therefore a totally different attitude to the question whether man is free.[1] The nineteenth century feared Determinism in terms of objective science. Ibsen developed his unique dramatic form in order to avoid facing the problem of decision. Connexion between an intellectual misconception and dramatic inadequacy is clear. I am prepared to agree with Steiner that there has been a "Death of Tragedy". I disagree that the conditions apply today.

The remaining writers I shall discuss with reference to four trends: the attempt to ask tragic questions while showing modern man in more or less naturalistic setting, as in plays by Miller and Sartre; the re-use of Greek myths by all the remaining authors mentioned; the attempt to create analogous myths in the context of our society, which I shall discuss with reference to Anouilh, Sartre, Ghéon, and Eliot; and the attempt to create a drama founded on Christian ritual in the way that Greek tragedy was founded on ritual. All these writers have acknowledged a debt to the Greek idea of tragedy, and it is possible to pass at least provisional judgement on their work from the point of view of Greek tragedy. There are three important writers whom I have omitted: Claudel, Yeats, and Brecht. Although they were all aware of Greek tragedy, it was a relatively less important influence. To relate their purposes to this discussion would take up a disproportionate amount of space, more especially as too little of their work has been performed in this country. The importance of Brecht has only been recognized generally in England in the last few years; the importance of the other two is a matter of considerable dispute, since they have left no followers. They are clearly more important than their neglect warrants, but I do not think we need to discuss them in order to see the problems that face the modern tragic writer; the same problems are raised with reference to the writers I do discuss. It will be asked why I have not written about O'Neill. I do not think that he is a very important writer, and what is effective in his work has nothing to do with Greek tragedy. Some of his work stirs me, because I feel it as the record of a real personal experience. His experience of

[1] Cf. pp. 178–81.

222

the sea, and above all the experience recorded in *Long Day's Journey into Night*, affect me, as I am affected by a personal novel, or an autobiography. There is no social implication in the writing. Nor is there in *Mourning Becomes Electra*, which has a plot somewhat similar to the *Oresteia* without Zeus, Artemis, Apollo, the Trojan War, the problems of governing Argos, Athena, Eumenides, the nature of democracy, and all the facts which drove Aeschylus to present the Orestes story, and from which it derives its universality.

I have already suggested that naturalism in the theatre is unlikely to be a useful medium. But Miller has written two fine plays which are partly naturalistic and partly tragic. It is worth seeing that the lack of clarity over crucial decision, which is the mark of naturalism, and which rendered it such a suitable medium for the nineteenth century, is also present in an age not obliged to shrink from the problem of freedom. Some of Sartre's work also illuminates the problems of naturalism as a medium.

Secondly, there has been an impulse to use Greek myths in a modern context. In France this is no new thing. The French Classical dramatists based their work on what they considered Greek tragedy to be. Through the eighteenth century this drama became more and more artificial, more and more constricted. Through the nineteenth century there were a series of attempts to recover a spirit more akin to the Greek tragedies, and at the same time advances in scholarship brought a clearer idea of the plays and their historical context. There were 582 original plays based on Classical themes, translations, and adaptations of Greek plays, during the period 1840–1900.[1] But when we read Nostrand's account of these plays we realize that the writers concerned did not really understand Greek tragedy very much. The outlook of the Greek poets was too far removed from that of the nineteenth century. Nor do the plays merit revival now. But at the same time as scholarship continued to illuminate the understanding of these plays the growing insecurity of life created a climate of opinion much nearer that of the fifth century than the nineteenth century had been. It would be a matter of arbitrary choice to date the beginnings

[1] H. L. Nostrand, *Le Théâtre Antique.*

of a real appreciation of the Greek tragedies being shown in a modern work. Claudel used his translation of the *Agamemnon*[1] to help him to create a new drama. But this *Agamemnon* is usually reckoned unstageable. Even Barrault, for all his admiration of Claudel, would not do it.[2] Cocteau's version of *Antigone* in 1922 is followed within a few years by a number of works which not only use Greek themes but also capture more of the spirit of the Greek tragedies than any works preceding the First World War. A number of these plays have been well received in England, but only Eliot has attempted to use the Greek stories in a similar way to these French writers.

We cannot talk to much purpose yet about the creation for our society of new myths analogous to the Greek myths; for it is not yet generally recognized what the Greek myths were, above all that they were believed to be stories which actually happened. One of the important questions about modern myth is whether our common modern religion, a belief in individual responsibility, and the virtues of scientific method is strong enough or specific enough by itself to create tragedy. Brecht's *Galileo* and Miller's *The Crucible* are relevant to this question. But there is not much point in discussing a writer in relation to a myth if not only he but all his audience is unaware that he is handling what could be a myth. Sartre is clearly aware of the need for myth. In an interview with Kenneth Tynan for *The Observer* he said:[3]

> The theatre's true battlefield is that of tragedy – drama which embodies a genuine myth.

It is not, however, clear what sense he gives to the word. There have been plays of Christian myth, though Anouilh has not realized the implications of what he has done in *L'Alouette* and *Becket*. Eliot also is presumably unaware that while he is not using myth in the Greek sense in *The Family Reunion* he is using it in precisely the Greek sense in *Murder in the Cathedral*; if he was aware I assume he would have said so. None of the plays

[1] 1894.
[2] Cf. Jean-Louis Barrault, *The Theatre of Jean-Louis Barrault*, translated Joseph Chiari, pp. 73–74.
[3] *The Observer*, 18 June 1961.

I shall discuss have a clear idea of myth; but the Greek idea of myth is clear. I shall deliberately judge these writers with reference to an idea none of them have fully recognized, in order to illuminate the notion of myth in our society. For it is generally agreed that the question of tragedy is very much connected with the question of myth.

Fourthly, there is the attempt to create Christian drama, based on Christian ritual as Greek drama was based on its own, and deriving inspiration from the two primitive Western dramatic traditions, the Greek and the Medieval; the pioneer of this attempt was Ghéon. We have seen that the purpose and the effect of Greek tragedy was more like that of the Miracle Cycles than of any subsequent tragedies. Clearly our understanding of one tradition will be illuminated by studying the other.

The Christian tragic poet has three advantages over the tragic poet of all other modern Western religions. His religion is doubly determined; it is possible from a distance to detect God's action in the world, somewhat as you can see that a field of corn once contained a road if you look from the air. Secondly, Christianity is ritualistic, more obviously so in some sectors of the Church than others, but in all sectors founded on a particular communal action, the eating of bread and wine, which is both itself and more than itself, in accordance with particular rules. The sacramental outlook makes it very easy to understand the need for a poetry of images, things both themselves and more than themselves. Aeschylus' net which is also doom, and not the less net for being doom, is immediately intelligible to those who have a sacramental religion. Thirdly, the Christian poet has a chance of writing for performance in a Church, before an audience of all classes who are not especially interested in the theatre. The commercial theatre is on the whole incapable of performing any of the great dramas, except Shakespeare. One of the ways in which those concerned with the commercial theatre will be made to realize its inadequacy is by seeing religiously or politically committed groups doing better jobs than many ordinary theatres.

It is sometimes said that there can be no Christian tragedy. I am not concerned to argue whether Christianity and Tragedy are incompatible. Clearly Christianity is compatible with the Greek idea of tragedy, except that it will be based on Christianity, and not on the religion of the Greeks.[1] There have been bad Christian plays called tragedies, and they have been bad for the same reasons as have made people say that Christianity and tragedy are incompatible; Christianity has been distorted and bowdlerized, largely because of the split in the Church, and the resulting lack of any central tradition against which to refer unorthodoxy. I take two comments to the effect that Christianity and tragedy are incompatible, as typical. Lessing writes:[2]

> Is not the character of a true Christian something quite untheatrical? Does not the gentle pensiveness, the unchangeable meekness that are his essential features, war with the whole business of tragedy that strives to purify passions by passions.

Presumably a "true Christian" should be thought of as someone a little like Christ. Is there any character in the history of the ancient world more extravagant in language than Him who reckoned rich men's chances of heaven on a par with camels getting through needles, who offended the squeamish by telling them to eat His flesh and live? Where else do we find such violent extremes of worldliness and asceticism as in Him who could fast for weeks in the desert, and yet be called a glutton and drunkard? It takes more than "unchangeable meekness" to hold a crowd of five thousand, and confronted with business men in the Temple, He did not bother about "purifying passion"; He gave it full rein. Nor is "unchangeable meekness" or "lack of theatricality" a natural reaction to the stories of the saints: the ecstatic abandonment of St John of the Cross, the intellectual ruthlessness of St Bernard, the sudden enthusiasm of St Peter. Sewall writes:[3]

> The history of the universe for the Christian is in principle already told.

[1] Cf. pp. 158–64.
[2] G. E. Lessing, *Hamburgische Dramaturgie*, 1769, translated by E. C. Beasley and Helen Zimmern, quoted by Barrett H. Clark, *European Theories of the Drama*, p. 258.
[3] Richard B. Sewall, *The Vision of Tragedy*, p. 10.

He has forgotten to look at the Creed. Christians say each Sunday that they believe that Christ will come again to judge living and dead; the history of the universe has by no means been told. Bowdlerized Christianity concentrated on some texts from the Gospels and ignored others, stressed the gentleness of Christ and the saints, and ignored their energy, slurred over the Judgement and the nature of evil. This is very likely incompatible with tragedy. But it is also incompatible with Christianity.

The Christian artist faces a large-scale misunderstanding of what Christianity is, due to the sentimentalizing of Christian teaching in the centuries of the dismembered Church. He also faces the fact that most people do not understand the terms in which Christianity is expressed. Eliot has talked of this, as do many Church leaders. People outside the Church know the words used in theological discussion, and think that they know the meaning, but do not. This is only a fundamental difficulty to Idealists, who believe in some special relation between the word and the thing, and therefore some permanent significance in the word. But if the word has lost its meaning the sensible thing to do is use another word, or phrase. If there is real experience to be described it can be described in new terms. If there is no experience, then Church leaders had better stop misleading the people. Eliot and Ghéon are both Idealists, as indeed are most Church leaders. A Christian poet who is not an Idealist will see that new terms must be found with which to describe the Christian experiences, and realize that this is eminently a task for poets. The realization that much of what has been called Christian is incompatible with Christianity, and the resulting need to find out what Christian dogma really is, should act as a stimulus rather than an obstacle to a dramatist.

The discussion in this chapter and Part II should show that there will probably be different answers to the question, Can there be modern tragedy? The difference will be partly a matter of the religion of the people who answer, partly a matter of choice as to how one defines tragedy. The first is an important difference, the second utterly trivial. I myself am uninterested in whether we can have Tragedy today, if Tragedy is defined, as it often is, in such a way that the masterpiece of Greek tragedy has to be called not quite Tragedy. I am deeply concerned with whether we can be a society fit for a drama such as the Greeks enjoyed. Because of this I am criticizing the plays of Part III with reference to the model of Greek tragedy. Sometimes this means I criticize a play for not being what it was never intended to be. I do this deliberately, because I am interested in what our theatre might become. Nor is it a denigration of any writer to say that his play is smaller than one by Sophocles. If I seem to dismiss any of these plays with less than they deserve, this is not an arrogant young critic's contempt of important work; it is that I pay all these writers the compliment of judging them with reference to what is acknowledged as the highest standard. To condemn their drama for being less than Greek drama is to affirm a belief that our generation could produce drama as great.

CHAPTER NINE

THE NINETEENTH-CENTURY
BACKGROUND

(i) THE GENERAL SITUATION

I have argued that we need to return to a way of looking at life
in which all experience can be brought to bear on any one experience, in which we emphasize the connexion between playing Bach fugues, on the one hand, with doing problems in
mathematics and, on the other, with jiving. We should emphasize the interrelation of all human activities, artistic,
scientific, political, and religious. We should try and understand jazz in the light of Bach, and Bach in the light of jazz,
moral decision in the light of artistic experience and artistic
experience in the light of moral decision, politics as a part of
religion, and religion as involving politics. If we adopt this
attitude we shall inevitably be opposed to a separate science of
aesthetics, a belief that works of art can be judged as good or
bad by criteria independent of life.

It is easy for us to say this; because we have seen the confusion that has come about through an opposite point of view
which thought it right to see art and science and politics and
religion as separate activities. This was the attitude of the vast
majority of people in the nineteenth century. It is therefore
worth examining some of their best drama to see the effects of
this attitude, at a time when it was not obvious that it would
have disastrous results.

If a biologist goes to hear a Wagner opera he is clearly going
to attend in quite a different way from that in which he attends
to his experiments. The intention of Wagner is to "sweep his
audience up into the music", in a way in which it was not the

intention of Bach or Palestrina. We are not meant to hear all
the notes in Wagner; we are meant to try to do so in Bach.
Music, especially music conceived in terms primarily of harmony and orchestral colour, as opposed to counterpoint, is very
good at this "sweeping up". And the advances in music, the
developments in harmony and orchestration, are the outstanding artistic achievements of the nineteenth century. This has its
effect in the theatre through the work of Wagner, who is more
significant than dramatists who only used words. The effect of
Wagner is much more powerful than the effect of Ibsen.

Music of this nature is the best argument for saying that art
should or does appeal to the irrational in us. The success of
music as opposed to the comparative failure of the other arts is
part of the general feeling that both art and religion were to do
with the irrational, non-scientific parts of our nature. This feeling came about because of the advance of science, which seemed
to be explaining away all mystery out of life in terms of fixed
impersonal laws. I am talking in these crude general terms
because I assume that no one disagrees with this conclusion.

With particular reference to the material of drama, human
decisions, we find that there was a great interest in the relation
of morals to the laws of science, but a great fear for human free
will in a determined universe. Büchner, Ibsen, and Strindberg
are interested in the problem of freedom, but they do not write
in the way best calculated to illuminate it. We do not see into
the process of decision.

One way to avoid showing decision is to use naturalism. If
we can only hear a person's words we shall never really know
how he decides. I think of how I myself have taken decisions,
and how incapable people whom I know are of putting the
nature of their decision into words. Naturalism is a way for the
writer to avoid showing what he thinks the decision means.

Secondly, there is a very different attitude to poetry in the
theatre. Agamemnon's action in stepping on to the purple carpet is a moment which clarifies our understanding of how he
decided to sacrifice Iphigeneia; the messenger's description of
the sunrise over the shipwrecked Greek fleet prepares us to see
that the final manifest light of the Eumenides in procession
may not necessarily be to our taste. Poetry is an attempt to

clarify, to present images of something that could not otherwise be expressed. The images can be discussed at length in prose terms, though they are more than their explanations. With Ibsen and Strindberg poetry is to charm us, to stop us asking questions. If it is analysed its effect is lost. There is constant use of flowers as both verbal and physical image in *Miss Julia*. Their effect is to charm and hypnotize us; we cannot ask at each point in the play what function their introduction has there, in the way in which we can ask it of the light or the net in the *Oresteia*. We are not to stop and ask whether Rosmer and Rebecca must commit suicide in *Rosmersholm*. If we do, the tension of the play is lost. Ibsen and Strindberg use poetry as Wagner uses music, to sweep us up into an unquestioning involvement.

Thirdly, the writers in question, including Büchner, avoid showing decision by making plays in which the decision takes place off stage. The significance of Ibsen's retrospective action is that he does not have to show the nature of an important decision. His heroes have already lost their freedom. He does not have to ask whether this is true of everyone. Danton's important decision was that of the September massacres. Büchner starts his play after Danton has had time to feel the effect of that decision, after Danton has ceased to be free. If tragedy is to help us to see the nature of decision more clearly, then all these nineteenth-century plays are very much less than tragedy.

(ii) GEORG BÜCHNER: *DANTONS TOD*[1]

This play is important because it is impressive in its own right, and also because we can see the effects that the philosophy which led to theatrical naturalism had on a play which is not naturalistic. It is on its own, however. The importance of Büchner was hardly realized till this century, and his work was not used as a model until the Expressionists. This play was written when he was only twenty-three. Some faults of construction can be attributed to Büchner's youth. Perhaps we must also say that the likenesses which this play bears to Greek tragedy, unique in its time, are also the result of a young man's recklessness.

[1] 1835.

There is a strong feeling of tragic rhythm in the play. Büchner started life as a doctor, and we get the same impression with him as with the Greeks, of someone who wishes to see what nature actually is, and then what history actually was, as we find in the Greek plays. It is certainly life seen from the point of view of death. Büchner has a strong awareness of physical death. There is a sense of contact with actual people dying, that we do not get from the Wagnerian suicides of Rosmer or John Gabriel Borkman.

Büchner said:[1]

> In my eyes the dramatic poet is nothing but an historian, superior in that he creates history for a second time, and instead of giving us a dry narrative translates us directly into the life of an age, gives us characters instead of characteristics and living forms instead of descriptions. His highest task is to come as near as possible to history as it really occurred. . . . The poet is no teacher of morals, he invents and creates characters, he makes past ages live again, and people may learn from them just as well as from the study of history and observation of what goes on in human life around them. . . .

If people are to learn from what the poet presents to them, then clearly the poet is in some sense a teacher. Büchner's disclaiming of the notion of poet as moral teacher should be taken with the belief then current, that moral teaching was the expounding of moral truths. By his connexion of history and contemporary life Büchner clearly intended no narrow intellectual sense of "learn". His audience were to discover things that would illuminate their lives. In this the aim is not far from that of the Greek poets.

There is also a feeling that history is part of a larger process, the evolutionary development of the natural order. This is the way St Just justifies the cruelty of the Revolution, by comparing it with the ruthlessness of nature.[2] Whether Büchner would endorse that justification is doubtful. But he believed

---

[1] Quoted by Stephen Spender, Introduction to *Danton's Death*, p. 12.
[2] *Dantons Tod*, II, pp. 41–42.

that the evolution which is "nature" is continued at a faster pace by man's conscious actions.

His "god" is impersonal. With reference to the Revolution he said: "I felt as if annihilated by the terrible fatalism of history." In the play there is much talk of the Revolution in an almost personal way. This was the time when Rousseau's theories of the General Will and the consequent tendencies towards Idealism were gaining a hold on people. The idea of the ultimate force being an impersonal one is hard for a dramatist to represent; it is harder still when it is abstract; and Büchner's attempts to personify the Revolution and the march of history by means of the crowd, do not give a sufficient strength. In order to show this force in its strength he must show the human figures as helpless against it. Because his gods are impersonal he writes pathetic tragedy.

His aim to use history as a means whereby people might learn to live their lives is an aim to use myth in the Greek sense. The French Revolution has the effect of an event in sacred history, rising above history, in a way something like that of the Crucifixion, which explains the references to Robespierre as "bloody Messiah"[1] and other such ones. The point of the play is that the Revolution, though horrible, was necessary. Büchner does not need to stress the good results it had, because everyone in his audience would take that for granted. In England the Revolution does not have this effect, because we obtained the political advantages without the bloodshed. The quality of the myth is therefore much weaker for us.

Although Büchner almost certainly agreed with the strictures on theatrical conventionality he gives to Camille,[2] he achieves a sense of distancing by the very fact he is presenting an action which is past, however authentically presented. All the characters talk alike, in a highly artificial manner that almost reads like verse, and they constantly liken themselves to ancient Roman heroes, which gives an extra, artificial dimension to the action. This style is inherent to the period. Some of the most artificial speeches are those he took directly from the records.

We notice how well rounded the vision of the play is. This is

[1] *Dantons Tod*, I, p. 26.   [2] Ib., II, pp. 32–33.

partly due to some of the most effective comedy of grotesque juxtaposition since Shakespeare. Marion's moving account of her passions is immediately followed by Lacroix' account of the mastiff and the poodle copulating in the street.[1] Büchner is well aware of the importance of sexual love, but takes good care to show that this which is so high and wonderful is also ridiculous. After a scene in which whores get soldiers to go with them the elegant lady enters to talk of "the scent of a flower, the natural pleasures, this pure enjoyment of nature!"[2] In general, the heroics of the main characters are counterpointed with the mock heroics of the crowd.

In a speech which he gives to Robespierre, and which must reflect his own opinion, or otherwise there is little point in its insertion, Büchner says that everyone performs many actions in thought, of which a few happen to be actually performed. The sin lies in the thoughts.[3] In this lies the justification for an artificial drama, which will show people performing actions which we have all thought, but few of us have performed. There is a fundamental contradiction here. Actions that are performed are helpful to us for understanding our unperformed "actions". The story of Danton is helpful in this way. The most important action Danton took was the ordering of the September massacres. Büchner does not show this. The whole play takes place after it has happened. I have tried to explain why Büchner should have done this. But the effect is to make the play less of a unity, and less compelling than it might have been if written from a different point of view.

The action of the play centres on Danton, and Danton's central action was ordering the massacres. This is not the central action of the play as Oedipus' turning away from the Corinth road and coming to the cross-roads was; all the other action does not follow as inevitable consequence of the initial action. It is more that we are shown the way in which all revolutions inevitably move to the left. First the king falls, then Danton, and then Robespierre: no one can control the march of history. This course of events is beautifully summarized in the last scene, when Lucile, out of her mind, is arrested for shouting, "Long live the king!" We have been reminded of the king's

---

[1] *Dantons Tod*, I, pp. 16–18.   [2] Ib., II, p. 31.   [3] Ib., I, p. 24.

execution, and that of Robespierre is hinted at. The historical process goes on, but it is difficult to see the relevance of human decision. Danton, thinking of his action over the September massacres,[1] says that he had no choice, that men are only puppets, "the swords with which spirits fight". Because we are not given more than Danton's view of the matter, and therefore do not know the truth, we are justified in complaining that Büchner has shirked the central issue of the play. But the impression we unconsciously assimilate is certainly that Danton was not free, and that the characters are only puppets.

The action is set under way by chance, the caprice of the mob. A citizen loses his temper at his daughter's bread-winning by whoring; this leads into a scene of mob justice directed at a man innocent except that he has a handkerchief. Robespierre appears, and they all resolve to make the Revolution stern again. The scene at the Jacobin club follows naturally, and there Robespierre directs this feeling against those who dress well, especially against Danton. This is Büchner's logic of events. It is unlikely that he would have such a tight construction as Sophocles. He does in fact put in several set pieces which are not particularly relevant to their immediate context, though giving a general flavour of the period; such is Payne's argument about God,[2] and Camille's remarks on the theatre.[3]

The constant reference to death as a woman,[4] and the connexion of death and sex in general, has something of the quality of an image, though it is far from clear what its exact function is, except that both are clearly intense experiences. But Marion's action is meant to be seen as a type of Danton's, though it is not an exact parallel.

The characters are shown in accordance with history, except that Danton was in fact faithful to his wife. We are never shown Danton making his momentous decision, and the impression of the play is that events happen whatever human beings do; so there is little sense that the action is as it is because Danton or Robespierre is as he is. Danton is a libertine, Robespierre a puritan, and Büchner has exaggerated history to point the contrast. But both will fall in much the same way. We are hardly

[1] *Dantons Tod*, II, p. 37.   [2] Ib., III, pp. 43–45.
[3] Ib., II, p. 32–33.   [4] E.g. ib., III, p. 46; III, p. 57.

235

shown Danton's greatness and not at all until his speech to the tribunal. This would not matter so much to the original audience, for whom Danton was a great figure in a way in which he is not for us. It is a long time since European history has been myth for Englishmen, and this is in some sense a play of myth. It is the only play that makes me wonder whether there could have been tragedy in the nineteenth century, or whether Büchner would have grown up to realize that the fatalism of history was incompatible with it. Let us by all means speculate on whether Büchner would have written a body of tragedy if he had lived; especially if it leads to a production of this grossly neglected play.

(iii) IBSEN

I have never yet met anyone who cared greatly for both primitive drama such as Greek tragedy and for Ibsen. I do not think that a critic is necessarily wrong to treat Ibsen with disrespect. After all, he has been a minority taste for a century. Surely, even the most dedicated Ibsen supporter must admit that his plays have dated. While it is almost impossible to make *Hamlet* seem a bad play, and while the *Oedipus Tyrannus* will always horrify, even in the truncated versions presented, when groups of people stand and speak what should be a singing dance, *The Wild Duck* needs superb acting to prevent it being boring. There are clear indications to show that Ibsen is not very relevant to a study of tragedy after the Greek manner. But it would be dishonest to pretend that apart from these "faults" I find him a congenial writer.

His significance is that he had a strong moral purpose, a concern to show his audience what they were, hypocrites. He also saw drama as having a social function, helping to unify an emerging nation. This is similar to the function of the Greek dramas. He himself combines this strong moral and social purpose with a nostalgia for the past, the heroic age, though his longing is more for a time when men were larger in stature, than for a time of greater moral coherence. His last plays are full of the atmosphere of a heroic world recognizably the same as that of his early work. I feel that this is what he enjoyed; his work with a special purpose was the result of conscious decision.

The deficiency of the naturalistic convention is that it cannot show enough of the minds of the characters. But its chief deficiency is in the moment of decision. This Ibsen avoids. We never see the moment of the most important decision the hero makes in his life; it has always happened sometime before the play begins. The retrospective method enables Ibsen to avoid facing up to the question as to whether human beings are free or not. I have argued earlier that freedom is connected with the notion of right decision.[1] It is likely therefore that a writer who did not make it clear whether his hero was right or wrong in his own opinion, and at what stage right or wrong, would not be able to understand the problems of freedom. We see this in *Brand*,[2] although here the convention gives opportunity for the writer to enlighten us completely. But we do not know at what point Brand is supposed to be wrong. At the end the crowd turns against him, but they do so for the wrong motives.[3] Brand is wrong at the end, but how soon before? Because of this lack of moral insight on Ibsen's part, we are shown pathetic studies of people who have gone wrong. We are never affronted in our beliefs, by facing their decisions.

People condemn Ibsen sometimes because he is a "moralist". They are those who do not approve of moral drama. But the truth of the matter is that Ibsen is a bad moralist. *The Pillars of the Community*[4] is a play written against hypocrisy. The play describes people, all of whom have lost their freedom. Their morality and their religion are both purely conventional. Dina surprises Johan by saying[5] that she hopes that America is not "proper and virtuous" but "natural". Lona is made to mock "the parson" Rörlund with a similar purpose.[6] Vigelund's conventional religion carries ironic point when he is twice made to say of the Indian Queen's voyage that it will be "in the hand of the Almighty", once when Bernick has decided to let it go,[7] and once when he has just discovered that his son is on board.[8] The climax of this development is when Bernick admits to

---

[1] Cf. pp. 178–82.   [2] 1865.   [3] *Brand*, v, pp. 227–43.
[4] 1877.   [5] *The Pillars of the Community*, II, p. 66.
[6] Ib., II, p. 63.   [7] Ib., III, p. 103.   [8] Ib., IV, p. 125.

Lona that they whom she has called "Pillars of the community" are all corrupted, but that the community has no other means of surviving.[1]

The most obvious way of showing this and at the same time focusing the action, as Ibsen does, on Bernick, would be to show Bernick taking the decision to marry Betty, whom he does not love, as opposed to Lona, whom he does. The question we ought to be made to face is the one he faced. If I can only fulfil my responsibilities by a lie, am I justified in lying?

Another way of meeting this purpose would be to show how Bernick regains his freedom. He could be made to realize the rottenness of his life by realizing his love for Lona, until he declares the truth, and his fortunes crash in ruins. We should see how truth must be adhered to, come what may. Here we are shown truth being adhered to, and the profits resulting. Clearly, right action does not normally lead to the happy ending, and to put a happy ending in a realistic play whose point is that truth must be adhered to, whatever the cost, is clear dishonesty, the worst fault in a moralist. Because Lona is meant to be a sympathetic character, and her advice is both right and clearly profitable, we are intended to identify ourselves with her. We do not see the action from all round, from a general point of view, but only from hers. Accordingly, by letting her solve the problem, our own moral insight is not advanced at all. It is sheer escapism. Like *Little Eyolf*,[2] the other play Ibsen wrote in which the hero regains freedom, it is a play of wishful thinking which pretends to be one of real life.

The point of *The Wild Duck*[3] is that one cannot always tell the truth. But we do not get this conflict presented at full strength because Gregers is a fool, caught up in the nonsense of his own life of "idealism". Hedvig's death for a lie is useless. It tears our heart-strings, and the fact that it is useless tears them even more; but because these characters stand for nothing our beliefs are completely unaffected.

This play also shows us Ibsen's moral incoherence, and the way in which this is bound up with the naturalistic convention. Miss Ellis-Fermor has remarked on the ambiguity of Gina.[4]

---

[1] *The Pillars of the Community*, IV, p. 120.
[2] 1894.   [3] 1884.   [4] *Three Plays*, Introduction, p. 16.

This is of great importance for our judgement of the whole situation. Is Gina, she asks, of a "coarse-grained placidity" or an "almost divine, inarticulate wisdom and charity"? We never know. Choice between these two conceptions should not be left to the producer. It makes far too much difference to the play.

The Wild Duck shows the one really satisfactory use of an image. The bird in captivity has all the symbolic qualities that Ibsen requires, and yet exists in its own right, for each character to take an attitude towards. The image of the white horse in *Rosmersholm*[1] is far less effective. It is vague; there is nothing about a white horse which connects inevitably in a poetic way with death and the supernatural. If I thought instinctively of an image of that nature I would think of an owl, or bat perhaps; something that flew. But certainly I would not say that any one image was inevitable for this enormous complex of experience. The white horse will do intellectually, as a short-hand to remind us of when it occurred before, and it has a vague resonance, but no more.

I have used the metaphor of vision when describing the different tragic poets. Aeschylus has eyes like a bird of prey. From miles away he sees a speck in the sky, and tells us, who cannot see, that it is two specks, a hawk chasing a nightingale. Euripides has quick eyes. Suddenly he notices snakes licking a woman's cheeks, tells us, and we realize what's going on. Ibsen says there is something vast looming up in front of us, and we are afraid. But he has defective vision, and soon we realize that it is quite harmless. He has an inaccuracy of the imagination. Mountains have strong associations; they suggest the power of nature, unearthly beauty, and so on. For Brand to die in the mountains is appropriate, because they connect with will power and heroism, and the wild parish where he has worked. For John Gabriel Borkman to do so is inappropriate. When he leaves the house it is a moment of high emotional tension. He refers to the mountains as his "kingdom".[2] We are caught up in his death wish. But he also says that he has now done with dreams.[3] But for an old man to go out hill-

[1] 1886. [2] *John Gabriel Borkman*, IV, p. 367.
[3] Ib., III, p. 349.

walking on a cold night is not reality at all, but a boy's dream. If Borkman was to return to reality his reality was the world of business success, the world of money. The power of the mountain image arises from associations which have nothing to do with the power of Borkman. Ibsen half realized this, but the additional associations of this scene, the suggestion that Borkman is a troll, charming metals out of the earth, the resemblance to the temptation of Christ, are even less relevant to Borkman the tycoon; admittedly he is made to talk of the mountains as the place where ore is mined, with which the commercial kingdom is built. But the activity of being a commercial king has nothing to do with ice-climbing. He says that he is dying because a cold metal hand is clutching him.[1] But this is just a metaphor for the cold. The image is resonant but evasive. Thinking about it causes it to lose its power.

The end of both *John Gabriel Borkman*[2] and *Rosmersholm* are ineffective as soon as we allow ourselves to think for a moment about them. We are meant to see these suicides as ennobling, and the effect is spoilt if we see them as ridiculous as well. If Rosmer and Rebecca are true to their rationalist selves they will see that the hardest task is to go on living, after rethinking all they believed in. If the point is that gentle rationalism is not strong enough to withstand this sort of crisis, then we must be shown an ending which is a loss of control, an outburst of passion, not a wedding march. Rebecca is a passionate creature, and if her passion did break out, after having been long subdued, it would hardly take the form of wedding without bedding. We see her triumphant atonement. We never see the despair without which the atonement is nonsense. Rosmer is not the stuff of heroes; if he is to commit suicide in this way it must be obvious that it is a desertion of his normal self, under pressure. We are shown two small characters, a murderess who couldn't stand the consequences of her crime and a rationalist who couldn't use reason when he came under real pressure. Mrs Helseth's "messenger speech" is intended to convey something of Greek solemnity. A more appropriate ending would be as someone has suggested Chekhov might have written. They would leap off the bridge to find the water frozen, and return,

---

[1] *John Gabriel Borkman*, IV, p. 369.   [2] 1896.

bruised and undignified. Then when they had been shown ridiculous we might be moved by their indignities; they might acquire a truer dignity than this Wagnerian end.

I find *Hedda Gabler*[1] Ibsen's most satisfying play, because it is totally ironical. It engages no tragic issues, and the interest is entirely on the pathetic character of Hedda. She thinks she can manipulate people, cannot realize that she is no longer able to do this, but is less and less able to live in the illusion. To Brack she comes to admit that she married Tesman because she had "danced herself out",[2] though she refuses to accept this in the next sentence. But she admits that she is a coward to Lövborg;[3] then she who prided herself on never getting into anyone's power finally allows herself to become completely in Brack's power; at the same time poor weak silly Thea, who has, however, made Lövborg write a great book, something that Hedda could not do, is clearly revealed as having more power even over Tesman. The illusion is shattered, and she cannot live with it. So she, who has dedicated her life to a kind of aestheticism of morals, commits suicide in the grand manner, and makes herself ridiculous. Brack's last words must be spoken lightly: "But good gracious, that sort of thing just isn't done." This makes an interesting play, and does not require the portentous solemnity of Ibsen's other work, but it is nothing to do with tragedy.

In the later plays especially there are several of the things which are associated with the view of life of Greek tragedy. There is a strong awareness of the demonic in man, a strong awareness of other than human powers around us, which Ibsen refers to as trolls and devils, and means more than a mere metaphor. This is particularly true of the last three plays,[4] but there are many allusions in *Rosmersholm* also. There is a strong awareness of human life as part of nature. Allmers in conversation with Rita recharges a stale metaphor:[5]

RITA (*angrily*): Oh, words! Good lord, we're creatures of earth after all.

[1] 1890.
[2] *Hedda Gabler*, II, p. 299.
[3] Ib., II, p. 317.
[4] E.g. *The Master Builder*, II, p. 171.
[5] *Little Eyolf*, III, p. 276.

ALLMERS: We have some kinship with sea and heavens too, Rita.

There is a constant reference to kingship. Solness promises Hilda a kingdom,[1] though it is a kingdom of the imagination. The king who is the focus of the ritual society of the old tragedies is here the man of vision, the focus of the romantic world which is Ibsen's equivalent. Borkman is also a "king",[2] and the chief function of so calling him is to draw attention to his heroic nature, to his lordliness. Borkman had wielded power; but we are not shown him in power. Ibsen comes near to adapting the image to a modern context, where the man who wields power is the tycoon, but his interest does not really lie in matters of power and decision. When we read this play a moral problem does present itself. If Borkman alone could bring happiness to the community by mining the hills, then is he right to marry his wife instead of Ella, to sacrifice himself to the community, or to sell his soul, according to our point of view; and secondly, should he embezzle the money, if only by that can the schemes be launched? That play might have affronted our beliefs, as the Greek tragedies do. It would also have justified Ibsen's title of moralist because it would have been a play about a moral problem, not about an individual, pathetic for all his megalomaniac poses. Instead, in this, and most of the plays, we are asked to respond to prose dialogue in much the same way as to Wagner's chromatic harmony, and sheer pressure of sound. The only thing that is at all tolerable about Wagner is his music. Ibsen is Wagner without music.

(iv) STRINDBERG: *MISS JULIA*[3]

Strindberg's influence as a formal innovator in the theatre has not been fully assimilated even now. He is a very important writer, though his work is not in general relevant to this inquiry. But he wrote one play which more than any other has been thought of as naturalistic tragedy, *Miss Julia*. With the exception of *The Dance of Death*, his later work is not in the naturalistic convention. *Miss Julia* must be judged somewhat in

[1] *The Master Builder*, I, p. 151.
[2] E.g. *John Gabriel Borkman*, I, p. 299.   [3] 1888.

isolation. There are aspects in which it is very like the Greek tragedies, but it is significant that both it and *Dantons Tod* have not been used by later writers as models.

In his preface Strindberg attacks the desire for comforting plays. We need to grow mentally tougher.[1] He is aware of the unpleasant conclusions of the philosophical developments of the time. He does in fact say:[2]

> I have had a feeling that, in our time, when the rudimentary thought processes operating through our fancy seem to be developing into reflection, research, and analysis, the theatre might stand on the verge of being abandoned as a decaying form, for the enjoyment of which we lack the requisite conditions.

He is aware of the implications of Determinism as understood then. Not only are they frightening for our views of freedom, and therefore are unlikely to help us in a philosophy devoted to the pursuit of happiness, but they suggest that all the personal instinctive activities will be seen to be pointless. The original preface to *Miss Julia* contains the words "like religion" after "the theatre". Strindberg excised these from his collected works; which were published when he had rejoined the Church.[3] But the implication, even without the words, is that once reason has progressed further, and more areas of human activity are brought under scientific laws, all that is thought of as the highest human activity, art, and religion, will be abandoned as pointless. His later plays are more irrationalist, signifying the natural reaction of an artist who believes that the activity of reason is gradually doing away with the need for his art.

We do get a feeling of tragic rhythm in this play, very similar to that of *Dantons Tod*. An impersonal force of nature crushes Julia to make way for a new type of being. Strindberg wishes us to see an analogy between what he presents and the natural order.[4] But there is an inconsistency in his preliminary think-

---

[1] August Strindberg, *Miss Julia*, translated by Edwin Björkman and N. Erichsen, Preface, pp. 104-5.

[2] Ib., p. 103.

[3] Cf. Hugo Gebers Vörlag, 1903.   [4] Preface, p. 104.

ing. He admits that he was interested in Julia as an unusual case. His interest in the oddness of Julia's background will prevent the feeling of universality he wishes to convey. If his point is that the new will oust the old, then he should show us the new ousting a strong representative of the old, not a neurotic specimen like her.

The play gives a good example of the inevitable failure of clarity resulting from the naturalistic convention. When Julia speaks in such a way as to sum up the play[1] she says that she is not to blame, she could not help it. Is this Strindberg's own view? We need to know; but there is no way in which he can show where the responsibility and blame lies. Further, in order that we should feel maximum pity for Julia, we need to see her incoherent and helpless. To rouse our emotions without engaging our reason and to fail in clarity over matters of decision seem inevitable concomitants of naturalism.

Structurally the play has many affinities with Greek tragedy. Julia lets herself be attracted to Jean, provokes his desire for her, until he naturally seduces her. As she tries to discover ways of escaping the disgrace that will follow, she comes to realize her moral disintegration, and makes him hypnotize her into committing suicide. All the action is contained in this. It is a tight, well-constructed play, in which the lack of an interval helps to make it resemble Greek tragedy more closely.

The play is about the fall of an ancient family who have outlived their social purpose, and have anyhow become degenerate. It is not a universal theme, because its universal implication is that the aristocracy has outlived its day, and if Strindberg had wished to show this clearly he should have taken a flourishing example of an aristocratic family and shown its fall. It is only about this general issue indirectly. We are meant to see Jean as a representative of the rising class; he has command of language.[2] Christine is dull and submissive; she will never get on. We come across the way in which here, too, the idea of the king is made to stand for the old order. Jean wants to go to Switzerland "where they have a republic".[3]

When Julia has gone into Jean's room a group of drunken peasants enters and performs a ballet in which they make a mess

[1] *Miss Julia*, p. 156.   [2] Ib., p. 123.   [3] Ib., p. 135.

of the kitchen. This is one of the few occasions on which an effect of the Greek chorus has been obtained in a modern play. Dramatically it is possible that drunken peasants should enter, but it has also the poetic purpose of generalizing the action. We see an imitation of Julia's debauch, which shows what is going on next door and at the same time conveys the mockery of the ordinary people and foreshadows the total collapse of Julia and her house. To show this at this point in this play a dance is perfectly adequate. But there are limits to the situations in which dance without words is enough.

The action is knit together at several points by fine images. It is foreshadowed by the behaviour of the bitch. Julia is first seen showing her disapproval of her animal's sexual activity, when she will do exactly the same herself. It is the gatekeeper's pug, too; the bitch is lowering herself.[1] Secondly, the relationship between Julia and Jean, and its alteration after the seduction, is shown by the two occasions on which they drink. Before, they drink the beer that Julia prefers to wine; after, they drink the burgundy Jean has stolen from the Count and concealed until now. Thirdly, we see a foreshadowing of Julia's death when Jean first orders her to kill the finch, and then when she falters, kills it himself.

Flowers are used throughout the play with symbolic effect, but it is not possible to relate the effect to the point of the play. Flowers to Strindberg are a general symbol of the irrational; they work on us as a charm.[2] The nearest this ever gets to being significant is when Jean says that Julia's disgrace hurts him as it does to see flowers beaten with the autumn rain.[3] But the flowers do not stand for Julia.

The accounts of the dreams of both Jean and Julia have obvious poetic significance, showing that he will rise and she will fall. It is one of the easy ways in which a naturalistic medium may be transcended while still remaining within the naturalistic limits.

The three characters exist both in their own right and as types, fulfilling a function in Strindberg's scheme. Julia is the decadent aristocrat, Jean the rising middle class, and Christine the subservient peasant. It is said that the effect of naturalism is to

[1] *Miss Julia*, p. 119.   [2] Preface, p. 106.   [3] Op. cit., p. 139.

make us identify ourselves with the characters. Here Strindberg is very careful to alienate our sympathies from them all, at the beginning. We are told of Julia's treatment of her fiancé in such a way that we shall not sympathize with her.[1] Christine is shown as dull, and Jean unattractively pompous. Christine playfully pulls his hair, and he replies crossly: "Don't pull my hair! You know how sensitive I am."[2] After Julia has collapsed completely to the extent of asking Christine to come to Switzerland with them, we are shown that both Christine and Jean steal.[3] This is done so that we shall not be tempted into identifying ourselves with Christine. Her respectable Church-going is only a façade.

Jean is prosaic, and in command of himself. He is loyal to his class, not letting Julia wake Christine from a sleep she has earned with a hard day's work,[4] and hardly able to shake himself out of subservience in order to tell Julia to kill herself, because he is hypnotized by the bell.[5] He orders Julia to prepare to leave the country, because he thinks she may have conceived; she goes to pack; he settles to do his accounts.[6] He is contemptuous of her sense of dishonour,[7] and makes it clear that he would never kill himself. In contrast, Julia is a much more complex creature, beyond his understanding. He can't see how she can hate and love at the same time, and he is shocked at the way she has flung herself at him.[8] He is genuinely moved at her collapse,[9] but he does not see far into this woman who was brought up to look like a boy, whose mother was an incendiary, who can lose control completely, and yet who acquires a kind of dignity in her ending. It is the contrast of mongrel and pedigree, and this is a contrast we often see. There is nothing universal about this play in what it does to us, or what it asks us to do. But there is a feeling that we are watching something more than what we actually see. It is not the effect of Greek tragedy, but there is something analogous to the effect of Greek tragedy. It can be called naturalistic tragedy if we remember that the features which it has in common with Greek tragedy are none of them naturalistic. It is right to call it naturalistic

[1] *Miss Julia*, p. 118.   [2] Ib., p. 118.   [3] Ib., p. 154.
[4] Ib., p. 125.   [5] Ib., p. 156.   [6] Ib., p. 146.
[7] Ib., p. 143.   [8] Ib., p. 138.   [9] Ib., p. 139.

tragedy, for that is a contradictory notion, and in the conception of this play is a contradiction, which luckily for the theatre Strindberg, thinker as he was, was not thinker enough to see.

(v) CONCLUSION

When we see Greek tragedies we ask of the actions represented, Was it right, Was it wrong? How was it right, how was it wrong? And we shall be shown how to make up our minds. All the poetry leads towards insight. In the nineteenth century we are asked to become involved with a surge of emotion in the hero's misfortunes while the poetry whirls beside us in obscure clouds. I might say that the early poets were surgeons, poring over the human predicament in sheer joy at the complexity of its nerves and veins, but with the aim to cure as their driving motive, and that the latter ones were magicians. But that is to be hard on magicians. When magicians were honoured, it was because their spells achieved something. The nineteenth-century writers are hypnotists, performing to impress us. However impressive their work is, we are left wondering about its relevance. Granted that we do not believe that men can cause rain by banging cymbals. Still, we need the rain.

CHAPTER TEN

MILLER

Miller has written three extremely successful plays, and is pre-occupied with questions akin to those that provoke a writer to tragedy. He is concerned with modern problems, and has on the whole used naturalistic or semi-naturalistic forms. In his introduction[1] he points out rightly that tragedy is a matter of the sort of questions a play asks, rather than of any particular theatrical form. By his remarks to the effect that he does not always use the "realistic style", which is his adjective for "naturalistic", he shows that he is aware that naturalism is only one of many conventions. But whether we call *Death of a Salesman* naturalistic or not, it and *A View from the Bridge* illuminate the problems facing a writer who wishes to ask the tragic questions without straying too far from ordinary modern life.

In this introduction he announces his refusal to adhere to the nineteenth-century doctrine of determinism which he rightly points out to be still current today. But he announces it rather as a cry of defiance than as part of a reasoned belief:[2]

> this dictum cannot be accepted as final and "realistic" any more than man's ultimate position can be accepted as his efficient use by state or corporate apparatus.

If he is right in rejecting Determinism in this sense, then perhaps it will not matter so much that he is not quite clear why he rejects it. The view of life that we get from his drama is that human actions are important, and can have effects. His plays will show decisions.

He started to be successful at a time when there was a brief

---

[1] Arthur Miller, *Collected Plays*, Introduction, p. 5.   [2] Ib., p. 53.

fashion for a kind of poetic drama "whose ultimate thought or meaning is elusive".[1] He attacks the concept of poetry as something vague and misty, and says:[2]

> I am simply asking for a theatre in which an adult who wants to live can find plays that will heighten his awareness of what living in our time involves. I am tired of a theatre of sensation, that's all.

This is to attack the notion of poetry that we find in Ibsen and Strindberg. It is the notion of poetry of much of the recent writers of "poetic drama", and Miller is right in his attack. It has nothing to do with the general question of poetic drama. The plays in question may show an inadequate sense of drama, but they show as inadequate a sense of poetry.

He realizes that a play must have a unifying idea,[3] though by saying that the idea may mean something different to him when he wrote the play and after some interval, he admits its ineffability. This realization was probably sparked off by the very varied receptions of *Death of a Salesman*,[4] and in the two later plays Miller took more care that the audience should understand the issues. He does not make it quite clear what he regards as the "idea" of a play, and I am not quite sure therefore whether it is nearer what I have referred to as the "action" or the "issues". However we regard it, there is a lack of clarity about the centre of *Death of a Salesman*, but Miller need not have worried about the varied receptions it had. It is not necessarily lack of clarity that makes different people see different things in a play. If a writer's vision is good he will present on stage something as many-faceted as life itself. Inevitably people will take different sides over who is right and who is wrong; they do so in real life. They will do so, even if the writer makes clear whom he sees as wrong. So it is irrelevant to the question of whether *Death of a Salesman* fails in clarity, that it should provoke different reactions in American salesmen and Spanish

[1] *Collected Plays*, p. 12.
[2] "The State of the Theatre", *Harper's Magazine*, ccxxi (November 1960), p. 66.
[3] *Collected Plays*, Introduction, pp. 8–9.   [4] 1949.

priests. If the central issues were made really clear it is quite likely that the reactions would be even more sharply different.

The action of *Death of a Salesman* is the suicide of Willy Loman. Such universality as the play has is caused by our involvement in his misfortunes. We are asked to look through Willy's eyes, but they are the eyes of the ordinary man. The play is held up as a contrast to the usual notion of tragedy as involving heroes, but is not such a contrast to the Greek tragedies, whose viewpoint is that of the ordinary chorus. But because we are asked to see through Willy's eyes we cannot see more than he can. The impression is bound not to be clear.

The play is of universal validity to the extent that it shows us our frustrations at contemporary society. Everything that Willy does turns against him. No one can live in industrial society now without feeling at some time that it is destroying him. But not everyone commits suicide. The play is built round an actual physical suicide and we are asked to see through Willy's eyes. To the extent that we become involved with Willy, the play ceases to have universal application. To the extent that we become involved in Willy's special plight and special characteristics, to that extent we shall come out saying, Poor Willy, instead of, What a society we accept. The more this play stirs our emotions, the less it will create awareness.

Furthermore, the suicide motive is so mixed. It is complicated even more at the last moment by the introduction of the new motive, the life insurance, whereby Biff will get 20,000 dollars.[1] This has very little to do with the issues that the play up till then seems to have involved. Certainly in real life suicide will involve extremely complex motives. To show why particular people kill themselves is a worthy artistic aim, though horrifying. But if the point of the play is to use a suicide to show some aspect of society, then the suicide's actual motives must be simplified, or the audience will not be able to take everything in. The naturalistic desire to show a particular suicide as fully as possible conflicts with the tragic intention to say something about our society which will hit home to all audiences in that society.

The issue involves the contradiction between our belief that

[1] *Death of a Salesman*, II, p. 218.

we must succeed in life and our sympathy for those who fail. There are occasions when we are responsible for getting a job done, and therefore for getting it done as well as possible. This may involve ruthless treatment of individuals. This is the conflict that we see in the decision of Howard, whether or not to sack Willy. But this conflict is weakened because we see Howard as an inattentive, small-minded individual. Miller talks of "the Law" which compels Willy to be treated as he is,[1] and if he means such a strong compulsion he should show us a reasonable man like Charley deciding to sack Willy, because Willy is incompetent, and the business must be done.

In order to feel sympathy for Willy as the inarticulate victim of a society he does not fully understand, we must see him inarticulate. As Miller has no means of illuminating us except through Willy, there is bound to be a lack of clarity. At the moment of crisis Willy goes round saying "Sh!"[2] That is all. The epilogue has a sentimental effect, and weakens the point of the play. If we are to be truly stirred with what Miller is concerned about we should not be allowed to go away saying, He is at peace now. We should not be at peace. This is a moving play, and it touches on important issues. But if the issues were presented more forcefully it would have to be a completely different play.

The action of *A View from the Bridge*[3] is the betrayal of his honour by Eddie Carbone. As in *Death of a Salesman*, the central action is not that from which all the rest of the play develops, but the climax of the development. The way to make sense of the form of Greek tragedies or Shakespeare is to think of the initial action; all other actions are performed as a result of people's reactions to the initial wrong. In this play no particular action sets events in motion. Miller has to make Alfieri say that he could see what was happening, what was going to develop;[4] it is an attempt to give an impression of something larger than the human beings moving them along in spite of themselves. It would be less necessary with a construction that showed everything as a natural reaction to one positive act,

[1] *Collected Plays*, pp. 35–36.
[2] *Death of a Salesman*, II, pp. 219–20.
[3] 1955.   [4] *A View from the Bridge*, I, p. 410

like poisoning a brother and marrying his wife, or building a
bridge. With both Shakespeare and the Greeks, the important
unifying factor is the action, not the hero. It does not matter
that the action is initiated by someone who is not the principal
character. If the tragedy is to be focused in one man, and we
are to see him active for the time that he is on stage, as opposed
to suffering the consequences of his wickedness or folly, then
making a play grow out of the consequences of one wrong act
will force the writer to make the main character perform two
climactic actions, that which sets everything in motion and the
last desperate act of defiance with which a play of this sort is
bound to end. Because this would be difficult, the play is given
a different shape. We can see what this play would be like if it
was in the form of Greek tragedy. It would resemble the *Ajax*.
Both plays are about the betrayal of the heroic code. But the
development of the *Ajax* all stems from the principal betrayal
which has already taken place. To rewrite Miller's work to
make it like Sophocles would mean that the play would begin
with Eddie ringing up the Immigration Authority, would show
the scene in which he kisses first Katie, and then Rodolpho,[1]
as a parallel to the refusal of Ajax to attack Troy and fall before
the walls in atonement, to signify even further his degradation
and show how he has lost his honour. All the material which
goes into the preliminaries to this would have to be crammed
into the short space of time between the betrayal and the recoil
on to Eddie's own head of his wrong action. This will convey
something of the difference in the two methods.

The play is about possessive love. That is to say, if it is about
anything it is about that. The drive in Eddie that made him
"hustle" to get work so that Catherine should eat[2] is the very
drive that makes him reluctant to let her go, and so leads to the
disaster. But in the play this is complicated by the sexual
element. Eddie is sexually attracted to Catherine, though he
never knows it. This unusual situation helps to make Eddie
more sympathetic, but it weakens the universality of the point,
which must surely be intended to apply to fathers as well as
uncles. Sometimes there's "too much love".[3] There is a hard

---

[1] *A View from the Bridge*, II, p. 422.
[2] Ib., II, p. 409. [3] Ib., II, p. 409.

truth here, and it applies whatever we mean by love. Here it is not made to apply with the force that it might have done.

The play is also about "settling for half".[1] It is a contrast between two societies, the old one, with its aristocratic moral code of honour, and the new one, with its insistence on the law. The Sicilians believe that all wrongs should be punished; modern Americans realize that some wrongs must be left unpunished, but they are not necessarily the less wrong for that. But though we will agree with Alfieri when he tells Marco not to be God in his vengeance on Eddie,[2] we will also agree that the tendency of modern society is not to be so aware of wrongs, once they no longer punish them with their own hands.

Because he thought that his audience had failed to get the point of *The Crucible*, and indeed as part of the progress towards greater explicitness from *Death of a Salesman* onwards, Miller used an engaged narrator. Alfieri is involved in the action, but is also chorus, commentator. This play reveals the dangers of this method. Granted that Alfieri is not like the chorus in Anouilh's *Antigone*, an all-knowing figure in evening dress. He still has to tell us things, and we may be annoyed both if we know them already and if we don't. In the first case we shall be bored; in the second case we will feel he is being superior for all his appearance of being a little man like ourselves. The Greek chorus is a group; it is much easier to ally oneself with a group reaction. Secondly, the Greek choruses use poetry. The meaning of what they say can be taken on different levels. There is something for every reaction in the audience. This is in bald prose. It means no more than what it obviously says; this is why these speeches sometimes sound portentous. There is no way of implying the overtones; they have to be stated, and therefore sound crude.

The New York version contained passages in verse, similar in form to that in *A Memory of Two Mondays*. It is bad verse, rhythmically unexciting, and there is little point in the end-stops. This is shown by the fact that Rodolpho's speeches in his scene with Catherine were in verse in the original version. There is no alteration; they are now simply written as prose.[3]

[1] *A View from the Bridge*, II, I, p. 379.   [2] Ib., p. 435.
[3] Ib., II, pp. 419–20.

Some of Alfieri's speeches of comment were in verse; they are more literary than the present version; the effect is to make Alfieri less real. I have had to rely on Welland's summary,[1] with extensive quotations; the New York version is not available in print.

The play contains one of Miller's finest pieces of dramatic poetry, and indeed one of the finest moments in twentieth-century drama, the first-act curtain. At a moment when the structure of the play demands a scene to show Eddie's impending fall we see Eddie working off his anger against Rodolpho by giving him the boxing lesson in which Rodolpho is hurt. Marco then challenges Eddie to lift the chair, which Eddie cannot do. We see Marco holding it up in triumph while Catherine and Rodolpho start to dance defiantly. Marco's loyalty to his brother is shown, and his greater, but less obtrusive, strength is perfectly imaged by wrist strength, which is of vital importance in knife fighting. Eddie is not as strong as he looks.

I was impressed when I saw the film of this play by the added depth Beatrice acquired. She has very little dialogue, and yet somehow she must give the impression of understanding more of what is going on than anyone else. The climax of her scene with Catherine is as follows:[2]

CATHERINE (*strangely moved at the prospect*: [of giving up Eddie]): All right . . . If I can.
BEATRICE: Honey . . . you gotta.

Without the help of the camera it is impossible for anyone to convey enough with so little dialogue.

Marco also is not written in quite fully enough. From the start he is the one that Eddie respects. Marco himself betrays his code. He gives his word to Alfieri that he will not harm Eddie if he goes out on bail,[3] and he breaks it. This is what Eddie has done, made someone like Marco break his word, intentionally. Either we need to know in the scene in the prison that then and there he decided to break it, or we must see into his thoughts as he prays in Church.[4] We never do, and an important dimension of the action is lost.

[1] Dennis Welland, *Arthur Miller*, pp. 92–107.
[2] *A View from the Bridge*, I, p. 406.   [3] Ib., II. p. 435.   [4] Ib., II, p. 436.

The conflict is seen at its strongest if Rodolpho is shown as a harmless, not especially abnormal person. Miller never makes it absolutely clear that he is definitely not a pansy, and the one moment when we see him moved to anger by the discovery that Catherine is testing his love for her on instructions from Eddie there is not enough dialogue to make clear what he is really like.

There is ambiguity in Eddie also. It is necessary to make him as sympathetic a figure as possible, or otherwise there is no play. The New York one-act version failed because Eddie appeared as a monster. A producer must be careful not to make the opening scene with Catherine, and in particular the sequence starting with his remark that she's "walkin' wavy", lose sympathy for Eddie.[1] When Beatrice worries about the cousins he must comfort her through gentle teasing, not appear querulous. We must see that when Beatrice flings her arms round him and says "You're an angel", she has good reason.[2] But this interpretation is not inevitable from the dialogue.

The inarticulateness of Eddie is used to good effect in the scenes with Alfieri. The catastrophe would not happen if Eddie was more self-aware. At the moment of crisis Beatrice shouts at Eddie demanding his "name":[3]

> You want somethin' else, Eddie, and you can never have her!

Eddie disclaims this with every fibre of his being. He does not realize, and the play would be horrible if he did. But the inarticulateness of Eddie makes for a general inarticulateness. Miller sometimes tries to fill out his dialogue with stage directions. Inevitably these give a different, more explicit effect when read from what they do on stage, however well acted. When he lets Catherine go to work we read:[4]

EDDIE (*with a sense of her childhood, her babyhood, and the years*): All right, go to work.

At the end there is an even greater sense of incoherence, inevitably bound up with the naturalistic convention.[5]

[1] *A View from the Bridge*, I, p. 381.   [2] Ib., I, p. 383.
[3] Ib., II, p. 437.   [4] Ib., I, p. 386.   [5] Ib., II, p. 439.

CATHERINE: Eddie I never meant to do nothing bad to you.
EDDIE: Then why – Oh, B!
BEATRICE: Yes, yes!
EDDIE: My B!

With this he dies, and we are left feeling that we do not know enough, stirred in our emotions, but unable to form judgement, unable to reach awareness.

I have said elsewhere that we are not yet capable of judging *The Crucible*'s[1] relevance to the problem of modern tragedy. The story has something of the effect of a myth; it tells of a past wrong that typifies a present one. But because the nature of the Greek myths is not generally known, no one has understood this, not even Miller. He is aware that by setting his play in the old Puritan New England he has achieved greater moral articulateness than would be possible in a modern setting. Even though he is writing naturalistically, he is writing about a society "immersed in the questions of meaning and the relations of men to God".[2] He is aware of the greater clarity obtained by using myth, and he is aware that the Salem story typifies part of modern American life. He has not put these two things together, and realized that this is myth, history used to illuminate a present crisis. The religion from whose viewpoint he writes is a belief in freedom and democracy; he uses nothing more specific than that. It remains to be seen whether this is a strong enough religion to create a mythology.

Although he has a strong social purpose, Miller asks us to see his plays from the viewpoint of a hero; there is not the social viewpoint of Greek tragedy. In this, as in the other two plays I have discussed, the social implications are weakened, because he is concentrating on his hero. The climax of *The Crucible* is Proctor's personal salvation, not the utter corruption of the judges; but Miller intended to show how supposedly rational men could hand over their conscience. For us, it is the way the judges behave that is important. *The Crucible*, like the other two, has a narrower focus, and less didactic impact than Miller wanted. As it stands, it is no nearer Greek tragedy than them. But it raises a new set of questions, of extreme importance.

[1] 1953.   [2] *Collected Plays*, Introduction, p. 47.

The impression of all of Miller's work is that there is a contradiction between the social purpose he believes in and the emotional tension of the particular situation he is describing. None of his forms has been entirely satisfactory, though the intensity of his writing has meant that he has left three very gripping plays. It is some time since he wrote a play, and *The Misfits* did not live up to the expectations it had aroused, either as film or half novel, half film-script as it was published. The question of how his approach to theatre drama can be developed, by Miller or anyone else, is still very much an open one. But in so far as theory can be of help, it would seem that his form is not a satisfactory one, and that his example is not therefore one to be followed too closely. He has achieved his success in spite of, rather than because of, his medium.

CHAPTER ELEVEN

COCTEAU, GIDE, GIRAUDOUX

(i) INTRODUCTORY

These three writers have produced the best plays based on
Greek myths during the twenties and thirties. We shall find
that there is a different flavour in Anouilh's writing, since he is
a generation younger. These writers, too, seem very different
from those who wrote before the First World War. It is partly that
more people were prepared to follow Cocteau in turning away
from a theatre primarily of talk, as the French theatre before
the war had been; it is partly that scholarship had advanced the
understanding of what Greek drama was really like. It is not
unreasonable to say that it was these men who set in motion a
revival of Greek drama, as opposed to a neo-classical drama.
There is far more of a Greek atmosphere, less of an undifferentiated Antiquity.

We shall find these writers treating themes of Greek tragedy
in a setting which is partly that of boulevard comedy. It is
trivializing comedy; we are not asked to take things too
seriously. When we see heroes on stage there is always a danger
that we shall think them artificial, not really alive. In the Greek
tetralogies there was a chance to laugh at the conventions you
had respected for the first few hours of the performance. In
Shakespeare we are constantly changing our viewpoint. In
French Classical tragedy we must always respect the convention. Otherwise there is no play. In the plays I shall discuss in
this chapter the heroes are presented as frankly artificial; the
tradition in which these plays are written is that of sophisticated comedy. But because there is this tradition, which was the
whole theatrical tradition of France and still is the most signi-

ficant thing about it even now, there is also a tradition of saying serious things lightly, of discussing everything in tones which suggest that it does not matter, even when it does. It is something which has far less hold in England, and has lost what hold it had since the coming of the Welfare State. When we watch French plays in this tradition it is like listening to the conversation of diplomats. Automatically we think that it is insincere. But it is sincere sometimes, though it is hard to tell. And we may feel that if you always talk like a diplomat you will lose some discrimination.

This ability to treat serious things lightly goes with an attitude to the theatre as something unique in itself, to which its own proper attitude belongs. The paraphernalia of the theatre all acquire a ritual significance. This is well expressed by Cocteau, who in *Les Monstres Sacrés* makes Esther say:[1]

> Le théâtre, c'est une sorte de couvent. On sert un dieu. On répète les mêmes prières. On ne va jamais au théâtre. Le jour on ne sort pas. On recommence les mêmes petites farces entre camarades. Et les visites sont très, très rares. J'ajoute qu'il y a de l'encens, des cierges et des fleurs.

Because of this attitude to the theatre we find the stories which have been part of the theatrical tradition take on a significance simply by their connexion with the theatre. The same attitude is expressed by the chorus in the opening speech of Anouilh's *Antigone*.

The theatre acquires its own reality as a closed world governed by aesthetic laws. It is therefore appropriate that we should be asked to see the action of these plays, not through the eyes of ordinary people but through those of the artist himself. This is the significance of the individual who plays chorus, who knows the course of the action beforehand. De Romilly says:[2]

> Le chœur est revenu pour commenter l'action, ou il a été remplacé dans ce rôle par un personnage privilégié, comme le Mendiant.

[1] *Les Monstres Sacrés*, I, iii, p. 24.
[2] *Mercure de France*, 1 May 1954, p. 80.

It is essential that the Greek chorus are not privileged, because they provide the viewpoint of the ordinary man; it is essential that the action of Greek tragedy really happened. In modern French drama we are asked by people who regard art as separate from life to engage in an experience which only touches life through aesthetic experience. The result may be stimulating theatre. But the Greeks had no word for "aesthetic experience".

(ii) COCTEAU

Cocteau is primarily important as having once again made the theatre a place for more things than just talk. His distinction of *poésie du théâtre* and *poésie au théâtre*[1] has reminded people that a play is more than a text. Clearly the poetry of the Greek tragedies is *poésie du théâtre*, especially such devices as Aeschylus' embodiment of images. In the theatre poetry must be the whole complex of music, dance, spectacle, and words. But this had been forgotten, and still is not properly realized.

He has written[2] that poetry should learn from sculpture more than painting now, should concentrate, so that its rhyme and rhythm can make maximum effect, and should avoid being "prose in evening dress".[3] He is preoccupied with science, and the responsibility of the artist in the age of quantum physics,[4] and he has said that art should keep in touch with the ordinary man. In his critical thought he is very advanced for his time, but he has not acted up to this in his actual writing. His most enthusiastic admirer could not say that the ordinary man will find much that is understandable in the ingenious theatrical tricks of *Orphée* or the high-flown talk of the gods in *La Machine Infernale*. Is it fair to convict him out of his own mouth?

> Gradually I fell into the sleep of a somnambulist. This became my normal state, and no doubt I shall continue to sleep this sleep until the end.

[1] *Les Mariés de la Tour Eiffel*, Preface.
[2] *A Call to Order*, translated by Rollo H. Myers, p. 12.
[3] Ib., p. 131.
[4] Ib., p. 1, and cf. "On Distance" in *The Hand of a Stranger*, translated by Alec Brown, pp. 132–51.

This comes from *A Call to Order*.[1] A few pages further on we read:[2]

A dreamer is always a bad poet.

Cocteau has said that he likes the cinema because it is like a dream,[3] and he is more at home in films where his talent finds greater scope, and his lack of intellectual ability is less noticeable. But that is not our subject.

Outstandingly the greatest work based on Greek myth from this period is Stravinsky's *Oedipus Rex*.[4] To me this seems a masterpiece in a way which none of the plays I shall discuss are. And Cocteau wrote the libretto. The Latin text gives it a remoteness, and also helps the religious associations, because sung Latin is *par excellence* the language of ritual. Cocteau also wrote an *Antigone*.[5] The text is merely a prose abridgement of Sophocles. The effect of the poetry of the original was to be obtained by music and dancing. There is little point therefore in passing judgement on a text which was never intended to stand alone. The effect of ballet is much less articulate than the effect of poetry. The advantage of the Greek dramas was that both music and dance had all the impact, and more, that our music and dance has, but were in themselves less elaborate, and served the verbal rhythm of the poet.

Orphée[6] is called a tragedy by Cocteau in the preface to the play, but it is a fantasy. It is better known in the film version, where the magical effects can be conveyed more easily. The main difference between the implications of play and film is that the former contains Christian symbolism. Cocteau had left the Church when he made the film.

The action of the play is Orphée entering death. This is not a central action from which everything else derives, as in Greek tragedy, or a climactic action to which everything leads, as in Miller. It is merely the main event of a story where every event follows surprisingly.

It is about the nature of the poet. Early versions of the story have used it as an image of love. Orpheus' skill in song is

---

[1] *A Call to Order*, Preface, p. vii.　　[2] Ib., p. 12.
[3] *Cocteau on the Film*, pp. 25 ff.
[4] 1926–7.　　　　[5] 1922.　　　　[6] 1926.

instrumental to his purpose in seeking Eurydice, whether in Virgil or the anonymous Middle English *Sir Orfeo*. The point of the latter concerns kingship. Only by putting off his kingship, by living as a hermit in squalor, can Orfeo reign again with his refound queen. Clearly the story might easily be made into an image of poetry. Only by sacrificing everything, by ceasing to be a poet, can one truly be a poet. The Orpheus story can be easily made into a Christian legend of sacrifice and applied to any activity, love, kingship, poetry. This is in a sense Cocteau's point. He has at any rate no other.

Our difficulty stems from the image of the horse. Because this is a Surrealist play we assume that the horse's phrase must be taken seriously. Then at the end we are told it was the Devil. We feel cheated; we only took its nonsense seriously because we thought that was what the poet wanted. We never have a scene where we see Orphée reorientate his ideas. Without that scene we are lost as to how to take it. Nor do we see any change in Orphée after he shakes off the Devil's influence. He is as unattractive after his return from the dead as before, and after his own death there is no opportunity to see him.

There are some clever uses of metaphors, which in the context are more than metaphor. We are prepared for Heurtebise to be an angel when he stays in the air, and Eurydice says:[1]

Vous êtes demeuré une bonne minute entre terre et ciel.

This is like a dream, when sometimes the meaning of what we dream can be expressed in a metaphorical sentence, but we dream the physical event the metaphor once meant.

Most of the imagery is imprecise; its effect is merely theatrical. The connexion of the mirror and time is understandable. But a mirror means more than just mortality. And what is the point of Death borrowing a watch from a member of the audience? Sometimes we feel Cocteau is hampered by the limits of the stage. The description of the set is far more explicit than any visual representation could ever be,[2] "*ce salon cerné par des forces mystérieuses*". The crux of the play is mainly carried by stage direction:[3] "*L'envoûtement du cheval est fini. Orphée se trans-*

---

[1] *Orphée*, Sc. v, p. 46.   [2] Ib., p. 14.   [3] Ib., Sc. ix, p. 99.

figure." *Orphée* is a fascinating *jeu d'esprit*. But it has nothing of the tragic spirit claimed for it in the prologue.

La Machine Infernale[1] can hardly be called tragedy, since most of it is set firmly in the idiom of boulevard comedy. Inevitably its impact is incomparably weaker than that of the *Oedipus Tyrannus*. We are bound to feel that a man who could turn the story of Oedipus into something trivial must be a trivial person. We are bound to be dissatisfied with an Oedipus who is less both as person and as type than the Oedipus of Sophocles. The climax of the play, however, is exciting, though perhaps this climax could not fail to be. Cocteau tries to keep the shock of the *dénouement* by making Jocaste die before Oedipe discovers the truth. He is puzzled. Why should she kill herself, because he is not a king's son? It is a chance for an actor to wring pathetic irony out of the part. But as Oedipe is about to discover the truth Cocteau gives a free translation of Sophocles.[2] The use of the same words as in the Greek gives a ritual effect to the discovery that we are all waiting for:[3]

OEDIPE: Je suis près d'une chose impossible à entrendre.
LE BERGER: Et moi d'une chose impossible à dire.

Anyone making a play about Oedipus after Sophocles is bound to show his awareness of the *Coloneus* as well as the *Tyrannus*. Cocteau does this by an epilogue which conveys the point of the *Coloneus* but in terms of literature not life. This difference sums up the different viewpoint of the two schools of writing. The point of the *Coloneus* is to show the numinous power acquired by those who suffer greatly, independently of whether they deserve it or not. Oedipus acquires power because he has done and suffered terrible things. Cocteau's point is that the story of Oedipus has power in this way, because it is a terrible story. Tiresias will not let Créon interfere with Oedipe and Antigone as they depart, for, he says, they belong now *"Au peuple, aux poètes, aux cœurs purs"*.[4] Créon thinks that they will belong to dishonour rather than to *"la gloire"* as Tiresias claims. The priest replies:[5] *"Qui sait?"*

But the main point of the play is that implied in the title and

[1] 1934.   [2] *O.T.*, 1169–70.   [3] *La Machine Infernale*, IV, p. 208.
[4] Ib., IV, p. 217.   [5] Ib., IV, p. 218.

alluded to by the opening speech of the Voice who comments on the action.[1]

> Pour que les dieux s'amusent beaucoup, il importe que leur victime tombe de haut.

When the Sphinx pities Oedipe, Anubis orders her:[2]

> Efforcez-vous donc de vous souvenir que ces victimes qui émeuvent la figure de jeune fille que vous avez prise, ne sont autre chose que zéros essuyés sur une ardoise, même si chacun de ces zéros était une bouche ouverte criant au secours.

Cocteau says that he altered the myth:[3]

> ... turning Oedipus's victory over the Sphinx into a false triumph born of his pride and of the weakness of personality of the Sphinx, a half-divine, half-feminine creature, who acts here as the princess was to act in my film *Orpheus*, when she thinks herself condemned for the crime of free-will. The Sphinx ... is duped by the Gods. ... Precisely by this betrayal of the Sphinx I underline to what extent the drama is in the Greek conception outside Oedipus, and in *Orpheus* I develop this idea further. The Gods prompt the death of Orpheus to ruin him, making him immortal and blind, *so robbing him of his muse*.

The story of Oedipus is the story of a trap in which both gods and men are caught. For Anubis says to the Sphinx:[4]

> Les dieux possèdent leurs dieux. Nous avons les nôtres. Ils ont les leurs. C'est ce qui s'appelle l'infini.

The Sphinx' protest is like that of Madness in the *Heracles*. But it is quite clear what Euripides is protesting against. It is not clear with Cocteau. He is protesting against gods he has invented himself. We are left with a vague image of the universe

---

[1] *La Machine Infernale*, IV, p. 14.   [2] Ib., II, p. 85.

[3] "On Being Invisible", *The Hand of a Stranger*, translated by Alec Brown, p. 25.

[4] *La Machine Infernale*, II, pp. 82–83.

as governed by spiteful warring fairies, and because this is an eccentric view we need to be shown it more clearly than we are.

Atmospherically the play is very effective. The red bedroom of Jocaste, full of animal furs, is a very powerful visual image. But it is only incidental. It does not have structural function.

Jocaste is made into a splendid part for an actress. Cocteau has had a chance to elaborate the character derived from the myth, and in particular has taken trouble to make the wedding psychologically credible. Another alteration is also effective. He makes Oedipe say that he only used the oracle about killing his father and marrying his mother as an excuse. Really he just wanted adventure. This seems to add something that is in keeping with the spirit of the original myth. Oedipus is the type of the rational man. He would not believe in oracles. This is the sort of thing that a modern writer can do for his time. But it is something very much less than what the Greek poets did. There is strength in this play, but all the strength lies in what remains of the Sophocles version.

(iii) GIDE

Gide's importance is primarily as a literary rather than a dramatic writer, but his *Oedipe* has had some success, and is worth consideration. He also wrote *Perséphone*,[1] a ballet in verse, but this bears about as much relation to Greek drama as eighteenth-century neo-classical sculpture does to the work of Pheidias. The ballet belongs to the world of Dresden shepherdesses not to that of Dionysus.

He also wrote *Le Roi Candaule*,[2] based on the story of Candaules told by Herodotus.[3] This is a work in the tradition of earlier French writing, choosing a story dignified by Antiquity, rather than because it has anything in it which makes it suitable for serious treatment. Herodotus tells it lightly; there is an Eastern, fairy-tale atmosphere about it, which makes it unsuited to Gide's solemn handling.

Jouan[4] says of *Oedipe*,[5] that it lacks "*vis tragica*". Compared

---

[1] 1934.   [2] 1901.   [3] Herodotus, I, 8–12.
[4] F. Jouan, "Le retour au mythe grec dans le théâtre français contemporain", *Bulletin de l'Association Guillaume Budé*, 6, 1952, p. 67.
[5] 1932.

with other retellings of the Oedipus story, it is relatively dull, though it can be made to grip the audience, as any staging of this story must. The action of this play is that of the *Tyrannus*. Oedipe is someone who values self-knowledge above all things, and who comes to see that he is completely unknowing. The action is seen much more from the point of view of Oedipe himself than it is in Sophocles. We are more expected to agree with his attempts at self-knowledge than we are to sympathize with Oedipus in the *Tyrannus*.

The play is about various attitudes to religion. Tiresias is "*vêtu en religieux*"[1] and Antigone is going to become a nun. The discussions in Act II are about "God" not gods. Later in that act Oedipe says:[2]

> J'ai compris, moi seul ai compris, que le seul mot de passe, pour n'être pas dévoré par le Sphinx, c'est: l'Homme.

His argument with Tiresias after that suggests that the point of the play is to show the way in which Man is trapped by God. But in this case it is an undoubted weakening that at the end of the play Tiresias is talking about gods, not God. There is a blurring of the outlines which weakens the attack on the Christian Church that is the undoubted intention of the play. Gide was always doubtful in his mind as to what attitude he should take to Christianity, and certainly did not totally disapprove of it. He does not mock Antigone for her faith, and it is certainly significant that Oedipe leaves with her finally. She decides to give up her calling as a nun and live with her father. This is an image of action which Gide does approve, someone who believes in God living up to her belief, but in her own way, not the Church's.

The chorus is a group of people, unusually. They are divided into two halves, and they speak in prose. This is probably the least promising way of all to tackle the chorus, when it comes to production. Choral speaking is hard enough. Choral speaking in prose is near impossible. The point of having a group is to show the ordinary man's viewpoint; the chorus are not privileged with insight into the future. Gide's chorus is very self-conscious; they say for example:[3]

---

[1] *Oedipe*, p. 68.　　　[2] *Oedipe*, II, p. 283.　　　[3] Ib., I, p. 255.

mais l'action de ce drame ne saurait s'engager sans que nous te fassions part d'une nouvelle très lamentable.

The spectacle of a group of people, who know everything that is going on, is too much. Perhaps it is less so for the French, who are notoriously cleverer than everyone else in the world.

(iv) GIRAUDOUX

A highly intelligent and humane man, an extremely skilful writer of elegant and frequently beautiful prose, Giraudoux was able to preserve something of the atmosphere of the old civilized Europe which the First World War blew away. This is not to say that he was deficient in feeling, simply that he had so many gifts that he would have died a gentleman, however great the catastrophe. He is a truly civilized writer, and he has dated, partly because Europe is no longer a civilized place.

Le spectacle est la seule forme d'éducation morale ou artistique d'une nation.

So said Giraudoux to his old school. The passage is quoted by Henri Godin in his introduction to *La Guerre de Troie n'aura pas Lieu*,[1] who is there concerned to show that Giraudoux believed that men's passions could be cooled by intellectualization, and that therefore his inclination was towards a philosophical drama.[2] He was inconsistent. He writes continually so that we do not really know whether he is serious or not, and wraps his meaning in contradictions, not all of which are demanded by the subtlety of his thought. He makes the actors say in *L'Impromptu de Paris*:[3]

JOUVET: Le mot "comprendre" n'existe pas au théâtre . . .

RENOIR: Le bonheur est que le vrai public ne comprend pas, il ressent . . .

BOGAR: Le théâtre n'est pas un théorème, mais un spectacle; pas une leçon, mais un filtre. C'est qu'il a moins à entrer dans votre esprit que dans votre imagination et dans vos sens . . .

Giraudoux certainly sympathized very strongly with this view, that the theatre was not a place for thinking. Clearly it is not,

[1] p. 41.   [2] Ib., p. 15.   [3] Sc. iii, p. 187.

if thinking is regarded as something separate from feeling. Clearly it is such a place if we realize that philosophical problems can only be discussed in terms of human experience, and that therefore the theatre is one of the few available media.

The last quotation gives a small example of the Idealist thought which bulks so largely in Giraudoux' writing. *"le vrai public"* is a phrase typical of such thinking. What does *"vrai"* mean? Not the majority. The majority do not go to the theatre at all. It presumably means the majority of those who do at the present time go to the theatre. But there seems little reason for setting them up as criteria for what should happen in the theatre except that they affect the box-office. It is a commonplace in Idealist thinking to find the notion "the real public", "the true Englishman" invoked as evidence in argument, because it is part of Idealist thinking that one can acquire an idea of such entities by intuition. If this is a wholly erroneous notion, then it is likely that it will have an adverse effect on a writer who holds it. Giraudoux is thoroughly Idealist in his thought, and this has definite effects on his drama. Sartre has gently ridiculed the way in which a Giraudoux character either is or is not, either is in love or is not. They never become anything, never grow except in sudden jerks.[1] A character is not as he is because he has stomach trouble, but has stomach trouble because he is of such a character. Sartre talks more in terms of the novels than of the plays, but examples can be given just as easily from the latter. Sartre, too, is confused about Giraudoux' derivations from the Greeks; he muddles Plato and Aristotle. But this does not affect the main point of the essay.

If there is a "true nature" of things which we can intuit there is also a "true nature" of ourselves. Everyone has an "essence" of their character, of which on occasions they may become aware, when they will be "their true selves". An "essence" is static, something that exists outside time. If that is the real basis of a person's nature, then the development of character is less important, because development is not of one's "true self". A dramatist who adheres to this notion might well turn out his best work in a totally artificial setting, some timeless world

[1] J.-P. Sartre, "Jean Giraudoux and the Philosophy of Aristotle", *Literary and Philosophical Essays*, translated by Annette Michelson.

where characters are, or are not, and do not change. This is the case with Giraudoux. A clearer vision of his thought comes over in *Ondine*[1] than anywhere else, and it has no less impact for being set in a fairy-tale world, because the effect of his thought is to make all his settings have something of a fairy-tale atmosphere. Granted that the setting of *Ondine* is artificial, yet there is a sense of man surrounded by forces which he does not understand and cannot control. It is a sense we all have at times, for all the advances of industrialization, and it is akin to the sense of some of the Greek tragedies. The region where human virtues count is such a tiny proportion of the universe. And the universe is merciless. One of the strongest expressions of this, because one associated with an expression of what looks like human sexual love, is in the scene between Ondine and Yseult:[2]

YSEULT: Ils oublieront. Ils changeront d'avis.

ONDINE: Oh! ne croyez pas cela. C'est tout petit dans l'univers, le milieu où l'on oublie où l'on change d'avis, où l'on pardonne, l'humanité comme vous dites ... Chez nous, c'est comme chez le fauve, comme chez les feuilles du frêne, comme chez les chenilles, il n'y a ni renoncement, ni pardon.

Giraudoux wrote that "Only God is without pity".[3] We feel that we are surrounded by eternal forces far greater than ourselves. Giraudoux connects their unchanging nature with his idea of the unchanging nature of the essences of things, and his drama is perhaps at its most powerful when he is free to make his own myth with which to express the idea.

The importance of Giraudoux in this discussion can best be seen by looking at his two plays on Greek myths which have something of the feeling of tragedy about them. *Electre*[4] inevitably has something of the quality of the Greek plays on the Orestes story, simply because it recalls the treatment by the Greek poets. *La Guerre de Troie n'aura pas Lieu*[5] has some of the quality of myth, because it is a play about war. To a

---

[1] 1939. [2] *Ondine*, II, xi, p. 311.

[3] *Amica America*. Quoted Donald Inskip, *Jean Giraudoux. The Making of a Dramatist*, p. 81.

[4] 1937. [5] 1935.

modern audience the Trojan war is not real; it has a fairy-tale quality about it. But the situation of war is so basic that it does not seem to matter so much what war the dramatist takes as his type of all war. If we see a play about people resisting an enemy or trying to prevent war starting we can easily see how the situation is parallel to our own resistance or attempts to preserve peace. Other political decisions are more complicated. It is harder to find the right myths for them. The tragic effect of *La Guerre de Troie n'aura pas Lieu* is due to its being about war, not especially to its use of a Greek story.

War is a subject highly suited to Giraudoux' philosophy. We are more prepared to hear of what he calls *"le Destin"* in this context. It does seem that sometimes a whole people becomes possessed by madness, and a force urges the separate evil thoughts of people together into an urge towards mass evil action. The heroes of *La Guerre de Troie n'aura pas Lieu* are moved along by *le Destin*, but it is easier for us to accept this in the context of war, since we do see that people are moved by something, even if we choose not to think of it in quite the way Giraudoux does.

Secondly, war is a suitable subject for him because it is easy to understand how men can become like *theoi* in war, pitiless forces that strike back automatically when struck. Giraudoux writes about special people, who have heroic qualities, unlike those of ordinary men, but he represents Hector in *La Guerre de Troie n'aura pas Lieu* as being turned into a *theos* in war. The best instance of this is his description of how he feels for his enemy – and then kills him:[1]

> on est tendre parce qu'on est impitoyable; ce doit être en effet la tendresse des dieux.

Otherwise the two sorts of people are distinct by nature. We should notice the way le Président talks of *"femmes à histoire"*.[2] Also in *Electre* there is the gardener's speech:[3]

> On réussit chez les rois les expériences qui ne réussissent jamais chez les humbles, la haine pure, la colère pure. C'est

---

[1] *La Guerre de Troie n'aura pas Lieu*, I, iii, p. 254.
[2] *Electre*, I, ii, pp. 15–16.   [3] Ib., Entr'acte, p. 61.

toujours de la pureté. C'est cela que c'est, la Tragédie, avec ses incestes, ses parricides: de la pureté, c'est-à-dire en somme de l'innocence.

This is something common to a considerable body of writing; it is the Romantic notion of the hero as a being apart, a substitute in a more democratic age for the way in which the heroes were always aristocrats in earlier writing. But at least the aristocrats governed. The Romantic hero is of a particular nature, and has no responsibilities except to himself. We find extreme examples of this in Anouilh, but it is in Cocteau and Giraudoux equally strongly, though not so blatantly. In Giraudoux, these people are under *le Destin*. It is a useful device for avoiding the general question of Determinism. He does not write about people who are not under *le Destin*, but his implication is that ordinary people are not.

These plays are the best way in which we can see Giraudoux' preoccupation with questions of political and moral decision and the artificial way in which he expresses them. They also provide sufficient examples of his skill as a writer, though examples of this could be taken from all the plays. Most of his poetry is verbal. On occasions he can produce a memorable use of plain language, as at the ending of the scene when Oiax has been insulting Andromaque, and through her Hector. Hector, to save Troy, endures all the insults.[1]

OIAX: *le giflant*. Voilà . . . Si Madame est ta femme, Madame peut être fière.
HECTOR: Je la connais . . . Elle est fière.

There are frequent delightful phrases such as the description by Paris of the kiss meant for Troilus, "ce baiser inédit".[2] But sometimes his language and his images run away with him. An example of the latter is to be found in the description of the hedgehogs and their Original Sin of crossing the road to make love.[3]

The action of *La Guerre de Troie n'aura pas Lieu* is the rape of Helen by Paris, which leads to the Trojan war. But the events

---

[1] *La Guerre de Troie*, II, ix, p. 308.
[2] Ib., II, ii, p. 285. [3] *Electre*, I, iii, pp. 22–25.

of the play are not the consequences of the rape and the interest is not on Paris as the representative of the Trojan crime. Paris' act is shown as a mad escapade, and the interest is on Hector's sane common sense, which tries to prevent the war, but is somehow overwhelmed. Finally, without really intending to, Hector kills the poet Demokos, who shouts out that Oiax has done it, and so starts the war, as it were by accident.

The Trojan war is used as an image of a war that just had to happen. Ulysse [1] says that it is a matter of *le Destin* having made two peoples complementary to one another, for a particular purpose, to destroy each other. Giraudoux is, of course, thinking of the French and Germans. The destruction can arise from an apparently trivial cause: [2] *"du fait que sec citoyens coupent méchamment les arbres"*. Ulysse does not want war,[3] "Mais je suis moins sûr de ses intentions à elle." Andromaque says:[4]

> Je ne sais pas si les dieux veulent quelque chose. Mais l'univers veut quelque chose.

Expressions such as these do reflect the atmosphere in a country waiting for war, and not knowing how to prevent it.

We get a little of the Greek double determination, though here it is rather that every now and then Giraudoux says that what he talks about in terms of gods and destiny really exists, though not quite in those terms. Cassandre accounts for her prophetic gifts:[5]

> Je ne vois rien, Andromaque. Je ne prévois rien. Je tiens seulement compte de deux bêtises, celle des hommes et celle des éléments.

A little later we find:[6]

ANDROMAQUE: Je ne sais pas ce qu'est le destin.
CASSANDRE: Je vais te le dire. C'est simplement la forme accélérée du temps. C'est épouvantable.

This should make us think about real war as well as that which we see on the stage. When we do, we may feel with Ulysse that

---

[1] *La Guerre de Troie n'aura pas Lieu*, II, xiii, p. 322–3.
[2] Ib., II, xiii, p. 324. [3] Ib., II, xiii, pp. 321. [4] Ib., II, viii, p. 303.
[5] Ib., I, i, p. 249. [6] Ib., I, i, p. 250.

destiny is malicious.[1] But in general we shall feel only a great pessimism. What can men do?

The point is quite definitely weakened by the supernatural apparatus that Giraudoux introduces, and in particular by the appearances of Iris.[2] This is put there for purely theatrical reasons; its ancestry is the successful nineteenth-century comedy, *La Belle Hélène*; it distracts us from the serious point Giraudoux is making.

Giraudoux does sometimes produce an image in the Aeschylean sense, to give us the point of the play in miniature. Here we have the ode to war,[3] when war is likened to the face of Helen. This sums up what he is saying, but the trivializing comedy of the medium weakens the point. The image is given to the ridiculous Demokos, but what Giraudoux is trying to say in general terms is surely that good poets make war like the face of Helen. We have only to think of the writers before the First World War who welcomed war as the opportunity for heroism.

All the characters are shown as trivial people except for Hector and Ulysse. Helen is a brainless woman, but she is someone who causes everyone to fight over her. Because we can see her as worthless, we feel greater sympathy for the Trojans. But however wonderful she was, to go to war for her would still be beastly. The impact of the play is weakened by trivializing Helen. If all the characters are trivial except for Hector and Ulysse the effect of their debate will cause the coughs to stop in the auditorium. If it is not possible to make an audience listen all the time, it is probably a good thing to make them listen hard for a short while. At this point we are made to think and feel, as we are during Hector's speech to the dead.[4] But that is not the case with all the play. We are asked to change our reactions so often that we never quite know what to think or feel. The final impact of the play is a long way from a matter of life and death.

The action of *Electre* is much as in the Sophocles play. What Egisthe and Clytemnestre do to Electre makes her into the sort

---

[1] *La Guerre de Troie n'aura pas Lieu*, II, xiii, pp. 322–5.
[2] Ib., II, xii, pp. 319–20.   [3] Ib., II, iv, p. 289.
[4] Ib., II, v, pp. 298–9.

of person who will prefer to destroy her city rather than forgo her opportunity for vengeance even for one day. But it is not shown like that. Because Giraudoux thinks in Idealist terms he thinks of Electre with a fixed character, not as developing. So he is able to make a play roughly like that of Sophocles but make her not know the truth about her father's murder. Electre is as she is, because that is how she is, not because of brooding over her situation. True they have treated her badly, and she had a traumatic experience when her mother dropped the young Oreste on the floor, but this is not advanced as reason for her present character. It is more that Giraudoux is saying that, given a character like Electre, if you tell her such a piece of news she will automatically act in this way, because that is her nature. Electre is then an abnormal character and the play ceases to be typical. There is no equivalent moment to the Sophocles urn speech, when we see what Electra might have become. And so the point of the play is not at all that of Sophocles, because Sophocles is concerned with showing how Clytemnestra and Aegisthus' acts recoil on them. He is concerned with a developing process. Giraudoux is showing someone who has a heroic view of life, and how she is sparked off to destroy. It is reasonable for Giraudoux to change the end as he does. The ultimate vindication of Orestes in the *Eumenides* has made people think that the killing of Clytemnestra was justified, to such an extent that they forget how horrible it is. Because of the literary effect of the tradition the matricide has lost its horrific quality. Giraudoux increases the destruction Electre does, in order to make sure that her horrific nature is fully apparent.

Superficially the play has considerable resemblances to the Euripides *Electra*, notably in the inclusion of Euripides' peasant husband of Electra, here made into the palace gardener. Both figures serve to provide a contrast to the loathsome royal family, being virtuous simple folk. But Euripides is making a protest against the attitude of mind that accepted the matricide as inevitable. In a modern context this particular protest is pointless, because the myth is not part of our history. Euripides is saying, This is what it was really like. Giraudoux, like Sophocles, is more concerned with thinking in terms of, "If x, then y."

It is about the terrible consequences of following *la justice*. It is Giraudoux attacking a manifestation of the Intuitionist ethics that usually accompany Idealism. It is a better play for the fact that it calls into question the author's philosophy. This is shown by the contrast of kingly, pure Electre and lying, compromising Clytemnestre and Egisthe. At the end Electre is more wrong, though Clytemnestre has a mean motive for saying to her children when they press her for the truth about her lover:[1]

> ... veillez à vos actes. Tout le mal du monde est venu de ce que les soi-disant purs ont voulu déterrer les secrets et les ont mis en plein soleil.

The weakness is that we do not know clearly what Electre stands for. At one time it may have been possible to say that you were defending Truth, and immediately you were thought a hero. Now we ask what is meant by saying you are defending truth. An abstract noun is no longer a possible battle cry.

It is about the contrast between the kingly person, the person of absolutes, and the man of compromise, Egisthe. Although he lacks "*huile sainte*"[2] he is the man best suited to rule, because he will serve the city best. Giraudoux' Idealist thought again leads to confusion. Egisthe is almost a different person, once "the king has declared himself in him".[3] Because of this we do not know whether he is genuinely repentant for what he has done, or not. The change in him is absolute; this is necessary if he is to represent the city which Electre will destroy. It is partly true to say that Giraudoux would not worry too much if his repentance is genuine. The important thing is the contrast between the benefit to the city from his command, in contrast with the truth on which Electre insists.

The Mendiant fulfils some of the function of the Greek chorus. He has a connexion with the beggars of the city, the people who will suffer for what Electre does, and he also conveys a sense of some power supervising the action. At the beginning they honour him, since he "may be Jupiter".[4] But as we would expect with Giraudoux, the religious implications, and the nature of the powers behind the action, are kept obscure.

---

[1] *Electre*, II, iv. p. 74. [2] Ib., II, vii, p. 90.
[3] Ib., II, vii, pp. 88–90. [4] Ib., I, iii, p. 19.

There is constant reference to the Aeschylean image of light, though it is used with considerably less precision. We should especially compare the remarks made over the sleeping Oreste and Electre with the words with which the play ends. It is "*l'aurore*", says the Mendiant. The last line is not ironical, but more with the effect of the Aeschylus description of the dawn breaking over the shipwrecks. Light shows some terrible things. The best image is that of the bird, which Agathe sees first in Act I, vi, and is eventually seen to fly lower in II, viii, when the Mendiant points out that it is a vulture. This image conveys most of the point of the play, tersely and yet with reverberance. It is the better for being something real, whose meaning the characters in the play need not know.

Apart from the Mendiant, the catalyst in the action is Agathe. She is a character in the tradition of boulevard comedy, and her main function is to provide amusement irrelevant to the main point of the play. But it is chiefly through her that Electre intuits the truth. It is appropriate that she should see the bird first. Both Egisthe and Electre develop in jerks, in the same way that the Eumenides are at one moment one age, at another five years older. Egisthe becomes a totally different person once he is king,[1] and Electre suddenly "gets the answer".[2] We do not need a feeling of double determination, because the whole atmosphere is artificial, but we do get an impression of actions being dictated by forces we never see, that have never been mentioned. But it is impossible to press Giraudoux to be too explicit. The ambiguities are summed up in the gardener's entr'acte speech. He says that if he called on God to send storms of tenderness God would reply that the secret of the world was "*Joie et amour*". Further, he continues, it is useless for a gardener to call for such storms:[3]

> On sent tellement qu'en ce moment, et hier, et demain, et toujours, ils sont tous là-haut, autant qu'ils sont, et même s'il n'y en a qu'un, et même si cet un est absent, prêts à crier joie et amour.

Tragedy is a thing of joy, because it implies the affirmation of what it appears to deny. The ambiguities of Giraudoux'

[1] *Electre*, II, vii, p. 91.　[2] Ib., II, vii, p. 92.　[3] Ib., Entr'acte, p. 62.

thought make it hard to grasp exactly what he is affirming, but the warmth of his heart makes us confident that he is affirming something, and in this play he may be said to have succeeded in writing a tragedy after the Greek model, in so far as it is possible to do so, omitting all that part of tragedy without which Greek tragedy would be nothing.

(v) CONCLUSION

The effect of all these plays in the theatre confirms that the Greek tragedies on which they are based have lost none of their impact. Nothing can make the blinding of Oedipus anything but horrifying. But there is an unreal atmosphere about these modern versions. They are based on what is no longer thought of as history, they do not seriously affect our attitudes to contemporary politics, or our own religion. The writers I have talked about have served a very useful purpose in helping to illuminate our understanding of Greek tragedy. Only by trying to transfer it to a modern context can we see what is essential and what incidental. But as we might expect, it is not necessarily work which copies its model most exactly in form that will be seen to achieve an effect most nearly analogous.

CHAPTER TWELVE

ANOUILH

Anouilh is chiefly important as a great theatrical craftsman. I find his frothy comedy pieces to be his best; but he has developed a style which makes it easier for tragedy to be shown on the contemporary stage, largely by developing the notion of theatrical artificiality which he took over from the writers discussed in the last chapter. He is not a philosophical, but a highly instinctive writer. He does reflect some of the philosophical ideas current in France at the time of his writing; but his philosophy expresses itself more in terms of mood and temperament than in ideas. He does not base his writing on a system like Giraudoux, and is therefore more immediately congenial to a generation which does not tolerate philosophical systems, even in philosophy.

His outlook on life is one of rebellion, the instinctive feeling of revolt that we must all experience confronted with much of contemporary industrial life. Certain of his plays, the *pièces noires*, are sometimes called tragedies of sensitive people crushed by insensitive surroundings. But these are not tragedies in the sense I have been using the word. The characters concerned are abnormal, the play involves no wider issues; there is no religious, political, or social significance. There is nothing that the audience is asked to do as a result of seeing them.

He has, however, written plays based on Greek myth, and has also written two plays on Christian myth, though without quite realizing what he was doing. These five plays gain in strength by embodying a myth, and it is worth seeing how they do so. For if the notion of myth means anything at all, then clearly the strength of the myth will be independent to a certain extent of what the dramatist does to it, and even of his awareness of its being a myth. Tragedy like that of the Greeks could well develop out of a need felt by writer and audience to learn the nature of the society out of which modern Europe grew, in order to understand modern Europe better. This would involve a need to question the Christian attitude to history and society, as shown in the development of Christian Europe up to the time when the Church broke up. To discover its nature is equally incumbent on Christian and non-Christian, because one of the reasons for deciding on our religion will be that we discover that it provides a better interpretation of particular events in history.

Anouilh, however, mainly uses these plays of myth, as he does his plays in a modern setting, to put over his own idiosyncratic view of life, rather than trying to see what are the issues of the particular crises he describes, and then putting them over in universal terms. All his plays tend to coalesce. They are shouts of defiance at society; they couldn't involve political decisions, since all his heroes are politically irresponsible. Tragedy for Anouilh is to shout at the top of your voice when hope is lost.[1]

His philosophy can best be shown by seeing the characteristics his heroes have in common. It is almost true to say that he never has an old hero; at any rate they are all "spiritual adolescents" as Marsh describes them.[2] They are existentialist in the way in which existentialism is an extension of Romantic self-centredness. They are contemptuous of life, especially of any intellectual activity, since intellectual activity inevitably involves compromise. They all say "no" to life, and this word becomes a mark of their nature. Humanity is divided into "yes" and "no" sayers. To say "no" is to perform an "absurd" act, and in Anouilh the existentialist absurd act is much the same as Gide's "*acte gratuit*". Antigone says "no" to Créon, Jeanne says "no" to her judges, so that the Inquisitor can say that the real evil is not the Devil, but man who "will say 'no' without lowering his eyes".[3] Becket tells Henry at the climax

[1] *Antigone*, p. 161.
[2] Edward Owen Marsh, *Jean Anouilh*, p. 196.
[3] *L'Alouette*, p. 177.

of their last meeting that he has only to say "no"; he needn't be logical, simply act, "absurdly", to the end. Those who act absurdly are described as *"orgueilleux"*, Antigone,[1] Médée,[2] Orphée,[3] Jeanne.[4] They have rejected *"l'espoir"* and *"le bonheur"*. It is the mention of the word *"bonheur"* which rouses Antigone,[5] and *"heureuse"* Jeanne,[6] and Orphée[7] to resist after they had decided to submit. The conception is so firmly embedded in Anouilh's writing that he can even joke about it. M. Henri, the figure of Death, embodying on stage the act of saying *"non"*, says that he "really likes *le bonheur"*.[8]

There are strong physical resemblances between the representatives of the two types. The heroes are usually girls, who want to be boys,[9] whose relationship with their lover is that of comrade.[10] They are not conventionally beautiful, though fascinating in an odd way, like Antigone;[11] Eurydice is clearly not conventionally attractive as her mother was;[12] her appeal is different. They are thin and pale and usually dark. They are either virgins or utterly promiscuous, but detached in their promiscuity, which characteristic is also true of Becket, the one male hero in the group. They love childhood and wish to return to its simplicities. Both Antigone[13] and Médée[14] have scenes of recollection with their nurses, and Jeanne's mother is a very similar character.[15] Those who say *"oui"* are represented as tired; both Créons, in *Médée*[16] and *Antigone*[17] are tired; so is Cauchon.[18] There is a recurring image. Both Médée's nurse[19] and Créon in *Antigone*[20] think of the good things in life as resting in the sun on a bench. They accept the indignity of being happy. Anouilh presents two races of men, and it is appropriate that their differences should be summed by M. Henri.[21]

[1] *Antigone*, p. 170.
[2] *Médée*, p. 382.
[3] *Eurydice*, IV, p. 528.
[4] *L'Alouette*, p. 181.
[5] *Antigone*, p. 186.
[6] *L'Alouette*, p. 210.
[7] *Eurydice*, III, p. 497.
[8] Ib., II, p. 468.
[9] *Antigone*, p. 144 and *L'Alouette*.
[10] *Médée*, pp. 384–87 and *Eurydice*, II, pp. 461–62.
[11] *Antigone*, pp. 131–32.
[12] *Eurydice*, I, pp. 418–19.
[13] *Antigone*, pp. 145–49.
[14] *Médée*, pp. 355–67.
[15] *L'Alouette*, pp. 43–50.
[16] *Médée*, pp. 368–74.
[17] *Antigone*, p. 132.
[18] *L'Alouette*, p. 185.
[19] *Médée*, p. 366.
[20] *Antigone*, p. 186.
[21] *Eurydice*, II, p. 470.

Mon cher, il y a deux races d'êtres. Une race nombreuse, féconde, heureuse, une grosse pâte à pétrir, qui mange son saucisson, fait ses enfants, pousse ses outils, compte ses sous, bon an mal an, malgré les épidémies et les guerres, jusqu'à la limite d'âge; des gens pour vivre, des gens pour tous les jours, des gens qu'on n'imagine pas morts. Et puis il y a les autres, les nobles, les héros. Ceux qu'on imagine très bien étendus, pâles, un trou rouge dans la tête, une minute triomphants avec une garde d'honneur ou entre deux gendarmes selon: le gratin.

This is what all Anouilh's plays are really about, saying *"oui"* or saying *"non"*. All his myths ultimately coalesce into this single question, and in every situation it is right to say *"non"*.

The delights of Anouilh's theatrical technique, and the simplicity of his dialogue, which sometimes achieves moments of an almost poetic intensity, have given him a deserved reputation. If *L'Alouette* gives more of the impression of being a tragedy than Shaw's *St Joan* it is because the whole action is staged within the trial of Jeanne. In a trial some facts about a man become less important, some immensely more so. A capital trial is an obvious occasion in which we will be asked to look at life from the viewpoint of death. Arthur Miller has remarked on the similarity of tragedy and a trial.[1] *L'Alouette* contains one of the finest moments that a prose drama has ever produced, when Jeanne and La Hire recall their early morning rides together, danger making sight and smell more acute.[2] It would be intolerable if it was actual experience, since actual danger blots out the enjoyment of the sensations; but it gives a unique edge to the sensations remembered, and this Anouilh has captured superbly. A great moment of dialogue, again about as good as prose can be, is when Antigone says that she would have liked to be Hémon's wife:[3]

Et je voulais te dire que j'aurais été très fière d'être ta femme, ta vraie femme, sur qui tu aurais posé ta main, le soir, en t'asseyant, sans penser, comme sur une chose bien à toi.

[1] Arthur Miller, *Collected Plays*, Introduction, p. 6.
[2] *L'Alouette*, pp. 162–71.   [3] *Antigone*, p. 153.

He can produce excellent and highly theatrical entertainment as in the scene between the mother of Eurydice and Vincent,[1] when they make love, partly in the dialogue of Musset, whom they have acted so often, a scene which has the same effect as the entire course of *La Répétition*. But Anouilh does use images without caring what their point is. There is no need for the scene where the Dauphin teaches Jeanne cards;[2] all that is said in it has been already shown; but the scene is effective in its own right. But why does Death not drink cognac?[3] The action of M. Henri in refusing to drink acquires a resonance which is irrelevant. Sometimes, too, Anouilh is obscure. Neither on stage nor in the text do I see the point of the little monk in *Becket*. As theatre poet Anouilh has considerable skill; he seems to lack the understanding to use his poetry to best advantage.

The action of *Antigone*[4] is that of the Sophocles play, though there is no forgetting of Antigone herself. The end comes much more quickly after she has gone, and there is no Teiresias. Créon is central. Sophocles' Antigone is inarticulate, but there is no doubt that her action is in keeping with the will of heaven, because of the treatment of the body, the impact of the chorus, especially in the ode on man,[5] and the words of Teiresias. Without these, the effect of the play is different. Antigone in Anouilh's play just resists, "absurdly". This is why the play was more of a success in Occupied France. After the Liberation Mme Dussane said:[6]

> It was now necessary to sympathise with Antigone by an intellectual effort, whereas formerly one had been in a conspiracy with it.

War and Anouilh are both great simplifiers. Now there is a danger that we shall see this as another play about an Anouilh hero who wants to die. Créon is right when he says that Polynice was only a pretext.[7]

This was why Lewis Galantière did not directly translate the play for its first production in English,[8] but adapted it. His

---

[1] *Eurydice*, I, pp. 409–11. [2] *L'Alouette*, pp. 111 ff.
[3] *Eurydice*, II, p. 468. [4] 1942.
[5] *Antigone*, 332–75. [6] Hobson, *French Theatre of Today*, p. 45.
[7] *Antigone*, p. 191. [8] New York, 1946.

most important change occurs in the great scene between
Antigone and Créon. When Créon has described the travesties
of the burial ritual as practised by the priests Antigone admits
that the whole thing is *"absurde"*. Why did she do it? For those
who do believe? No. *"Pour personne. Pour moi."* [1] This famous
climax has been changed. She says instead, "No, Créon. There
is God and there are His priests. And they are not the same
thing." [2] Antigone becomes a martyr, and the play is half
turned into a Christian one, by extending the chorus' part. It
has not been done well, or completely. Galantière has thought
it right to water the character of Antigone down, to make her
less "irritating", and so has cut out her beautiful "Comprendre . . ." speech, [3] about the black water. This is not in
keeping with the spirit of Greek tragedy. Euripides in particular, having shown that a character is right, will go out of his
way to show that apart from the rightness of the action, the
person has nothing necessarily to commend him. The adaptation also makes Créon more of a villain. At one point he is
described as "loving being king". [4] In the original he "gets on
with the job". [5] The point of the play is that Créon is wrong,
not that he is a bad man; by making him a bad man, the point
is weakened. Nor has Galantière taken trouble to turn the play
properly into a Christian one; he never makes up his mind
about the right emphasis to give to the views about immortality. It is extremely surprising that Anouilh should still allow
his adaptation to be in print, even though he might have con-
sented to it at first, as the only way of getting his play produced
in English. The fact that he does allow something which has
been changed enough to make a completely different point is a
very serious charge against his artistic integrity.

The play as he wrote it is about his idea of the hero, his idea
of kingship. Antigone at the end has a kingdom which Créon
cannot enter. [6] Créon thinks of kingship as the job of ruling. [7]
The two conceptions cannot be reconciled. But it is the fairest
statement of Anouilh's philosophy. Créon once was a man who

[1] *Antigone*, pp. 173–74.
[2] Samuel French ed., p. 47.
[3] *Antigone*, pp. 141–42.
[4] Samuel French ed, p. 15.
[5] *Antigone*, p. 132.
[6] Ib., pp. 179 and 187.
[7] Ib., pp. 171 and 177.

said *"non"* and decided to say *"oui"* and accept responsibility. Here the two ways of life are represented as the result of choice, not an inevitable birthright. Créon is the most sympathetic of all Anouilh's sayers of *"oui"*.

This play expresses best his ritual view of the theatre, which we see in the opening speech of the chorus, and the feeling "this is so" that we get from Greek tragedy here finds its happiest expression in the modern French *nécessité littéraire*. These characters will act their roles to the end. The use of the artist-figure chorus gives Anouilh a chance to give his views on tragedy.[1] We should notice how, like Giraudoux, he believes it starts from something tiny, a moment's glance at a passing girl.[2]

Much of the play is taken up with showing the special nature of Antigone, who is contrasted with Ismène and Hémon, neither of whom understand her, and who is seen to have all the characteristics of the Anouilh heroine in her scenes with the nurse, to love dawn, her childhood, and her dog. Much of the main scene between her and Créon is equally spent in showing what sort of people they are. This makes for interesting character study, but is irrelevant to any new tragedy based on Antigone, which is to make the same point in a new context as Sophocles does for his own context. For clearly the myth is one of situation. Whatever sort of man Créon is, he has made a mistake. Any natural girl would do that for her brother unless she is frightened. Of all Sophocles' plays the *Antigone* is the one which touches our most basic instincts. More than any other it is about what is natural and unnatural. Anouilh has found the story the best myth for putting over his peculiar view of life, his unusual heroine. The plays appear so similar but are worlds apart. The distance between them is the distance between a knowing individual in white tie and tails talking about drama and a group of citizens singing about man.

The action of *Médée*[3] is once again apparently similar to its Greek model, but in final impact very different, because Médée is another Anouilh heroine. It is a less successful play, because she is frankly immoral, she can do wicked deeds and feel no remorse. The adjective *"noir"* applied to all the heroines now

[1] *Antigone*, pp. 160–61.   [2] Ib., p. 160.   [3] 1946.

takes on moral significance. The people who say *"oui"* are called:[1]

> Race d'Abel, race des justes, race des riches, comme vous parlez tranquillement.

Although our sympathies have been detached from her at the beginning, for example by her treatment of the nurse, whom she will leave in a hole at the side of the road if need be,[2] we must become involved with her point of view if the play is to take effect. We need never do this with Euripides' Medea, who is fiend from start to finish.

Although Anouilh's Antigone dies for no principle, we cannot help feeling that her death has value as an act. Its value is heightened by the ironic ending, in which we see the guards left in possession of the stage at their card game. We feel that the death has value, all the more because no one cares. The ironic ending of *Médée*, in which guard and nurse are left chatting as the curtain falls, is intended to distance our sympathies from Médée. But it does not have the impact of the earlier play, because here the death involves no issues. The irony has no strength because there is nothing to be ironical about. The death is horrific or merely theatrical, according to the amount of our involvement with her. It is interesting to see that this is the most naturalistic of the Anouilh plays which I discuss here. Unless we are made to feel that the fire with which the play ends is a real fire, we shall be disappointed. The end of *L'Alouette* gives us plenty to think about. There is no need to do more than suggest the fire.

There is a moment unique to Anouilh in which it is suggested that the character who does and suffers terrible things is not free.[3] Médée soliloquizes, suggesting that she is the victim of circumstance. It is a soliloquy and we are bound to take it as reflecting more than her belief. Anouilh probably put this in, to lessen our horror at Médée's action. We should feel she is not really responsible. This is a direct consequence of trying to write something akin to tragedy, but making the audience involve itself in the character who performs the terrible actions of tragedy, instead of watching the character through the eyes

[1] *Médée*, p. 389.   [2] Ib., p. 358.   [3] Ib., p. 396.

of a chorus of ordinary people. The suggestion that the characters are victims of fate is necessary to stop the audience being too horrified. The result of this technique is that intellectually we are not horrified at all. The technique of the Greek poets means that we can never cease to be horrified, even if we squirm less in the theatre.

Eurydice[1] has much less resemblance to a tragedy. It is a romance. The plot is much the same as that of some of his plays in a modern setting, and what resemblance the story bears to the Greek original concerns the fairy-tale elements, which were never used in any Greek tragedy, since tragedy was incompatible with fairy-tale.

But Anouilh even abuses the fairy-tale convention. Orpheus through his gift of song wins Eurydice, provided that he observes the conditions imposed. Anouilh's Orpheus does not observe the conditions, and wins his Eurydice all the same. Death loses its seriousness by being turned into a happy-ever-after land, and the impact of the ending is sentimental because it offends our sense of justice. The ethics of fairy land are strict; logical according to the logic of fairies.

The story is primarily an image of love, and this is what Anouilh makes his play about. Eurydice is said to love Orphée in a unique way. But she has had other lovers, and we can see the effect Dulac has on Eurydice. Now it is interesting to explore the notion of whether Eurydice can be pure in spite of what she has done, and it might be interesting to attack the question of whether she could be right to sleep with Dulac to save the little stage manager,[2] though Anouilh does not deal with that question, by making out that she was definitely wrong to do so. These problems are worth discussion, but in a different play. Only if the love of Orphée and Eurydice is total could we excuse their conduct towards everyone else. It is clearly meant to be, but there is the scene when after protestations of passion as extravagant as those we have been laughing at when uttered by Vincent and the mother,[3] Eurydice says that she has had lovers, and Orphée takes it quite calmly.[4] Anouilh thinks of love as completely possessive, demanding, and consuming

[1] 1941. [2] *Eurydice*, III, pp. 500 ff.
[3] Ib., I, pp. 414 ff. [4] Ib., I, pp. 423 ff.

How could a lover of this kind tolerate his woman having had other lovers?

Their love is inadequately portrayed, and as a result they appear as monsters. Orphée's father is shown as despicable, but it is done contemptuously. When Orphée leaves for his "rendezvous with death" the father's snores increase in volume.[1] Eurydice starts to *tutoyer* Orphée as soon as she has heard of Matthias' suicide because of her.[2] With this, Anouilh makes a subtly horrible point. We are asked to admire the hero and heroine, the ones who say "*non*", but there is no sympathy in the portrayal of those who say "*oui*". Orphée's father and Eurydice's mother have a very different effect from Créon in *Antigone*.

There is a toughness about a genuine fairy tale that is totally missing from this play. The best example of it is Orphée's music. It was a mistake to make him a violinist. We cannot imagine him playing anything much better than Saint-Saëns. To move death would require the Bach Chaconne at least. It would be different with a singer; an untrained singer can produce enormous effect on an audience through *hwyl*. A violinist needs technique. This may seem a trivial accusation, but it affords substance to the criticism that Anouilh's imagination is too facile, that he is a "man of the theatre" in the pejorative sense of that term. He has not bothered to think what being a musician like that would mean; he makes it all too easy, as he makes love too easy, and death trivial. *Eurydice* is very far from possessing the realness of tragedy. It is not as real as the fairy tales it imitates.

The action of the myth of St Joan is Joan's yielding to the persuasion of the saints she hears; she goes to the Dauphin and persuades him to fight the English. This leads to her commanding the battles herself, and so to her eventual capture and burning. It is an action like that of the *Heracles*, a catastrophe set in motion by a good action, but it is not quite the same, because the good action achieves the results at which it was aimed. With or without the Christian doctrine of the Resurrection of the body, the story of Joan of Arc is one of triumph, so long as we are not too closely involved in her personal fate.

[1] *Eurydice*, IV, p. 535. [2] Ib., I, p. 440.

This is the action in Shaw's *St Joan*, but the play is not organized as a poetic development in which one act follows another as direct consequence. The issues of the play are discussed; they are not part of a poetic development, because there is no poetic development. The structure of *L'Alouette*[1] is much tighter; there is less change of mood; and there are several scenes which are not necessary to the structure,[2] it is more the case that the death of Jeanne is seen to be the natural consequence of all that has gone before.

But the lines of the story are all taken from Shaw, though it is likely that Anouilh was also influenced by *Joan of Lorraine*, a play by Maxwell Anderson.[3] The Inquisitor is made important, though he was not so in historical fact, so as to emphasize the basic conflict of individual against institution. Both have the joyous ending. There are incidentals in common, the remark that God fights on both sides, the reasons given for Joan dressing as a man, the sudden showing of the executioner in the middle of the trial, the remark of Charles that he does less harm than an earnest Republican. Anouilh's developments are in the direction of creating greater pathos, more sympathy for Jeanne's plight.

The issue of the myth in Christian terms is the paradox that sometimes the will of God will seem to flout the law of God, the conflict between the demands of the ritual through which the Holy Spirit best comes and demands of the Holy Spirit acting direct upon an individual. The story of St Joan is that of someone led by God to flout the natural order of things which was laid down by God; it shows us that Christianity must be both Catholic and Protestant at the same time. The point of the story for an anti-Christian writer would lie in examining the phenomenon of spiritual power for which it is incumbent on him to give an explanation.

The issues presented by Anouilh are those of the Christian myth. But Anouilh avoids presenting them with any force. He lets his interest in the character of the Inquisitor run away with him. The Inquisitor represents the anti-humanist side of Christianity, Ladvenu the humanist. The story of Joan involves this conflict. The conflict is broached:[4]

[1] 1953.   [2] Cf. p. 282.   [3] 1947.   [4] *L'Alouette*, p. 154.

L'INQUISITEUR: Et qui aime l'homme, n'aime pas Dieu.
LADVENU (*doucement*): Il a voulu se faire homme, pourtant . . .

But then the Inquisitor becomes the victim of personal emotion, and the point is slurred over. The person of the Inquisitor is uninteresting in this situation; what is interesting is his office. In the same way we are made to feel sympathy with Cauchon as a person, not to see what right he had on his side. Again, when we are beginning to realize how dangerous Jeanne is, Anouilh avoids making us face this issue. He introduces the pathetic interlude, when we hear why she wears male clothes in prison. While we feel sorry for her, and laugh at Warwick's inability to control English lust, we lose the point of the play, the conflict between rationalist and authoritarian Christianity, expressed by the accusation that Jeanne does not believe in miracles and her counter that all life is one continual miracle.[1]

There is some highly effective use made of the artificial theatrical convention. Jeanne chases her brother and bumps into Beaudricourt[2] thus shortening the action and avoiding the need for transitions. There is an example of the convention protesting against itself, similar to the chorus' interjection of protest against Créon in *Antigone*,[3] when Ladvenu protests against the beating of Jeanne by her father and is told by Cauchon that they can do nothing, since they are not yet in the play.[4] There is an image which a writer in a more fully poetic convention might have put to greater use. Warwick tells Cauchon that he loves animals and yet he hunts them.[5] Jeanne and La Hire have much the same attitude to the *godons*.[6] It is natural to destroy what one loves, and sometimes it may be right. And perhaps this might apply to the Church destroying Jeanne.

Warwick provides an effective chorus, by the nature of his detachment as unbeliever and Englishman. He provides ironic counterpoint by denying the miraculous nature of Jeanne's success. Only because it was success, at his expense, he talks of *l'impondérable*.[7] Cauchon is like Créon; he has said "*oui*", and

---

[1] *L'Alouette*, p. 142.   [2] Ib., p. 52.
[3] *Antigone*, p. 191.   [4] *L'Alouette*, p. 41.
[5] Ib., p. 133.   [6] Ib., pp. 169–70.   [7] Ib., p. 132.

is tired; but he is drawn sympathetically. Jeanne is another Anouilh heroine, very similar to all the others. The play is about saying *"oui"* or *"non"*, but the nature of the myth has meant that Anouilh has not been able to avoid saying something a bit more than that. The strength of the myth gives the details of the play strength, but we are finally left dissatisfied. It is a brilliant device to make the ridiculous Beaudricourt order the play to end with the Coronation, and ending like this gets all the effect of Shaw's epilogue with far greater economy. But the text ends with Anouilh's stage direction:

> Le rideau tombe lentement sur cette belle image de livre de prix . . .

If that is all that he thought of this story, then this discussion has been so much waste paper.

The myth of St Thomas à Becket is the story of the consequences of Henry's decision to make his Chancellor Archbishop in order to have control over both Church and State. The issues involved are those of the conflict of Church and State, typified by the conflict as to who should be supreme, king or pope. Anouilh is not concerned to make a play on these lines. It is not chance that *L'Alouette* ideally is played without interval, as one action, while *Becket*[1] is in four acts. The development of the play is not the development of an action's consequences. The events are held together because they follow one another in time. There is no central action as in Greek tragedy. There is much less significance in the telling of the story by flash-back than there is in fitting the events of *L'Alouette* into Jeanne's trial.

The play is not about the central issue of the story, because Henry is made a pathetic figure, incapable of an original idea of his own, grabbing Church money because he is hard up. This is untrue historically, and makes the whole play smaller.

Becket's death is shown as pointless, by the parody of the Church. It is in a sense an anti-Christian play. But it has no edge. There is no point in attacking the Medieval Church by showing two Renaissance prelates[2] who have read Machiavelli

[1] 1959. [2] *Becket*, III, pp. 153–59.

290

When Becket comes to see that his violent austerity was wrong[1] it is difficult to see what all the fuss is about. Why should the "honour of God" and that of the king not become one?

It is clearly not a study in sainthood, or if it was intended to be, it is a very bad one, with a badness comparable to the badness of *Eurydice* as a study of either love or musicianship. Presumably Anouilh wants to show that Becket is not a saint, or that sainthood is a meaningless concept, but he has not taken the trouble to find out a few basic things about the concept as understood by those who find it useful. He makes Becket say that he is not worthy of grace[2] and is therefore not touched by it; so one would imagine that this is to indicate that Becket is to be damned, since a man who offers himself as martyr without being touched by grace will be damned if anyone is. But in fact this remark has no significance of this kind. It is that Anouilh hasn't bothered even to read a book which would tell him that ecclesiastics would not talk about grace like that. And this also explains his parody of a robing scene.[3] It is clearly not meant to be funny; it is just that he hasn't bothered to find out the attitude to priesthood which he is presumably attacking; priests do not hold conversations while robing, or when robed. If the play is intended as anti-Catholic it clearly loses its force by its lack of comprehension of Catholic dogma, in sharp contrast to Brecht's *Galileo*, for example, where Brecht has taken trouble to understand the force he is attacking.

Anouilh says that it is the story of two men who couldn't understand each other. There is no suggestion that we are going to learn how to understand history, because the two men are to all intents and purposes invented characters. It never appears conceivable that Henry should understand Becket, because the latter is presented as immeasurably superior in every way. The only interest lies in the pathetic study of the helpless Henry, though Anouilh has made Becket's conversion psychologically plausible. The nature of the play is well shown by the end. Here Anouilh needs no stage direction; the end is ambivalent in itself. We can see the end as a triumph for Henry: a brief flogging, and then control of the Church. Or we can see it as the apparent eclipse of the saint, but with the knowledge

[1] *Becket*, III, pp. 160–62. [2] Ib., IV, p. 179. [3] Ib., IV, pp. 202–4.

of his ultimate triumph. But we do not, because we have ceased to think in these terms at all. Anouilh has said in a programme note to the play that he is a man of the theatre, and therefore should not be taken seriously.

Becket seems to me to be a very clever, very bad play indeed. It is bad in the same way that some virtuosi's performances of Bach are bad, because it turns into a display piece something which was not achieved without cost. Henry and Thomas were people who honestly tried each in their own way to achieve something. I do not know what artistic responsibility means if it does not mean that one should try when writing about real people to understand what they were really trying to do. That will mean that a writer will have to take the trouble to make up his mind where he stands on such issues. In the case of the story of Becket he will have to decide to take up one of four attitudes, or not write. He will have to look at the story from a Christian viewpoint, or an anti-Christian viewpoint, or he will have to say that he honestly suspends judgement, or that it does not matter one way or the other. What he will not have to do is haver between all four viewpoints. A sense of responsibility towards the myth he uses is not often thought a very important aspect of the criticism of a contemporary writer. As far as we can see, it was the most important aspect of the criticism of the Greek tragic poets. Few will deny that there is a tension and a sense of moral urgency in Greek tragedy that is lacking in the modern theatre. Could the two facts not be connected?

CHAPTER THIRTEEN

SARTRE

(i) INTRODUCTORY

"The theatre's true battlefield is that of tragedy – drama which embodies a genuine myth."[1] This is what Sartre has said recently. Before he has been reluctant to use the word "tragedy" because it conjures up the idea of the seventeenth-century French theatre. But he said that we should return to a theatre of "Situation"[2] in 1946, and meant by that a kind of drama which involved issues, and illuminated people's lives rather than stimulating their emotions, or merely entertaining them.

He has said that literature, and especially drama, should concern itself with life, and has flung himself into politics, though not necessarily with success. He has tried to make a drama which should be about philosophy and politics, and may have realized more or less, though he has not expressed it explicitly, that some things just cannot be said at all, unless there is a theatre of this kind in which to say them; for they cannot be said in any other medium.

By this I mean that he has an idea of an "engaged" theatre, and he has a religion which involves a total commitment to experience. Whether his idea of theatre is adequate, or his religion adequate, is another matter. But such an idea of the theatre, and such a religion, are necessary conditions before anything like Greek tragedy can be written.

Aware that the theatre cannot compete with film in naturalism, he has said it must compete by cultivating ritual qualities.[3]

---

[1] "Sartre talks to Tynan", *Observer*, 18 June 1961.
[2] "Forgers of Myths", *Theatre Arts*, June 1946, pp. 324–35.
[3] Ib., p. 332.

Its greatness derives from its social and, in a certain sense, religious functions: it must remain a rite;

This is the third necessary condition for a modern drama in any way akin to Greek tragedy, a religious attitude to the theatre.

Sartre has not defined his use of the concept "myth", and his religion involves denying the external application of most of the terms usually involved in religious discussion, so that it is difficult to see exactly what he means; since Sartre does not define his terms, it is tempting to think that he has not always quite worked out their significance in the unique context that they have in his unique philosophy.

I have expressed my attitude to Sartre as a philosopher, and what is true of his philosophy seems to be true of all aspects of his thought. In philosophy he has turned other philosophers' attention to the important questions, has reorientated inquiries which looked as if they had lost any general sense of direction. But what he himself has said is full of inconsistencies. His logical disciplines are not rigorous enough. In religion he has drawn attention to some aspects of religious experience which have been recently neglected, but he has not been able to formulate his atheist religion without using terms like "transcendent" which have resonance, but no application in an atheist metaphysic. In the theatre he enjoys a ritual which derives from an attitude of mind he believes we have outgrown. My own feeling is that Sartre has made an enormously important contribution to that complex of activity which is necessary before tragedy can be written, but that he is important even if we do not read his philosophy, assimilate his religion or his attitude to politics, or even think his plays are good.

Sartre's contribution to religious thought can be most briefly understood, first, by thinking of him as the founder of a new atheist religion, and secondly, as drawing attention to certain features of Christian and other religious experience by inventing terms for experience which many people no longer use Christian terms to describe. Much of what he says is derived from other people; it is more that Sartre has acquired the status of prophet, and it saves time to discuss the ideas as if they were all his own. In his first capacity he cannot yet be judged adequately. It is too early to see whether he can make any real effect on atheist thought and channel it into something with explicit formulations of belief, and rationalized morals based on that belief. I quote two passages, however, to show his dangerous use of metaphors from other religions. This is highly misleading atheism. He ends *Existentialism and Humanism*[1] by saying of Man:

> It is by pursuing transcendent aims that he himself is able to exist.

He ends *Being and Nothingness*:[2]

> Man makes himself man in order to be God, and selfness considered from this point of view can appear to be an egoism; but precisely because there is no common measure between human reality and the self-cause which it wants to be, one could just as well say that man loses himself in order that the self-cause may exist.

All these terms seem to be highly misleading, and far harder thought needs to go into explaining them. The obvious concrete sense of the last sentence is that it is a paraphrase of the words of Christ, "He that loseth his life shall find it." Sartre has not rid himself of Christian terminology. He is a useful writer for Christians, since he emphasizes the fact that many facets of religious experience are common to many religions, not only to Christianity, though of course Kierkegaard, who is regarded as the founder of Existentialism, was a Christian. I instance a few: existentialist Despair is very nearly the same as the Dark night of the Soul of mystic writings. Bad Faith is that aspect of Original Sin which is talked about in phrases such as "the Devil is the father of lies". It is seeing evil as good, a universal corruption. We find similar attitudes to life expressed in Sartre and Eliot. Celia, in *The Cocktail Party*,[3] needs:

> The kind of faith that issues from despair:

Oreste in *Les Mouches* believes[4] that "human life begins on the

---

[1] Translated Philip Mairet, p. 55.
[2] Translated Hazel E. Barnes, p. 626.
[3] II, p. 140.   [4] III, ii, p. 102.

far side of despair". Celia's choice is surely "absurd", though the word is not used:[1]

CELIA: I don't in the least know what I am doing
               Or why I am doing it. There is nothing else to do:
               That is the only reason.

REILLY: It is the best reason.

CELIA: But I know it is I who have made the decision:

Sartre says "act without hope", Eliot "wait without hope". We could multiply examples. For Christians to understand this is important, because it makes for a deeper grasp of the nature of the actual experiences to see how they are described by writers of an opposite religion. And it is important for atheists to realize that these so-called "modern" experiences have been described by Christians for many centuries.

Sartre's thought on all matters is full of inconsistencies, arising out of the conflict of his philosophy and his sympathies. Two seem worth selecting. First, in spite of his insistence on the metaphorical quality of religion as described by believers in the great religions, and his insistence that we must start with what we know, our own consciousness, he says "the real is never beautiful". This is best seen in a passage from *L'Imaginaire* which is quoted by Iris Murdoch,[2] who points out that this contradicts what Sartre says elsewhere. There is likely to be an inconsistency in the writing of a man who denies himself the luxury of an external God, and yet hankers after an other-worldly Beauty. Secondly, he insists on the rationality of his contemporaries and believes in democracy, but does not allow the rationality of his predecessors. The point of view of history is the point of view of Bad Faith. His belief in democracy has no rational justification. We may expect inconsistencies in his political outlook. These inconsistencies I could try to enumerate, but they are too many. I shall try and show how a few of them have influenced his plays.

But it is first worth noticing that there is a clear inconsistency between his stated aims and his actual practice in that aspect of a dramatist's work which I have referred to as his poetry. Now

[1] *The Cocktail Party*, II, p. 144.
[2] *Sartre. Romantic Rationalist*, p. 46.

no one has called Sartre a great or even a good poet, either of
the theatre or of language. There are no outstanding theatrical
moments in his work comparable to those in Anouilh's. The
incantation of the Furies in *Les Mouches*[1] is not exciting poetry.
His memorable lines are abstract, not concrete, memorable for
their thought rather than their imagery. But apart from this he
has made clear his aim as a writer, and has not practised in accordance with it. He has said[2] that in an age corrupted by propaganda and the mystifications of "isms" a writer must "call a
spade a spade", and has deplored poetic prose in consequence.
But he uses misleading metaphors constantly. What religion is
he attacking in *Les Mouches*? What use can he make of the
notion of infinite duration in *Huis Clos*? He mixes history and
fairy tale in *Le Diable et le Bon Dieu* until we do not know what
effect he intends. He has admitted that the shellfish in *Les
Séquestrés d'Altona* are a private image.[3] It may be said that
Sartre has not enough technique for his purpose; but it is also
clear that he might have fulfilled his aims better if he had considered a little more carefully what he was trying to do first.

(ii) THE PLAYS IN MODERN DRESS

Huis Clos,[4] *Morts sans Sépulture*,[5] *Les Mains Sales*,[6] and *Les
Séquestrés d'Altona*[7] have something of the tragic atmosphere,
while being cast in more or less naturalistic form. The other
two plays I shall discuss are more obvious attempts to use myth.
But there is a considerable variation in Sartre's theatrical form,
and it is best to discuss each play on its merits without paying
too much attention to classification.

Huis Clos has been called Sartre's best play by several critics.[8]
It shows three people who refuse to escape from their own
nature by turning their backs on their past, and instead prefer
to rest in their own despair. This is to take the general impact
of the play rather than Garcin's cry as central. "*L'enfer c'est les*

---

[1] III, i, pp. 88–89.
[2] *What is Literature?*, translated Bernard Frechtman, p. 210.
[3] *Observer*, 16 August 1961. [4] 1944. [5] 1946.
[6] 1948. [7] 1959.
[8] Cf. Hobson, *The French Theatre of Today*, p. 96.

autres"[1] may not be intended to sum up the play, though most people have taken it as doing so, and Sartre has not contradicted them. Perhaps we should say that other people can be used to fix an image of ourselves as we want to be. These three want to be in Hell: they prefer the laziness of despair.

A person who is in despair is highly unsympathetic, because it is the hardest case of suffering for the outsider to understand, and the sin of despair is the least attractive of all the seven deadly sins. Accordingly, if the play is to make much impact we must feel sympathy for the characters. We must feel sorry that they have lost their freedom, or we are not involved in the action.

The crux of the play is the closing of the door. To make this play a success it is necessary to persuade the audience that people, apparently still free, will of their own volition choose to stay inside. But in fact they will only do so if they have already abandoned their freedom of action. The closing of the door is only psychologically possible if the characters are really and truly in Hell before the play starts. The point Sartre wishes to make is that men choose their own Hell. The closing of the door can only make its theatrical effect if we forget the philosophical point of the play.

In a naturalistic convention it is hard to suggest a very long passage of time. But it is necessary to the point of the play that we should have seen that all the possibilities of the various relationships have been explored before we can say that they have reached impasse; and only if they have reached impasse is it right to talk of Hell. Estelle is hardly allowed to realize what Inez is, and certainly not to do anything about it. Garcin has far more to say to Inez. It would only be plausible to say that the possibilities of the relationships were exhausted if they were schizoid, unable to come out of themselves. Clearly they are not. The play ends before it has really begun.

What is the point of talking about Hell if you do not believe in Hell? Sartre seems to say that the torture of Hell in the old myths was physical, and torture is really mental. But what is the point of saying this if you believe the whole concept a metaphor? If it is a play about the state of mind called being in Hell,

[1] *Huis Clos*, v, p. 167.

then Sartre cheats, since he brings in the notion of infinite duration. Either men are creatures who in some way live for ever or they are not. If they are not, then eternal punishment is nonsense, and talk of Hell misleading and pretentious.

If Sartre really thought of these people as the worst sinners he is a very naïve thinker. Inez is pathetic in her need to torture people. It is the only way she can become aware of herself.[1] Garcin is obviously ineffective; and Estelle, though completely selfish, is not dedicated to evil. She killed her child almost without noticing, but there is no suggestion that she would go on killing. There is no sign in any of them of a wilful choice of evil, kept up for a long time. These are very small-time sinners, and if it is said that these are the worst "sins" in existentialism, then we must say that existentialism gives a very inadequate account of evil. We are, however, more likely to say that the characterization of this play is very thin and that Sartre has not remembered when writing it that "human life begins on the other side of despair".[2] Sometimes in order to begin again it is necessary to plumb the utmost depths. There is never any indication that these people have got near such depths.

Morts sans Sépulture is a much simpler play. It is not a tragedy because we are not confronted with any choice. The Resistance is represented as certainly right, and the Vichy torturers are shown as monsters, decadent or ultra-savage, but all corrupted by power. The play is important as an example of something for which the theatre is not the best place. It is often said that there can be no tragedy without heroic situations, and the implication is that a heroic situation is sufficient to make a tragedy. This is not the case. There also needs to be a conflict of ideas to justify the author putting dialogue into the mouths of his characters. Without the ideas there is no justification for the dialogue. For in these situations people do not talk. The situation of this play is a tense and moving one. I can believe easily in the possibility of men becoming like the torturers, and so I can believe in the situation of the captives. But the only purpose of showing this play is to make me imagine this situation more clearly, and the more clearly I imagine it, the more I want to say, "Shut up."

[1] *Huis Clos*, v, p. 144.   [2] *Les Mouches*, III, ii, p. 102.

With much of the dialogue cut out this might make a fine film. In the artificial atmosphere of the theatre we feel that real people are being played with; for the people represent nothing except themselves. Sartre has not imagined sufficiently strongly what it would be like to be in the position of the captives. Especially unconvincing is the moment when Jean comes in and starts saying that he would rather be tortured.[1] At this point I fail to believe in him as a leader. He is not utterly demoralized and even if he were he wouldn't talk so much. Later Canoris tries to persuade Henri and Lucie to live.[2] The will to live in a human being is very, very strong. These people have been tortured, but not to breaking-point. I do not believe that they would just accept death like that. No actress should be asked to say Lucie's line:[3]

Je suis sèche, je me sens seule, je ne peux penser qu' à moi.

There are some fine moments, when the dialogue is very spare, for example in the short scene between François and Lucie when she tries to cheer him up through her joy in Jean's love. It ends with François saying of his love for Jean, scornfully: "*Pas comme tu l'aimais.*"[4] Lucie replies: "*Non. Pas comme je l'aimais.*" The scene has been so written that an actress will have no difficulty in letting us see right inside her. It could be a great moment illuminating the inadequacy of sexual love in a real crisis. But in general the dialogue has not been sufficiently pared down. Has Sartre realized what every writer should remember all his life, that there are many situations in life, and those not the least important ones, where all his craft of words is totally inadequate?

Les Mains Sales tells the story of Hugo's mission to kill Hoederer. This action is central and climactic. On the interpretation of it hangs Hugo's ultimate fate. But at the climax of the play we are asked to be interested in Hugo, not in the issues involved, and at the end we are thinking of Hugo, not the issues. It is not really theatre of "Situation".

The only issue that the action could involve is that of the

[1] *Morts sans Sépulture*, sc. iii, 1, pp. 214 ff.
[2] Ib., sc. iv, 3, pp. 244–49.   [3] Ib., sc. iv, 3, p. 248.
[4] Ib., sc. i, 1, p. 178.

question of compromise. If one believes in a cause must one follow the cause with utter single-mindedness, or may one compromise with the principles if compromise will help the attainment of the end? The play ceases to be about this, because at the end we learn that Hoederer, the compromiser, has been rehabilitated. The play could still involve this issue if there was anything to show that Hugo's suicide was for the principle that there should be no compromise. All we should need would be for Olga to ask him to agree that Hoederer's death meant nothing, and him to say, No; that would be a lie. But there is no such moment.

The play is written for a non-Communist audience, who will sympathize and agree totally with Hoederer. Hugo is weak, and his principles are badly thought out and despicable;[1] he has no idea of what political action really involves, and prefers his principles to people. Hoederer has not tried to claim his hands are clean; he is "steeped in guilt". Hugo thinks he can keep himself clean, being in love with an idea of what men should be, not with what they are. So the play becomes a pathetic study of the unwisdom of the intellectual, ineffective in everything, including his ridiculous attempts at heroics at the end of the play. If this is the structure of the play, then the business with the photographs[2] fulfils a useful double function, advancing the plot by explaining Hugo's odd behaviour, giving Hoederer reason to think he has summed Hugo up, and so to trust him; while at the same time it throws excellent light on Hugo's character. But this business does not in any way illuminate the situation. So the play is not of the kind that Sartre thinks should be written.

I have assumed that the ending is meant to be ironical, and it is possible to produce it so that it is. But there is no clear indication that Hugo's death is a complete waste, nothing equivalent to Brack's last remark in *Hedda Gabler*. Olga shouts to the assassins to go away. Hugo has made remarks which seem to indicate that he is an existentialist spokesman, and his last remark could be taken as a heroic one. Unless the ending is ironic, it is a very bad one. But I am not entirely sure how

[1] *Les Mains Sales*, v, 3, p. 212.
[2] Ib., iii, 4, pp. 112–14.

much Sartre did intend us to admire Hugo, and I find this ambiguity a great weakness.

The central action of *Les Séquestrés d'Altona* is old Gehrlach letting the Rabbi be killed when he has promised his son Franz that the Jew would be saved. Franz performs a similar action when he lets his prisoners be tortured. Both actions are shown as typical of the actions of Germany in submitting to the Nazis, but the course of the play is not a development of the consequences of the original action, since that was only a reaction to the already existing horrors of the Nazi government. These so-called central actions are not central in the way that the central actions of Greek tragedy are, because they have so much less influence on the course of events; they only influence internal psychological developments in the few people we actually see on stage.

It is more profitable to see it as a pathetic study of two people who have lost their freedom by a wrong action in the past. The play bears obvious resemblance to *John Gabriel Borkman*, with the function of Borkman shared between Franz and his father. There is, for example, the same use of the image of kingship applied to the world of business[1] as we saw in Ibsen's play. We are not to take sides and see whether an action was right or wrong if it is a pathetic study we are watching. And we never have to face the decision that Franz faced over the prisoners, because we are told, after all, that it would not have been profitable to torture them. To us, comfortably outside the situation of the characters, it is obvious which way one ought to choose. There is no affront to our moral sense. It is a study in Franz' corruption. How far he must have sunk, to give way like that.

But the play seems to touch on several issues that are never raised squarely. We have allusions to the Gehrlach game, "loser wins", and then the father says[2] of Germany, that they had to play "loser wins". In a sense what the father has done is typical of what Germany did. He did not act for freedom; he went with the Nazis because someone would do the work even if he did not, and by doing this he kept some power. He runs his family as he wants, and finally gets his way with Franz. He

---

[1] *Les Séquestrés d'Altona*, V, i, p. 215.   [2] Ib., V, i, p. 213.

ends by arranging a Wagnerian suicide for himself, as well he might, since he has nothing to live for, except excruciating pain. He has wielded power, and the firm no longer wants a king; he will have no successor. He has played "loser wins" with extreme success. Then we should be able to watch the end in a detached spirit. We could say, Look at these Germans. They have ruined Europe, they are detestable. But there is something magnificent about them. But that would be to make the father the central character, not Franz. Franz' reaction is so unusual that he ceases to typify in any way, and so the play is not theatre of "Situation". It seems to touch on issues when Franz asks what the difference was between their family, who hated Hitler, and others who loved him, since old Gehrlach built Hitler ships, and he killed enemy soldiers.[1] But the play does not present this issue squarely.

It almost says that all Germany ought to be mad like Franz, while in fact Germany is the richest country in Europe, and this is connected with the way in which the mad Franz is shown as speaking the truth which the sane fail to recognize.[2] But if the purpose of the play is to show that this horrible family is doing what one might expect anyone who had been involved with the Nazis to do, Sartre should have taken more trouble to show that they were normal before the Nazis took over. We feel that they were always mad and horrible.

The play almost says that Europe is finished, however much she may cover up by building ships and so on. Then Franz is speaking the truth when he says the century was a jumble sale when the liquidation of the human species was decided on in high places,[3] something which is confirmed by the play ending with his speech on the tape, when this thought is uttered at greater length. But if Sartre really wanted to show that Europe was dead he should have taken a family more obviously of the 1960s, a Gehrlach who thinks of a good future for his business, a family not brooding or incestuous, and show Franz telling the truth there.

These issues are not presented squarely, because Sartre probably did not intend to say these things with quite such strength.

[1] *Les Séquestrés d'Altona*, I, ii, p. 44.
[2] Ib., III, iv, p. 146. [3] Ib., II, i, p. 78.

Their effect is to suggest at first that the play is about important things, and then to disappoint those who look closer, by not offering any illumination on the important questions we think the play is raising. Because the play offers us no real illumination we are irritated when we are asked to regard the melodramatic double suicide at the end as a heroic consummation. Leni's clairvoyance[1] means that we are certainly meant to involve ourselves in the death in the manner of Wagner, or Ibsen. But this death solves nothing, and nothing has been put before us which needed solving. We might compare Iris Murdoch's judgement on Mathieu's death in the tower, from *Les Chemins de la Liberté*.[2] She says that "his final achievement lies in sheer violence", "action which excludes reflection", "the old familiar, romantic answer to the problem". *Les Séquestrés d'Altona* conveys a strong atmosphere of evil, but its success lies in things which have nothing to do with tragedy or theatre of "Situation".

(iii) THE PLAYS OF MYTH

The story of *Les Mouches*[3] is the story of Oreste arriving at Argos to discover the town wallowing in collective guilt for the murder of Agamemnon, and coming to the decision to take the guilt on his own shoulders by killing Egisthe and Clytemnestre. It is Oreste becoming an existentialist hero who can kill his mother without flinching, and becoming a man free from the oppressive shackles of religion. For men are free, but do not know it;[4] gods and kings live in fear of them finding out. Oreste has led the way. The ending shows us Oreste leaving Argos with the flies, the symbols of the people's feelings of guilt, and the Furies, the symbols of the gods' vengeance, following him ineffectually.

The ending is effective because we see Oreste apparently carrying away the town's guilt. But the point of the play is that the guilt is imaginary, and this is confirmed by the fact that the rationalist tutor is quite unperturbed by the Furies. The theatrical effect directly contradicts the point of the play.

The play was performed during the Resistance, when censorship prevented the production of most plays which dealt with

---

[1] *Les Séquestrés d'Altona*, V, iii, p. 221.   [2] *Sartre*, p. 25.
[3] 1942.   [4] *Les Mouches*, II, ii, 5, p. 77.

political themes and were set in the present. The myth was chosen originally so that the play could be produced, and the play was taken as saying something about the Pétain régime. Egisthe is Pétain, Zeus the German occupation. But there is so much about repentance, which seems to have wider connotation than that of the immediate contemporary situation, that it is reasonable to take the play as an attempt to reflect some universal problem.

It is an image of the discovery that man is free of God, who has no power over someone who refuses to acknowledge any power. It is the argument that because we must interpret miracles ourselves, therefore miracles are a meaningless concept. It is an image of an "atheism" like that of Lucretius who believed in gods, remote and powerless to affect the world. Oreste[1] rejects the sign of Zeus that he should go home, because that would be to do the gods' will. He sees the gods as ineffectual, not as non-existent. It is not an image of Sartre's normal religion, which is genuinely atheist.

The play also presents a series of images of the disgusting nature of ritualist religion or the ritual instinct. Zeus is not the Greek god, since Sartre, for example, makes him to have created the world.[2] He must presumably stand for the God of Christianity, and the play be intended as an attack on that part of Christianity which has meant that money is spent on Churches and vestments, not on the poor, and time is spent lamenting past sins, instead of building houses. It is, as it were, an attack on the Catholic Church in Spain, or Southern Italy. If this is part of his purpose, the effect is considerably weakened by the lack of clarity. No one would deny that some religions are disgusting and horrible; but to say that all religion is disgusting is rather like saying that all art is beautiful. The descriptive adjective ceases to have any application. Similarly some repentance is obviously morbid; some is not. If you say that all repentance is morbid, then the word loses its force.

Sartre is inconsistent in his attack. Mostly he seems to be attacking the cruelties and nastinesses that come from practising a ritual life. But in the scene between Zeus and Egisthe, which we are meant to take seriously, we hear that Zeus committed

---

[1] *Les Mouches*, II, i, 4, p. 63.   [2] Ib., II, ii, p. 98.

the first crime, that of making men mortal.[1] It appears that Sartre is drawing to our attention the cruelty of God, the source of the cruelty of religion. This is all it can mean. But Sartre is an atheist. One cannot both curse God and disbelieve in Him. This ambiguity is not resolved. We sometimes feel Sartre is attacking God, and sometimes attacking the religious instinct, which causes men to act foolishly and cruelly, although its exercise is entirely purposeless. Either point would be worth making a play about. But failure to make clear which point he is making means that the play is nonsense. It is not surprising that he does a theatrical cheat. Having aroused our emotions with the summoning of the dead from the cave,[2] we are then told in the next act, that this is all mass hypnosis.[3] Naturally we will start to doubt the convention, since we assumed that Sartre's convention meant that the dead were walking round. We shall therefore doubt the nature of the Furies, and that of Zeus. The play will cease to be about anything.

The effective pieces of writing are those which contribute to the atmosphere. We are not shown clear reasons for choosing freedom, because the forces opposing freedom are built up emotionally and not rationally. We see flies sucking the yellow muck from a boy's eyes at the beginning,[4] we hear of Clytemnestre's spotted underclothes,[5] which Electre will wear at the end, as symbol of her repentance.[6] This is nasty, and it makes us feel that Argos is a beastly place; but it has no reference outside the theatre, because we are not clear to what it is referring. Zeus tells of the death of Agamemnon to Oreste and the tutor. The whole town then was "like a woman on heat". The connexion of sex and violence is well known, and often occurs in Sartre. It stirs us here, but it has no exact point. It contributes to a vague oppressive atmosphere, but does not illuminate the situation which Sartre wishes his drama to put over.

Le Diable et le Bon Dieu[7] is admitted not to be a complete success. We feel a sense of confusion; a great many issues are raised, but Sartre never remains concentrated on any of them. It is difficult to trace a logic of events by which we can assimi-

---

[1] *Les Mouches*, II, ii, 5, p. 75.   [2] Ib., II, i, 2, pp. 46 ff.
[3] Ib., II, ii, 3, p. 71.   [4] Ib., I, i. p. 14.
[5] Ib., I, iv, p. 29.   [6] Ib., III, ii, p. 97.   [7] 1951.

late what the form of the play is. There is no one central action whose consequences are the course of the play. The most important event is Goetz' wager that he will be good for a year and a day. After making this wager, cheating so that he lost it, and calling off the siege that would have meant a massacre, he makes various ineffectual attempts to do good, until he finally discovers that he can't be good, and that God does not exist. Then he returns to the life he led before.

We can see Goetz as a corrupting influence. Everyone with whom he comes in contact goes to pieces. This is shown by his kiss. He kisses Heinrich, Nasty, a leper who would much prefer an indulgence to a useless kiss, and he tells his peasants in the City of the Sun to give Karl the kiss of peace. This has a suitably disgusting effect in the theatre, but it has no more than a vague impact.

A fundamental obscurity of the play is that we do not know whether Goetz is ever meant to be good. Sartre has written of the play:[1]

> I have tried to show that Goetz, a free-lance captain of mercenaries and an anarchist of evil, destroys nothing when he believes he is destroying the most. He destroys human lives but cannot disturb society or social judgements . . . Whether he tries to achieve the absolute through good or through evil, he succeeds only in destroying human lives.

This appears to indicate that Sartre believes that it is more destructive to overthrow social organization than kill human beings, which would make Hitler not so very destructive a person. If he really thinks this, then perhaps he thinks that Goetz' actions while he is being "good" are good. I don't know if he could think that; but there seems little point in the play otherwise. All we see of his "goodness" is his preparation to give his lands away, when he blasphemes by comparing himself to Christ.[2] Later we see his treatment of the leper,[3] when Heinrich rightly says:

Tu prends les âmes pour des légumes.

[1] *The Contemporary French Theatre*, p. 162.
[2] *Le Diable et le Bon Dieu*, sc. iv, 4, p. 132.
[3] Ib., sc. v, 2, pp. 155–8.

The goodness is the death of Catherine. If the City of the Sun is meant to be a Utopia, it is a bad description; the Utopia is shown as insipid. It may be, however, that Sartre cannot describe goodness. If this is intended to be goodness, then the play partly asks whether there can be goodness founded on a lie, that of the cheating wager, the miracle Goetz fakes so that he may appear to be able to take Catherine's sins.[1] There is also a challenge to our moral sense when it is announced that Goetz' refusal to fight for Nasty's revolt has meant the death of 20,000 peasants. His "goodness" has killed more people than ever his evil did. Neither of these points strike home, because we are not sure if Goetz' "goodness" is genuine. But clearly this is intended to be one of the issues of the play, since it is given such prominence in the argument between Goetz and Nasty,[2] when the two do not reach a conclusion, and the argument is left at deadlock, Goetz saying that one must not wait till the world ends to see if good is possible, Nasty saying that one must not do good if as a result the world perishes.

By setting his play at the time of the Reformation, which coincided in Germany with the peasants revolting in much the same way as they had in England in the fourteenth century, Sartre must have intended to make it about the issue of individualism, the conflict between order and the individual conscience. And we do get something of this conflict, particularly in the scenes with Nasty. But it is not the central point of the play.

Sartre has said that the play mirrors the situation of modern Europe, torn between the U.S.A. and the U.S.S.R. But this is a very obscure parallel. The U.S.S.R. is the revolutionary side, and so presumably the side of Nasty. The U.S.A. will then be the Church. But Nasty stands for the individual, and whatever one may say about the faults of Capitalism, at least the U.S.A. stands more for individualism than the U.S.S.R. Perhaps Sartre did not mean this seriously. But if his intention was really to mirror that conflict, then he has certainly failed to put over his point.

It is an attack on the Church. There is no point in starting the

---

[1] *Le Diable et le Bon Dieu*, sc. vi, 6, pp. 192–93.
[2] Ib., sc. iv, 5, pp. 134–42.

play by showing the siege of Worms, except to mock a worldly and peevish prelate. It is in keeping with the Indulgence-selling scene, one of Sartre's most theatrical conceptions. But in addition to the attack on the Church, the play is full of attacks on the cruelty of God, especially at the beginning by Heinrich, and later by Hilda. This leads very oddly into the conclusion that God does not exist, and, as in *Les Mouches*, it looks as if Sartre is arguing from the cruelty of God to His non-existence.

All these issues are made less important by the fairy-tale atmosphere of the story. Goethe wrote a *Götz von Berlichingen*, based on the story of a real man. Sartre's debt to Goethe or to history is slight, and the result is to make us take the play less seriously.

The characters in this play are much more important in their own right than elsewhere in Sartre. Heinrich distracts attention at the beginning because it seems as if his dilemma whether to follow his Bishop or to save the people[1] will be central to the action, and he is built up as an immensely sympathetic character, trying to do the best he can in terrible circumstances. But then he becomes unimportant, and wanders round with the Devil, taunting Goetz. Nasty is the completely confident fanatic, certain that revolution must come, but at the end he has to admit that he is doing all the things that he considered anathema.[2] Hilda is meant in some way to be parallel to Heinrich, and her collapse is unsatisfactory, because we do not see into her properly. Goetz is not a man utterly dedicated to evil. He is a blusterer, as his attitude to the sack of Worms shows.[3] He has partly become as he is because he is a bastard and people have patronized him.[4] Heinrich calls him *"le bouffon"*. We cannot be sure whether this is Sartre's intention, or whether he meant to show Goetz as utterly evil, and has failed. We might be enlightened by the final "trial" between him and Henrich, but nothing is revealed by that. The issues remain obscure, and the play, though full of interesting moments, makes sense neither as fairy story, history, drama of situation, or drama of character.

[1] *Le Diable et le Bon Dieu*, sc. i, p. 45.   [2] Ib., sc. xi, 2, p. 280.
[3] Ib., sc. iii, 3, pp. 86–87.   [4] Ib., sc. ii, 4, p. 66.

(iv) CONCLUSION

An unbelievable number of critics have appeared to approve or disapprove of Sartre according to whether they approved or disapproved of "philosophical drama". The Greeks would have simply laughed at this situation. It is as if art critics decided whether they approved of an artist or not, by whether they approved of red pictures. Unfortunately, our muddled generation cannot simply laugh; there are art critics who judge on these grounds, and they are not always laughed out of a job. There is good philosophy and sound philosophizing, and bad philosophy and misguided philosophizing. Critics have said they approve or disapprove of "philosophical drama" without thinking it necessary to distinguish between good and bad philosophy, because they are too lazy to study the philosophy and discover whether it is sound or unsound, good or bad. People argue about Sartre rather as they argue about Ibsen as "moralist". Those who object to an unattractiveness in both writers weakly assume that it is because the former is "philosophical" and the latter a "moralist". If they went into the matter further they would probably see that they found the two writers unattractive because one was an unsound philosopher and the other a bad moralist. Sartre is inconsistent as a philosopher, and inconsistent in his approach to the theatre, and to myth. Believing in the uniqueness of the contemporary situation, he allows himself to indulge his love for the pageantry of the past in the theatre. An opponent of Christianity, he tries to give philosophical status to his belief in democracy, by pretending that he deduces the existence of others with mathematical logic, when this highly dubious deduction is only possible with reference to God; an opponent of Christian ritual, he uses the two justifications for Christian ritual, the fear of God, and the fear of Hell, so that his audience will be in a ritual frame of mind. This attitude to Christianity is one of the best examples of an exactly similar inconsistency in his philosophy and his drama. The one is illuminated by study of the other. Sartre is an important writer, and it is especially important to discover whether his example should be followed or avoided. He has produced a philosophy which is in parts thoroughly unsound and in other parts highly commendable. His plays show us much of what a writer ought to do, and much of what he ought not. Perhaps his greatest significance will be that study of his work should convince the most hardened critic of the futility of "aesthetic" criticism; and to have helped our generation to turn from this misguided and futile outlook is a considerable achievement.

CHAPTER FOURTEEN

GHÉON

To criticize Ghéon in the fashionable aesthetic terms, only asking whether he expressed his philosophy adequately, not asking about the philosophy itself, is even more ridiculous than it is with the other writers I have mentioned. The significance of Ghéon is simple. He said that Western Europe had lost touch with the origin of its culture, the Mass, and that therefore its art had decayed. Now clearly European culture did originate with the Mass; composers set its liturgy; architects built places where it could be celebrated; sculptors and dramatists illustrated aspects of it. Clearly also European culture has decayed. If the fundamental dogma of Christianity is correct, then our culture can revive by returning to its origin. If Christian dogma is correct, then Ghéon was the first to practise in terms of the theatre an attitude towards art which most Europeans had forgotten. He is either significant because he is the beginning of a revival which has not yet gathered momentum, or he is a lost figure, making a protest against the boulevard theatre, someone whose plays have never been performed on the professional stage. Either way it is an ideological matter.

His was the first attempt to create a theatre which would be both popular and religious, as was that of the Greeks. It would not have an audience of the whole population, but unlike all other theatres, it would at least have an audience of all classes. Nor would someone who wrote for the *peuple fidèle* be writing for people who were "interested in theatre". The latter are those who will criticize in the aesthetic terms incompatible with serious drama such as there has been in the past, incompatible with any idea of the poet as teacher.

He was the first to study both primitive European dramatic traditions, the Greek and the Medieval. He calls Shakespeare Medieval.[1] His Christian purpose enabled him to see the greatness of the Medieval drama which had for so long been unnoticed, and his understanding of the Medieval drama helped him to understand certain elements of Greek drama, which others did not. Notably this meant that he got nearer than anyone else to understanding the function of the chorus.

In his own right he is a fine theatrical craftsman, though like the Medieval masters, his best effects are very much *poésie du théâtre*, not so much purely verbal ones. Free from the confines of the proscenium stage, and profiting from the insistence of Copeau that the actor must sing and dance and use his body, he can convey a more varied theatrical experience than that found in most theatres even now. A most moving example of a play with two levels of reality occurs in *Noel sur la Place*, when the gipsy girl who plays Our Lady tells her old father-in-law, who is representing the Magi, to get up from his knees, or his rheumatism will suffer. The third scene of *Le Mystère de* ''*Invention de la Croix* is a totally unnaturalistic dialogue between Helena, mother of Constantine, and the coryphaeus. It presents the battle between Maxentius and Constantine briefly and in such a way as to excite us. It is a good example of the truth that if a writer has a strong purpose to get over in the theatre, a theatrical form will be found. The desire to say something will normally precede the choice of means to say it.

Ghéon did not evolve a language suitable for his purpose. He wrote for people to whom the old idioms still had meaning, and so to us now his imagery has the limp effect of Victorian hymnology or the many statues of Madonnas based on three centuries of copying Raphael. His philosophy is firmly Idealist, as we can see from his theories of art advanced in the opening pages of *L'Art du Théâtre*, and the Idealist respect for the actual words used to name experiences connected with Christian belief and practice would have done much to prevent him seeing the need to find new terms for the experiences Christian dogma is designed to explain. It is not surprising that he should have thought in this way; his generation of Catholics did. He was not

[1] Henri Ghéon, *L'Art du Théâtre*, p. 64.

sufficiently sophisticated philosophically to see that there was no necessary connexion between Catholicism and Idealism, and as a result the impact of his writing suffers.

Most of his work is more obviously inspired by Medieval drama than by Greek, and his best plays are those in which he has captured some of the folk atmosphere of the Miracle Cycles. But he wrote two plays deriving inspiration from Greek drama, one on a Greek and one on a Christian myth.

Le Mystère de l'Invention de la Croix[1] was written in response to a request from a monastery to write a play for performance in the open air, to celebrate the Cross, a theme which appealed to Ghéon's desire for a reunion of Eastern and Western Christendom under the Cross. It has an epic form, being in three parts, and representing the situation that in spite of the Crucifixion the world is not wholly changed. The first part presents us with the history of the world from the Crucifixion to the victory of Constantine over Maxentius in the sign of the Cross. It is preluded with a chorus alluding to the entire history of the world up to the Crucifixion, the climax of history. The second part tells the story of the misunderstanding and wickedness as a result of which Constantine ordered the death of Crispus, his innocent son. In spite of Christ's death, innocent men will still be wrongly killed. The third part is the search of Helena for the True Cross, and her eventual finding of it. The play ends in a triumph which includes Constantine.

The second part begins with a chorus which says that we have seen the sign of the Cross, but not its effects. The actual loss of the physical wood of the Cross is taken as a symbol of the way that people ignore what has been made available to them. Reconciliation is only possible if everyone treads the Way of the Cross as we see Helena doing during her search in the third part.

As Helena comes to Calvary the chorus "gets muddled". Half say "she is weeping for Crispus", the other half, "she is weeping for Jesus". As the Medieval writers made plays about those figures in Old Testament history whose sacrifice could be shown as a type of the sacrifice of Christ, so Ghéon makes the story of the death of a comparatively innocent Christian into a

[1] 1932.

type of the completely innocent death of Christ. This is the Christian account of history, the story of the folly and wickedness of men causing the senseless death of innocent people, as a result of which deaths new glories become visible.

This is an enormous scope, and Ghéon has not had the technique to make a masterpiece. Nothing less than a masterpiece would have done. There are some magnificent theatrical moments, and it would be highly effective in an audience of *peuple fidèle*. But it needs an audience which already assumes the ultimate triumph of Christianity; it does not force its audience to accept the Christian triumph whether they like it or not, as the greatest Christian art does. There is an aspect of the thought of the play which helps to explain this. Ghéon has mixed history and legend, the history of Constantine's political intrigues, and the legend of the Finding of the Cross. He has used the finding to show the ultimate victory of Christianity. But he has shown it in earthly terms, which is untrue. He has allowed his story to represent a permanent triumph for Christians. But there was nothing permanent about Constantine's conversion even, and it is dangerous to say that when Christianity is most obviously accepted then the world is most obviously Christian. It presents that Christian attitude which has made non-Christians say that Christianity is incompatible with tragedy. The non-Christians think that this is so because Christianity talks of ultimate triumph. But it is more the case that too many Christians have talked of the triumph too easily, forgetting that it is not a triumph in earthly terms, and that it costs everything. The Christian message of the first and second parts of this play represents a Christian view of history. Moments of Christian worldly triumph are irrelevant interruptions, not culminations.

One of the purposes of this play was to present an image of Reunion. This is embodied in the set, which has three areas, representing Rome, Byzantium, and Jerusalem. Jerusalem is not used until the last part when Helena goes for the Cross. Reunion can only come through the Cross. This purpose is not, however, in the forefront of the play, which has so much to say anyhow.

He uses both a speaking chorus and a singing choir. The chorus is just "*chœur*", and not as integrated in the action as the chorus of a Greek tragedy. The choir chant, though he does not always specify what they are to chant. What he does specify is one chant which recurs:

> Crucem tuam adoramus, Domine, et sanctam resurectionem tuam laudamus.

It appears after the opening chorus, telling of history up to the Crucifixion. It is heard again when Helena and Constantine are to be baptized after the battle which he won in the sign of the Cross. It is heard again when Helena has just prevented Constantine, crazed with grief at his mistake over Crispus, from killing himself. It is sung by the actors on stage at the end of the Way of the Cross, and again sung by the choir after the miracle when the dead child is restored to life by the True Cross. All the action is judged in terms of the Cross, the image of utter defeat, and utter triumph. The meaning of the chant changes with the context of its utterance. It fulfils a function analogous to the Greek choruses. A chanting choir is a much more powerfully evocative force than a speaking chorus, one much more like the Greek choruses. And a chanting choir is something that is familiar in Christian worship. It is most likely that if there is any drama written to resemble Greek tragedy it will use the tradition of liturgical music, especially plainsong, which being musically simple allows prominence to the words.

The significance of this play lies in the theatrical form it takes as a result of its liturgical purpose and in the fact that it uses something like a Christian myth, though perhaps not entirely consistently. It is a new venture; we could hardly expect a masterpiece. But it is a highly significant model.

At one time in his life he was much influenced by Gide, and it was natural that he might try and write another *Oedipe*.[1] His play is subtitled *Le Crépuscule des Dieux*. It is the story of Oedipe coming to self-realization, and the development of a growing dissatisfaction with the gods who have made him as he is, as a preparation for the God who is to come. It is an internal action. The events of the Oedipus story are incidental to the development of Oedipe.

The first act shows Laios and Jocaste on their wedding day,

[1] 1942.

faced with the oracle which forbids them to have children. Jocaste is prepared to abandon her hope of pleasure, but Laios revolts against such tyranny. Jocaste gives way, and then decides to get rid of the child, casting doubt on the status of gods who could allow such a thing,[1] and emphasizing, as everyone does, the innocence of the child. The second act shows a Jocaste who cares nothing for the gods, and desperately wants sex, and a modest Oedipe, who refers his victory over the Sphinx to the will of the gods. The third act is the story of the *Tyrannus*. Oedipe is furious with the gods for the outrage they have inflicted on him. Why did it happen, he asks. Jocaste replies:[2]

Parce que vous naissiez et que vous ne deviez pas naître.

He blinds himself as an act of despair and defiance; it is too late to die. The last act takes place in the wood where Oedipus met the Sphinx. His self-realization comes while we learn about the battle in which his sons are killed, whom he has cursed in the previous act, so that the line may perish. At first he says that Thebes is dead, but then he realizes that Thebes will live again, and this realization is the beginning of his salvation. This act is his searching for "the secret", which finally the innocent Antigone suggests, that there is another God, who waits, until there will be people to do His Will of love. This will perhaps be the secret, and in this knowledge Oedipe can die peacefully, while Antigone ends the play by saying:

Veillez sur la nouvelle Thèbes, Dieu inconnu.

The play presents an image of inadequate religion, the despair of a pagan confronted with gods who do not act for love. Unlike the other retellings of the Oedipus story, Ghéon has worked out a clear and consistent interpretation, and fitted it into his own religious thought. To do this he has taken a point of view nearer that of the *Coloneus* than the *Tyrannus*. Oedipe was innocent at first; even though he was wrong to curse his sons, yet his curse fulfilled a divine purpose, since clearly the line had to die out. As Sophocles uses the story of Oedipus finally to present an image of something mysterious, wonderful, and beyond our ken, so Ghéon suggests that this terrible

[1] *Oedipe*, I, ii, p. 161.   [2] Ib., III, vi, p. 213.

event had a function in some mysterious vast purpose which we cannot understand, but which is related to the purpose of the world as he sees it, that purpose being love.

He uses imagery to put over his point. The sun is used to stand for the power behind the world, and for example when Jocaste, at her wedding, speaks of her desire for children, Laios says:[1]

> Vous parlez comme le soleil quand il crie: Midi! à la terre.

It is glorious but terrible. The opening chorus presents the image of man walking to his destiny like a traveller going south into the sun. All that is certain is his shadow behind him. This fine image is repeated word for word at the end of Act I.

The chorus is spectator, commenting as they do in *Le Mystère de l'Invention de la Croix*. Ghéon never fully succeeded in integrating them in the action, which he could hardly have done here, since the action is internal to Oedipe; he did not want to show the whole of Thebes preparing for Christianity, because his point is that only very exceptional circumstances could bring people as near Christianity as Oedipe was brought, until the Crucifixion. This play has some fine theatrical moments, such as the beautiful moment of quiet in the middle of the wedding festivities,[2] and Ghéon has come nearer than anyone else to making religious sense of the Oedipus story in any terms other than those of its original religion. But it is not his most successful play, and his work in general has been sufficient to show that there is no need for a Christian dramatist who wishes to do for his audience what the Greek poets did for theirs to return to the Greek myths which have long since ceased to be myths for us.

Deléglise summarizes several of Ghéon's statements about his artistic intentions by saying: "*L'art a le droit et même le devoir de nommer Dieu*".[3] It is not an exaggeration to say that in terms of the theatre, which had totally lost its connexion with its origin in a way that music never has, he reclaimed the right, and restated the duty. With a humility which contrasts favourably

---

[1] *Oedipe*, I, iii, p. 140.   [2] Ib., I, iii, pp. 140–41.
[3] M. Deléglise, *Le Théâtre d'Henri Ghéon*, p. 282.

with some of the more pretentious claims of other writers he
said:[1]

> Je ne dis pas que mes pièces sont bonnes; je dis que mon
> idée est bonne; d'autres la reprendront et feront mieux.

His plays are far more successful than those who are tied to the
conventions of the bourgeois theatre, and who have therefore
never seen them, will admit. But he did not succeed in developing a language sufficient for the needs of his drama. He wrote
in a vulgar and tasteless idiom. But then so did the early Greek
tragic poets, if we may trust Aristotle. His is not a rough-hewn
vulgarity, but one worn smooth with age. But it is at least an
idiom of the people, as was that of Thespis and Phrynichus. One
of the achievements of Ghéon has been to draw our attention
to the greatness of the Medieval masters, who are known by no
name, only by their work. We shall honour his achievement
less by remembering his name than by continuing his work.
Let him be forgotten, and thus be made part of the great company of his Medieval predecessors. Or let him be remembered
as name and nothing more, a second Thespis.

[1] *L'Art du Théâtre*, p. 193.

ELIOT

(i) INTRODUCTORY

Of all the writers I have mentioned Eliot is probably the most obviously significant in a discussion of this kind. So much has already been written on his work, that the brief space available in this general discussion will seem to many critics to do him an injustice. Much of the criticism which has gathered round him in a way unprecedented in the case of a living writer gives the appearance of delivering final verdicts on his work. I do not believe that such criticism is possible, nor will it be for a long time. A century is not long enough; two centuries' perspective may be. I have tried in this inquiry to criticize modern writing in a different way from that in which I criticize the Greeks. I certainly intend my criticism to be received in a different spirit. Ibsen and Eliot are the only writers I discuss who have already acquired a critical canon. I do not intend that my criticism should be added to a canon, since I do not think such a thing is desirable or really possible. Future developments prove critics wrong; no judgement about contemporaries should be treated as sacrosanct; I regard the job of a critic of contemporary or near contemporary work as stimulating thought for the future, rather than summing up the present. We cannot sum up the present, we can only live in it; and that means looking forward.

Eliot is an important writer, and also a critic. He has a clearer idea of his artistic aims than most artists, and he has been prepared to state them in print. But a writer is not necessarily the best judge of his own work. Eliot has made pronouncements about his poetry; but he may have been wrong. Too much criticism has taken it for granted that he must be right. I have instanced one example,[1] where he has underrated his own achievement, and most critics have followed him blindly.

Without Eliot's work, the question which I have written the book to raise could not have been asked in terms of the English theatre. He has made it possible to think of a modern English tragic drama; all criticism must start with his achievement. He has reintroduced a poetic drama which for a short time was even successful in the West End. Discussion of the possibility of poetic drama must include an appraisal of his method in writing it. He has also reintroduced a drama which like that of Ghéon could mention the name of God, though *Murder in the Cathedral* presents a totally different attitude to the problem of Christian drama than his later plays.

(ii) PHILOSOPHY AND POETRY

As a playwright Eliot puts over an orthodox Christian view of life, based on an Anglican Thomism. But he was brought up in the Idealist tradition; Bradley is the philosopher who has most influenced him. Most of his Christian contemporaries still think in Idealist terms, and the destruction of Idealism as a system by the Logical Positivists was hailed as a defeat for Christianity, or slurred over in fear, according to the religion of the person concerned. It is only the post-war Christian philosophers who have begun to see that the destruction of the Idealist scheme is not only right, but also advantageous to Christian thinking, purging it of much that is unnecessary and even wrong.

This is, of course, a large subject and needs far fuller treatment. But there is one central feature of Idealism we ought to note which must have an effect on a poet who adopts it. The system suggests a Reality which is outside time, and static. Now of course Bradley spent much effort talking about time, and Eliot is very much aware of time in his poetry. But the tendency of Idealists is to pay less attention to the natural world, to time and change and growth; inevitably they will do so, since they say Reality is outside time. We have seen the effect Idealism has on Giraudoux' treatment of character. The incompatibility of this philosophy with any view which sees life as a process of

[1] Cf. p. 208.

growth may explain partly why Eliot drew less attention to his notion of the scheme of things as he became more interested in the development of character in his later plays.

Sometimes Eliot, writing as a Christian, still seems to put over a view of this static Reality.[1]

> Love is itself unmoving,

But could one not say that the point of the doctrine of the Trinity was precisely to assert the opposite, that love must keep moving? Certainly the one thing we can say with confidence about the vision of the love of God as expressed in the *Commedia* is that it is a vision of continual movement:[2]

> e l'un dall' altro, come iri da iri
> parea riflesso,

So does Dante describe the three wheels of light. A little later he says:[3]

> O luce eterna, che sola in te sidi,
> sola t'intendi, e da te intelletta
> ed intendente te, ami e arridi.

To go further into this would involve detailed examination of mystical writing and take me far out of my depth. I do not wish to suggest that Eliot invariably despises the natural world or ignores time, though this has been suggested by some critics. But there is this intellectual influence which must cause a tendency in this direction. In addition, he was brought up a Unitarian, in a religion which denies the divinity of Christ, and so denies the importance of time and the natural world. For the Unitarians God did not become man at a particular point in time. Temperamentally he has more affinities with the Negative than the Affirmative Way of religion; his work is full of references to *The Cloud of Unknowing*, which is held up as one of the great Negative works. All these things combine to produce an outlook on life which must make it far harder for him to express his religion in dramatic terms than someone whose intellectual or religious practice was more instinctively outward-directed. I am sure that this is extremely important for the

---

[1] *Burnt Norton*, v.   [2] *Paradiso*, xxxiii, pp. 118–19.
[3] Ib., xxxiii, pp. 124–26.

understanding of Eliot's work; but I hold it an impertinence to probe much further into the spiritual state of someone who is still alive. However, it is necessary to add that by criticizing the influence a misleading philosophy has had on his work, and suggesting that he has partly assimilated concepts which conflict with orthodox Christianity, I am not attempting to belittle his influence as thinker, poet, or Christian. Our generation is so full of misleading philosophies that it must be very difficult for anyone to write without being influenced for the bad by some of them. And after four centuries of a divided Church it is perhaps impossible for any one man to put over a view of life which would unquestionably be called orthodox Christianity; perhaps there is someone somewhere, no doubt thought highly eccentric.

There is a sense of detachment in his writing, which everyone can notice, though different people will refer to it in different ways. A producer should always bear in mind these lines from *Burnt Norton*:[1]

> . . . not in movement
> But abstention from movement; while the world moves
> In appetency, on its metalled ways
> Of time past and time future.

In all the plays the still spectator is very important, especially Agatha in *The Family Reunion*; through her everything happens. She is the catalyst; it is a favourite image of Eliot's. We think of Reilly watching the other actors in the first act of *The Cocktail Party*. Colby, also, should be made to stand as still as possible throughout *The Confidential Clerk*, while all the others rush in and out round him.

Sometimes we find what seems a deliberate avoidance of theatricality. A good example was noted by *The Times'* critic reviewing *The Elder Statesman*.[2] When Claverton decides to submit to Monica's judgement, he is already absolved. Less action is shown on stage than might have been. With the exception of Lady Elizabeth, Gomez, and Mrs Carghill, he demands restraint from his actors. Even in *Murder in the Cathedral* there is need of restraint. For the first half of the play the actor

[1] *Burnt Norton*, iii.   [2] *The Times*, 26 August 1958.

playing Becket should take all the opportunities offered to show character, otherwise the play is dull. But after the temptations we see a martyr, not a man. There should be a complete contrast, and the lines should be delivered more impersonally, as in the liturgy. I was involved in a production, which seemed to convey precisely that Becket fell into the fourth temptation. The chorus screamed "The Lords of Hell are here" and "Destroy yourself and we are destroyed".[1] At this moment the man acting Becket was told to rise to his feet and "play the speech big": "Now is my way clear, now is the meaning plain." If Thomas says that in tones of triumph it suggests that he has found the way; the point is that the chorus, suffering, find it for him. Eliot's lines demand a quiet delivery; one must not seize the obvious theatrical advantage.

Fergusson[2] criticizes *Murder in the Cathedral* as having a "mechanical feel", and attributes this rightly to Eliot's Idealist conception of the divine plan. Eliot, he says, starts with the theological idea of a martyr, not with a man. As Fergusson hardly mentions the chorus, his remarks about "mechanical feel" are worth little, but he is right that Eliot seems to start from an idea. For we have to say, this is a play about a saint. If we do, then it makes sense, and Eliot has time over for saying other things. If we ask proof of Thomas' sanctity we are not really shown it. In the same way we are asked to take Eggerson's sanctity for granted. The play makes nonsense unless we do. But it is reasonable to object that it would be easier if we did see more evidence on stage. And it is part of the Idealist attitude that the word "saint" has a fixed meaning. In fact, there are many different sorts of saints; we will have different reactions to them all.

It is difficult to know where this Idealist habit of preconceived reaction ends and a tendency to private imagery begins. Eliot uses imagery in *The Family Reunion* whose full appreciation demands that we know its use in *Burnt Norton*. His dedicatory poem in *The Elder Statesman* admits that the poetry has a private meaning beyond the public one. This is always dangerous for a dramatist, whose work must be public.

[1] *Murder in the Cathedral*, Part I, pp. 43-44.
[2] *The Idea of a Theater*, p. 217.

(iii) MURDER IN THE CATHEDRAL

Hailed as the one great play in English of this century, translated into most European languages, made into an opera and a film, this work needs none of my justification. And the time has not come to examine it as a classic, though of all the plays which I have discussed in this part of my inquiry, it is the most likely to be one, in my reckoning.

Clearly also this is the play which is most near in spirit to Greek tragedy, of all the plays written in English or French in this century. It is formally similar; it uses a myth in the same way as the Greek tragedies did, and the myth bears the same relation to the religion of Eliot's audience as the myths of the Greek poets did to their audience's religion. It is based on ritual, and the action is carried principally by the chorus, not by an actor. It was performed at a festival, not before a theatregoing public. Because Eliot became interested in another sort of drama, he emphasized the exceptional aspects of this play, to my mind wrongly. It is very likely that this will be called his masterpiece; is it not also time that we examine it as a model for future writing?

The action is simple; it is the crushing of Thomas into a martyr, first spiritually, and then physically. There is a slight feeling of likeness to the form of the *Choephori*, where there is the same preliminary spiritual action, so strongly presented that it almost seems to include the following physical action.

Thomas then is not active himself. A martyr is someone who has surrendered his will to God.[1] The "tragedy" is set in motion by God's will. There is not a parallel natural cause, one human action from which everything stems. This gives a very different effect from that of Greek tragedy. The pattern of God's will is shown very clearly; it is not left to be gathered from the pattern of events. *Murder in the Cathedral* does not then present doubly determined history in quite the way of the Greek tragedies or indeed the Miracle Cycles.

The action is developed in the chorus. They are as closely integrated in it as they could be. They are participants even more than the chorus is in most Greek tragedies. The action of

[1] *Murder in the Cathedral*, Interlude, p. 49.

the play is really internal. It is an offering of the will to be crushed into conformity with the will of God. This the chorus can do, as Thomas does. In the first part they act with him, act or suffer, we cannot distinguish. It is only the actual martyrdom that they fear, and so they become guilty of Thomas' blood, as everyone who consents to a killing becomes guilty of it. But the physical death of Thomas is relatively unimportant in the development of Eliot's pattern; and the chorus suffer with Thomas everything except the actual physical death.

The chorus are drawn in against their wishes; their last words before Thomas enters are a prayer to him to go away.[1] Then as Thomas is brought to his knees by the Fourth Tempter, the chorus become overpowered in their reason as he is in his. In a riot of animal imagery they see the "Lords of Hell".[2] Crowd and saint are overpowered together, and in the overpowering grace comes to Thomas. We do not see his suffering, only that of the chorus. It is a wonderful vision. Anyone's spiritual torments can help to make a saint. As the knights approach, the chorus panic while Thomas remains calm,[3] but immediately before the killing they experience the utter void, beyond death, and at the killing they realize the total corruption of the entire world, including themselves. Having gone through this despair, having been destroyed spiritually and known physical terror, they may join in the praise with which the play almost ends. Right at the end the chorus kneel in penitence, for the audience, confess their responsibility for the murder, and pray for forgiveness to the Trinity and St Thomas. The audience are drawn in to the action as well, as closely as they can be, short of physical involvement. We are all made to realize that we can only join in the praise if we admit our share of the guilt. If we do not admit our share in the guilt we cannot join in the praise and the Church triumphant must go on without us.

And we must think no further of you

says the third priest.[4] The point of this scene and the implications of the end are often slurred over in performance. The rejoicing is only conditional on the penitence.

[1] *Murder in the Cathedral*, Part I, p. 20.   [2] Ib., Part I, pp. 42–44.
[3] Ib., Part II, p. 68.   [4] Ib., Part II, p. 85.

The play does raise the issue of whether people should be governed by sacred or secular authority, but it is not central, though it is the obvious issue of the actual historical story. Put differently, it is the question as to whether the Church should try and influence politics or not. It is the point of the second temptation, but Eliot is not so interested in it. The second temptation is more important than the third in terms of outside effect, and therefore we may feel a sense of anti-climax about the third, more petty one. But the rhythm of this play is a gradual increase of confidence in Thomas. He becomes more and more secure, until the unexpected fourth temptation shatters his confidence. This rhythm shows that Eliot is not really interested in the political issue, a clear difference of outlook from that of the Greek poets.

The struggle with Henry is shown obliquely and we need to know the historical allusions. Clarendon[1] was an occasion of compromise when Thomas took an oath of loyalty, "saving his order".[2] Northampton[3] was the council, after which Thomas left for France. This council is shown in the film version,[4] but when he wrote the play Eliot felt that to show Henry would be a distraction from the main theme.

The play therefore remains as an image of martyrdom, and the other issues become irrelevant because Eliot's outlook stresses the difference between saint or martyr and ordinary person, and the incomprehensibility of the martyr's death. At the death the issues seem irrelevant. It is something detached from time. The significance of the death is that it is a type of the death of Christ, and that is the point of the sermon for the Christmas Eucharist. Christ's birth and death are celebrated at the same time, the peace He brought involved his followers in torture, imprisonment, disappointment, and death. By design we follow this celebration with that of the first martyr St Stephen, so that we may remember what sort of peace Christ brought us. And this is Eliot's justification for writing this play. Every martyrdom holds some clue to the meaning of the life and death of Christ.

The most important structural image is that of the animals.

---

[1] *Murder in the Cathedral*, Part I, p. 26.   [2] Cf. ib., Part II, p. 60.
[3] Ib., Part I, p. 26.   [4] *The Film of Murder in the Cathedral*, pp. 25–33.

There are allusions to hunting and trapping by Thomas and the tempters[1] which prepare us for the moment when the animals, the "Lords of Hell", overpower the chorus after the fourth temptation.[2] After the climax of the first scene with the knights, the chorus are completely overwhelmed and the animal imagery takes on a surrealist appearance.[3] They become "United to the spiritual flesh of nature". The priests in their panic see the knights as beasts,[4] and the knights sing for "Daniel" to enter "the lions' den".[5] Finally, while the choir sing *Te Deum* in the background the chorus speak of hawk and wolf and worm taking part in the final praise.[6] It is a point we shall find again in Eliot; the angels of destruction are also instruments of praise. It is central to the play.

An interesting, effective, and unique structural device is the repetition of Thomas' words[7] by the Fourth Tempter.[8] Thomas thinks he knows what it is to "act or suffer", but he does not. He can say, to the priest, "the women know in their hearts, though they cannot express it". But the tempter will hurl his words back, "You know in theory, but have not experienced it." Production must make this clear, but it is quite possible to do this, and it is an excellent piece of theatre.

There are indications of character in the poetry of both Tempters and knights, and there is every reason for a production to emphasize their individuality, since their function as part of the pattern is made so obvious. The fluid theatrical form which Eliot employs to great effect never allows us to worry about whether they are meant to be old friends of Thomas or allegorical figures. It does not matter. Sometimes they are doubled with the knights, though Eliot has said that he prefers them not to be. The knights' speeches are allocated differently in different editions, presumably in an attempt to align the characters of the knights as there revealed, with that of the temptations they have represented before. The alignment is not exact, but the idea of the doubling is attractive, helping to emphasize the unity of the play.

[1] *Murder in the Cathedral*, Part I, pp. 23, 25, 29, and 34.
[2] Ib., Part I, pp. 42–44. [3] Ib., Part II, pp. 66–68.
[4] Ib., Part II, p. 73. [5] Ib., Part II, p. 74.
[6] Ib., Part II, pp. 85–86. [7] Ib., Part I, p. 21.
[8] Ib., Part I, p. 40.

Critics who do not understand the method of a poetic dramatist who has small time to indicate character have called Thomas
characterless. There are plenty of indications of character in the
first part, but as in Greek drama they are only given in a half
line of text. They need the actor to fill them out. Becket has a
sense of humour.[1] He is popular, a bit of a showman.[2] It is very
uninteresting to play him as austere; all martyrs will inevitably
seem somewhat austere; and the shock of the fourth temptation
will be greatly lessened if he has been shown as a haughty man.
"Merry" is the first adjective I should give an actor. But after
the temptations he must appear partly out of the world; the
difference of first and second part is the difference between a
man, and a priest celebrating Mass. From then on, we can only
take part in the action through the intermediary chorus, the
centre of the play's development.

The play has many incidental merits, some of which are obviously significant when we consider it as a model for future
writing. The fluid staging is very effective and economical of
time. It is put to most successful use in the original beginning
of Part II, the entry of the priests with the banners for the
Saints' days following Christmas, which now follows the added
chorus. This device reminds us of the three sorts of martyr, and
thus emphasizes the point of the sermon and enables Eliot to
make the point that really every day is a day of crisis when he
comes to 29 December.

I have drawn attention elsewhere to the great strength of the
dialogue's verse form.[3] He exploits some of the many potentialities of this line. There is the way that the Langland or Old
English line is sometimes lengthened to one of three stresses
each side of the caesura:[4]

To see how doughtilich Deth sholde do· and deme her
    botheres righte.
The Juwes and the Justice· ageine Jesu they were,

---

[1] *Murder in the Cathedral*, Part I, pp. 22 and 31.
[2] Ib., Part I, pp. 15–16 and 22.　　　[3] Cf. pp. 207–9.
[4] Langland, "Christ's Dying and Descent into Hell", from *Piers Plowman*, taken from Boris Ford (ed.), *Pelican Guide to English Literature*, I, *The
Age of Chaucer*, II, 39–40.

This is the principle behind lines such as these:

> I'll remember you at kissing time below the stairs.[1]

and:

> And last at Montirail, in Maine. Now that I have recalled them.[2]

This effect is easier when there is a rhyme as in the first example.

Purely artificial lengthening is used with good effect for the First Tempter:[3]

> Fires devouring the winter season,
> Eating up the darkness, with wit and wine and wisdom!

Wisdom, with the extra stress, is an afterthought, excellently dramatic. These effects must, of course, be used sparingly, or they will destroy the verse form.

He never uses the pure eight-syllable iambic at all. This song-like effect is not exploited, though he almost uses it in two climactic moments, both spoken by Thomas:

> It is not I who insult the king,[4]

and:

> Unbar the doors! Throw open the doors![5]

He uses rhyme, and the avoidance of rhyme, sometimes with great skill, notably in Thomas' speech at the end of Part I. After the still couplets of the opening the rhymes become freer, as Thomas becomes aware of his colourful past, which he is now leaving. Then at the end the rhymes tighten, but before the last couplet there is an unrhymed line, which breaks the static quality of the couplets and looks forward to the next act.

In general, Eliot has made use of most devices in the verse, alliteration in the Second Tempter's scene, puns and word play,[6] parody,[7] and repetitions whether liturgical or colloquial as in the later plays. There are other important images besides that of the beasts, especially those of the wheel, and the seasonal

---

[1] *Murder in the Cathedral*, Part I, p. 26. [2] Ib., p. 26.
[3] Ib., p. 24.   [4] Ib., Part II, p. 65.   [5] Ib., Part II, p. 72.
[6] Ib., Part II, p. 66.   [7] Ib., Part II, p. 74.

change from winter to spring. Above all, the chorus verse is a masterpiece of *vers libre*. Eliot had the experiences of the choruses he wrote for *The Rock* behind him and he drew on the tradition of the English psalter. They are unique in English poetry. But that is not the effect of a Greek chorus, who sang something in a very strict metric, to which they moved in time. The Women of Canterbury are a magnificent conception, but Eliot would have been closer to his Greek models if he had stayed closer to his own liturgical tradition, with a singing, even an antiphonal choir.

It is harder to show saints than sinners. Eliot shows us a passive saint. Greek tragedy, as it were, showed us active sinners. It is easier to make a singing choir effective than it is to make a spoken chorus. If Christian followers of Eliot try to make Christian tragedies after the Greek model and stick more closely to the model than Eliot does in these two respects, they will surely find it easier to produce Christian tragedy. Where it will be produced or whether it will ever get professional production is another matter. Good or bad, it will probably be disregarded by theatre critics. But Eliot has made a model which shows us how Greek tragedy could be imitated in a modern context. Once there has been one imitation, it is possible to see how to do further imitations. Out of such imitations could grow a dramatic renaissance. It might then even penetrate the theatres.

(iv) THE LATER PLAYS

The importance of these plays was that with them Eliot succeeded in putting over a religious vision couched in poetic form, in spite of using the conventions of the naturalistic drawing-room comedy. Drama need no longer be written in this convention and we can only regret that so much of Eliot's valuable energy was used up trying to overcome the inevitable deficiencies of this inadequate and dreary medium. Most of the problems that arise in discussion of these plays concern this difficulty. Detailed discussion of them is therefore less relevant here.

They are not, of course, called tragedies; *The Cocktail Party* and *The Confidential Clerk* are called comedies, and there is a sophisticated lightness of touch about them all, similar to that of trivializing comedy. It is the same tone as that of Giraudoux, the tone of a civilized upper class, still fairly leisured.

It is this tone and the naturalistic setting which made Eliot put his poetry "on a thin diet".[1] In justification of this course we hear it said that today is not a time for rich language. It is clearly not a time for decorative and rhetorical language, but that does not mean that a writer should not use structural imagery, imagery for character, or vivid visual writing. No comments that I have seen distinguish between the two. It might surely be said that our complicated age needs every possible resource to describe it, not a "thin diet of poetry".

Almost the only rhetorical device Eliot allows himself is an exaggeration of the colloquial use of repetitions; this can be best seen in the opening of *The Cocktail Party*. Otherwise it is a poetry of plain statement, with a very gentle rhythmic beat. His line is one of three stresses and many unstressed syllables. It is so free that he has to have most lines ending with a sense stop. It is also sometimes ambiguous in prosody.

> And the night unfeared and the day expected

must surely be scanned with four stresses.[2] The verse is necessary; without the lines the words would be spoken wrongly. But it is difficult to say exactly what its effect is. Sometimes, however, it is very beautiful, in a way like nothing in English. I find the second act of *The Cocktail Party* and parts of *The Elder Statesman* intensely moving. It is a kind of austere perfection, a purist insistence on a black and white, not a coloured picture. It is like Bruckner's austerity, surrounded by the lush orchestration of his Romantic contemporaries.

As is the poetry, so is the religious experience; less intense, and nearer to ordinary life. He wanted to present the crises of religious experience in terms nearer to those in which they actually occur to most people. His aim was to approach as closely as possible to actual everyday experience.

His greatest mistake in this aim seems to have been his use of metaphor. Too much fuss has been made about the Eumenides in *The Family Reunion*. They could easily be staged, prob-

---

[1] T. S. Eliot, *Poetry and Drama*, p. 32.
[2] *The Family Reunion*, Part I, p. 11.

ably in masks. But in the Christian terms in which Eliot is talking they are metaphor. They might be said to be angels, or they might be said to represent that aspect of God's will which is horrible when you flee it and glorious when you submit. And there is a parallel between this notion and the notion of the Eumenides in Aeschylus. But Aeschylus accepted these beings as actual; they were worshipped. Eliot's Eumenides can only be understood indirectly, by means of a literary understanding of the Greek myths. By avoiding obvious Christian terminology he made it harder, not easier, for his audience.

This applies to his ritual, both in *The Family Reunion*[1] and *The Cocktail Party*.[2] The runes can only be taken as allusions to Christian ritual. They will only be understood in the way that Eliot wants by Christians who see them as Christian rite, which apparently they are not. The non-Christians will think them nonsense, and if they understand the Christian significance, will think that Christian ritual is similar mumbo-jumbo. The image of Christianity in these plays is not easier but much harder to grasp than that in *Murder in the Cathedral*.

The action of *The Family Reunion*[3] is Harry being confronted with his salvation. It is passive, and internal, and there is no great development, since he arrives at Wishwood already far advanced in the necessary suffering. We are to assume from the scene with Downing[4] that he did *not* push his wife overboard, but only dreamt it, though this is far from clear. It is a poem of gradual illumination. First it is through Mary, who sees the Eumenides but pretends not to, for his sake, as she admits to Agatha,[5] and then it is through Agatha that he comes to full realization of what he is. After that his decision to leave follows naturally.

This personal, interior story is complicated by much material irrelevant to the theme, but needed for the structure of a naturalistic play. All the story of Arthur and John is irrelevant; the scene between Harry and Warburton does not advance the action at all.[6]

---

[1] *The Family Reunion*, Part I, iii, p. 70.
[2] *The Cocktail Party*, Part II, pp. 149–50. [3] 1939.
[4] *The Family Reunion*, Part I, i, pp. 38–43.
[5] Ib., Part II, iii, p. 120. [6] Ib., Part II, i, p. 73.

The point of the play is that imagined sin is as bad as committed sin, but it is combined with an increasing awareness of the God who causes the guilt feelings. The occasion of Harry's sin is the event which stirs him to awareness of God. At first it is an awareness of loss, which makes him try to go back to childhood memories, but gradually as the past is filled in for him by Agatha, the loss becomes clearer, though Eliot has left his final salvation vague, which many think to be a mistake.

This is a theme very similar to the Quartets, or at least to *Burnt Norton*. It is better expressed in the poem than here, where so much seems irrelevant. Eliot thought wrongly that he had integrated the chorus better than in *Murder in the Cathedral*.[1] The real interior action touches them not at all. There is more naturalistic justification for their presence; but that is not integration in the action of a poetic play. The chorus do not do much except say that they do not understand. There is a conflict between the attempts to write a personal poem and a drawing-room comedy, which is apparent in the imagery of rose garden, hospital, cold spring; these can be understood fully only with reference to his other work. There is some fine verbal poetry in this play, and it has an important theme. But the theme has been better expressed elsewhere.

The women of Canterbury come to see that "the world is wholly foul". So does Harry. So do Edward and Lavinia, Celia, and eventually Peter Quilpe, in *The Cocktail Party*.[2] This despair is the prelude to self-awareness and a Christian way of life, and all Eliot's plays have to do with this theme. In *The Cocktail Party* a minor domestic crisis occurs. Lavinia walks out on her husband Edward. In the light of this, relationships which had looked real before are seen to be insubstantial, and because of the breakdown of the human props to their life, the characters are forced up against God. The action is supervised by the Guardians, a crazy man who travels everywhere and cooks anything, a gossipy society woman, and a psychiatrist. These are the developed Christians, who have gone through the stage that the remaining characters in the play must face. There is an element of the tragic viewpoint about the action because those who have chosen to go back to their ordinary lives have to live

---

[1] T. S. Eliot, *Poetry and Drama*, pp. 25 and 28.   [2] 1949.

their lives in the knowledge that Celia, confronted with the same situation, chose a way that led to a martyr's death. It is a way of putting over the idea that every Christian has to be prepared to die for his faith, though not all will be called to do so. But the play is written as comedy, and should be enjoyed as such.

Eliot has said that the story is based on the *Alcestis*. This does not help our understanding of the play. Celia makes her sacrifice after she has severed her connexion with Edward; Alcestis gives herself up for her husband. In addition, "Alcestis" has been split into Celia and Lavinia. The most noticeable effect is Reilly getting drunk at the party, like Heracles. And that is just Eliot's fun.

There are two principal difficulties. Peter is the last to be bought to realization; he needs Celia's death to shock him into awareness. But he is less fully characterized than the others. His conversation does not provide quite enough action for the last act, which becomes more of an epilogue. Secondly, it is very difficult to show the rebirth of the Chamberlaynes. In the last act they are in a state of grace, but they can still only talk in cliché. Eliot's medium is too naturalistic to convey this by poetry.

He shows the rebirth through the symbolism of the food. At the beginning it is inadequate; at the end abundant. The food symbolism must certainly be brought out in production. It ties with Alex' story of the monkeys,[1] the prelude to Celia's death; and it conveys a hint of the Eucharist.

An effect of unreality is ingeniously created by the comedy of I, ii. Numerous exits and entrances give us a sensation of not knowing what's happening. We all know the sensation in real life; this is a mad world – and the bottom may drop out. It is a way to effect a penetration through the surface of things, by means of near fantasy.

There is a vagueness about all the characterization; the Guardians have to be made mysterious, to seem powerful. We do not see very much of the relationship between Edward and Celia, none of that between Lavinia and Peter. Eliot would no doubt say that none of this is important for what he is trying to

[1] *The Cocktail Party*, III, pp. 159 ff.

say. He is interested in changes in people which have to take place in solitude. But to make plays always about these kinds of changes takes away most of the normal means of a dramatist's expression.

The Confidential Clerk[1] is constructed as a well-made play. The audience is kept in suspense up to the end. The tone is much nearer the ordinary tone of drawing-room comedy, and the verse is even less apparent. It is not important to know that the story derives from the *Ion*, but there is a greater affinity of tone. The *Ion* is about Ion, not Apollo; it is a play about a special person, round whom hangs an aura like that round Colby. Religious vision is less intense, and there is no continuous poetic action. Poetry is used on occasions to give the sensation of penetrating within the surface of things. We are not aware all the time of two levels of action.

The Elder Statesman[2] has affinities with the *Coloneus*. But instead of the ferocious pessimism of Sophocles, Eliot gives an atmosphere of reconciliation and peace. The action is extremely simple. It is Claverton repenting of two past sins and relinquishing his hold on life, his hold over his scapegrace son, and his loving daughter. Although it is far from the world of the *Coloneus*, we might say that it was the result of a Christian brooding on the tone of the last speech of Oedipus,[3] and amplifying it through his hope of a final redemption, somewhat as Ghéon meditated on the Oedipus story.

The action is set in motion by the malice of Gomez and Mrs Carghill. As these are involved in Claverton's sins, the action is more closely knit. It is more clearly doubly determined. It is natural that the arrival of Gomez will spark off reflection in Claverton. It is natural, and part of the poetic or divine plan. It is also more frequent that these sorts of realization are sparked off by people who intend to hurt.

The characters are carefully integrated in the pattern; but their function depends on their nature, and they are more strongly drawn than in the other plays. Michael needs to be clearly shown; his function is to humiliate his father into awareness; we must see exactly what he is. Because Mrs Carghill, and to a lesser degree Gomez, are acting from an irrational desire,

[1] 1954.   [2] 1958.   [3] *O.C.*, 1611–19; cf. pp. 105–6.

they provide stronger parts for their actors. But it is hard to act the lovers. From the start they must be radiant; but the opening scene is very difficult to make radiant. Only at the end does Eliot give them a rare and remote poetry. But if there were actors who could convey the quality he wants throughout the play there might be a moment in the West End theatre convention where as Eliot has hoped, an audience was led[1] "to a condition of serenity, stillness, and reconciliation"; there to be left "as Virgil left Dante, to proceed toward a region where that guide can avail us no farther".

(v) CONCLUSION

Two very different attempts to show modern English audiences a poetic drama; two very different attempts to make Christianity once again theatrical; one with a more conscious evangelizing purpose, and a more conscious awareness of Greek myth; the other without effort, making more people aware of the claims of Christianity, and also being more like Greek tragedy. The achievement of Eliot in his later plays will be discussed for a long time. If they are judged successful it will be the triumph of a man of integrity over a poor medium, the conventions of a social class that has outlived its usefulness, and a mode of philosophical thinking which is misleading. The achievement of *Murder in the Cathedral* in one aspect is clear. It should be to make Church leaders hang their heads in shame because they have not immediately encouraged the growth of festivals where drama could be presented in blatant challenge to the weak remnants of an English theatrical tradition as tarnished as the tawdry gold ornamentation of its crumbling Victorian playhouses. It should be to rouse writers to say that there is no reason whatsoever why this play should be treated as an isolated example, not the beginning of a new tradition, except their own lack of skill or lack of courage; it should be to make them realize that here is a medium which demands the highest excellence in every skill they possess, philosophical, poetic, musical, and theatrical, since nothing but the best could be ever good enough for such a cause as this. Let all whom it may concern despair, and then make a beginning.

[1] *Poetry and Drama*, final sentence, p. 35.

CHAPTER SIXTEEN

CONCLUSION

I have dared to claim that this is an age when tragedy once again might answer a need in our lives, as it has done in some periods of history. I have made this claim primarily because it is so easy to recognize the need. We are all aware of the insecurity of human life; we must all learn to live with this insecurity; it does not take wisdom or insight to say this, as it may have done in the recent past. It is easy for us to see the limits within which human action is free and the catastrophic consequences of overstepping these limits. It is easy for us to realize that we must learn to understand each other and ourselves, and understand how our society has become as it is. We can see that all is not well with it; we need to know what went wrong, and how it went wrong, and at what time, so that we may put it right if we can. If we do not discover these things there is a real chance that we shall destroy ourselves. We cannot but be aware of the possibility that we ourselves, the people we love, and the community which our ancestors worked to build, will be utterly destroyed. We can hardly fail to be aware of death; we can hardly fail to see the need to reach a clear idea of right and wrong within the conditions of our society; we can hardly fail to be aware of the limits of our understanding. Awareness in these three ways is the mark of Greek tragedy. So we may dare to hope that out of the realization of our need may grow the answer to our need.

I have spent what some may consider a disproportionate amount of time on recent developments in philosophy, because studying what has happened in philosophy is the easiest way of seeing something that has happened to every aspect of our thought, something which is irrevocable. I have called this the end of certainty. It is most easily seen in the collapse of all philosophical systems, the discovery that it is not possible to account for any experience, rational or sensory, except in terms of one's own personal experience or by analogy with one's own personal experience. It is connected with the fact that it used to be thought that the world could be described as made of atoms, minute physical objects, physical in the same way as trees and rocks. Now the world is described in terms of electrons, although we cannot say "electrons exist", and mean by the word "exist", the same as what we mean when we say that buffaloes exist, and dodoes do not. We have seen the end of philosophy as an intellectual system, and the end of the possibility of philosophers *qua* philosophers guiding our lives completely. We can see that we can never say of an action "that is right", or of a picture "that is beautiful", and know that we are not mistaken, and that what we say has complete objective validity. Nothing is certain, but we ourselves can become a little more certain. We know nothing except that we can learn to understand a little more, and that there are many ways in which we are helped to understand.

We are living in a society desperately in need of people able to take clear decisions. One of the ways in which we can learn to clarify our decisions is to see how other men in other societies have faced similar decisions, and how the society has been affected when the decision was wrong. If we all accept this, then we shall see the function tragedy can play in our lives. It will teach us how to think. We shall resort to myth; not because myth is pretty, but because if we do not understand the past we shall not understand the present. We shall not understand very much, and it will not help us with the present very much; but it is all we have. We shall use models, not syllogisms; we shall rely on our imagination; not because it is nice to use our imagination, but because the nature of the world is better described through the Indeterminacy Principle than by deductive syllogisms. Our imagination will fail; still, it is all we have. We shall not try and fence off a little garden of poetry with a few rotten aesthetic terms. We shall walk through the entire jungle of science where growth is faster, more horrifying, more exotically beautiful, and where there will be no temptation to believe we ourselves grew the plants.

I am claiming then, that our generation is able to see why imaginative activity is the most important activity of the mind, and why poetry is therefore not a pleasant decoration, but the centre of the intellectual part of life. I have suggested reasons for thinking that a tragic drama something like that of the Greeks is a necessary part of this imaginative activity which I have called poetry, and that in the condition of our society, in practice unfavourable to poetry, it is less unreasonable to hope for tragic drama than some other form of poetry. I am claiming that we need poets who are teachers in the Greek sense, and that we can see why we need them.

I have tried to show that the plays discussed in Part III are less important than the Greek tragedies because of their intellectual content or the philosophy of the writer. The weakness of nineteenth-century drama is that no writer dared to show the process of decision because all the writers feared that a close examination of the process of decision would reveal that man was not free. The triviality of Cocteau, Gide, and Giraudoux is due to their belief that one could apply in the theatre a set of aesthetic values, which were different from the values of ordinary life. The weakness of Anouilh is directly due to the way in which he has not thought out the implications of the story he is presenting. Sartre is inconsistent throughout his writing and the inconsistency of his drama is similar to that of his philosophy. We are somewhat worried by the characterization of Eliot and Giraudoux; this is because their idea of people is an Idealist one. We are left unmoved by the language of Ghéon, when he has thought it unnecessary to think of new words, owing to his Idealist belief that a particular word calls up a particular experience. With Miller it is more that his medium is not quite adequate for what he wants to say; but this is because he is using a medium evolved to evade the issue with which he wishes to deal.

I do not wish to suggest that all these deficiencies are of equal importance. I hope I have already indicated the merits and failings of these writers. Nor do I wish to denigrate their achievement; by drawing attention to the difficulties facing them, I hope to make us realize more clearly what they have achieved. I wish to suggest that we now are privileged with an understanding of much that has been wrong in Western thought for many generations and should therefore feel a responsibility commensurate with this privilege.

I have also tried to show that it is possible, and much more profitable, to criticize contemporary writing without using terms of aesthetic value. Most of the writers I have discussed have used their drama to express their view of life and society. I would not insult their efforts by thinking that there was no importance in what they said, only in how they said it. This seems to me a reasonable course of action; it is up to those who say that it is possible to have a separate set of aesthetic values to show how they derive these values. I have never seen this done.

I have seemed to suggest that we are on the brink of great new art. I have done so, because I think that it is theoretically possible, and has not been theoretically possible. What hinders us now are practical difficulties. The possibility of modern tragedy is a sociological question. I do not think that anyone is likely to maintain a belief in a separate aesthetics or to remain an Idealist once he has understood the developments of modern philosophy, or to adopt the Romantic attitude towards the artist once he understands that this attitude arose from a desire to safeguard the imagination from science, and that science is one of the best exercises of the imagination. I have not met anyone who has done so, or read any books which maintain these opinions combined with an awareness of the new developments. But a great number of people are still Idealists, and most theatre critics certainly seem to use some set of aesthetic values. To say that the poet should be a teacher is unfashionable; until it is widely accepted, there will be no tragedy like that of the Greeks.

Secondly, I have said that we are aware of danger, death, and the limits within which we are free. But in practice we see that many people are doing their best to forget these limits, to close their eyes to the possibility of death. To say that it does not matter what our government does is about as safe as saying that it does not matter whether one drives on a road or off it;

but the sight of cars speeding down a road frightens some people so much that they close their eyes. Wishful thinking is incompatible with tragedy, and our society is full of wishful thinkers.

Thirdly, we must consider the state of the theatre. I do not know if there could ever be anything like Greek tragedy in theatres whose function is said to be entertainment, and in fact is to make a profit for someone. The temptation to avoid unsettling the audience is too strong. But a more enlightened audience will demand plays that enlighten and not merely soothe them; concert audiences have become more discriminating, and theatre audiences are following them slowly. It may be different too if we have subsidized theatres. I do not know what will happen; no one knows. Sometimes we hear it said in this context that Shakespeare contrived to make money out of his plays. But the strength of his writing lies in what he was able to assume as a result of a long tradition of drama not dependent on the box-office. He did not face the same situation as a modern writer starting without such a tradition.

The great periods of theatre started with an audience gathered at a festival for something that they would neither have called art nor entertainment. In the fifth century at Athens, or in the fourteenth century in England or France, the audience was the population; it was not an audience of one class; it was not an audience of people interested in the theatre. To ask whether modern tragedy is a possibility is to ask whether there could be such an audience nowadays. I do not know; television reaches an audience which is in effect the entire population, but hardly has the same festival atmosphere. It is possible that education may create a demand for a television drama which will consciously aim to enlighten its audience's understanding of life in the community by means similar to that of the Greek poets. The effect of television is certainly to make our community smaller, to make us feel that we know all our important people personally; it is somewhat similar to the way in which they were known in ancient Athens. There are certainly opportunities for a revival of something like Aristophanic comedy, satirizing actual people. I find it harder to conceive anything strictly analogous to tragedy, but I do not think we should be let off so lightly as to be told that we could not possibly create tragedy, even on television. We have too many opportunities to be let off lightly.

We would all admit that there has not yet been a body of dramatic writing which can compare in scope and intensity with Greek tragic drama. We cannot yet say that there is modern tragedy. What hinders its development are certain features of our society which clearly can be overcome, and ought to be overcome if we want a responsible democracy. Everything is uncertain, and up to us. That is why I have introduced the entirely new question of the relation of television. How can a critic say now that there can be no tragedy? There is a new medium, which touches the mass of the population. We must see what happens, and try to guide what happens. Perhaps there cannot be tragedy; but it is too easy to despair.

If there is one lesson to be learnt from the Greeks it is for critics. Let them abandon their unsoundly based aesthetic judgements and take seriously the writers' attempts to illuminate the choices society must make. Unless poetry is fact, not fiction, and treated as fact, not fiction, we shall not have drama like the Greeks. A writer by himself cannot create tragedy; he can only guide his society on a way that they must choose. Can there be tragedy today? The first answer is: "Yes, if we care enough about the way our society is developing to take seriously those who are trying to understand it."

There are further questions. If a Christian asks, "Can there be tragedy?" the answer is quite straightforward, "Yes." There is the body of history that can fulfil exactly the same function as the Greek myths did for the Athenian audience. There is continuous musical tradition to use, and now a recently rediscovered dramatic tradition. There is the chance of writing for an audience of all classes and occupations, not especially interested in the theatre, gathered for a purpose not primarily theatrical. There has been one play which can reasonably be said to be Christian tragedy, and a great play, and there have been quite a number of others which are much better than it is fashionable to say, because the fashionable criticism has been anti-Christian. The challenge is simple, hard, and clear as the message itself.

There are two other questions contained in this one. Can drama which appeals to a parochial minority properly be called tragedy? I do not know. But it cannot be the size of the audience that is ultimately important, so much as the fact that it represents a society, large or small. Many people would agree with me in saying that the climax of all Western art was created in thoroughly parochial conditions. I allude to the Lutheran tradition of Church cantatas, and its culmination in the writing of the B minor Mass and the St Matthew Passion. The challenge to Christians is to create the conditions in which, even if unrecognized like Bach, writers can do with drama what the eighteenth-century Lutherans did with music.

Secondly, it will be asked whether this hypothetical tragedy can appeal to non-Christians. The crude answer is, "Yes, if it is good enough". The music of Bach and the sculpture of Chartres do. Christians should believe that they are given a greater understanding of what it is to be human than those outside the Church, but they have many times gone wrong in the past by using this belief as an excuse to shut their eyes, not as a challenge to open them; as a result they have produced bad art, and bad Christianity. We have the privilege of having our eyes forced open, even the laziest of us. The least we can do is face the challenge.

Can there be any other kind of tragedy? Let each person act and speculate for himself. Philosophical argument is abstract; it is easy to avoid its consequences. Tragedy is argument in terms of real people, and events which actually happened. Can men of all beliefs become willing to submit their beliefs to this sort of test? Can there be Humanist, Marxist, Existentialist, Christian writers who will submit their own religion to the most searching challenges they can conceive before an audience composed of people who hold opposite beliefs, realizing that their religion is being staked, and that to a small degree the truth of the religion will be judged by the effect of the play? Can there, above all, be audiences prepared to accept the responsibility of what we call a free society and submit to the challenge with their leaders? I do not know. But if this could happen we might have a great society.

I have talked throughout this book as though tragedy was

344

a matter for poets and actors and critics. This is because I have hoped to draw attention to some few points about the making of tragedies which may interest these craftsmen in particular. The real problem lies elsewhere; it is a matter for society as a whole, but in society as a whole poets and actors and critics can do a little. For I should insult the memory of the great poets about whom I have been writing if I talked as if tragedy was an end in itself, rather than one means towards the end of giving people a new vision of what their society might be. It is not a coincidence that Aeschylus' epitaph makes no mention of his poetry; the important thing to him was that he served his community, in whatever way he happened to be able. It is like Chaucer, repudiating his poetry at the end of his life, not because he wished to deny the value of poetry, but because he was so much aware of something before which even poetry, the best thing he knew, was utterly unimportant. It is not much to ask this generation to try and create the conditions in which we might be given such a vision in terms of our own society, for it is so easy to see our society's enormous potentialities. It is right to see what the vision of Aeschylus was, for it is so easy to translate his vision into our own terms. Let our generation, which has seen the discovery of electricity, the permanent conquest of darkness by light, consider also the other parts of Aeschylus' final vision. We, too, can say that what is good in our system of government is well typified by the principle of trial by jury. We, too, have received into our state powers whose capacity for destruction is unlimited, and without whom most of us would starve and go naked, even if we see these powers not as faces that drip poison and coils of snakes, but as mushroom clouds and coils of wire. Can we not, then, at least translate into our own terms the rest of the vision Aeschylus reached without benefit of predecessors? That final vision is a procession; all that is best in government and all the powers of nature, that bring total destruction if abused and untold benefits if well used, join together to receive divine blessing and, still linked together, leave the altar surrounded by the entire population, go into every part of the city and live in it for ever. This is the end of tragedy, that every person and every point of view should finally capitulate to a peace beyond understanding.

NOTES

CHAPTER ONE

a [cf. p. 21]. Friedrich Solmsen, *Hesiod and Aeschylus*, p. 222, note 166, has noted certain passages which seem to indicate that Aeschylus knew the work of Xenophanes. *Suppl.* 96 ff., for example, "shows a very interesting combination" of Hesiod, *Works and Days*, 6, with Xenophanes, Frag. 25. I should myself prefer to say that the ideas were generally being discussed at the time, in Athens and in the Ionian cities; scientists and tragedians each made use of them, in ways appropriate to their different purposes.

b [cf. p. 25]. To summarize Plato's religion is inevitably to oversimplify. I have assumed a development of his thought roughly as follows: at first he explored an idea of a *theos* apart from the world; with this in mind he makes Socrates say that we know nothing about *theoi* or their names, *Crat.*, 400 D; we should compare *Phdr.*, 246C–D, *Crit.*, 107 B, and *Epin.*, 984 D. Later, without necessarily abandoning this idea, he became more aware of the religious needs of the unphilosophical majority, who were incapable of understanding such a *theos*, and who could only worship something obvious. In the *Laws*, 717 A–B, he advocates sacrifice to the Olympians, to the powers who look after a city, to *daimones*, and to heroes. Elsewhere his language suggests that the descriptions of *theoi* are a matter of convention 885 B, 890 A, 904 A, 914 B, and probably 891 E, though the text is dubious. He ended by preferring to maintain the traditional forms of worship artificially, since he had been unable to find any better sanctions for right conduct in society.

c [cf. p. 26]. We know very little about fourth-century drama; we have to gather indications from Aristotle, and make guesses based on the tendencies of Euripides' later plays. The problem has been discussed by Kitto, *Form and Meaning in Drama*, pp. 239–42. He has also discussed the difference in the conventions of tragedy and tragi-comedy, *Greek Tragedy*, pp. 308–27. It is clear that there were many imitations of Euripides' tragi-comedies throughout the century. Menander owes much to this style of writing. If the conventions of tragedy and tragi-comedy are opposed to each other it is reasonable that the decline of one should accompany the rise of the other, this rise being part of a process in which the tragic poet became less of a teacher and more of an entertainer.

d [cf. p. 29]. The origins of Greek tragedy are fully discussed by Pickard-Cambridge in *Dithyramb, Tragedy and Comedy*, pp. 5–220. By collating all the available evidence he has clearly shown the limits of our knowledge, and successfully rebuffs the various theories which happily ignore those limits.

e [cf. p. 32]. cf. Jebb's Introduction to the *Philoctetes*, pp. ix–xx. He describes the plots of the plays Aeschylus and Euripides made about Philoctetes, basing his account on that of Dion, lii and lix. There are considerable differences of detail, but in all three the action is the attempt of Odysseus to get Philoctetes to Troy. The companion of Odysseus varies, however. In the epic version of the story it is Diomedes, not Odysseus. I find these differences of the same sort as those of the different handlings of the Orestes story.

CHAPTER TWO

a [cf. p. 35]. cf. K. J. Dover, "The Political Aspect of Aeschylus' *Eumenides*", *J.H.S.*, LXXVII, Part 2, 1957. He argues that to show the Areopagus as a court with no political powers is to accept the reforms of Pericles and Ephialtes in 462. There has been considerable discussion about Aeschylus' involvement in contemporary politics, but much of the evidence is still in process of being evaluated; full treatment of this question needs more space than I possess, if one is to do justice to it.

b [cf. p. 35]. There is no conclusive evidence that any well-known Ionian philosophers were in Athens at this time, though we may be sure that if they were Aeschylus would have met them. It is possible that Anaxagoras was at Athens for the period of Aeschylus' maturity as dramatist. Tradition says that Anaxagoras arrived in the year of Salamis. Burnet accepts this, *Early Greek Philosophy*, pp. 251–56 (3rd ed.). Kathleen Freeman, *The Pre-Socratic Philosophers*, pp. 261–62, argues against such an early date, and suggests that Anaxagoras arrived 465–0, and was exiled from Athens at the beginning of the Peloponnesian War.

c [cf. p. 36]. If we accept the evidence of the papyrus fragment, *P.Oxy.*, 2256 Frag. 3. 1b, then Aeschylus won first prize with this trilogy in a year when Sophocles came second and the archon's name began Ar . ., although it is possible that Ar . . is merely "archon". Sophocles' first victory, possibly with his first entry, was 468. In 464 the archon was Archedemides. E. C. Yorke, *Classical Quarterly*, 1938, pp. 117 ff., counted resolutions in the trimeters, and on the basis of this stylistic feature thought that the *Supplices* was later than the *Persae*. But F. R. Earp, *The Style of Aeschylus*, 1948, claimed the *Supplices* the earliest play on stylistic grounds. A. Diamantopoulos, *J.H.S.*, LXXVII, Part 2, pp. 200 ff., suggests it was written round 490, and not performed until twenty-five years later for political reasons. I do not think this play is nearly as primitive as some critics have thought, and therefore accept the papyrus. The question is discussed by Kitto, *Greek Tragedy*, 2nd ed., pp. 1–2.

d [cf. p. 43]. We may compare Heracleitus Frag. 67, in which God is described as: "day and night, winter and summer, war and peace, surfeit and hunger, taking different shapes like the different scents of fire mixed with particular spices", with the fragment from Aeschylus' *Heliades*, Frag. 70, quoted on p. 60. We may also compare Heracleitus Frag. 32 with *Agamemnon*, 160 ff.

e [cf. p. 51]. It is likely that the last scene of this play is spurious, since it requires three actors. The question does not

need discussion here, for the point of the play is not signifi-
cantly altered by its retention. Aeschylus is not so facile as
to imply that a funeral is a compensation for a death.

f [cf. p. 59]. I have thought it best to ignore as an aberration
the obelizing of 505–7 in the latest edition of the Oxford
text, and follow the earlier distribution of parts. Murray has
ended by following Verrall, who gives his reasons for obelizing in his edition of the *Choephori*, Appx. 1. 13, pp. 173–5.
Neither of them consider the importance of the image of
the net. Verrall wishes to give an exactly symmetrical
number of lines in the distribution of speeches after the
Commos and has noticed that these words are attributed to
Sophocles, Clemens Alexandrinus, *Stromateis*, p. 182, ed.
Syllburg, and are quoted in a lyric metre. It is easy to think
that speeches symmetrical in length mean something when
you read them off the page. What possible significance could
this symmetry have on stage? The audience would never
notice. Symmetry in the Commos is a demand for symmetry
of movement. And if Sophocles did write these lines, and
Clemens did not make a mistake, why should we not say
that Sophocles borrowed them from Aeschylus. He, after all,
was the younger.

g [cf. p. 62]. There is continual argument about the number of
the jurors. On balance it seems more likely that there were
twelve, six voting for each side. Then Athena will give the
one, casting, vote. It would be very odd if Athena voted
with them, and then, after equalizing an unequal vote, added
a casting vote to turn defeat into victory. The procession at
the end of the *Eumenides* is no guide to the numbers. The
propompoi must have walked with the Eumenides, one with
each, in a double column. The debate in the *Agamemnon*,
1348–71, has been used to support the idea of a chorus of
either eleven or twelve. Twelve is more likely; the last
twelfth couplet does not express the same opinion as the
first, nor is it a summary. Thomson in his commentary on
the *Oresteia*, vol. ii, pp. 298–300, quotes various passages,
and in particular *Aristid. Or.* 2. 24, which show that according to the tradition the votes were equal, and Athena added
hers for acquittal. There is a tradition that Athena made the

votes equal, but it is a late tradition, Lucian i. 591. The dispute concerns the production of 711–41. I am sure that when Athena says, I *will* give my vote to Orestes, 735, she should stand, holding up the pebble. This would give maximum tension on stage. She does not drop it straight in; the future tense is important. If this is so, the first juror will go up and vote in silence; the eleven two-line speeches, 711–32, will then be spoken as each of the remaining eleven jurors goes up to vote. The last speech of the Eumenides, 731–3, taking three lines, would mark the end of the voting. It would spoil the balance of tension if the Eumenides spoke during both first and last vote. If the aim is to show two sides evenly matched the presentation must be symmetrical. Surely too, the first voter must drop his pebble in silence; this action is far too exciting theatrically to allow of distractions like the speeches. I conclude therefore that the votes are equal as an indication that both Apollo and Eumenides are needed in the total world order, while Athena confines herself to a casting vote, an image of the way that the final synthesis of the two sorts of power is something new, and beyond them both.

CHAPTER THREE

a [cf. p. 87]. Jebb brackets 904–20, although he admits that these lines were in the text which Aristotle had (cf. *Rhet.*, 3, 16, 9). His main reason is that this special justification with reference to a brother is incompatible with the universal justification Antigone advances, 450–60. But for an individual to advance this special justification need not contradict the universal justification, and certainly it is not an adequate argument for saying that the passage is an interpolation. If an interpolator wanted to change Antigone's motivation he would have to cut out the earlier passage. It is impossible to see any purpose to be achieved by interpolating this.

CHAPTER FOUR

a [cf. p. 131]. It is the general opinion among scholars that while Sparta was the technical aggressor in the Peloponnesian War, the Athenians were moral aggressors. Clearly their power was a growing menace to Sparta, but a mere increase of power, even if wrongfully acquired, does not make an aggressor. We need not take Thuc. 1, 23, as meaning more than that if there is a situation such as the growth of a power like that of Athens, a reaction such as that of Sparta's is almost bound to follow. The Athenians had nothing to gain by starting the war; what could they achieve that they were not achieving already without war? Further, the Spartans were notoriously indifferent to what their allies wanted unless they wanted it too. It is unlikely that they would have gone to war because their allies were provoked. And all the so-called aggressive actions by the Athenians affected only the allies, not the Spartans: Corcyra, Potidaea, and the Megarian decree. There is more evidence, but it has not yet been collated and discussed in print. I am indebted to conversations with G. M. de Ste Croix, who is in the course of publishing his views. I do not wish to anticipate his work, more especially since the controversial nature of this issue would demand a lengthy discussion.

b [cf. p. 142]. If we read the text we shall see that the so-called "Palace miracle" involves no great difficulties in staging. The chorus sing how the king's halls *will* crash to the ground, 588, and then they "see" the architraves tottering, 591–2. Dionysus calls on them to set fire to the palace, and then they see flames leaping round Semele's tomb, which is off-stage. They hurl themselves to the ground. The main destruction therefore is something the chorus see, but we do not. It would be ridiculous production to make the architraves totter, as the chorus say they see them totter. The chorus is not a B.B.C. commentator. Very likely flames were simulated, and crashes heard, but we do not know how this was managed, any more than we know how Aeschylus produced the end of the *Prometheus Vinctus*. But we can say that Euripides does not ask for the destruction of the palace set.

CHAPTER FIVE

a [cf. p. 159]. cf. Glynne Wickham, *Early English Stages*, 1300 *to* 1660, pp. 114–17. He quotes the decision of the Diocesan

Court of High Commission at York in 1576, which in effect forbade the performance of the Cycles, and describes the various attempts since the dissolution of the monasteries to suppress this drama, which was considered too effective as propaganda for Catholicism. The Cycles did not decay because the people were tired of them, as used to be said. They had too much effect on the people, and were thought dangerous.

CHAPTER SIX

a [cf. p. 147]. I am indebted to Professor Powell, Department of Physics, University of Bristol, for this account of Ukawa's work.

APPENDIX

TERMS USED IN THE ARGUMENT

I have thought it necessary to explain my use of three different sorts of terms. First, there are concepts of archaic Greek religion which cannot be exactly translated. I have therefore merely transcribed the Greek. Here I attempt brief paraphrases of terms which require a great amount of study, primarily for the benefit of those who do not know Greek. Secondly, again for the convenience of those who know no Greek, I have explained the technical terms of tragedy which I have used. Thirdly, I have had to use some of those vague and high-sounding words which have lost their meaning through constant emotive use in critical and philosophical discussion. I have tried to use these terms with the same reference throughout, and as much as possible to avoid emotive uses. There is no implication that this is the only right way to use them.

(i) GREEK RELIGIOUS TERMS

theos. A power other than human, usually immortal, sometimes personal, sometimes impersonal.

daimōn. Often these two terms are interchangeable. On the whole, *daimones* are less powerful, causing particular experiences to particular individuals; the Olympians are always *theoi.*

erinys. A special power, more or less personal, whose primary task is to enforce the limits of *moirai*, whether for a person or for something like the sun.

moira. Originally this meant "share". It is one's "portion in life"; everyone and everything has a *moira*, including the totality of things. In human lives we are usually made aware of the notion when someone oversteps the limits of his *moira*. Awareness of one's *moira* is necessary to achieve excellence within it.

Dikē. What is natural. Rivers flow downhill. The logic of events. If you kill, someone will kill you. *Dikē* operates in both natural and moral spheres. It is something like the notion of Natural Law as basic moral instinct. Certain wrongs like killing offend it, and will recoil. It is a much more neutral, all-embracing word than "justice", but the adjective, *dikaios*, is much nearer in meaning to "just". The Greeks never quite worked out the relation of positive just acts to *Dikē*, and so in terms of *Dikē* they could never commend justice properly.

sōphrōn. The noun is *sōphrosynē*. An awareness of one's *moira*. A clear-headed humility; it is more intellectual than the normal connotation of "humility".

(ii) TECHNICAL TERMS IN GREEK TRAGEDY

Strophe. A stanza in a sung ode where the chorus moves in one direction.

Antistrophe. The succeeding stanza, not always immediately succeeding, rhythmically identical, where the chorus perform exactly the same movements as in the strophe, but in the opposite direction.

Epode. A stanza in a sung ode, which does not balance with another one.

System. *Strophe* and *antistrophe* together.

Parodos. The entry of the chorus, chanting in anapaests.

Commos. A lament, though the greatest, that in the *Choephori*, is also the moment when Orestes and Electra summon up energy for action. A passage in lyrics, partly solo, partly choral.

Anapaests. Short, short, long is the rhythm. This metre and its variants is used when the chorus march rather than perform a set dance, and chant rather than sing.

Trochaic tetrameter. Long, short, long short, four times. Probably it was the first metre used for a dialogue. Euripides

uses it for incantatory effect; Aristophanes uses it often
when he wants an effect half-way between verse and song.

Stichomythia. A passage of alternating speeches, each one line
long.

Protagonist, deuteragonist, tritagonist. First, second, and third
actors. There was a definite sense of seniority.

(iii) CRITICAL AND PHILOSOPHICAL TERMS

religion. One's fundamental attitude to life. In this sense everyone has a religion; some people's religions are wholly or
partly definable in terms of the well-known "religions",
others are not.

metaphysic. That part of one's religion which can be intellec-
tualized.

Humanism. Sometimes called Liberal Humanism, sometimes
Rationalism. An agnostic or atheist religion which advocates most of the Christian ethical code without the dogma.

The Problem of Pain. If someone, not obviously evil beyond
others, suffers acutely in a way which bears no relation to
previous events, anyone who believes in a loving, or just
God, or who wants so to believe, is bound to ask how and
why such things happen. A play which shows a comparatively innocent person suffering does not present the Problem of Pain fully, if the suffering is shown as the direct
consequence of someone else's wickedness or folly.

pathetic drama. A play which stresses the suffering of victims,
rather than the moral crisis of a free agent's decision.

poetic, dramatic, theatrical. Poetic drama such as Greek tragedy
has a central pattern to which all events and characters are
subsumed. To make sense of the structure it is necessary to
discover the pattern. I use *poetic* to refer to those plays
whose structure is of this nature, and to those parts of a
play whose first function is to create this structure, and in
general to think of the craft of poetry as a making of
patterns. I use *dramatic* to refer to the development of
character and story, and *theatrical* to effects aimed at an
audience. Clearly, however, the great theatrical moments in
a great play will be those that both reveal character, develop
the story, and form a part of the poetic structure. These

three terms are only aids to thought, not fundamentally separate.

myth. A story out of which tragedy is made, about an event which the audience believes to have actually happened, and which typifies some universal dilemma. Normally, it is not thought that a myth need be true; when I refer to this use I say "myth".

image. An object or event in the visible tangible world, which also stands for something invisible and intangible, only to be understood by analogy. On stage an image may be represented verbally, physically, or by means of gesture. I use "imagery" to refer to purely verbal representations.

symbol. I use this as a pejorative term, when a writer has not grasped how one thing stands for something else. I apply it when the object or event is not fully real in itself, or when what it stands for can be easily explained in paraphrase.

type. I use this as a word of praise, when a person or event stands for something wider than the immediate context of the play.

artificial. I intend no pejorative sense. The theatre is more artificial than the cinema, because in the theatre we may represent a room in any way we choose; in the cinema we will try and show a room as one would meet it in real life.

Romantic. In this discussion a pejorative term. This does not imply that the Romantic movement was a bad thing at the time. I use the term to imply an attitude where the artist is thought to be only responsible to his own art. Involved in this notion are those of aesthetic truth, and the artist as being outside the rest of humanity, and therefore not responsible to society, or a code of ethics.

BIBLIOGRAPHY

PLAYS

References to the plays of Aeschylus, Sophocles, Euripides, and Aristophanes are to the latest edition of the Oxford Classical Text (O.C.T.).

References to the fragments, unless otherwise specified, are to Augustus Nauck, *Tragicorum Graecorum Fragmenta*, 2nd ed., Teubner, Leipzig, 1889.

Reference is to the line number only.

Elsewhere reference is to Act, scene and page numbers. When a scene is subdivided, as for example in Sartre, I give the subdivision as well.

The sign ω in this section indicates an author's preface or introduction. The sign ωω indicates an introduction by someone else, which I have used and wish to commend to attention.

GEORG BÜCHNER, *Dantons Tod* and *Woyzeck*, ed. Margaret Jacobs, Manchester U.P., Manchester, 1954. ωω

HENRIK IBSEN, *The Collected Plays of Henrik Ibsen*, (11 vols.), translated and edited by William Archer, William Heinemann, London, 1906–12. ωω

Three Plays. The Pillars of the Community – The Wild Duck – Hedda Gabler, translated by Una Ellis-Fermor, Penguin Books, Harmondsworth, 1950. ωω

The Master Builder and other plays. Rosmersholm – The Master Builder – Little Eyolf – John Gabriel Borkman, translated by Una Ellis–Fermor, Penguin Books, Harmondsworth, 1958. ωω

I have referred to the Penguin translation, except where there is no Penguin translation.

AUGUST STRINDBERG, *Eight Famous Plays*, translated by Edwin Björkman and N. Erichsen, Gerald Duckworth London, 1949. ω, ωω

ARTHUR MILLER, *Collected Plays*, Cresset Press, London, 1958. ω

JEAN COCTEAU, *Théâtre, I: Antigone – Les Mariés de la Tour Eiffel – Les Chevaliers de la Table Ronde – Les Parents terribles*, Gallimard, Paris, 1948. ω

Théâtre, II: Les Monstres sacrés – La Machine à écrire – Renaud et Armide – L'Aigle à deux têtes, Gallimard, Paris, 1948. ω *Orphée*, Stock, Paris, 1927.

La Machine Infernale, Grasset, Paris, 1934.

ANDRÉ GIDE, *Théâtre: Saul – Le Roi Candaule – Oedipe – Perséphone – Le treizième arbre*, Gallimard, Paris, 1947.

JEAN GIRAUDOUX, *Théâtre, I: Siegfried – Fin de Siegfried – Amphitryon 38 – Judith*, Grasset, Paris, 1958.

Théâtre, II: Intermezzo – Tessa – La Guerre de Troie n'aura pas Lieu, Grasset, Paris, 1959.

Théâtre, III: Electre – Supplément au Voyage de Cook – L'Impromptu de Paris – Cantique des Cantiques – Ondine, Grasset, Paris, 1959.

JEAN ANOUILH, *Pièces Noires: L'Hermine – La Sauvage – Le Voyageur sans Bagage – Eurydice*, La Table Ronde, Paris, 1958.

Nouvelles Pièces Noires: Jézabel – Antigone – Roméo et Jeanette – Médée, La Table Ronde, Paris, 1958.

L'Alouette, La Table Ronde, Paris, 1953.

Becket ou L'Honneur de Dieu, La Table Ronde, Paris, 1959.

JEAN-PAUL SARTRE, *Théâtre, I: Les Mouches – Huis Clos – Morts sans Sépulture – La Putain respectueuse*, Gallimard, Paris, 1947.

Les Mains Sales, Gallimard, Paris, 1948.

Le Diable et Le Bon Dieu, Gallimard, Paris, 1951.

Les Séquestrés d'Altona, Gallimard, Paris, 1960.

HENRI GHÉON, *The Mystery of the Finding of the Cross*, translated by Frank de Jonge, A. and C. Black, London, 1956. The play is not available in the original French.

Oedipe ou le crépuscule des dieux, précédé de Judith. Tragédies. Avant-propos de Jacques Reynaud, Plon, Paris, 1952.

T. S. ELIOT, *Murder in the Cathedral*, 4th ed., Faber and Faber, London, 1959.

The Family Reunion, Faber and Faber, London, 1939.

The Cocktail Party, 2nd ed., Faber and Faber, London, 1958.

The Confidential Clerk, Faber and Faber, London, 1954.

The Elder Statesman, Faber and Faber, London, 1959.

SAMUEL BECKETT, *Waiting for Godot*, Faber and Faber, London, 1957.

TENNESSEE WILLIAMS *Four Plays: The Glass Menagerie – A Street-car named Desire – Summer and Smoke – Camino Real*, Secker and Warburg, London, 1956.

CRITICAL BIBLIOGRAPHY

GENERAL

BARRETT H. CLARK, *European Theories of the Drama*, Appleton, New York, 1929.

EDWARD GORDON CRAIG, *The Art of the Theatre*, Foulis, Edinburgh and London, 1905.

T. S. ELIOT, "A Dialogue on Poetic Drama," Introduction to *Of Dramatick Poesie* by John Dryden, 1668. Etchells and Macdonald, London, 1928.
Poetry and Drama, The Theodore Spencer Memorial Lecture, Harvard University, 21 November 1950. Faber and Faber, London, 1951.

UNA ELLIS-FERMOR, *The Frontiers of Drama*, Methuen, London, 1945.

FRANCIS FERGUSSON, *The Idea of a Theater*, *A study of ten plays. The art of drama in changing perspective*, Princeton U.P., Princeton, 1949.

T. R. HENN, *The Harvest of Tragedy*, Methuen, London, 1956.

ROBERT EDMUND JONES, *The Dramatic Imagination. Reflections and Speculations on the art of the theatre*, Duell, Sloan and Pearce, New York, 1941.

F. L. LUCAS, *Tragedy*, Hogarth Lectures no. 2, revised ed., Hogarth, London, 1957.

RONALD PEACOCK, *The Poet in the Theatre*, Routledge, London, 1946.

JEAN RACINE, *Théâtre*. Especially relevant are his prefaces to *Esther* and *Bajazet*.

FRIEDRICH SCHILLER, *Works*, translated from the German (4 vols.), Bohn, London, 1846–9.

Vol. iii, pp. 439–444, "On the use of the Chorus in Tragedy" (Preface to *Bride of Messina*), *Essays Aesthetical and Philosophical*, Bohn, London, 1875.

pp. 128–42, "On the Sublime" – pp. 142–68, "On the Pathetic" – pp. 333–9, "The Stage as a Moral Institution" – pp. 339–60, "On the Tragic Art" – pp. 360–72, "Of the Cause of the Pleasure we derive from Tragic Objects".

RICHARD B. SEWALL, *The Vision of Tragedy*, Yale U.P., New Haven, Conn., 1959.

ROBERT SPEAIGHT, *The Christian Theatre*, Burns and Oates, London, 1960.

GEORGE STEINER, *The Death of Tragedy*, Faber and Faber, London, 1961.

C. E. VAUGHAN, *Types of Tragic Drama*, Macmillan, London, 1908.

EUGÈNE VINAVER, *Racine and Poetic Tragedy*, translated by P. Mansell Jones, Manchester U.P., Manchester, 1955.

CHARLES WILLIAMS, *The Image of the City*, Oxford U.P., London, 1958.

PERIODICALS

A. M. QUINTON and MISS R. MEAGER, "Tragedy", Symposium, *Proceedings of the Aristotelian Society*, Supp. vol. xxxiv, 1960.

GENERAL TO PART I

R. C. FLICKINGER, *The Greek Theater and its Drama*, 4th ed., University of Chicago Press, Chicago, 1936.

H. D. F. KITTO, *Form and Meaning in Drama*, *A Study of Six Greek Plays and of Hamlet*, Methuen, London, 1956.

Greek Tragedy, Methuen, London, 1939; and 3rd ed., 1961.

RICHMOND LATTIMORE, *The Poetry of Greek Tragedy*, John Hopkins Press, Baltimore, 1958.

D. W. LUCAS, *The Greek Tragic Poets*, 2nd ed., Cohen and West, London, 1959.

GEORGES MÉAUTIS, *Sophocle. Essai sur le héros tragique*, Albin Michel, Paris, 1957.

GILBERT NORWOOD, *Greek Tragedy*, Methuen, London, 1920.

MAX POHLENZ, *Die Griechische Tragödie*, B. G. Teubner, Leipzig and Berlin, 1930.

PERIODICALS

H. D. F. KITTO, "The Dance in Greek Tragedy", *Journal of Hellenic Studies*, LXXV, 1955.

"The Idea of God in Aeschylus and Sophocles", no. v. in *La Notion du Divin depuis Homère jusqu'à Platon*, Fondation Hardt pour l'étude de l'Antiquité Classique, Vandoeuvres-Genève, 1954.

RICHMOND LATTIMORE, *The Poetry of Greek Tragedy*, reviewed in *Times Lit. Supp.*, 6 February 1959.

T. B. L. WEBSTER, "Some Psychological Terms in Greek Tragedy", *Journal of Hellenic Studies*, LXXVII, 1957.

CHAPTER ONE

ARTHUR W. H. ADKINS, *Merit and Responsibility. A Study in Greek Values*, Clarendon Press, Oxford, 1960.

JOHN BURNET, *Early Greek Philosophy*, A. and C. Black, London, 1920, 3rd ed.

H. A. DIELS, *Fragmente der Vorsokratiker*, 6 ste. Aufl. von Walter Kranz, Weidmannsche Verlagbuchhandlung, Berlin, 1952.

E. R. DODDS, *The Greeks and the Irrational*, University of California Press, Berkeley and Los Angeles, 1951.

G. C. FIELD, *The Philosophy of Plato*, Oxford U.P. (Home University Library), London, 1949.

KATHLEEN FREEMAN, *Ancilla to the Pre-socratic Philosophers*, A complete translation of the Fragments in Diels, *Fragmente der Vorsokratiker*, Basil Blackwell, Oxford, 1948.

The Pre-Socratic Philosophers, A Companion to Diels, *Fragmente der Vorsokratiker*, Basil Blackwell, 1946.

FRIEDRICH SOLMSEN, *Hesiod and Aeschylus*, Cornell U.P., Ithaca, New York, 1949.

J. A. STEWART, *The Myths of Plato*, translated with introductory and other observations, Macmillan, London, 1905.

A. W. PICKARD-CAMBRIDGE, *Dithyramb, Tragedy and Comedy*, Clarendon Press, Oxford, 1927.

The Dramatic Festivals at Athens, Clarendon Press, Oxford, 1953.

The Theatre of Dionysus at Athens, Clarendon Press, Oxford, 1956.

SOURCE MATERIAL

ARCHILOCHUS.

ARISTOTLE, *Poetics, Nicomachean Ethics.*

HERODOTUS, *Histories.*

HESIOD, *Theogony, Works and Days.*

HOMER, *Iliad, Odyssey.*

PINDAR.

PLATO, principally *Gorgias, Republic, Laws.*

THUCYDIDES, *Histories.*

XENOPHON, *Memorabilia.*

CHAPTER TWO

EDUARD FRAENKEL, *Agamemnon*,[1] 3 vols., Clarendon Press, Oxford, 1950.

GILBERT MURRAY, *Aeschylus, the creator of tragedy*, Clarendon Press, Oxford, 1940.

J. D. DENNISTON and DENYS PAGE, *Agamemnon*,[1] Clarendon Press, Oxford, 1957.

E. E. SIKES and ST J. B. W. WILSON, *Prometheus Vinctus*,[1] Macmillan, London, 1902.

GEORGE THOMSON, *Prometheus Bound*,[1] Cambridge U.P., Cambridge, 1932.

Aeschylus and Athens, Lawrence and Wishart, London, 1941.

[1] Edited texts.

PERIODICALS

E. R. DODDS, "Morals and Politics in the *Oresteia*", *Proceedings of the Cambridge Philological Society*, 1960.

K. J. DOVER, "The Political Aspect of Aeschylus' *Eumenides*", *Journal of Hellenic Studies*, LXXVII, Part 2, 1957.

H. D. F. KITTO, "The Prometheus Trilogy", *Journal of Hellenic Studies*, LIV, 1934.

HUGH LLOYD-JONES, "Zeus in Aeschylus", *Journal of Hellenic Studies*, LXXVI, 1956.

D. S. ROBERTSON, "The Prometheus," *Proceedings of the Cambridge Philological Society*, 1938.

CHAPTER THREE

C. M. BOWRA, *Sophoclean Tragedy*, Clarendon Press, Oxford, 1944.

R. C. JEBB,[1] *Sophocles: The Plays and Fragments*, with critical notes, commentary and translation in English Prose. In 7 vols. Cambridge U.P., Cambridge, 1883–1907.

G. M. KIRKWOOD, *A Study of Sophoclean Drama*, Cornell U.P., Ithaca, New York, 1958.

H. D. F. KITTO, *Sophocles, Dramatist and Philosopher*, Oxford U.P., London, 1958.

F. J. H. LETTERS, *The Life and Work of Sophocles*, Sheed and Ward, London and New York, 1953.

J. T. SHEPPARD, *The Oedipus Tyrannus of Sophocles, translated and explained*, Cambridge U.P., Cambridge, 1920.

A. J. A. WALDOCK, *Sophocles the Dramatist*, Cambridge U.P., Cambridge, 1951.

T. B. L. WEBSTER, *An Introduction to Sophocles*, Clarendon Press, Oxford, 1936.

CEDRIC H. WHITMAN, *Sophocles. A Study of Heroic Humanism*, Harvard U.P., 1951.

[1] Edited texts.

PERIODICALS

R. P. WINNINGTON-INGRAM, "A Religious Function of Greek Tragedy", *Journal of Hellenic Studies*, LXXIV, 1954.

CHAPTER FOUR

E. M. BLAIKLOCK, *The Male Characters of Euripides*, New Zealand U.P., Wellington, 1952.

O. R. A. BYRDE, *Heracles*,[1] Clarendon Press, Oxford, 1914.

A. M. DALE, *Alcestis*,[1] Clarendon Press, Oxford, 1954.

E. R. DODDS, *Bacchae*,[1] 2nd ed., Clarendon Press, Oxford, 1960.

L. H. G. GREENWOOD, *Aspects of Euripidean Tragedy*, Cambridge U.P., Cambridge, 1953.

G. M. A. GRUBE, *The Drama of Euripides*, Methuen, London, 1941.

W. H. S. JONES, *The Moral Standpoint of Euripides*, Blackie, London, 1906.

GILBERT MURRAY, *Euripides and His Age*, 2nd ed., Oxford U.P. (Home University Library), London, 1946.

A. S. OWEN, *Ion*,[1] Clarendon Press, Oxford, 1939.

DENYS PAGE, *Medea*,[1] Clarendon Press, Oxford, 1938.

M. PLATNAUER, *Iphigeneia in Tauris*,[1] Clarendon Press, Oxford, 1938.

A. W. VERRALL, *The Bacchants of Euripides, and other Essays*, Cambridge U.P., Cambridge, 1910.

Euripides the Rationalist. A Study in the History of Art and Religion, Cambridge U.P., Cambridge, 1895.

Four Plays of Euripides, Cambridge U.P., Cambridge, 1905.

R. P. WINNINGTON-INGRAM, *Euripides and Dionysus*, Cambridge U.P., Cambridge, 1948.

G. ZUNTZ, *The Political Plays of Euripides*, Manchester U.P., Manchester, 1955.

[1] Edited texts.

PERIODICALS

E. R. DODDS, "Euripides the Irrationalist", *Classical Review*, XLIII, 1929.

CHAPTER SIX

J. L. AUSTIN, *Philosophical Papers*, Clarendon Press, Oxford, 1961.

G. E. M. ANSCOMBE, *Intention*, Basil Blackwell, Oxford, 1958.

A. J. AYER, *The Foundations of Empirical Knowledge*, Macmillan, London, 1940.
Language, Truth and Logic, 2nd ed., Gollancz, London, 1956.
The Problem of Knowledge, Macmillan, London, 1956.

AUSTIN FARRER, *The Freedom of the Will*, Black, London, 1958.

A. G. H. FLEW (ed.), *Logic and Language*, Basil Blackwell, Oxford, 1st series 1951, 2nd series 1953.

STUART HAMPSHIRE, *Thought and Action*, Chatto and Windus, London, 1959.

T. P. R. LASLETT (ed.), *The Physical Basis of Mind*, Basil Blackwell, Oxford, 1957.

IRIS MURDOCH, *Sartre, Romantic Rationalist*, Bowes and Bowes, Cambridge, 1953.

K. R. POPPER, *The Open Society and its Enemies*, Routledge, London, 1945.

BERTRAND RUSSELL, *Introduction to Mathematical Philosophy*, Allen and Unwin, London, 1953.

GILBERT RYLE, *The Concept of Mind*, Hutchinson's University Library, London, 1949.

JEAN-PAUL SARTRE, *Being and Nothingness, An Essay on Phenomenological Ontology*, translated by Hazel E. Barnes, Methuen, London, 1943.
Existentialism and Humanism, translated by Philip Mairet, Methuen, London, 1948.

W. H. WALSH, *Reason and Experience*, Clarendon Press, Oxford, 1947.

G. J. WARNOCK, *English Philosophy since 1900*, Oxford U.P. (Home University Library), London, 1958.

MARY WARNOCK, *Ethics since 1900*, Oxford U.P. (Home University Library), London, 1960.

LUDWIG WITTGENSTEIN, *Philosophical Investigations*, translated by G. E. M. Anscombe, Basil Blackwell, Oxford, 1953.

PERIODICALS

NATHAN ISAACS, "On a Gap in the Structure of our General Psychology", *Journal of Child Psychology and Psychiatry*, vol. 1, pp. 78–86, Pergamon Press, London, 1961.

CHAPTER SEVEN

EDWARD GORDON CRAIG, *On the Art of the Theatre*, Heinemann, London, 1911.

PERIODICALS

EZRA POUND, "Vorticism", *Fortnightly Review*, September 1914.
"Prolegomena", *The Poetry Review*, vol. I, no. 2, February, 1912.

GENERAL TO PART III

JEAN-LOUIS BARRAULT, *The Theatre of Jean-Louis Barrault*, translated by Joseph Chiari, Barrie and Rockliff, London, 1961.
Reflections on the Theatre, translated by Barbara Wall, Rockliff, London, 1951.

ERIC BENTLEY, *In Search of Theater*, Dennis Dobson, London; Kingsport Press, Kingsport, Tenn., 1954.
The Playwright as Thinker, A Study of Drama in Modern Times, Reynal and Hitchcock, New York, 1946.

JOSEPH CHIARI, *The Contemporary French Theatre*, Rockliff, London, 1958.

D. L. GROSSVOGEL, *The Self-Conscious Stage in Modern French Drama*, Columbia U.P., New York, 1958.

HAROLD HOBSON, *The French Theatre of Today, An English View*, Harrap, London, 1953.

RAYMOND WILLIAMS, *Drama from Ibsen to Eliot*, Chatto and Windus, London, 1952.

W. B. YEATS, *Essays and Introductions*, Macmillan, London, 1961.

PERIODICALS

JEAN-PAUL SARTRE, "Forgers of Myths", *Theatre Arts*, June 1946.

"Sartre talks to Tynan", *Observer*, 18 June 1961.

CHAPTER EIGHT

H. L. NOSTRAND, *Le Théâtre Antique et à l'antique en France de 1840 à 1900*, Droz, Paris, 1934.

CHAPTER NINE

STEPHEN SPENDER and GORONWY REES, *Danton's Death*[1] (translation and introduction), Faber and Faber, London, 1939.

CHAPTER TEN

ARTHUR MILLER, "On Social Plays", Introduction to *A View from the Bridge*, Cresset Press, London, 1957.
The Misfits, Penguin Books, London, 1961.
"The State of the Theatre: A Conversation with Arthur Miller", reported by Henry Brandon, *Harper's Magazine*, ccxxi, November 1960, pp. 63–69.

DENNIS WELLAND, *Arthur Miller*, Oliver and Boyd (Writers and Critics series), Edinburgh and London, 1961. This contains a full bibliography on Miller.

CHAPTER ELEVEN

JEAN COCTEAU, *A Call to Order*, translated by Rollo H. Myers, Faber and Gwyer, London, 1926.

[1] Edited texts.

The Hand of a Stranger, translated by Alec Brown, Elek, London, 1956.

Cocteau on the Film, A conversation recorded by André Fraigneau, translated by Vera Traill, Dobson, London, 1954.

HENRI GODIN, *La Guerre de Troie*,[1] Textes Français Classiques et Modernes, London U.P., London, 1958.

DONALD INSKIP, *Jean Giraudoux, The Making of a Dramatist*, Oxford U.P., London, 1958.

NEAL OXENHANDLER, *Scandal and Parade. The Theatre of Jean Cocteau*, Constable, London, 1958.

JEAN BOORSCH, *Myth and Symbol in Jean Cocteau*, Yale French Studies, 1951.

F. JOUAN, *Le retour au mythe grec dans le théâtre français contemporain*, Bulletin de l'association Guillaume Budé, Paris, June, 1952.

BERT M.-P. LEEFMANS, "Giraudoux' Other Muse", *Kenyon Review*, Summer, 1954.

J. DE ROMILLY, "Légendes Grecques et Théâtre Moderne", *Mercure de France*, 1 May 1954.

CHAPTER TWELVE

EDWARD OWEN MARSH, *Jean Anouilh: poet of pierrot and pantaloon*, W. H. Allen, London, 1953.

MERLIN THOMAS and SIMON LEE, *L'Alouette*,[1] Methuen, London, 1956.

CHAPTER THIRTEEN

WILFRID DESAN, *The Tragic Finale. An Essay on the philosophy of J.-P. Sartre*, Harvard U.P., Cambridge, Mass., 1954.

JEAN-PAUL SARTRE, *Literary and Philosophical Essays*, translated by Annette Michelson, Rider, London, 1955.

What is Literature?, translated by Bernard Frechtman, Methuen, London, 1950.

[1] Edited texts.

CHAPTER FOURTEEN

HENRI BROCHET, *Henri Ghéon*, Les Presses d'Ile de France, Paris, 1946.

M. DELÉGLISE, *Le Théâtre d'Henri Ghéon*, Sion – Imprimerie – lithographie Fiorina et Pellet, 1947.

HENRI GHÉON, *L'Art du Théâtre*, Serge, Montreal, 1944.

CHAPTER FIFTEEN

MAUD BODKIN, *The Quest for Salvation in an Ancient and a Modern Play*, Oxford U.P., London, 1941.

DENIS DONOGHUE, *The Third Voice, Modern British and American Verse Drama*, Princeton U.P., Princeton, N.J., 1959.

T. S. ELIOT, *The Idea of a Christian Society*, Faber and Faber, London, 1939.

The Sacred Wood. Essays on Poetry and Criticism, 2nd ed., Methuen, London, 1928.

Selected Essays, Faber and Faber, London, 1951.

Selected Prose, Penguin Books, London, 1953.

The Three Voices of Poetry, Cambridge U.P., London, 1953.

T. S. ELIOT and GEORGE HOELLERING, *The Film of Murder in the Cathedral*, Faber and Faber, London, 1952.

HELEN GARDNER, *The Art of T. S. Eliot*, Cresset Press, London, 1949.

D. E. JONES, *The Plays of T. S. Eliot*, Routledge, London, 1960.

F. O. MATHIESEN, *The Achievement of T. S. Eliot*, 2nd ed., Oxford U.P., New York and London, 1947.

N. BRAYBROOKE (ed.), *T. S. Eliot. A Symposium for his 70th birthday*, Hart-Davis, London, 1958.

A complete bibliography on Eliot can be found in Jones' book.

The Proceedings of the Aristotelian Society are referred to as *P.A.S.* in the text; *The Journal of Hellenic Studies as J.H.S.*

INDEX

371